An Economic History of
Russia 1856–1914

An Economic History of Russia 1856–1914

W.E. MOSSE

I.B. Tauris Publishers

LONDON · NEW YORK

Originally published 1992 in hardback
as Perestroika Under the Tsars by
I.B. Tauris & Co Ltd
45 Bloomsbury Square
London WC1A 2HY

175 Fifth Avenue
New York
NY 10010

Paperback edition 1996

In the United States of America
and Canada distributed by
St Martin's Press
175 Fifth Avenue
New York
NY 10010
Copyright © 1996 by W.E. Mosse

A full CIP record for this book is available from the British Library

Library of Congress cataloging-in-publication card number: available
A full CIP record is available from the Library of Congress

ISBN 1-85043-519-7 Hardback
     1-86064-066-4 Paperback

Printed and bound in Great Britain by
WBC Ltd, Bridgend, South Wales

'All cases are unique – and very similar to others'   T. S. Eliot

'. . . no state that values its independence can ignore the need for defensive modernization'   Francis Fukuyama

'Experience teaches that the most dangerous moment for a bad government is usually when it begins to reform itself. Only genius can save a ruler who undertakes to relieve his subjects after prolonged oppression. Evils borne patiently as inevitable become intolerable the moment the possibility is conceived of escaping them.'
                                        Alexis de Tocqueville

'He tried to reform the unreformable'   Anatoly Sobchak

Plus ça change

Acknowledgement

The author gratefully acknowledges the assistance of the Leverhulme Trust in the completion of this study through the award of an Emeritus Fellowship.

Contents

Preface

This book is intended to show that perestroika in the Soviet Union (Russia) associated with the names of Mikhail Gorbachev and Boris Yeltsin is not the unique phenomenon it might appear. Similar attempts at restructuring have occurred repeatedly in Russia since at least the time of Peter the Great. Here, attention will be focused on those occurring between Russia's defeat in the Crimean War and the outbreak of war in 1914.

In this context, it may be desirable to try to define the too often loosely employed term 'perestroika' as it is to be used here. In common usage it denotes simply more or less radical changes in Russia introduced from above. It is, however, possible to define the term more precisely as a number of separate though interrelated processes. Economic perestroika involves a far-reaching change of the economic system by means of legislative and administrative action. In the present instance it is more particularly the introduction into a semi-feudal agricultural society of industrial entrepreneurship, urban financial institutions and, in short, early capitalism. Parallel political perestroika is marked by the replacement of centralized, secretive, monarcho-bureaucratic absolutism by a system of (pseudo) constitutional monarchy with a number of more or less freely elected institutions, a measure of decentralization and a degree of 'openness' (glasnost) combined with some guarantees of a rule of law and civil rights. The relationship between economic and political perestroika is a complex one. In particular, political perestroika does not necessarily favour economic 'restructuring', if anything the reverse.

A third aspect of perestroika, more elusive than the others, is the psychological adaptation to change involving the loss of old certainties and values and the need to come to terms with numerous unfamiliar and often distasteful innovations. Thus in Russia perestroika is almost invariably linked to a form of 'Westernization', 'the West' being the only available role model and one uncongenial to traditionalists and nationalists. Finally, in the somewhat longer term, there is the inevitable accompaniment to perestroika, the more or less radical transformation of society. Some groups or classes decline, others rise.

Although not necessarily synonymous with 'modernization' (whatever that term may mean) perestroika would normally be a modernizing or progressive influence whether measured by a bourgeois-liberal or by a Marxist yardstick. It is, however, not inevitably a positive force. In Russia in particular it could also be seen as a negative influence, as being ill-suited to the national character and alien to Russian traditions. The overall evaluation of the process must inevitably be subjective. Not everyone involved in or affected by it would necessarily see it as an influence for good. 'It was a quite ordinary everyday conversation', writes Tatiana Shcherbina, 'about what the future would bring . . . when a young Russian woman said quietly: "It will be the same shit as before."'[1]

Gorbachev's and Yeltsin's attempts to modernize an antiquated and inefficient economic, social and political system – the three aspects are of course interrelated – constitute in fact a variation on an old theme, the perennial Russian need (or urge) to catch up with more advanced societies. It is in their international setting among others that tsarist attempts at perestroika and those of Gorbachev, Yeltsin and Stalin invite comparison.

There are striking similarities in motivation. Like Stalin on the one hand and Aleksandr II, Witte or Stolypin on the other, Gorbachev is spurred on by a resolute determination to maintain and indeed enhance Russia's position among the Great Powers. To do this, it is necessary to strengthen a weak economy, to develop a 'military-industrial complex' and to fashion effective instruments of administration. Without the restructuring of an inefficient system with low productivity, Russia, it is clear, is doomed to drop out of the ranks of the Great (under Gorbachev, super-) Powers. The protagonists of perestroika realize that in Russia's overriding national interest there is no alternative.

The attempts, however, to make more or less radical changes in an old-established system run into formidable obstacles. These change little between the tsarist and Soviet periods. Some of the more important may be listed here. Perhaps foremost among them is the opposition of vested interests – whether serf-owners or privileged *apparatchiks* who, not surprisingly, defend their threatened property or privileges. Inevitably, in any major restructuring hitherto privileged groups stand to be hurt in pocket, status and self-esteem. They are likely already to be well-organized in large informal networks, ensconced in entrenched positions and ready to engage in a furious rearguard action in defence of their threatened interests. Where open opposition proves impossible, passive resistance and sabotage lie ready to hand.

A second cluster of obstacles lies in what, for want of a better term, one must call the Russian 'national character'. One element of this, by common consent, is a certain laziness, a reluctance to make decisions, a lack of initiative and the desire to avoid responsibility – in short *Oblomovshchina*, named after the antihero of Goncharov's famous novel. It was a Russian characteristic deplored by Lenin; the antithesis of successful entrepreneurial activity.

A further element of resistance to perestroika was a deep-seated attachment to collective forms of social organization combined with a profound strain of democratic egalitarianism. These indeed could be described as the dominant traits of the popular psyche which the *muzhiks* had transferred from their villages to other social groups including the urban proletariat.

Any removal of collectivist constraints inevitably increases inequalities – indeed like Stolypin's 'wager on the strong' it may be specifically designed to do so. By the mass of Russians, whether from envy of the successful or on spiritual or moral grounds, it is inevitably viewed with distaste. These underlying sentiments are linked to ideological opposition. Perestroika, in one form or another is associated with non-Russian features, with 'the West'. Protagonists of perestroika are of necessity *Zapadniki* ('Westernizers'). Patriotic Russians of slavophile disposition, however, feel perestroika – even when they recognize its practical necessity – as something alien and hurtful to 'true' Russian values and traditions. In consequence, perestroika will readily produce a nationalist-nativist reaction of the kind propagated among others by Aleksandr Solzhenitsyn.

In addition, there are numerous obstacles to perestroika on a more mundane plane: scarcity of resources, technological backwardness, vast military expenditure in relation to GNP, international adventurism, the distraction of the reformers by domestic politics and intrigue and the need to operate from an insecure base. More fundamentally perestroika has an unsettling effect, creating or aggravating as it does social, political and ethnic (or national) problems.

The cost of perestroika is high whether under Witte or Yeltsin, not least in a poor and backward country like Russia/Soviet Union. Perestroika, in fact, can be accomplished only by a drastic lowering of living-standards for the bulk of the population. The price may for a time be hunger and undernourishment, chronic shortages and, given the vagaries of the Russian climate, periodic famine. Nor do hitherto privileged groups escape. Living standards, whether of *pomeshchiks* or *apparatchiks* are inevitably lowered and their social position may be damaged beyond repair, as depicted in Chekhov's *Cherry Orchard*.

Perestroika is therefore difficult to bring about with the consent of the governed. It is inevitably unpopular and requires an element of coercion – the use of power symbolically described in Aleksandr Pushkin's *Bronze Horseman*. The would-be reformer is not necessarily strong or determined enough to confront the obstacles successfully and perestroika in practice is thus subject to severe constraints.

Several groups of protagonists of perestroika can be distinguished: realists of the 'there is no choice' school, who see an overriding necessity for perestroika in the interest of the national future; 'Westernizers' like Andrei Sakharov who wish to see their country take its place among the civilized nations of 'the West'; and technocrats impatient of inefficiency, sloth and *Oblomovshchina*. To these might be added liberals who are concerned with political structures, with civil rights, the rule of law (important also for commercial purposes); in short who wish for glasnost in the widest sense of the term.

In all these respects, there is little difference, as the present study seeks to show, between the tsarist and Soviet attempts at perestroika. *Mutatis mutandis* they present important similarities. In view of this, it appears unnecessary, with only occasional exceptions, to draw attention in the text specifically to detailed parallels. Every part of the story reveals the close similarities of comparable processes of perestroika whether under tsar or first secretary.

NOTES

1. Tatiana Shcherbina: 'Die ganz gewöhnliche russische Katastrophe', *Süddeutsche Zeitung*, No 80, 4/5 April 1992, p 10.

Part I

Introduction

1

The Background

The history of modern Russia presents a number of recurring features. Their recurrence is not fortuitous but is the product of underlying causes which have changed little over the centuries. They are independent of political régimes and were unaffected by the October Revolution of 1917. Among them are the phenomena known today as perestroika and glasnost. Like their opposites, stagnation and official secrecy, they are of long standing and deeply embedded in Russian history. The present study is more particularly concerned with the late tsarist period, but has light to throw on Soviet policy today.

Before turning to the underlying causes of perestroika and glasnost it is desirable to attempt a definition of the terms. Perestroika denotes a radical transformation of the existing order of things, principally with economic connotations but with political and social implications also. Perestroika normally originates in the centre of power and is imposed on the regions of the empire frequently over local opposition. Among the more famous practitioners of perestroika are numbered Ivan IV, Peter the Great, Catherine the Great, Aleksandr II and Stalin. Their number also includes Aleksandr I and his minister Speransky, Witte, Stolypin, Khrushchev and Gorbachev. However different in some of their aspects most of the periodic attempts at perestroika show a family likeness in methods of implementation, resistance encountered and degree of success achieved. The present study will concentrate on three major perestroikas of the nineteenth and early twentieth centuries, those associated with the names respectively of Aleksandr II, Witte, and Stolypin.

The term glasnost – openness – was first used in its modern sense in the year 1826 in connection with the show trial of the Decembrist

3

conspirators. There was then an argument in official circles as to whether the trial should be held behind closed doors or whether there should be publicity – an open door – glasnost. In the end, the curious, and perhaps symbolic, decision was reached to adopt a policy of a half-open door, one neither wide open nor yet completely shut.

Glasnost, however, could be used also in a wider sense as denoting a more general policy of openness. It could include a degree of freedom of expression, an absence or at least a limitation of censorship, and a sphere of activity, however circumscribed, conceded to local initiative. In all its different manifestations it would mean the recognition by central government of a domain left open for 'the public'. Glasnost must inevitably create a potential for pluralism. It implies some interaction between state and society, a measure of public choice in the cultural sphere, an element of initiative from below. Not least, it must necessarily allow members of 'the public' the right of at least limited criticism of the actions of government. It is clear that glasnost did not – and does not – denote political liberalism or democracy. It does not necessarily involve political pluralism. Whilst it may, in certain circumstances, contribute to political change also, it is not necessarily bound to do so.

It might be noted already at this point that, between perestroika and glasnost there exists, on the face of it, a logical contradiction. While perestroika implies, indeed requires, firm central direction (by preference some form of autocracy) and obedient executive organs, glasnost involves a certain relaxation of control. Perestroika means telling people what to do and requires obedience to its imperatives; glasnost involves the right of society to express its views on – and perhaps to oppose – official policies, including those of perestroika. With perestroika dividing the articulate part of society into reformers and conservatives, glasnost allows them to debate their differences in public. Glasnost can thus prove a retarding influence so far as perestroika is concerned.

Effectively perestroika and glasnost do not necessarily go in harness. Some architects of perestroika have abhorred glasnost and would have no truck with it. On the other hand, those trying to combine the two have invariably run into difficulties. Whatever the policies adopted, the juxtaposition of perestroika and glasnost presents peculiar problems.

*   *   *

The fundamental reasons for the recurrence of these phenomena over the centuries must first be examined. In brief, they are the product of a distinctive feature of modern Russian history, the combination of economic underdevelopment (eventually relative only) and the status of a 'great' and finally a world power.

The reasons for Russia's long enduring backwardness are to be found in the first place in her geography; in soil, climate and geographical location. These natural disadvantages were further compounded by man-made causes. Some of the factors involved are described by Trotsky in his history of the Russian Revolution:

> The population of this gigantic and austere plain open to eastern winds and Asiatic migrations, was condemned by nature itself to a long backwardness. The struggle with nomads lasted almost to the end of the seventeenth century, the struggle with winds bringing winter cold and summer drought continues still. Agriculture, the basis of the whole development, advanced by extensive methods. In the north they cut down and burned up the forests, in the south they ravished the virgin steppes. The conquest of nature went wide and not deep.[1]

Russia had fertile soils in the Black Earth Belt, the *chernozem*. The frozen northern tundra, however was impossible to cultivate. Further south, the vast forest belt of the *taiga* was more suitable for a hunting, trapping, and fishing economy than for an agricultural one. For a long time, as Trotsky points out, it was cultivated only by the primitive slash-burn method. The Black Earth Belt south of the *taiga* was subject to the scourges of eastern winds, drought and soil erosion and, until well into the seventeenth century, to destructive raids from the south. Lastly the southern steppe, historically wide open to the passage of nomad horsemen from the East, was more suitable for a pastoral rather than an agricultural economy.

Other disadvantages were aggravated for much of Russia by long and severe winters and a correspondingly short growing season. Nor was farming efficiency promoted by primitive agricultural techniques which continued into the mid-nineteenth century: shallow ploughing with wooden implements, lack of manuring, servile labour, strip-farming with periodic redistributions. Handicapped by unfavourable conditions, Russian agriculture was doomed to low productivity compared with better-placed competitors in central and western Europe and on the American continent. The state of agriculture was a major cause of Russia's poverty.

A different set of circumstances impeded the commercial development of Muscovy/Russia. Until the eighteenth century, it was virtually landlocked with the remote port of Archangel on the inhospitable shores of the White Sea (and frozen during a large part of the year) as its only outlet. Moreover, Archangel was connected to the North Sea only by the perilous sea passage around the North Cape. The acquisition in the sixteenth century of Astrakhan at the mouth of the Volga gave access merely to the Caspian, an inland sea. Subsequent territorial expansion did indeed bring Russia successively to the shores of the Baltic, the Black Sea and what is usually described as the Pacific. However, all were inland seas, the 'Pacific' being effectively the virtually landlocked Sea of Japan. None gave direct and unimpeded access to the major arteries or overseas trade. All the seas, particularly their exits, were controlled by other, potentially hostile powers. Muscovy/Russia remained throughout a large continental land mass with little indented coastline. Of such ports as Russia did develop, not one was permanently ice-free.

The consequences for Russia of her remoteness from the major venues of overseas trade were far-reaching. While more happily placed countries of the Atlantic seaboard were developing early capitalist economies through shipbuilding and navigation, maritime insurance and banking, colonial trade and industry, nothing comparable occurred in Russia. Not for her the great trading emporia with their self-assured merchant princes, fine buildings and patronage of the arts and letters. Where other countries developed flourishing commercial cultures, Russia long retained a primitive 'natural economy'. She remained an exporter of raw materials and an importer of manufactured and luxury goods.

Other reasons for Russian underdevelopment compared with more advanced Western countries were cultural. Russia lacked the heritage of ancient Rome with its legal codes based on concepts of private property, contract and inheritance. There was neither Canon Law nor commercial law. Russia had no Reformation, no equivalent to Calvinism with its ethic of hard work, thrift and saving, of capital accumulation and of wealth as the reward of piety. The Russian Orthodox Church tended to concentrate instead on spiritual values and problems of salvation. It was another element retarding economic development.

Unlike other underdeveloped countries Russia had, at the same time, also become a major European power. In 1709 at Poltava she had decisively defeated Sweden, until then the leading Baltic power. In 1760, during the Seven Years War, Russian troops had for a time bivouacked in the streets of Berlin. At the end of the century, Catherine the Great had claimed the lion's share in the partitions of Poland and established Russia firmly on the northern shore of the Black Sea. In 1814, Russian detachments entered Paris as part of the coalition forces which had defeated Napoleon. The following year, Tsar Aleksandr I had dominated the Congress of Vienna. During the European crisis of 1848–9, Nikolai I had played the decisive role in settling the affairs of Germany, the Habsburg monarchy, the Danubian principalities and the Danish kingdom. The Russian Emperor had become something like the arbiter of Europe.

Russia's relentless advance, in the course of a century and a half from the position of a relatively obscure regional power to European near-hegemony had been achieved by a series of wars that pitted her in turn against the Sweden of Charles XII, the Prussia of Frederick the Great, the Ottoman Empire and the France of Napoleon. Except in the Seven Years War, when her rulers had voluntarily foregone victory, Russia had gained territory and enhanced her status. She had become a great military empire.

*   *   *

How did Russia, despite her economic backwardness, achieve the position first of a major regional, then of the leading continental power? There are a number of reasons. In the first place, before the industrial revolution of the nineteenth century, size of territory and population were major military assets. Russia's size combined with severe climatic conditions had contributed to the defeats of both Charles XII and Napoleon. A large population meant a large reservoir of manpower. As they would demonstrate during the First World War, Russian commanders could always contemplate heavier losses than their opponents.

In the second place, until the technological revolution of the mid-nineteenth century with its railways, breech-loading rifled weapons and armour plating, military technology remained relatively unsophisticated. In an age of infantry battles and horse-drawn transport, Russian armies could hold their own at relatively little expense. Among Russia's other assets were the long cultivated skill in bayonet fighting, the hardiness (and often fatalism) of her peasant soldiers, a highly mobile cavalry with, at its core, Cossack units with their horsemanship and hardy mounts. Both peasants and Cossacks were able to live off the land reducing the need for commissariat services. Though their sophistication was low, Russia had economical and cost-effective land forces. Also, not being a significant maritime power, she was spared the expense of maintaining an effective navy which burdened some other countries.

Finally, ever since the sixteenth century, Russia had been adept at borrowing or copying more advanced tactics and techniques from her rivals and competitors. Swedes, French, Scots and above all Germans (both Baltic Germans and those from Germany proper) successively served the Russian armed forces in large numbers down to middle-echelons. Moreover from the mid-eighteenth century onwards Russia's rulers and the heads of her military establishment, were of

Germanic descent. During the Napoleonic Wars, close ties had developed between the Russian and Prussian armies. Towards the end of the nineteenth century, military co-operation with France replaced that with Prussia/Germany. Russia consistently had access to advanced technology and tactics and Russians, with limited resources, proved themselves apt pupils. However, they became increasingly disadvantaged when early industrialization and the concomitant revolution in military technology, the 'mechanization of warfare', got under way.

Russia's rise to the status of a major power had been favoured also by her political traditions. The autocracy of her rulers is, with justification linked to the two centuries (c. 1240–1480), during which the grand-princes of Muscovy had functioned as tribute gatherers for the Tartar Khans. Backed by their overlords in many of their enterprises, they had themselves copied Tartar methods of government. After the end of Tartar rule in the late fifteenth century, absolutism had been reinforced when the Muscovite grand-princes adopted the ideology and rituals of the Byzantine empire which asserted the supremacy of the ruler over a subservient church. The cult of autocracy as the ideal form of government was propagated and firmly established from this time.

Since the reign of Peter the Great, autocracy had been secularized, with the subordination of church to state being further strengthened. It had remained unaffected by the vicissitudes of biological accident, weak rulers, coups d'état, the rule of women, of minors, usurpers, or foreigners. The reason for the strength of the autocratic tradition lay in the absence of the three forces which, in the West had tended to contest royal power and to limit monarchic absolutism. As a result of the economic backwardness already discussed, no influential commercial bourgeoisie or powerful city states had ever developed once Novgorod had been destroyed. The 'baronage', such as it was had had its power broken at the end of the sixteenth century by Ivan IV. Finally the Orthodox Church, never a power, lost whatever influence it possessed during the seventeenth century. Peter the Great had merely completed its subjugation when he abolished the Patriarchate and replaced it with the Holy Synod, a college and later ministry of church affairs.

Unchallenged by burghers, barons or church, unhampered by estates or parliaments, autocracy in Russia with its servitors civil and military ruled supreme from the time of Peter the Great. It had in fact formed the basis – the only possible one – for his reforms, the first and most radical perestroika.[2] Peter, the first 'modernizing' autocrat, the originator of Russia's rise to the status of a great power had laid foundations on which his successors would build.

   With the establishment of Peter's modernized autocracy, a distinctive rhythm had developed in Russian government, an alternation of periods of severe repression with notable thaws when central control was relaxed in several spheres. Such thaws occurred roughly every 40 years, approximately once in each generation. The first followed the iron-fisted rule of Peter the Great, the second, in the early years of Catherine the Great, that of her tyrannical husband Peter III. A notable thaw was ushered in early in the new century by the young Aleksandr I after the murder of his martinet father. Another followed the death of Nikolai I in 1855. The rhythm however, was interrupted after the death of the autocratic Aleksandr III in 1894 when the widely expected thaw failed to materialize with fateful consequences. Subsequent thaws would be associated with the provisional government under Kerensky, to some extent with Lenin's NEP and, later still with the reforms of Khrushchev and Gorbachev.

   It is interesting to ask why such thaws should have occurred so regularly. Was this a matter of chance or was it an inherent feature of the system of autocracy itself? Perhaps the best answer is that it was a mixture of both. The accident of the personal temperament of the more liberal autocrats undoubtedly played a part. Equally so, however, did the desire of new rulers to dissociate themselves from oppressive predecessors. In some cases there was a recognition that the smooth running of the régime required some release of pent-up pressures. Again there might be a desire to enlist a degree of public support for an intended perestroika, a package of reforms. Indeed some new rulers may have courted a measure of popularity. There may also have been generational causes, the opposition of fathers and sons, predecessors and heirs. Some of the autocratic reigns ended in failure, encouraging a change of course. By contrast, the initiators of the thaws were frequently weaker personalities than their strong-willed predecessors. Thus though much was accidental, thaws were to some extent at least also built into the system. So also, therefore, would be a measure of glasnost.

*   *   *

From the late eighteenth century onwards thaws and glasnost would become associated with another issue, that of nationality. Since the incorporation of Little Russia in the seventeenth century, Muscovy/Russia had been a state including an ethnic minority. Early in the eighteenth century with the annexation of the Baltic provinces, she had acquired important communities of landowners and burghers of German descent. However, what made Russia a truly multinational state was her share in the spoils of the Polish partitions at the end of the eighteenth century. Henceforth, the Russian Empire would include large and compact populations both of Poles and Jews. The Napoleonic Wars and subsequent peace settlement added an autonomous Finnish component.

Of these minority groups, far and away the most important were the Poles. The Kingdom of Poland/Lithuania, Latin and Roman Catholic and linked at times with Protestant Sweden had, since the sixteenth century, been the traditional rival and enemy of Russian Orthodox Muscovy. Their Hundred Years War had been waged over the disputed territories of western Russia, inhabited by Little Russian (Ukrainian) and Belorussian peasants with a Polish landowning class and a clergy either Roman Catholic or Uniate (that is owing allegiance to the Pope while retaining the Orthodox ritual). Early in the seventeenth century during Russia's 'Time of Troubles', Polish forces had for a time even occupied the city of Moscow. Muscovites and Poles were bitter hereditary enemies.

The Polish partitions, under which Russia acquired the lion's share of the former Polish-Lithuanian state, did nothing to mitigate the enmity though the terms of the relationship were changed. If anything, Polish national sentiment was sharpened by vain resistance, as was Russian hostility towards the 'disloyal' Poles. Policies of conciliation and repression adopted in turn by Russian governments proved equally ineffective. In the last resort, the Polish aim would always remain liberation from the Russian yoke.

The issue had wider implications. After 1815, the Kingdom of Poland was Russia's advanced outpost to the West through which lay her lines of communication with Western Europe, notably with Prussia/Germany. An independent and almost certainly hostile Poland would isolate Russia from the rest of Europe. Furthermore, Poland occupied an important strategic position. Defensively, it constituted a Russian glacis against invasion from the West. An independent Poland, on the other hand, would be an ever-ready springboard for a potential invader. Offensively, Poland was a threat to the neighbouring capitals of Vienna and Berlin, both relatively close to the Polish border. Strategically, it could be argued, control of Poland was crucial to Russia's position as a European power.

There was also a related complication. For a long time, Poland had been closely associated with France. She had formed part of the French Eastern States System which was made up of Sweden, Poland-Lithuania and the Ottoman Empire and directed in the first place against the Habsburg monarchy but secondly also against Muscovy/Russia, hereditary enemy of all three states. For France, Poland was and remained an essential ally (eventually also against Germany). Owing to geographical distance and, eventually, to the Revolution,

France was too weak to prevent the dismemberment of Poland, though she by no means abandoned her interest in Polish affairs. The Grand-Duchy of Warsaw had served as a springboard for Napoleon's attack on Russia. When the Poles rose against Russian rule in 1830 (as they would do again in 1863), French public opinion was passionately 'Polish' even if the July Revolution and other events nearer home prevented the French government from lending active assistance. Russians, in a resulting outburst of xenophobia, turned on Western supporters of the Polish insurgents. An independent Poland, it was held, would be tantamount to a permanent French armed camp on the Vistula.

While Poles continued to strive for independence, Russian policy alternated between repression and attempts at conciliation. In this situation, any Russian thaw would raise Polish hopes, produce patriotic, and therefore anti-Russian, demonstrations and provoke a Russian backlash. What was true of the Poles, the quintessential 'subject nationality', would apply, if to a lesser extent, to other minority groups in the multinational empire. It was one of the hazards of thaw and glasnost.

*   *   *

Overall, Russia's basic problems arose from its inescapable coexistence with the more advanced nations of the West. One aspect of this was a culture gap between East and West. Some privileged Russians were in a position to compare their own culture with that of Europe and, eventually the USA. They could compare political systems, read Western works on political and economic matters. They could contrast lifestyles and cultural amenities. Most of those capable of making such comparisons would find Western culture and Western political systems the more attractive. They would borrow and import from the West its dress, manners and fashions, architecture and theatre, literature, periodicals and modes of thought. They would import Western luxuries, from the champagne that so often flowed in nineteenth-century Russian novels to rock 'n roll, jeans and Coca Cola. The most 'dangerous' imports however, were 'subversive' political theories – and in the Russian political context, almost any Western idea was of necessity subversive. This had been the case with Roman Catholicism in the Western provinces, with the eighteenth-century Enlightenment and, above all, with the ideas of the French Revolution.

In dealing with the problems posed by unavoidable cultural and intellectual coexistence, Russian rulers pursued alternating policies. During the rare periods of thaw, they looked benignly on the Westernization of the more educated among their subjects. Much more frequently and over longer periods, their reaction would be the reverse. Every effort would be made to inhibit or at least to minimize Russian contact with the dangerous centres of infection. Travel abroad by Russians was discouraged and obstacles put in its way. Foreigners, except those it was impossible to do without, were not encouraged to visit Russia. The most effective attempt to control Westernization was through preventing the introduction and diffusion of intellectual 'contraband' by means of censorship of publications and correspondence; a policy of anti-glasnost. At the same time, some intellectuals would evolve anti-Western ideologies, extolling the superior virtues of Russian Orthodox culture, of autocracy as a system of government, of Russian social organization, and finally of Marxism-Leninism. The attempt to minimize Western contacts and to pursue a policy of counter-glasnost could be seen as a defensive reaction of the Russian government and sections of Russian opinion against the dangerous temptations of the West and its magnetic attraction for many Russians, some of whom chose to settle abroad.

However, the attitude of Russian governments and opinion towards the West was consistently schizophrenic. Western achievement was admired, from Swedish military techniques to the writings of Adam Smith, and from Western engineering to the cultivation of maize. Whatever the feelings of misgiving, distrust and even aversion, it was consistently accepted that Russia could not do without the fruits of Western achievement.

Under Peter the Great and earlier, borrowing from the West had been mainly in the military sphere, relating to tactics and armaments. Military requirements and the need to keep up with Western advances so far as possible would remain at the core of Russian relations with the West. It was, and would remain, a precondition of the acquisition and preservation of Russia's great power status. The industrial and technological revolutions of the 1850s and 1860s merely intensified the need, as would be glaringly revealed in the course of the Crimean War. It then came to be understood that military competition and great power status required a strong industrial and economic base, something in the nature of a military-industrial complex. This could not be created in a country like Russia without assistance – both financial and technical – from outside. Foreign engineers and capital had to be invited into Russia to help develop her industries.

It had been optimistically assumed by Peter the Great that the foreign 'teachers' might be needed for a generation or two, after which the Russians would be able to manage on their own. But the idea of 'catching up' with the West, an idea sustaining generations of Russians, was destined to remain a chimera. Two and a half centuries after Peter the Great, Khrushchev would still talk boastfully but vainly about catching up with the USA and overtaking it. The rate of Western technological progress remained faster than the Russian; the hope of catching up definitively proved illusory.

Though continuous, the attempt to catch up proceeded at an uneven pace, marked by periods of relative stagnation and others of frantic endeavour. It is these accelerated attempts to maintain Russian competitiveness which constitute the essence of the successive perestroikas of Aleksandr II, Witte, Stolypin, Stalin, Khrushchev and Gorbachev. Though the methods might differ, the underlying motivation was the same – as was the perceived need. Only by forced effort could a naturally stagnant society given to routine, and conservatism be dragged into the restructuring needed to preserve Russia's position among competing powers. It was a position successive rulers and large parts of the Russian élite were unwilling to forego.

*   *   *

The relation of perestroika to glasnost is complex. A policy of glasnost is, of course, entirely feasible without perestroika. For a large part of the Russian population other than relatively small groups of intellectuals however, glasnost was normally a matter of secondary importance. In the eighteenth century indeed, rulers like Peter or Catherine the Great had to force their 'enlightened' educational policies on a recalcitrant gentry. Even under Aleksandr I the thirst for glasnost was still modest. It was only with the growth of '*obshchestvennost*', or an educated public, after the middle of the nineteenth century, that the professional classes and their journals began to involve themselves seriously in public affairs and to clamour for a policy of openness.

There is no doubt either that, in the short term, glasnost impeded perestroika. If major changes had to be imposed on a reluctant or indifferent population in the face of conservative resistance this could clearly be done most effectively by an autocratic power which could break down all resistance regardless of opinion. Any attention to public opinion and especially opinion that was relatively free would be, at worst, an obstacle, at best, a distraction and a dissipation of energies. Given the fact that any perestroika was bound to hurt strong vested interests and disturb established habits, glasnost geared to the needs of perestroika was barely conceivable. Views publicly expressed were likely to be critical or hostile. Propaganda effort in favour of radical reform on the other hand was unlikely to convert major sections of the population.

Overall, glasnost, or freedom of expression, while theoretically neutral in relation to perestroika, would tend to make it more, not less, difficult to achieve. Glasnost would almost inevitably, weaken the authority which a government needed to carry out a policy of perestroika. It involved of necessity some degree of voluntary relaxation of central control. It permitted the airing of grievances, notably by disgruntled nationalities. It was likely to involve public criticism of government policies which would otherwise have been prohibited. Not least, it would encourage opposition to test the limits of official tolerance. Glasnost, in fact, would allow freedom of expression both to those who did not desire perestroika and to others who considered that it did not go far enough. To the extent that opinion could influence official policy and its execution, glasnost, for a government intent on perestroika, was thus likely to be at best an unwelcome diversion, at worst a potential danger. While Peter the Great, Lenin and Stalin, proponents of perestroika without glasnost, were on the whole able to achieve their goals, those whose reforms included an element of glasnost (Aleksandr I, Aleksandr II, Stolypin, Kerensky, Khrushchev) either had to abandon or at least tone down perestroika, or lose power. Whether a perestroika may or may not achieve results was probably largely independent of its association with a policy of glasnost. But, so far as perestroika was concerned, glasnost may not only be a nuisance but also a threat.

In broad terms, the juxtaposition of autocracy, perestroika and glasnost created a number of contradictions or paradoxes. In the first place, autocracy and centralized control stifled individual initiative, a prerequisite of effective and lasting perestroika. Yet such perestroika was impossible without a strong and virtually unfettered central authority. At the same time the relaxation that was perhaps necessary for the success of true reform weakened the authority needed to achieve it. There was also an element of contradiction between a policy of thaw and one of modernization. What were the chances of catching up with dangerous competitors in a relatively short period of time under a relaxed regime?

There was a deep ambiguity also about Russia's relations with the West. For centuries Russia required and acquired vast inputs of Western capital and technology in order to 'catch up'. Western military technology and other skills were needed for Russia to hold her own with the aim always to overtake or to defeat a competitor. The West, therefore, was invited to contribute materially to a policy intended ultimately to weaken or undermine its own position. Russia's psychological attitude to the West was schizophrenic, a compound of admiration, envy and detestation, often found together in the same individual. Russians had reluctantly to recognize an inferiority extending over many generations. Dearly as they would have liked to stand on their own feet, this would prove consistently impossible. So long as Russia had to coexist, she had, however unwillingly, to borrow and to copy. That the disunity among Western countries could be exploited for the purpose was only a minor consolation.

A further paradox lay in the ambivalent interaction between autocracy and centralized control on the one hand, and glasnost and perestroika on the other. Both policies in their longer term effects, would tend to undermine autocracy, and upset the political status quo. In the case of glasnost it is clear that this encouraged publicity and hence public criticism of the government and its policies. Almost inevitably, this would promote political opposition, leading possibly to radical change or even revolution. In its turn, perestroika inevitably involved longer term social changes, a weakening of some social groups, a strengthening of others, which would also have profound political consequences. For the powers that be therefore, glasnost and perestroika were alike dangerous instruments. In adopting them, yielding to perceived necessity, Russian régimes of whatever complexion were in the longer term helping to undermine themselves. When their dangers became too apparent, perestroika and glasnost would be jettisoned by those who had earlier promoted them – only to be resumed later by others who again saw the imperative need for them. Could perestroika and glasnost ever succeed under such political autocracy? Could they succeed without it? These are among the paradoxes involved in what, on the face of things might appear fairly straightforward policies.

It is within these broader parameters that three instances of perestroika, those associated respectively with the names of Aleksandr II, Witte and Stolypin will be examined in detail.[3] The last statesmen of the tsarist régime, their activities span the half century or so preceding the Revolution. The methods and to some extent the aims of the three men differed. They operated, however, within the same political system. If the term perestroika has a meaning, it must apply to the policies of all three, whatever the differences of detail and emphasis. Certain contrasts between them, moreover, are as instructive as are the similarities. Their combined experiences throw much light on the problems, possibilities, perils and limitations which re-emerged in the policies of the Soviet government and indeed its successors today.

NOTES

1. Leon Trotsky: *The History of the Russian Revolution* (London, 1932), vol I, p 23.
2. How far Ivan IV's restructuring, his *oprichnina*, can be described as a perestroika must remain a matter of opinion.
3. To these names might be added that of the less well-known Loris-Melikov.

2

The Old Order

To understand the Great Reforms of Tsar Aleksandr II, it is necessary first to note some essential features of the old order which preceded them. This, in essence, was an unsophisticated socio-political structure resting essentially on three basic institutions. The first of these was autocracy; unlimited, hereditary monarchical absolutism, equally operative in church and state, civil and military administration. In theory, all decisions on policy and personnel were the ruler's, in practice at least all the more important ones. The operative feature of autocracy – a good deal of ideological verbiage apart – was that the autocrat chose (and at his pleasure dismissed) all ministers. They reported to him on their activities at regular intervals, more or less frequently in accordance with the perceived importance of their office. Until Westernization supervened, they had been wont to describe themselves as the tsar's serfs or slaves. Abject servility and super-deference persisted, at least officially, among their successors. The tsar was thus effectively his own prime minister. Ministers held office only so long as they continued to enjoy his confidence. The dangers of such a system under a mediocre, let alone a subnormal autocrat are obvious. However, the accepted mystique of the tsar's office with its quasi-religious aura could conceal and to some extent mitigate a mass of human shortcomings. Autocracy, once a feature of many European monarchies, was a symptom of political underdevelopment. In Russia it was widely held to be superior to Western institutions, allegedly avoiding their divisions, faction and strife. Protagonists of this form of government also argued – possibly with some justification – that it alone could keep together a vast and increasingly heterogeneous empire. Autocracy was also defended as

16

the specifically Russian form of government adapted to the national character and traditions.

The second core institution of the old order were the service gentry in their double capacity as state servants, both military and civil, and as local agents of the central government, described by Nikolai I as his 'unpaid hereditary police-masters'. The relaxation and eventual abolition of compulsory state service for members of the *dvorianstvo* by Peter III made little practical difference. The service gentry, partly replenished by newcomers from other 'free' classes of the population, continued to provide the bulk both of officers and *chinovniks*. It remained the backbone of a heavily bureaucratized, hierarchically structured ruling class. At the same time, the individual *pomeshchik* (landowner) under the old order fulfilled a number of important public functions. In the first place, he ensured the maintenance of law and order in his village or villages by the exercise of a form of primitive manorial jurisdiction over his serfs. Secondly, he provided from among their number a quota, fixed annually, of recruits for the Russian army (condemned to serve for a period of 25 years). Finally, the landowner was responsible for the payment by his serfs of a poll or capitation tax, with himself having to make good any shortfall. In effect, the landowning *dvorianin* was the local administrator providing the Russian state with local government at no cost to itself.

The third pillar of the old order was the institution of serfdom. Regarded during its consolidation under Peter I as the compensation to the gentry for compulsory state service, it survived the abolition of that service in 1762 as an economic and socio-political institution in its own right. As such, it fulfilled a double purpose. In the first place, it provided unpaid agricultural labour for up to three days a week on the estates of noble landowners. In mainly non-agricultural regions, owners would receive money payments, *obrok*, in lieu. Originally a device for paying the noble landowner for lifelong state service with land and unpaid labour to work it, it would later be justified as his reward for the performance of unpaid administrative duties or as a supplement to meagre salaries earned in state employment. Serfdom, moreover, was integrated into a system of domestic service often indistinguishable from slavery. According to the whims of their owners domestic serfs (*dvorovie liudi*) could be treated abominably, tolerably, or with kindness in a patriarchal fashion – but always in a completely arbitrary manner. Moreover, as a large-scale landowner, the state had its own serfs administered by officials, as had the imperial family on its estates.

The structure of the old order was basically a simple one. At the bottom there was a mass of serfs, administered by landowning gentry or, more rarely, by state officials. Above them, there rose a class of

landowners and officials with the two becoming gradually differen-
tiated. At the apex of the pyramid was the autocrat, surrounded on the
one hand by his family and court favourites, and on the other by his
chief executive agents. Notwithstanding occasional palace coups and
despite the great peasants' rising (1773–5) associated with the name
of Pugachev, the structure was essentially a stable one. Its basic
strength was demonstrated by the consummate ease with which
Nikolai I crushed the half-baked Decembrist rising of 1825. Moreover, it was an order buttressed by the prestige of brilliant military and
diplomatic achievements, notably under Catherine II (1762–96) and
again under her grandson Aleksandr I (1801–25). Whatever the
internal shortcomings of the system, Russians glowed with patriotic
pride at the exploits of Suvorov and Kutuzov, their military heroes.

Nevertheless the rising of part of the military aristocracy in 1825
administered a shock to the régime. It generated in the new emperor,
Nikolai I, a premature but persistent siege mentality. Among his
policies, not the least important had been the setting up of the Third
Division of His Majesty's Own Chancery, effectively a Ministry of
State Police, with the Corps of Gendarmes as its paramilitary executive
arm. Although a secret police had long existed in Russia, as in many
other states, the creation of the Third Section by Nikolai I lent a new
emphasis to the preoccupation with state security. It may indeed be
said to have turned the Russian old order into something of a police
state.

An accompanying innovation was militarization. Nikolai I, himself
trained as a field officer, would consistently refer to the empire as his
'command'. Everyone, from schoolboy and university student to the
most senior official, was put into uniform and subjected to a hierarchical quasi-military discipline. All social relations were organized on
the basis of subordination and unquestioning obedience. Soldiers, the
tsar's adjutants-general, were used extensively to supplement and
sometimes supersede civil administrators even at the highest level.
With a standing army of little less than a million men, Russia was
turned into something like an armed camp. She became a militarized
society from the court downwards.

A further feature of Nikolai's reign was an extensive and unprecedented attempt at thought control through a sharpening of censorship regulations, the examination of private correspondence and the
widespread use of police agents and spies. What finally emerged
during and after the revolutions of 1848 is usually known as 'the era
of censorship terror'.[1] Any free expression of opinion was stifled –
though dissidents still found clandestine means of propagating their
ideas. Censorship, operating at times with less than total effectiveness,
was supplemented by the propagation of an official ideology, summed

up by the Minister of Education, Count S. S. Uvarov in his well-known slogan of 'Orthodoxy, Autocracy and Nationality'.[2] It was this which became the keynote of educational policy and the inspiration of official pronouncements, decrees and proclamations. National chauvinism linked on the one hand to the Orthodox religion, on the other to a paroxysm of monarchical devotion ran high, at any rate in official circles.

The repressive régime set up by Nikolai I following the Decembrist shock, intensified after the Polish rising of 1831 and reached its apogee during the year of revolutions, extending well beyond the confines of the Russian Empire. In co-operation with Metternich and reactionary Prussian rulers the tsar had assumed the role of 'policeman of Europe'. In the revolutions of 1848, Nikolai I helped to suppress the Hungarian revolt against the Habsburgs, maintained order in the Danubian Principalities, forced the Prussian government to yield to Austria in the Punctuation of Olmütz and ensured the survival of the historic Danish monarchy. Had it been physically feasible, he would have intervened also in the affairs of France. Effectively, Nikolai I ensured the survival of the Habsburg monarchy by contributing to the defeat of national-liberal movements in Germany, Italy and Hungary. Poland had hardly stirred.

What Nikolai I succeeded in imposing, at least superficially, during the 30 years of his reign (not only on the Russian Empire, including Poland, but also on Eastern and Central Europe) was a deep political freeze of an unprecedented kind. With his allies, he had succeeded in containing the rising tide of liberal and national sentiment. The freeze had of necessity been extended to the social and economic spheres. Serfdom, the basis of Russia's social and economic structure, had been preserved in the interest of social and political stability. Economic development – elsewhere in Europe this was the age of early industrialization and railway construction – was deliberately held back. The reasons were both economic and political. The maintenance of a vast standing army in a poor backward country left few resources for economic development. Private entrepreneurship and investment scarcely existed. The domestic market was supplied mainly by the cottage industries (*kustar*), which occupied the peasantry during the long winter months. Fiscal constraint, moreover, coincided also with political intent. It was understood that industrial development might lead to social change and political unrest. Thus Count Kankrin (originally Krebs) the tsar's long-serving Minister of Finance, rejected proposals for the building of some railway lines on the grounds that railways encouraged 'frequent and useless travel, thus fostering the restless spirit of our age'.[3] The only major line built in Russia during the first half of the nineteenth century, was the administrative link between the two capitals of St Petersburg and Moscow. This so-called 'Nikolai Railway' was constructed by American engineers and on instruction from the tsar in virtually a straight line. Thus Nikolai ruled over his empire of 'Dead Souls' (Gogol's classic novel was published in 1842).

And yet, even Nikolai I was on occasion prepared to tinker with some of the basic institutions. Thus a succession of secret committees staffed by senior officials debated endlessly and without result the possibility of modifying serfdom. His motive for such efforts remains unclear. Was it concern for the public opinion of Europe, the wish to present the world at large with a more civilized face? Was it on the other hand genuine indignation at some individual outrages widely known and periodically publicized? Or was there growing unease at recurring peasant riots and acts of violence against individual land-owners with distant echoes of Pugachev? Or perhaps a dawning realization of the low productivity of servile labour both in agriculture and industry? Whatever his motives, and they were probably mixed, even Nikolai I (like his brother before him) did show some desire for the modification – and even contemplated the eventual abolition of serfdom at some time in the future.[4] The subject of reform had not been completely taboo even under the 'Iron Autocrat'.

Nikolai I impressed on the old order certain specific features reflecting his own siege mentality. Yet there is little reason to doubt that the order was essentially stable and secure. It was not an accident that the upheavals of 1848–9 passed Russia by. Her prestige in Europe stood high with friend and foe alike. With her tall and imposing ruler and his vast armies, Russia appeared to the outside world as an invincible giant. There was little to suggest that the old order would not persist for decades to come.

Hubris overtook the mighty tsar when in 1853–4, ignoring the advice of Nesselrode, his cautious Foreign Minister, he blundered and blustered ill-prepared into war; first with Turkey and then, more fatefully, with her allies Britain and France. He showed misjudgment, relying on the benevolence and gratitude of the proverbially fickle Habsburgs and also arrogance, primarily in his dealings with Turkey but also with the 'upstart' emperor of the French. Diplomatic inepti-tude was compounded by faulty strategy when Nikolai decided to defend at all costs the new naval base and fortress of Sevastopol in the remote Crimea. The Russian command proved its incompetence not least in permitting Anglo-French forces to establish a bridgehead in the Crimea. The pusillanimous Prince Menshikov and his successors were on a par here with their British and French counterparts, none showing significant military talents except for General Totleben, an engineer and architect of Sevastopol's prolonged defence. Of course there was little military experience on either side, the last major battle in Europe having been fought at Waterloo in 1815.

What decisively tipped the scales against the Russians, however, was their technological inferiority. That of their Black Sea fleet proved very damaging, allowing the Allies to maintain their lines of supply and communications to the Bosphorus and the Dardanelles. Still more serious was Russian inferiority in infantry weapons, the lack of rifled breech-loading rifles. Perhaps most significant of all was Russian inferiority in the field of transportation. While the Allies constructed a narrow-gauge military railway in the Crimea, Russian supplies and reinforcements had to be brought into Sevastopol over distances of hundreds of miles and the wounded evacuated by road-using ox carts. This lack of adequate communications combined with the effectiveness of French artillery bombardment, in the end, made the fortress untenable. Its loss was a shattering blow especially to the tsar who had staked his prestige on its successful defence.

In fact, Nikolai I did not live to see the final defeat. A healthy man in his prime, he was demoralized by impending Russian failure. Broken in spirit, he neglected a chill and was carried off by ensuing complications. Indeed people would speak of suicide. At his death, autocratic power passed into the hands of a relatively young and untried heir. It was to him that fell the thankless task of liquidating the war and burying the earlier glories of the campaigns against Napoleon, the Congress of Vienna and the successes of 1848–9.

Russia's international situation was alarming. Sweden began hostilities the following spring and Austria was also adopting a threatening attitude, issuing an ultimatum. The King of Prussia, Russia's last friend, warned that he might be unable to maintain his sympathetic attitude. A grand anti-Russian coalition was in the making. There was no choice but to make peace. This was concluded in Paris on 30 March 1856. Russia had to accept terms which the new tsar and the bulk of his subjects considered dishonourable. Two provisions of the peace treaty in particular rankled. The neutralization of the Black Sea, severely limiting Russia's naval presence was one. The other was a modest cession of territory in the border province of Bessarabia, the first wrung from Russia since Peter I's 'Capitulation of the River Pruth' in 1711. Its object was to sever Russian communications with the mouths of the River Danube. Compared to these provisions the abrogation of the special rights claimed by Russia to protect the Christian populations of the Ottoman Empire may have been less painfully felt. At the same time, the bankruptcy of the old order and, more particularly, the 'system' of Nikolai I stood glaringly revealed. The need for far-reaching changes – perestroika – was widely recognized.

NOTES

1. Michael T. Florinsky: *Russia* (New York, 1955), vol II, p 813.
2. The untranslatable *narodnost* – from *narod* (people).
3. Florinsky: *Russia*, vol II, p 789.
4. Some improvement in the lot of the state serfs was actually achieved thanks to the activities of a conscientious Minister of State Domains, Count P. D. Kiselev, who enjoyed the tsar's confidence.

Part II
Aleksandr II

3

The 'Tsar Liberator'

The beginnings of the new reign were marked by a thaw, a relaxation of discipline after a period of severe repression. Two particularly unpopular ministers, those of the interior and communications, were sacked. Within a few months of his accession, the new tsar withdrew vexatious legislation directed against religious dissenters (sectarians), while a more tolerant régime was introduced also for the Catholic Church in Poland. Restrictions on university admission disappeared. Young scholars were, once again sent abroad at public expense. Works previously banned by the censors were permitted to appear. A general review of censorship regulations was instituted. The coronation manifesto cancelled tax arrears for the tsar's poorest subjects. Provinces which had suffered during the war received tax exemptions. The hated system by which the sons of conscripts were consigned to military orphanages to be brought up as soldiers was abolished, as were similar arrangements for often kidnapped Jewish boys. Restrictions on Polish landowners in the western provinces were removed. Jews were relieved from special taxes. A major amnesty for political prisoners included the surviving Decembrists. Heavy passport fees, part of Nikolai I's 'Iron Curtain' against the West, were abolished. In short, it was made abundantly clear, in the manner typical of the inauguration of a reform period, that the spirit of government had changed.

More fundamental changes were foreshadowed in the manifesto announcing the conclusion of peace:

> With the help of divine Providence, which has always protected
> Russia's welfare . . . may her internal wellbeing be strengthened

and perfected: may truth and mercy reign in her courts: and may there develop in all spheres the urge towards enlightenment and every form of useful activity. May everybody under the protection of laws equally just for all and giving all equal protection, enjoy the fruits of his honest labour.[1]

It was a proclamation which seemed to hold out the vague promise of some reform of Russia's corrupt, dilatory, capricious and often cruel judicial system. It even proclaimed the concept of equality before the law at least as an aspiration. There was thus some promise of 'organic' change, perestroika.

Moreover, Aleksandr II embarked, almost at once, on another far-reaching innovation: the construction of several major railway lines. Already in the autumn of 1855 he set up a committee charged with studying European railway legislation. On the day the conclusion of peace was officially confirmed, he told Baron Stieglitz, Russia's leading financier: 'The peace is signed; we must profit by it.' Thus encouraged, Stieglitz departed forthwith for Paris to discuss railway financing with French banking interests. Agreement was speedily reached by Stieglitz and finance houses in Paris, Amsterdam and London. With mainly French capital the great Russian Railway Company was formed with the object of constructing a number of arterial lines serving both economic and military needs. The Russian government guaranteed a minimum return on the capital invested so long as an agreed maximum cost per mile was not exceeded. Though the company and its largely French engineers would meet with many difficulties, and though major completions would not materialize for years (1868–74), Aleksandr II had, perhaps without fully realizing its implications, taken a giant step towards the destruction of the old order inherited from his admired father.

*   *   *

Soon Aleksandr II would take a yet more decisive step: the ending of serfdom, Russia's basic social institution.[2] His conversion to the need for abolition had been a gradual one. As a member of his father's secret committees he had, on the whole, inclined to the side of the serf-owners. However, several factors led him to change his views. As he himself would confide to the writer Ivan Turgenev, the latter's abolitionist *Sportman's Sketches* (*Zapiski Okhotnika*) published in the late 1840s had impressed him profoundly. A growing realization by the educated Russian public of the need for a radical perestroika following the Crimean debacle hastened his conversion. So did the stirrings of unrest among conscripts returning from the Crimea. Last but not least was the influence of abolitionists in his entourage. These included his wife, a German princess he consistently neglected, his mistress, Princess Aleksandra Dolgoruky, his younger brother, the ultra-liberal Grand-Duke Konstantin, and the Grand-Duchess Elena Pavlovna, a Württemberg princess, widow of one of his uncles. Thus in his immediate circle, whether at soirées or during the nights which followed, the tsar was insistently pressed to 'take the plunge'.

Conscious of the size of the task, lacking confidence in his own abilities and by nature easy-going, pleasure-loving, indeed lazy, Aleksandr II hesitated. Rumours circulated soon after his accession, to the effect that serfdom was to be abolished. He had countered them with an ambivalent declaration to representatives of the Moscow nobility (April 1856):

> For the contradiction of certain unfounded reports [he announced] I think it necessary to tell you that I do not at present intend to abolish serfdom; but certainly, as you well know yourselves, the existing manner of owning serfs cannot remain unchanged. It is better to abolish serfdom from above than to await the time when it will begin to abolish itself from below. I request you, gentlemen, to consider how this may be achieved, and to submit my words to the nobility for their consideration.[3]

It was the tsar's first public pronouncement on the subject of serfdom and it had several significant features. While disclaiming any intention of abolishing serfdom immediately, he at the same time, expressed his conviction that the existing system had ceased to be tenable. Using the dreaded spectre of a future *jacquerie*, a new *Pugachevchina*, he tried to convince Moscow *dvoriane* that necessary changes must be introduced from above. At the same time, however, he called on his listeners to submit their suggestions for necessary changes. Invitations to the premier estate to co-operate with the autocratic power would from then on be repeated, so long as hope remained of enlisting the serf-owners' voluntary co-operation. There was also an implied undertaking that the modifications and eventual abolition of serfdom would be a gradual process rather than a single cataclysmic act.

In fact, shortly after his address to the Moscow nobility, the tsar consulted Lanskoy, the Minister of the Interior, about the best means for initiating 'gradual endeavours towards the liberation of the privately owned serfs'. In reply, Lanskoy proposed the drawing up of a plan for liberation by stages. He was then instructed to gather relevant information from the ministries involved and also to prepare a historical résumé of the evolution of serfdom since the days of Peter the Great together with an abstract of the numerous proposals for its modification. He was furthermore to take advantage of the forthcoming coronation for informal soundings of visiting marshals of the nobility.

The attempt to enlist the assistance of the nobility in the proposed perestroika, however, produced little result. Neither the Moscow address nor similar promptings to some marshals visiting St Petersburg brought the desired response. Neither did repeated hints from Lanskoy. Spokesmen of the *dvoriane* replied, not wholly unreasonably, that ignorant as they were of the principles on which the government intended to proceed, they were unable to devise these for themselves. Faced with the failure of his efforts, the tsar then resolved to take the initiative. He did this – in the time-honoured manner of his predecessors – by assembling a secret committee composed of senior bureaucrats under his own chairmanship. In his absence it would be chaired by the President of the State Council, Prince Aleksei Orlov, an aristocrat of 71 known as a determined defender of serfdom. The majority of members also opposed abolition. Among its few abolitionists was Lanskoy, a Freemason and erstwhile Decembrist sympathizer.

At the opening meeting, the tsar announced that the time had come to consider 'with due care and deliberation' arrangements that would pave the way for the eventual abolition of serfdom. He then enumerated the major issues raised in a memorandum prepared by Lanskoy. Was all the land, including that at present allotted to the village communes for their perpetual use, to remain the property of the landowner? If yes, should the serfs' customary right of use be legally recognized? Should landowners be compensated for the loss of free labour services and of such land as they might have to give up? If so, how far should the cost of compensation be borne by the Exchequer? These, said the tsar, were the questions to which members of the committee had to address themselves.

The majority of the committee, influential and wealthy landowning aristocrats, were resolved to prevent emancipation altogether or, should this prove impossible, to reduce its impact to a minimum. Orlov, Adlerberg Senior, an erstwhile favourite of the late tsar, Gagarin, Panin (Minister of Justice) and Muraviev (Minister of State Domains) spared no pains to obstruct, indeed to sabotage the efforts of Lanskoy and some senior officials of his mainly reformist ministry. As the deliberations of no fewer than seven secret committees on the matter had in the past run into the sands why should not the eighth do so too?

While the secret committee was stalling, the Ministry of the Interior decided to prepare its own draft project. This gave privately owned serfs their personal freedom with possession of their huts and farmyards (for which they would indemnify the landowner over a period of 10–15 years) but left the entire estate as the landowner's property. During the elaboration of this project in the summer of 1857, the tsar, at a German spa, observed to P. D. Kiselev, former Minister of State Domains and a confirmed abolitionist, 'I am more determined than ever but have no one to help me in this important and pressing task.' As Kiselev noted in his diary, Aleksandr II was clearly determined to press on but was meeting with difficulties at every step. In fact, on returning from his German holiday the tsar discovered to his annoyance that in his absence no progress whatever had been made. To expedite matters he now appointed to the committee his brother Konstantin under whose prompting some slight progress was at length achieved.

While matters were thus advancing at a snail's pace, the governor-general of the three Lithuanian provinces, General V. Y. Nazimov, arrived in St Petersburg (November 1857) bearing a petition wrested with much arm-twisting from his local nobility. In it, they requested permission to prepare local projects for the abolition of serfdom. Presently, similar petitions would arrive also from other provinces. All were referred by the tsar to the secret committee. The petitioners, in fact, were entertaining hopes of a landless liberation similar to that introduced earlier in the century in the Baltic provinces without adverse effects for the landowners. The tsar, however, had other ideas. He issued orders to prepare forthwith a draft law following the lines of Lanskoy's proposal. After liberation, the ex-serfs were to receive their homesteads which would become the property of extended families. They would retain the right to farm the land they currently cultivated in return for a regular fixed payment in cash or in labour. Three meetings of the committee sufficed to produce the desired draft.

On 20 November the tsar instructed Nazimov to convene in each of his provinces, representative committees of the nobility to prepare detailed proposals for emancipation. These must incorporate certain basic provisions. Landowners would retain (legal) ownership of the whole of their estates. The peasants, however, must be assured of the *use* of as much land as would be needed for their subsistence and for the payment of taxes. For such land, they would have to compensate the landowner in either cash or labour. They would acquire legal ownership of their homesteads after payment of redemption dues spread over a fixed number of years. Seigneurial jurisdiction would continue. In a supplementary instruction Lanskoy informed Nazimov that personal bondage would cease after a 12-year transition period. Steps should be taken first to limit and finally to abolish the institution of domestic slavery.

Within a few days, Lanskoy despatched copies of the tsar's rescript (an order addressed to a named individual) and of his own accompanying circular to the governors and marshals of nobility of every province in European Russia 'for information and action should the nobility of your province express a similar desire'. Some days later, the tsar spoke to representatives of the St Petersburg nobility. Their governor-general, he said, had explained to them his wishes on the peasant question which, it was his firm resolve, must be settled. The principles that had been enunciated would be ruinous to neither party. 'I hope,' he concluded, 'that you will show a sincere interest in this matter, and will turn your attention to a class of people who deserve that their situation should be justly assured. Further delay is impossible; the matter must be dealt with now not postponed to a distant future. That is my unshakable resolve.' And, turning to the governor-general, he added, 'I ask you to co-operate with the nobility and to lead them; help them if there are difficulties'.

Two further steps followed. The hitherto 'secret' rescript to Nazimov was officially promulgated and, early in the New Year, the until then secret committee became the clumsily named official 'Main Committee on the Peasant Question for the Review of Projects and Suggestions concerning the Peasantry'. In this way, Aleksandr II made public his intentions and committed the prestige of the autocracy to their realization. At the same time he had, at least by implication, appealed to the Russian public to second his efforts. Though he may not have realized it at the time, this act of glasnost ranks among the most momentous decisions taken by the Russian autocracy.

The public declaration of the tsar's intention to liberate the serfs divided Russian society from top to bottom. The ruling class, land-owning and bureaucratic, split into two bitterly hostile camps with an abolitionist minority facing a 'planter' (opposed to emancipation with land) majority. The intelligentsia (journalists, publicists, academics, professionals) was also split, if in very different proportions. While a majority of senior bureaucrats and landowners either openly or secretly opposed the tsar's intentions, the bulk of the numerically small intelligentsia led by the radical publicist Aleksandr Gertsen living in exile in London greeted the tsar's announcement with enthusiasm. 'Thou has conquered O Galilean!' Gertsen's *Kolokol* (*The Bell*) exulted. The anarchist Peter Kropotkin would recall that all of intellectual St Petersburg 'was with Gertsen and especially with Chernyshevsky ... The whole disposition of St Petersburg, whether in the drawing rooms or in the streets was such that it was impossible to draw back.'

In fact, it would take a grinding three-year struggle for the tsar to accomplish his purpose. The conservative opposition with which he and his supporters had to contend was formidable. A group of wealthy aristocratic officials inherited from the previous reign aware that liberation especially with land, would sound the death knell of the old order, formed the planters' high command; both lower cadres and rank and file were recruited from provincial gentry. These were in many cases heavily in debt and feared that losing part of their land, their free labour services or payments in lieu, their domestic slaves and seigneurial jurisdiction would destroy their status and way of life. Only an idealistic minority mainly of younger men was prepared to carry out the tsar's intentions. On every provincial committee set up under pressure from local governors, to prepare projects of emancipation, planters formed a majority. It long remained uncertain to what degree the tsar's authority would prevail.

In his struggle with the serried ranks of the planters, the tsar was sustained by two small groups of people, besides public opinion which could only help psychologically. One consisted of members of his family and entourage whom we have already mentioned. The other was a group of officials, with the Grand-Duchess Elena as the link between the two.

During the early and mid-1850s, the grand-duchess's regular Thursday soirées had provided a meeting place for reform-minded officials recruited during the previous reign by enlightened chiefs in the Ministries of the Interior and State Domains, and a number of liberal intellectuals from both St Petersburg and Moscow. 'There, conversation flowed freely and, most important, sensitive reform questions, which could not be discussed either in the press or in official circles were often the topic of conversation.'[4] 'At all of these gatherings', one participant would note in his memoirs, 'in spite of differences of opinion, everyone agreed on one general feeling: the desire for a better order'.[5] This and other similar discussion circles were beginning to create an 'enlightened bureaucracy' composed of younger officials 'who realized that reform would involve society as a whole and who had begun to share the social conscience of the moderate intelligentsia'.[6]

Most were well acquainted with the administrative routines of the old order which they criticized savagely. Several had made a special study of economic and social conditions either of towns or of the peasantry. Among them were men with practical experience. Prominent in this group of enlightened younger officials, and emerging as their natural leader, was Nikolai Miliutin, nephew of the reforming Minister of State Domains of the preceding reign, Count P. D. Kiselev. Offspring of an impoverished but well-connected noble family, Miliutin could look back on a rapid bureaucratic career as a statistician in the Ministry of the Interior (1841–52) under the enlightened L. A. Perovsky. In 1842, he had been placed in charge of a body clumsily named Provisional Section for the Reorganization of Municipal Government and Economy, presently to be absorbed into the Economic Department of the Ministry of the Interior. Through his work in the Provisional Section, Miliutin had risen above the rank and file of middle-ranking bureaucrats. From this moment, he never looked back. While heading the Provisional Section, Miliutin had begun to gather round him a circle of enlightened colleagues destined to play an important part in the future perestroika. There would emerge 'a group of men with a knowledge of Russian conditions and practical experience in planning and implementing change, who saw reform as being more far-raching than mere improvements in the state administrative machinery.'[7]

Behind Miliutin's reformist views lay a statist political philosophy. This appeared prominently in his attitude towards serfdom. Echoing the views of Aleksandr II 'his primary concern was the interest of the state and not that of any one social class.' He therefore opposed serfdom 'mainly because of the negative effect he considered it to have on the state as a whole . . .' as 'a major hindrance to social and economic progress in Russia'.[8] Only emancipation of the serfs would make it possible 'to improve the productivity of Russian agriculture and thus produce the capital needed for industrialization of the Empire'. As a bonus, Miliutin saw in emancipation the possibility 'of destroying the absolute power of the aristocracy [gentry would perhaps be more appropriate] in the countryside which stood as a challenge to the power of the central authority in St Petersburg'.[9]

As an interested spectator with a ringside seat, Miliutin had observed the tsar's early efforts to overcome the resistance of bureaucracy, aristocracy and gentry to emancipation with land. In the spring of 1858, he wrote in a letter to his uncle Kiselev:

> The nobility is self-interested, unprepared, underdeveloped . . . I cannot tell you what will come out of all this, without leadership and direction, faced with the most crude opposition from the highest officials . . . It is impossible not to be amazed at the rare firmness of the Emperor who alone curbs the present reaction and forces of inertia.[10]

Among the most harmful reactionary influences Miliutin counted the tsar's confidant General J. I. Rostovtsev, an influential member of the Main Committee on Peasant Affairs. To blacken Rostovtsev's character and perhaps weaken his influence, Miliutin did not scruple to transmit a note denigrating the general to Gertsen's émigré *Kolokol* in London. Miliutin, moreover was closely connected with plans worked out during 1858 for the reform of local administration designed to reduce the influence of the nobility. The conservatives counter-attacked by agitating for his removal. Late in 1858, discouraged about the prospects of reform and feeling that he had lost the tsar's confidence, Miliutin contemplated retiring from the state service.[11] Only the persistent pleading of his patrons, his chief Lanskoy and the Grand-Duchess Elena prevented the tsar from accepting the proffered resignation.

To co-ordinate the proposals to be received from the provincial committees the tsar, on the advice of Lanskoy, set up the so-called Editing Commissions in February 1859. It would be their task to draft a general emancipation statute and they were headed by Rostovtsev, who would be answerable directly to the emperor alone. By this time, Rostovtsev had become convinced of the need for emancipation with land. Not knowing whom to appoint to the new commissions he turned to Lanskoy. He also consulted a young relative P. P. Semenov, who happened to be both a member of Miliutin's circle and a regular visitor of the grand-duchess's soirées. Both drew Rostovtsev's attention to Nikolai Miliutin. Early in 1859, Semenov had brought about a reconciliation between Miliutin and Rostovtsev, who would henceforth work in tandem. On the joint recommendations of Lanskoy, Miliutin and Semenov, the commissions were then packed with enlightened bureaucrats, and abolitionist landowner-experts. At least ten belonged to Miliutin's circle and were regular visitors to Elena Pavlovna's salon. Fourteen had recently held office in the reformist Russian Geographical Society. Out of a total of 38 members a solid nucleus of 16 had known each other for years and shared a common passion for reform. They were already agreed on the form the legislation should take and were more than a match for the disunited planter opposition.

In March 1859 Lanskoy recommended Miliutin for the vacant post of Deputy Minister. To overcome the tsar's distrust of Miliutin, the grand-duchess arranged for him to be received by the empress who, in her turn, succeeded in dispelling her husband's doubts. Miliutin was appointed acting deputy minister. In that capacity, he would now dominate the proceedings of the commissions. He would chair both the crucial economic and the financial section. He would also preside over the codification section set up later to draft the actual statutes. Within the space of six months, with Miliutin as the driving force, the Editing Commission (now amalgamated into a single body) had completed the first part of its task, the preparation of a draft law for the abolition of serfdom in Russia.

Two critical obstacles remained. Late in 1859 and early the following year two groups of representatives of the provincial gentry came to St Petersburg to express their views on the commission's draft proposals. It was clear that they would try to emasculate the project. On the instructions of Lanskoy and with the approval of both Rostovtsev and the tsar, Miliutin convened a secret informal meeting of his most trusted supporters. They agreed, after much discussion that only parts of the draft, to be selected by Rostovtsev, should be submitted to the provincial delegates for their comments. It was decided also that the gentry representatives must neither present counter-proposals nor act formally as a group. They must be prevented from holding formal meetings. They should confine themselves to expressing an opinion on such questions as would be presented to them by Rostovtsev. In short, the spokesmen of the provincial gentry would be muzzled. Glasnost would be sacrificed to the interest of perestroika.

Before the critical point was reached Rostovtsev, the crucial link between the commission and the tsar (to whom he reported almost daily), fell seriously ill (October 1859). This occurred when the arguments between the commission and the first group of gentry representatives were at their height. The tsar was also being bombarded with memoranda and petitions condemning the proposed legislation. There was a constant fear among reformers that his determination might weaken in the face of concerted gentry resistance. To replace at least in part Rostovtsev's declining influence, Miliutin and his ally Prince Cherkassky used the grand-duchess's salon, frequented also by Aleksandr II, to urge him at every turn to stand firm in the face of gentry attack.

While protagonists and opponents of emancipation were thus fighting for the tsar's support, Rostovtsev died on 6 February 1860. Six days later, the reformers learned with consternation that his place on the commission would be taken by the Minister of Justice, Count V. N. Panin. A wealthy aristocratic landowner (he owned over 20,000 serfs), Panin had the reputation of being a reactionary planter. Several prominent members of the Editing Commission including Miliutin contemplated resignation but were dissuaded by the joint efforts of Lanskoy and the grand-duchess. Both parties, conservatives and reformers, considered that the appointment marked a shift in the stance of the tsar in favour of the rejoicing planters. In fact, this was not the case. What neither conservatives nor reformers knew was that, prior to appointing him, Aleksandr had exacted a promise that Panin would carry the work of the commission to the conclusion he desired.[12] Panin's appointment was therefore not the consequence of a shift in the tsar's attitude but resulted from the conviction, inculcated in him by Speransky, that the autocracy had a mediating function. And was it not politic to involve in the impending legislation a prominent conservative like the Minister of Justice? Notwithstanding some deviations Panin would, on the whole, abide by his undertaking to bring the work of the commission to the conclusion favoured by the tsar.

After he had assumed the chairmanship of the commission (end of February 1860) it fell to Panin to ward off the onslaught of the gentry delegates of the second summons. These would remain in the capital until 8 May 1860. Panin vacillated, caught between the delegates, 37 of whom presented to him a petition to the tsar, and 19 reforming members of the Editing Commission who also submitted a memorandum. The gentry petition with which he no doubt sympathized argued 'that any enactment of an emancipation with provisions for the perpetual usage of gentry lands for a fixed payment by former serfs would undermine the principle of the inviolability of private property, would reduce the income of the nobles significantly, and would throw the entire landowning class into disorder'. To obviate possible difficulties in plenary sessions under Panin's chairmanship, Miliutin and his friends resorted once again to the tactic of private unofficial meetings, now held in Miliutin's apartment. Eventually, the work of the Editing Commission was formally completed at a general session on 10 September 1860 though the winding up process took a further month. With this, Miliutin's direct involvement in the legislative process reached its term.

The draft law was then presented to the main committee where the aristrocratic planter leaders were preparing a last-ditch stand. The tsar informed Grand-Duke Konstantin, now the committee's president, that he would not permit major changes. The draft was duly passed with the addition of one significant provision that the Editing Commission had had no time to complete. Thus amended, it went before the State Council. Here, the tsar brushed aside strong opposition though the opponents of the measure were able to slip in a last-minute provision about the so-called 'beggarly allotment' to be considered presently. Finally, on 19 February 1861, the statute abolishing serfdom was officially promulgated.

On 21 April, the tsar dismissed Miliutin as acting Minister of the Interior. He would be employed again but in a very different capacity. Lanskoy also retired. This was part of the tsar's endeavour to propitiate the *dvorianstvo* as well as of his balancing act. The four year long struggle for emancipation was over for Russia's Abraham Lincoln.

Before considering some details of the emancipation legislation, the methods employed in its preparation must be analysed. The first and most significant feature is the role of autocratic power. Without its intervention at every stage of the long drawn-out legislative process, no emancipation of the serfs with land could possibly have come about. It was a reform no elective body in Russia at the time could conceivably have achieved. Autocratic power had interacted in the process with the two leading and partly overlapping elements of the ruling class: the higher bureaucracy, and the landed aristocracy and gentry. Autocracy and bureaucracy appear, in this instance, as mainly antagonistic forces. In the contest between the two, the entrenched aristocratic officials employed obstruction and procrastination as principal weapons in the defence of their material interests. Against such obstruction, favoured by the time-honoured Russian practice of preparatory legislative activity by secret interdepartmental committees, the autocratic power found itself in an apparently weak position. If the precedents of previous reigns were a guide, Aleksandr II must have lost the battle or been forced to compromise very considerably.

What came to his assistance, and helped to save him from almost certain defeat, was the small but compact nucleus of middle-ranking reformist officials and their like-minded allies among liberal (often Slavophil) landowners and in the moderate intelligentsia. With Miliutin as their leader, they had been debating and planning for years in the Ministries of the Interior and State Domains as well as in Elena's salon. These were the indispensable allies of an autocratic ruler fearful of offending the 'premier estate' of the Empire whether in its aristocratic, bureaucratic, or gentry manifestation. Two generations earlier Aleksandr's grandfather Paul I had paid with his life for doing just that. However, through the abolitionist influence in his family and entourage, Aleksandr was persuaded to persevere. The curious alliance of autocracy and radical bureaucratic reformers would in the end carry the day.

The reforming element in the bureaucracy, acting for what it conceived to be the common good in opposition to vested interests, had originated in the days of Nikolai I. It would, in one form or another, remain a force for modernization and perestroika, almost to the end. Liberation of the serfs with land was its first and arguably its greatest achievement. It was, however, a force which could be activated only from the outside, usually by the autocracy; it was incapable of taking the initiative. The reformers, moreover, invariably remained outsiders among senior bureaucrats preoccupied primarily with routine administration, with careers, power and perks, and devoted to the defence of their privileges. They would always remain a small public-spirited minority able, in favourable circumstances, to exercise an important influence.

Miliutin and his associates were inspired primarily by concern for the public good. Serfdom was seen by them as the major obstacle to Russia's economic and cultural progress. So were the outmoded privileges enjoyed by members of the *dvorianstvo*, in particular its serf-owning element. The enemy for them, were the representatives of gentry interests. Among themselves, they professed radical democratic views and sympathy for the underprivileged downtrodden majority. Their preoccupation with economic progress apart, their wider concerns were social and cultural rather than political. It was this which made possible their co-operation with the autocratic power. Both saw the state of which they considered themselves the servants, as standing above the particular selfish interests. In the name of the public good they were, as bureaucrats, prepared to act even against the interests of what, for most of them, was their own class or estate.

It was at this level of public concern (or needs of the state), that their strivings coincided, at least for a time, with the objectives of the autocracy. A late convert to emancipation with land, Aleksandr II had become convinced of the need for drastic modernization largely under the impression of the Crimean defeat. If Russia was to recover her position among the nations, extensive changes were imperative. This was a conviction which had superimposed itself on earlier predispositions of a different kind. A sentimental and humanitarian child of the romantic age Aleksandr had from his youth been receptive to abolitionist arguments on humanitarian grounds like those of Turgenev's *Sportsman's Sketches*. Both his mother, a Hohenzollern princess, and an early tutor, the liberal romantic poet Zhukovsky, had encouraged this strain in his personality. Moreover even Nikolai I had recognized the need first to modify and ultimately to abolish serfdom. Again, the tsar's warning to the Moscow nobility that serfdom might one day begin to abolish itself from below may well have reflected an actual fear. The Crimean War had seen an increase in endemic peasant unrest, provoked mainly by the levying of recruits, a fruitful source of many and varied abuses.

Once Aleksandr II had resolved on emancipation with land, it had been his principal concern to achieve the reform he considered imperative in co-operation with, rather than in opposition to, the *dvorianstvo*. It was this purpose which underlay his repeated speeches, indeed a whole whistle-stop tour of several provinces, in which he had vainly urged representative landowners to help him in his endeavours. Again and again, he reiterated that his proposals were injurious neither to landowners nor serfs but fair and just to all. His authority eventually prevailed over gentry opposition, for the landowners lacked prominent spokesmen in the imperial family and the immediate entourage. The elderly Orlovs, Panins and Gagarins were imbued with sentiments of monarchical loyalty and perhaps also lacked the qualities needed to lead an effective last-ditch stand.

For the aristocratic conservatives and the bulk of the provincial gentry alike, the bitter and prolonged struggle over emancipation had been a traumatic experience. In their great majority, they had opposed the tsar's perestroika and it would indeed have been a near-miracle had it been otherwise. Most felt their vital material interests threatened at a time when, in any case, their economic situation was far from rosy. As was customary among Russian landowners, they were living beyond their means and many estates were heavily mortgaged to official credit institutions. While they might have accepted a landless liberation and the loss of seigneurial authority, the transfer of land to their erstwhile serfs, at any rate in the fertile agricultural regions, appeared to them an act of unpardonable spoliation.

An additional element of resistance was the force of inertia, the natural preference for the 'good old days', with a consequent fear of radical change, a future without the familiar landmarks. A particular cause of anxiety was the likely reaction of the former serfs once manorial authority had been removed. At best, the old deference would be gone for ever; at worst ... Whatever emerged from the tsar's designs, it was certain to bring inconvenience, discomfort, danger. With limited exceptions, the Russian *dvorianstvo*, bred in the comfortable days of serfdom, was not an adaptable class.

Such feelings were accompanied by an understandable sense of grievance. Forgetting that estates with peasants living on them had once been granted to their forbears in return for lifelong state service, the landowners had long since come to treat them as hereditary private property. They were now being deprived of part of this, many believed, by 'red' landless St Petersburg officialdom. And their sense of grievance was exacerbated by the cavalier treatment which their representatives had received in St Petersburg. Was this their reward for generations of loyal service? Overall, the ruin of the *dvorianstvo* was widely anticipated.

The magnates, still numerous in the ministries and on official committees, were as a rule sufficiently wealthy not to have to worry too much about the purely economic effects of the impending reforms. Yet they also could not but be apprehensive. Firmly rooted in the old order they felt that the coming emancipation would spell the end of an age – their age. They resented too the role played by renegades of their own class like Miliutin and his friends, their juniors in the bureaucratic hierarchy and often their social inferiors.

The reactions of the landed gentry as a whole, were both under-standable and predictable. If they were influenced to some extent by residual feelings of monarchical loyalty and the exhortations of the tsar, such influences were rarely decisive. In essence, the fight over emancipation had been one between the autocratic power and the premier estate with victory for the former and consolation prizes for the latter. It was the second decisive defeat suffered by the Russian nobility following the failure of the Decembrists in 1825. To a limited extent, it also marked a partial success for two other groups in society: the bureaucracy which had determined both the mechanics and some of the legislation's content, and nascent public opinion with parts of the intelligentsia rendering useful assistance to the architects of reform. The age of the landowners was drawing to a close.

Under the provisions of the emancipation statutes consisting of 22 separate enactments with over a thousand sections and covering 360 printed pages, an immediate end was put to personal bondage. Seigneurial jurisdiction was abolished. The former serfs would become owners of their homesteads. Provisions of great complexity regulated the transfer of part of the land to the peasant communities. Norms were laid down for the size of allotments in different regions. During a transition period of 20 years, the villagers would enjoy the use of this land in return for an agreed rent (or labour services in lieu). After 20 years, the redemption operation proper would begin. It was expected to take decades, after which the land would become the property of the village commune. The Exchequer would pay the landowners 75 or 80 per cent of the price for the land they were to lose in the shape of interest-bearing bonds. The rest was to be made up by the peasants over a period of years. They were expected also to repay eventually the sums advanced by the government.

The arrangements would impose a heavy financial burden on the newly-liberated peasantry. In many cases payment would exceed the rental value of the land, especially as the price to be paid included a concealed element of compensation to the landowner for the loss of labour services or of money payments (*obrok*) in lieu. Some peasants would lose some of the land they had hitherto cultivated. Peasant communities which opted for the 'beggarly allotment' – a quarter of the maximum norm for the region free of all charges – would be inexorably doomed to progressive pauperization. Domestic serfs who gained their freedom would receive no land allocation. The financial provisions of the statutes, while imposing an exorbitant financial burden on the ex-serfs, did little to benefit the landowners. The government bonds in which they had been paid depreciated rapidly, while free instead of bonded labour involved expense and created serious managerial problems. Landowners as well as peasants would be impoverished.

The liberation statutes contained further provisions tending to perpetuate the low productivity of peasant farming. Though many of Miliutin's supporters recognized the economic advantages of individual farming operations, the old communal arrangements traditional mainly in the central provinces were retained. Peasant land which had been redeemed would become the property of the village commune to be allocated by it to individual households. Where this was the current practice, the repartitional tenure would continue with periodic redistribution of strips in the communal fields to accommodate changes in the size of households. The persistence of strip farming involved not only common crop rotation but also some common – or at least synchronized – farming operations. Traditional disincentives to more efficient farming thus persisted with a severe discouragement of individual initiative or innovation. The village commune, furthermore, remained collectively responsible for the payment of taxes and redemption dues. The village authorities, under the guise of peasant self-government were given draconian powers including corporal punishment and even banishment. Thus the collectivist features of village life would continue. Peasant farming in consequence remained primitive and inefficient.

There were, however, several reasons for preserving a system of communal land ownership which was widely recognized as unproductive. Some were of an administrative nature. Thus Rostovtsev in opposing individual household ownership argued that the peasants still needed a strong authority to replace that of the squires. Without an effective commune, the landowners would never obtain the payments and services to which they were entitled. Nor, Rostovtsev might have added, would the government be able to collect taxes or levy recruits. These considerations dictated the preservation of an effective rural organization whether at village level or at that of the *volost*, a newly created administrative unit embracing a number of villages. A further practical consideration was the fear of uncontrolled and excessive peasant mobility. The authority of peasant institutions combined with an internal passport system would, it was held, provide a safeguard, against these perceived dangers.

It was also argued by defenders of the communal system, that it had evolved over a long period of time and could not be abolished suddenly without serious economic, social, or even political consequences. Slavophil ideologists also argued for the land commune as Russia's most distinctive social institution superior morally to the 'rotten individualism' and competitive selfishness of the West. Socialists in their turn saw in the village commune the germ of a future socialist society. Only economic liberals favoured individual household ownership.

Perhaps the most cogent reason for preserving the village commune, however, would become apparent only in retrospect. Its destruction would have been a revolutionary operation, a further instalment of perestroika, and one that would have split the peasantry from top to bottom. Furthermore, the transition from one system to the other would have been beset with an array of practical difficulties. To have superimposed a second change of this magnitude on the one entailed in separating peasants and landowners would have been a sure recipe for total chaos in the Russian countryside.

A different question sometimes raised concerns the terms of emancipation. Could these have been more favourable to the peasantry? The solution favoured by members of the radical intelligentsia and, it seems, the bulk of the peasantry would have been to transfer to the peasants free of charge all the land they had until then been working for themselves. This would have been possible only on one of two conditions. Either the landowners would be compelled to give up roughly one-third of the land they considered theirs without any compensation (even autocratic power could hardly have imposed this without provoking a political upheaval), or the Treasury would have to make itself responsible for all compensation payments. But the chronic problems of state finance had recently been exacerbated by the cost of the Crimean War. Retrenchment had become the order of the day. As it was, the payment to landowners of compensation in depreciating bonds would prove a severe burden.

Terms for the peasantry might conceivably have been improved, but only marginally, and principally through somewhat larger allotments. The ones allocated were in most cases adequate in relation to the size of the then peasant population. Again burdens imposed on temporarily obligated peasants, those awaiting the conclusion of redemption agreements, might have been made somewhat less onerous. The difference would have been slight. Even somewhat more generous arrangements would still, as events turned out, have reduced many peasants to misery. It is difficult to see how provisions significantly more favourable to the privately-owned serfs could have been made. It is true that in 1864, more favourable terms would be conceded to the peasantry of the Polish kingdom. That, however, was a political act designed to punish rebellious Polish landlords for the rising of 1863. State peasants and those on estates belonging to the imperial family were liberated in 1863 and 1866 on somewhat more generous terms, but then both state domains and imperial appanages were relatively extensive. Nor did the state or the imperial family depend wholly on their lands for revenue or livelihood. Both could more easily afford to give serfs somewhat larger allotments in return for slightly less onerous redemption payments.

Overall, whatever their shortcomings, the statutes of 1861 formed a major landmark in nineteenth-century Russian history. Almost by a stroke of the pen, the autocrat had destroyed the old social order of which serfdom had been the centrepiece. Aleksandr II accomplished a major feat of social engineering and drastically altered the relationship between the two basic classes of Russian society. While the legal change was immediate and dramatic, the economic and social effects would make themselves felt only gradually. The implementation of the emancipation statutes and the adjustment to them of the local population would be a lengthy process. By the emancipation, an element of dynamism was introduced into a hitherto static society. Emancipation was largely a leap in the dark; its results anticipated by the government with a degree of apprehension. In fact, the dangers against which the statutes' authors had sought to guard; rural disorders, even a *jacquerie* or *Pugachevchina*, and the rapid creation of a rural proletariat materialized only to a limited extent. Instead, new problems emerged which were not, and perhaps could not, be foreseen. The main question for the government was whether, following a period of inevitable upheaval, a new, stable and more productive rural order would emerge from the ruins of the old.

* * *

Following the labours of the emancipation struggle, the bureaucratic machine turned its attention on the orders of the tsar to further basic reforms. The first of these, as foreshadowed in Aleksandr's early manifesto, was a thorough-going overhaul of the empire's judicial system. This had long been notorious for its secrecy, procrastination, its gross injustices and its venality. A secret committee chaired by the aged Count D. N. Bludov, had for years been wrestling ineffectually and in dilatory fashion with the thorny problem of legal perestroika. The abolition of serfdom had lent this some urgency. With the disappearance of seigneurial jurisdiction, peasants and peasant communities were likely to be brought increasingly within the purview of the courts, even if petty cases involving only peasants were to be handled by special low-grade institutions confined to the peasantry. In the autumn of 1861, impatient at Bludov's lack of progress, the tsar reinforced his committee by the addition of a number of competent jurists and reform-minded officials, prominent among them S. J. Zarudny and D. A. Zamiatnin. Offspring of an impoverished family of Ukrainian gentry and trained in the Ministry of Justice, Zarudny would become the Miliutin of the judicial reform. Zamiatnin would replace Panin as Minister of Justice in the autumn of 1862.

As he had done for the emancipation laws, the tsar himself laid down guidelines for the work of the rejuvenated committee. He had instructed its members to reorganize the judicial institutions of the empire in the light of 'those fundamental principles, the undoubted merit of which is at present recognized by science and the experience of Europe'. The coming reforms would thus be a measure of Westernization. 'The "Chinese Wall"', a Russian historian has observed, 'which for 45 years had separated our legislators from the direct influence of European science and contemporary progress collapsed. The principles of Europe in public law and science ... were at last freely admitted into our legislation.'[13]

In accordance with its brief, a major report of the commission listed no fewer than 25 radical defects of the Russian legal system and proposed remedies. Among the latter were the complete separation of the judiciary from the rest of the administration; the introduction of the jury system in criminal cases; the election of magistrates (Justices of the Peace) to deal summarily with petty cases and a drastic simplification of cumbersome court procedures. The most important recommendation however, was for the replacement of court proceedings in writing and behind closed doors, by public ones based on adversarial pleading.

The government then, embarked upon a process of public consultation. In a bout of glasnost – the term was coming into widespread use in connection with the reforms – a memorandum outlining the basic features of the proposed innovations was published in the autumn of 1862. Legal officials, universities and even private individuals were invited to comment; 446 separate comments were received and these too presently published in six bulky tomes. The comments were then co-ordinated by a further committee, an Editing Commission, staffed by some of the empire's best jurists. Within 11 months the commission with the aid of a wealth of detailed preparatory studies compiled over the preceding decade, produced not only draft proposals for the reorganization of judicial institutions, but for good measure also draft codes of both civil and criminal procedures. Following some revision in the Imperial State Council, the judicial statutes received the imperial assent on 20 November 1864. In an *ukaz* (imperial decree) of the same date addressed to the Senate the tsar explained that the new legislation was the outcome of his wish to establish in Russia 'expeditious, just, merciful and impartial courts for all our subjects; to raise the judicial authority by giving it proper independence and in general to increase in people that respect for the law which national well-being requires, and which must be the constant guide of all and everyone from the highest to the lowest'.[14] If these were counsels of perfection, to be only imperfectly realized in practice, the *ukaz* did proclaim the two principles, novel in Russia, of the independence of the judiciary and the rule of law, in principle binding, at least in theory, even on the autocrat and his agents.

Perhaps the key provision of the statutes was that on the irremovability of judges except for misconduct in office. Though occasionally circumvented by means of 'postings', this would help to insulate the judiciary from executive and bureaucratic pressures. Other significant innovations included the replacement of police agents by examining magistrates in criminal investigations, the introduction of a recognized hierarchy of appellate jurisdictions and the abolition of barbarous punishments. The equality of the tsar's subjects before the law was established in theory and to a large extent in practice.

The judicial reform would also generate two by-products of major significance for the future. Under the Zamiatnin régime (1862–6) many idealistic young men, possibly the cream of Russian officialdom, flocked to his ministry to participate in the implementation of the reforms (ministers effectively selected their own senior subordinates). In the course of their subsequent careers, some of these would move on to other institutions, the Senate, the cabinet office, the Law Department and Secretariat of the State Council, even sections of the Ministry of the Interior. The bureaucracy, thus became permeated to a degree with a spirit of legality and judicial impartiality, and a repugnance for arbitrary executive action. Still more important perhaps was the emergence of a bar of practising lawyers, defending counsel in criminal and even in political cases. This would become in time a fertile recruiting ground for political activists including much later Aleksandr Kerensky. Lawyers, both practising and academic became the backbone of the (higher) professional intelligentsia, even if some like Pobedonostsev or Bogolepov would in the end espouse reactionary views.

The judicial reforms have been unjustly criticized on two main grounds. The first was the unavoidable gradualness of their introduction. Not until 1866 were the new courts set up in ten provinces constituting the judicial districts of St Petersburg and Moscow. The system was then progressively extended to the remainder of European Russia. The official explanation for the relative slowness was lack of resources both material and human. This rings wholly true, though under Zamiatnin's successors political considerations also may have played a part.

The second charge was that the new judicial institutions worked imperfectly, that abuses persisted, that the executive interfered, more particularly in political trials. In some areas, notably Poland, the Western provinces with their mixed populations and the Caucasus, the jury system was never introduced. However, what is surprising is not that the new institutions worked imperfectly in an underdeveloped country like nineteenth-century Russia, but that they worked at all, let alone with considerable success. The gradual implantation in Russia of rudimentary concepts of the rule of law, and of some degree at least of equality before the law, amounted to a cultural and social revolution. The days of Gogol's Government Inspector and his like, of the abuses pilloried by Gertsen and Saltykov-Shchedrin were gone for ever. Even the less than perfect operation of the judicial system described by a jaundiced Tolstoy in *Resurrection* at the end of the century was a far cry from the judicial horrors of the old order which Nikolai I had been unable to reform. In the judicial sphere, as in that of rural relations, the reforms of Aleksandr II thus marked the beginnings of a new era.

*   *   *

The last of the Great Reforms, that of local government was, to some extent, linked to the abolition of serfdom. Indeed the two had been prepared almost *pari passu*. On the one hand, some provision now had to be made for the welfare of the former serfs, for whom their owners were no longer responsible. On the other, some landowners were seeking compensation for the decline in their authority following the abolition of seigneurial jurisdiction and of serfdom in general. Finally, the government needed some administrative agency to supplement the thinly spread network of local officials and to take over some of the tasks previously carried out on its behalf by the local landowners. Thus a number of causes arising from liberation combined to make a radical reform of local government an urgent necessity.

Since for a variety of reasons no one wished to increase the number of local officials, the major issue concerned the form local self-government should take. On this, there was a fundamental difference of views between oligarchs who wished to preserve the gentry monopoly and democrats who desired to break through the class and estate principle by creating 'all-class' institutions. In addition, there was the issue of relations between central and local government. While centralizers believed in control of any new institutions by the St Petersburg ministries, their opponents took the view that local people must to a large extent be allowed to run their own affairs. A subsidiary but related issue concerned the scope of any new institutions, the division of functions between them and agents of central government.

All these matters became the subject of years of bitter argument on both broad principles and detail between democrats and oligarchs. Prominent among the former were the Miliutin brothers, first Nikolai and, after his fall his brother Dimitry, the reforming Minister of War. The opposite party had as its most prominent representative P. A. Valuev who, in 1861 had succeeded Lanskoy as Minister of the Interior. In the preparation of the draft statute, while Nikolai Miliutin had been in the ascendant, the views of the democrats had prevailed. Then, under the guidance of Valuev, the oligarchs gained the upper hand. The draft that finally emerged from the Main Committee was designed, on the one hand, to ensure the preponderance of the larger landowners in local government, on the other to restrict the activities and limit the authority of the new bodies to be set up, the local councils or *zemstva*.

Battle was finally joined when the draft came before the State Council. The reformers were led by the Miliutin brothers and included among their number the Minister of Finance, Reutern and Kovalevsky, a former Minister of Education. During discussions extending from 1862 to the beginning of 1864 they again and again criticized Valuev's draft and sought to secure amendments. Valuev, had among others the support of Panin and, fatefully, also that of the tsar, though in the State Council, the parties were evenly balanced. One crucial division occurred over the method of selecting chairmen of the *zemstvo* assemblies at the lower tier of the *uezd* or district. Were they to be chosen by the deputies or would the local marshal of the nobility become the chairman ex officio? The resulting vote was a tie. The tsar decided for the oligarchs. When it came to the chairmanship of the higher tier provincial assemblies, the democrats were again outvoted. Dimitry Miliutin, Kovalevsky and a third democrat Baron Korff, fought hard against clauses limiting the competence of the *zemstva* and subordinating their activities to control by the Ministry of the Interior and its agents. In the final resort, the oligarchs with the tacit support of the emperor, were able to carry the day on all major issues. On proposals involving political change however modest in scope, the tsar in every instance sided with the conservatives.

The statute which was finally promulgated early in 1864, while bearing the imprint of Valuev and his supporters, yet contained important democratic innovations. In more than one respect, it involved major breaks with Russian administrative tradition. As a result, the *zemstva* emerged as hybrid institutions, combining elements of genuine local self-government with those of bureaucratic organs of the state. Though the numerical preponderance of landowners in the *zemstvo* assemblies was assured, the gentry lost its monopoly of local government. For the first time, the estate principle would be broken through the representatives of peasants and burghers, joining in all-class elected bodies, even if as junior partners. The *zemstva*, as their name suggested, would be representative of all 'the land'.[15]

A second novelty was a necessary corollary of the first. *Zemstva* were officially charged with supplying the needs of local populations in fields like health and hygiene, elementary education, veterinary services, storage of grain reserves and road repairs. Presently, they would add matters like agricultural improvement, rural credit, fire insurance, the encouragement of co-operatives and statistical services. The sense of social responsibility motivating many *zemstvo* activists would distinguish them radically from the majority of class-bound gentry in the parallel assemblies of the nobility.

Another feature distinguishing the *zemstva* from earlier bodies was the continuity of their operations. During intervals between the annual plenary sessions, *zemstvo* affairs would be directed by a board (*uprava*) of four or five members elected for a three-year term. Members, often from impoverished gentry families were to be paid a salary fixed by the *zemstvo* assemblies. Under their direction *zemstva* would employ growing numbers of often semi-trained medical personnel; midwives, teachers, veterinary surgeons, agronomists and statisticians. Usually drawn from young and idealistic members of the radical intelligentsia, they would become known collectively as the Third Element, the other two being officials and *zemstvo* gentry. Both boards and Third Element, were innovations in Russian local government of considerable importance.

A further innovation, bitterly contested by conservatives, was the right of *zemstva* to levy rates on land and dwellings. *Zemstvo* rates would rise in due course to almost ten per cent of total national taxation. It was their rating power which assured for the *zemstva* at least a degree of autonomy as well as the ability to satisfy local needs. This was something very different from the existing right of assemblies of the nobility to tax themselves for purposes of the noble estate, a privilege sparingly used in practice.

Other changes resulting from the creation of the *zemstva* had political implications. While the old assemblies of the nobility were and continued to be dominated by class-conscious conservatives, *zemstvo* service, on the whole, tended to attract public-spirited landowners of liberal and often Slavophil disposition. The *zemstvo* was destined to become the nucleus of opposition to officialdom, both central and local. It was also a fruitful training ground for future public men. For the first time Russia had all-class elective bodies – still unthinkable under Nikolai I – only partly under administrative control and with power to raise their own finances. Circumstances would endow many *zemstvo* members with an ethos of public service contrasting sharply with that of a self-seeking officialdom. At least potentially, this was an alternative political elite.

Zemstva, almost from their inception, were inevitably drawn into activities at variance with official policy. Their assemblies would increasingly be tempted to express opinions on broad political issues. Evading government prohibitions, board members from different provinces would tend to co-operate, to begin with over innocuous matters like loyal addresses, commemorative celebrations, official presentations. They would go on to joint insurance operations, food supplies, famine relief and the fight against epidemics. Increasingly, there would be contacts and 'private' meetings – frowned on by the authorities – of chairmen of *zemstvo* boards. Scenting danger, ministers could do little more than scold, obstruct, or issue occasional bans. Whatever they did, however, and in spite of all their attempts to bureaucratize the *zemstva*, these would remain an alien element within the bureaucratic-autocratic state.

One source of future friction would be the *zemstva*'s increasing use of their rating powers and the employment of their fiscal resources. The Ministry of Finance, faced with growing financial stringencies, would look with a jaundiced eye at the potential revenue siphoned off by *zemstvo* rates. Nor did instances of *zemstvo* extravagance or misman- agement help to improve matters. This, with time, would become a major source of friction. *Zemstva* would frequently be criticized from the Right as inefficient and extravagant. But, given Russia's low cultural level and flawed administrative traditions, the imposition of legal restrictions and persistent bureaucratic obstruction, it is hardly surprising that the new and untried institutions often worked imper- fectly. Inexperience also played a part. It would take years of painstak- ing endeavour before *zemstva* would become fully equal to their task.

Criticism from the Left regarding the domination of the *zemstva* by gentry landowners was equally misplaced. Which other group of the rural population would have been capable of running them? Neither village priests nor local officials, let alone peasants, were qualified to do so. Landowners, with all their faults, were the only rural group containing cultured or educated elements, some with a degree of administrative experience. In short, if there was to be any improve- ment, by means of self-government in the condition of the local populations, the gentry would have to take the lead. The composition of the crucial *zemstvo* boards was, by and large, appropriate to their duties.

What did gravely weaken the effectiveness of the *zemstva*, however, were a number of structural flaws. The first of these concerned relations with local agents of central government, above all with the local police authorities. The previous administrative structure was left completely intact. No links of any kind were established between the *zemstva* and local representatives of the various ministries. Lacking executive organs of their own, *zemstva* were entirely dependent upon the goodwill of local officialdom for levying rates and the enforcement of their regulations, and this was frequently lacking. *Zemstva* were further weakened by the absence of any close links with the people whose interests they were supposed to serve. At the lower end, the two-tier *zemstvo* structure ended at *uezd* or district level which, owing to the size of districts, made the *zemstva* remote from their charges. What would come to be described as the 'small *zemstvo* unit', an all- class vestry, parish or township meeting, was lacking. The correspond- ing administrative unit, the *volost'* was confined to peasant affairs. It has been suggested that the reason for the ommission was bureaucratic distrust of local landowners and the wish to circumscribe their influence. Whatever the reason, the result left the *zemstvo* devoid of local roots. A third weakness, stressed by political reformers was the lack, at the other end, of 'a roof', that is a link with legislative processes at the centre. In a different perspective, the absence of a national *zemstvo* prevented the expression of common *zemstvo* concerns. All proposals to link the *zemstva* with the legislative work of the State Council were shelved.

As a result of these structural defects the *zemstva*, were 'floating in the air', suspended between the people and the central government and closely involved with neither. Their relations with officialdom remained ambiguous, ill-regulated and ill-defined, with the St Petersburg *chinovniks* enjoying the upper hand.[16] 'The new wine of self-government', it has been observed with truth, 'was poured into the old skins of the bureaucratic order which was by its nature incompatible with self-government.'[17]

While the early introduction of the *zemstva* was greeted with hopeful anticipation, that enthusiasm would steadily wane. For a decade, they would concern themselves with 'small deeds'; setting up schools and surgeries and promoting agricultural improvement. However, faced with a variety of difficulties, *zemstvo* deputies and administrators lost heart. Apathy spread. Meetings were poorly attended. Public opinion also became disillusioned. Publicists began to complain of the unsatisfactory state of *zemstvo* affairs. Only their undoubted achievements during and after the great famine of 1891 would give the *zemstva* their second breath.

*   *   *

One further aspect of Aleksandr II's reforms deserves mention. Late in 1861 the tsar had appointed as Minister of Education A. V. Golovnin the 'right hand' of Grand-Duke Konstantin, and a radical reformer. His appointment coincided opportunely with the presentation of a report on higher education by a committee which had been collaborating since 1858 with professors of the University of St Petersburg on the revision of its charter. This, together with the observations of other universities which had been consulted, was submitted to a further mixed group of officials and academics, this time to prepare new regulations for all universities of the empire. The activities undertaken by the new committee were thorough. Its draft proposals, translated into English, French and German, were submitted for comment to Russian and foreign academic institutions, to educational specialists and to officials of both state and church. K. D.

Kavelin, a distinguished professor of law, was sent abroad to study the organization of higher education in Germany, France and Switzerland. All the information collected was made public in two bulky tomes. The draft, revised several times, was approved by the State Council and finally promulgated in June 1863.

The new statute restored university autonomy, removing many of the restrictions which had been imposed in 1835. University councils consisting of members of faculty with their own elected officials were given wide powers to deal with both academic and administrative matters. Every university would be headed by a Rector elected from among the professors for a term of four years. A new institution, a university court, was set up with jurisdiction over students in matters of discipline. It would be presided over by a law professor assisted by two members of faculty elected by the council. While government-appointed curators would exercise a general supervision over the universities, the inspectors appointed by the Ministry of Education lost many of their earlier powers. Golovnin had favoured the legalization of student unions and of corporate student activities but this, in the end, did not figure in the final draft. Though several universities advocated the admission of women students, this was also denied. At the same time, the ministry under Golovnin tried to promote the training of future university teachers. Promising students received stipends for postgraduate studies. There was unprecedented encouragement of contacts with foreign educational institutions. Whatever the shortcomings of the new university statute, Russian universities experienced a rapid development under its operation. The period between 1863 and 1880 can be considered the most brilliant in the history of Russian universities.

In the area of censorship, mainly within the ambit of the Ministry of the Interior, the record of the authorities was mixed. The fearsome censorship committee of Nikolai I had been wound up at the end of 1855. Under the thaw inaugurated by Aleksandr II, there had been an increase of glasnost. Whereas between 1845 and 1854, only six newspapers had been licensed, between 1855 and 1864, this number would rise to 66. At the same time, the number of periodicals permitted to start publication had swelled from 19 to 156. A review of censorship regulations had been begun in 1857. Until its long delayed completion eight years later, the situation with regard to censorship procedures had remained unclear and practice arbitrary. By the time new regulations were published in the spring of 1865, earlier reforming impulses had partly evaporated.

The new regulations, described as 'provisional' – they would remain in force for 40 years – were a jumble of old and new elements. Two seeming innovations were the partial abolition of preliminary censorship and the replacement of administrative punishment for press and publishing offences by judicial proceedings before the courts. However, in neither case did the authorities fully abandon the earlier methods. Effectively, therefore, the operation of the censorship would depend almost wholly on the spirit of the administration and the general intellectual climate. So long as relatively liberal attitudes prevailed, the new regulations would favour a degree of glasnost. Should official dispositions change, however, the former methods of censorship and partial repression lay ready to hand. Yet even though the government would presently turn to reaction, Russian literature at least, flourished under the new regulations. The age of Turgenev was not yet over, that of Dostoyevsky, Tolstoy and Chekhov was at hand.

*   *   *

The Great Reforms of Aleksandr II, his perestroika, elaborated between 1858 and 1864 were far-reaching in their effects. Few areas of Russian life remained untouched. All changes, predictably, encountered bitter opposition from conservatives, both landowning and bureaucratic. While some opponents would defend the old order on ideological grounds, the greater number were fighting for vested interests. Active protagonists of reform were relatively few in numbers. They were to be found, as has been seen, in the tsar's immediate entourage, among a cluster of reform-minded officials, locally among some idealistic younger landowners and finally, in the ranks of the intelligentsia. It was not a strong constituency. However, the imperial prestige commanded the reluctant acquiescence of many who disliked the changes. They felt that the imperial command must be obeyed. It was thus the autocratic power alone that made perestroika possible. The reforms were a revolution from above carried out by a man of mediocre talents but convinced of the need for change and capable of a degree of determination, in the early years of his reign at least.

Half a Hohenzollern and an admirer of Prussia and things Prussian, the tsar wished, in broad terms, to 'Prussianize' Russia by reforming at least some of her institutions. Though a reformer, he was not a liberal. Indeed there is evidence to suggest that his disposition was scarcely less autocratic than that of his late father. However, the need for perestroika after the Crimean debacle was self-evident and widely recognized. A continuation of the régime of Nikolai I might well have eliminated Russia from the ranks of the great powers. However, while recognizing that perestroika had become an imperative necessity if Russia was to regain her international prestige, the tsar was determined that it should in no way diminish his autocratic power. In fact, he had correctly sensed the possible threat to that power, represented by even the relatively modest *zemstvo* institutions with their principles of local self-government, election and decentralization. Accordingly, he had consistently backed Valuev and the oligarchs, against Miliutin and the democrats. He was determined that perestroika should be brought about without basic change in the political system.

The attempt at perestroika with a minimum of political change would, however, store up trouble for the future. The new institutions that were being created would somehow have to fit into the rigid framework of centralized bureaucratic rule. This would inevitably become the source of future friction. In fact, what emerged from the tsar's perestroika was a ramshackle structure, an old building, patchily reconstructed. As summed up by a perceptive French observer:

> The emancipation was followed by numerous reforms, administrative, judicial, military, even financial, yet all these reforms, prepared by different commissions subject to rival or hostile influences, were undertaken in isolation, in an incomplete manner, without coherence and without a definite plan. The task was to build a new Russia, the edifice was constructed upon the old foundations. Building operations were carried out without a blue-print, without a general plan, without an architect to co-ordinate the different operations. By introducing here and there particular innovations while neglecting near-by indispensable repairs, by incorporating everywhere his innovations into the ancient structure, Alexander in the end succeeded after immense labours in making of the new Russia an incomplete and uncomfortable dwelling where friends and opponents of innovation felt almost equally ill at ease.[18]

However true, this fails to explain how Aleksandr II could have brought about still more radical changes even had he wanted to do so. Was he to abolish at one fell swoop autocracy, *dvorianstvo*, bureaucracy, centralization, the established hierarchical structures, challenge even more massive hostile vested interests? And what would replace everything being abolished? There can be little doubt that a root and branch perestroika going significantly beyond what had been done was not within the realm of the possible. The choice for Aleksandr II lay not between a halfway house and a brand new structure for which Russia in any case was totally unprepared, but between a reconstructed house and continued existence in the old, ramshackle and outmoded building.

However incomplete and unsystematic the perestroika, its impact on the future through the initiation of a dynamic of change in a hitherto stagnant society would be immense. Railway construction, the liberation of the serfs, free labour, rural education, the strengthening of legal institutions, the introduction of effective local government and the social consequences of all of these taken together were destined in succeeding decades to alter the face of Russia. The régime would have to adapt itself as best it could to far-reaching changes set in train by the Great Reforms. Moreover, the consequences of perestroika, intertwining with those of glasnost would in due course come to pose a threat to the very survival of the tsarist régime itself.

NOTES

1. A. Kornilov: *Kurs Istorii Rossii XIX Veka* (Moscow, 1912) Part II, p 136.
2. The main works in English dealing with the abolition of serfdom are: Terence Emmons: *The Russian Landed Gentry and the Peasant Emancipation of 1861* (Cambridge, 1968); Daniel Field: *The End of Serfdom: Nobility and Bureaucracy in Russia, 1855–1861* (Cambridge, 1976); and W. Bruce Lincoln: *Nikolai Miliutin: An Enlightened Russian Bureaucrat of the 19th Century* (Newtonville, MA, 1977). The standard work in Russian is P. A. Zaionchkovsky: *Otmena Krepostnogo Prava v Rossii, Provedenie v zhizn krestianskoi reformy 1861g* (Moscow, 1958).
3. Jerome Blum: *Lord and Peasant in Russia: From the Ninth to the Nineteenth Century* (Princeton, 1961), p 578.
4. Lincoln: *Nikolai Miliutin*, p 36.
5. *Ibid*, p 35.
6. *Ibid*, p 36.
7. *Ibid*, p 31.
8. *Ibid*, p 30.
9. *Ibid*, p 40.
10. *Ibid*, p 44.
11. In a debate in the State Council on a peripheral issue, the tsar silenced one of his senior ministers: 'You are interceding in vain. For a long time Miliutin has had a reputation as a "red" and a dangerous man' (quoted in Lincoln: *Nikolai Miliutin*, p 46). The tsar never completely lost his distrust of Miliutin. The view of him as a 'dangerous red' was echoed by the Prussian Minister in St Petersburg, Otto von Bismarck.
12. Panin was credited with having said on one occasion: 'If I discover by some means direct or indirect that the sovereign's attitude to something is different from mine, I consider it my duty to abandon my convictions and even to work against them' (quoted in Lincoln: *Nikolai Miliutin*, p 58).
13. G. A. Dzhanshiev: *Epokha Velikikh Reform*, 10th edn (St Petersburg, 1907), p 402.
14. *Ibid*, p 409.
15. The term *zemstvo* is connected with the Russian word for land, *zemlia*. *Zemstvo* has an equivalent in German, *Landschaft*, but none in English.

The Russian plural, *zemstva*, though more rarely used in the relevant literature, may be preferable to the anglicized *zemstvos*.

16. *Chinovniks* is a term used widely to describe the holders of ranks or grades (*chin*) in Peter the Great's Table of Ranks, which included upper- and middle-range officialdom.
17. I am unable to trace the origin of the quotation but feel – with sincere apologies to the unidentified author – that it is too good to be omitted.
18. W. E. Mosse: *Alexander II and the Modernization of Russia* (London, 1958; R/pb, London, 1992), pp 105f. Translated from Anatole Leroy-Beaulieu: 'L'Empereur Alexandre II et la mission du nouveau Tsar', *Revue des deux Mondes*, 1 April 1881; extract in P. A. Zaionchkovsky, ed: *Dnevnik D. A. Miliutina* (Moscow, 1950), vol IV, p 99.

4

Perils of Glasnost:
The Failure of 'Liberal' Autocracy

According to de Tocqueville's famous dictum, the most dangerous moment for a bad government is usually the one when it begins to reform itself. The Russian régime as the 'tsar-liberator' would soon learn was no exception to the rule.

The extravagant expectations raised by the tsar's early measures persisted for a time. To pacify the planters Aleksandr sacrificed Lanskoy and Nikolai Miliutin, but he also appointed protagonists of reform to ministerial office. Most were protégés of the Grand-Duke Konstantin and the Grand-Duchess Elena, and had belonged to the Miliutin circle. With a brief reactionary interlude, two liberals succeeded each other at the Ministry of Education. A liberal reformer replaced Panin as Minister of Justice. The financial portfolio went to M. Kh. Reutern, another member of the Miliutin group. Dimitry Miliutin, a brilliant staff officer and radical democrat, became Minister of War, while Grand-Duke Konstantin himself took charge of naval affairs. Reformers became presidents of both the State Council and the Council of Ministers, another was put in charge of the Second Division of His Majesty's Own Chancery, the body concerned with drafting legislation. Even Valuev, the new Minister of the Interior could be described as an oligarchic liberal, a Whig. The team was completed by Aleksandr Gorchakov, a man of liberal dispositions appointed Foreign Minister already in 1856. Thus, during the winter of 1861–2 Aleksandr II appointed what amounted to a reforming and even a liberal ministry.

Discriminatory measures against minorities: Poles, Jews, old believers and sectarians were either removed or at least relaxed. The constitutional rights of the Grand-Duchy of Finland were scrupulously respected. Cruel and degrading punishments were abolished particularly in the armed forces. Elementary education was largely freed from clerical control. Three major enactments followed, the university statute of 1863 and the judicial and local government acts of the following year. A greater regard for civil liberties seemed assured. There was lively public discussion of further changes to be made; an atmosphere of glasnost prevailed.

*   *   *

Some reforming and liberal measures coupled with relatively free discussion had raised many expectations. Together with high hopes, however, the changes also created an atmosphere of uncertainty. Typically, the old censorship arrangements, now partly in abeyance, had not been replaced by new guidelines. Perestroika with glasnost threw the empire into a ferment. Soon manifestations appeared that aroused the tsar's misgivings, while providing ammunition for conservative critics. Two developments in particular, the emergence of nihilism (the term popularized through Turgenev's *Fathers and Children* in 1862) and the growth of the Polish national movement were designed to cause alarm.

Members of the small radical intelligentsia who had hailed the early thaw and the decision to liberate the serfs with enthusiasm, soon became disillusioned with the terms of emancipation. As early as 1858 Nikolai Chernyshevsky, their mouthpiece, expressed regret at the premature confidence he had placed in the tsar. The revival of Polish nationalism had wider reverberations. Russian radicals were espousing the cause of Polish nationality as well as that of the peasants. At a requiem mass in Moscow, a Russian speaker declared that Russians and Poles shared a common enemy – the tsarist government. Under the impact of these developments students were becoming restive. The tsar's instructions that minor breaches of discipline on their part should be overlooked did little to calm the situation. Gertsen's *Kolokol* was fanning the flames from the banks of the Thames by its support for students, radicals and Polish patriots.

Russia, following the relaxation of controls and the introduction of a measure of glasnost was in ferment. Socialist propaganda was flooding the military academies. Leaflets circulating in the capital were calling for social revolution and/or the convocation of a Constituent Assembly. In May 1862 one of these, 'Young Russia', called *inter alia* for elective national and provincial assemblies, elected judges, public ownership of factories, the dissolution of monasteries, free universal education and, to crown it all, the abolition of the institution of marriage. There was a need, it declared, to 'change radically and without exception, all the foundations of contemporary society'. In case of resistance from the ruling classes 'the people' must strike at them without pity. A few weeks later, a wave of fires swept different parts of the empire. One conflagration, in the market quarter of St Petersburg gutted two thousand shops and stores. There was a suspicion of arson. While public opinion suspected Polish and socialist extremists, others blamed right-wing *agents provocateurs*.

Still more alarming from the tsar's point of view, was the discovery of subversive propaganda in the army. In May 1862, four junior officers and two NCOs were arrested in Warsaw. After investigation, they were charged with having spread among the soldiers under their command 'lying and impertinent slanders about the tsar and the ruling dynasty'. Further, they had read and passed on to other ranks 'books and pamphlets of a subversive nature . . . with the object of undermining their loyalty and obedience to the lawful authorities'.[1] Of the accused, three were condemned to death, a fourth, an NCO, to flogging through the ranks (a punishment not yet abolished). The incident touched a raw nerve in the tsar, as revealed by a passionate outburst during a passing-out parade of cadets the day before sentence on the disloyal officers was carried out.

In November 1860, the thirtieth anniversary of the Polish rising was commemorated by the singing of patriotic hymns in the streets of Warsaw. In February 1862 during the second of two huge demonstrations, crowds skirmished with the police. Russian troops opened fire, killing five demonstrators and wounding many more. Meanwhile the Polish national movement was proceeding from street demonstrations to insurrection. Early in 1863 Polish partisan bands began to resist superior Russian forces. It was becoming clear that nothing short of complete independence from Russia would satisfy Polish nationalists. The parallels with recent history hardly need pointing out.

Faced with revolutionary manifestations inside Russia proper, and also with militant Polish nationalism, Aleksandr II persevered in his chosen course. While repressing overt revolutionary activities he simultaneously appointed a whole bevy of liberal-minded and reforming ministers. One can only speculate on the reasons for his persistence in a policy of perestroika in the face of hostility from both the Right and the Left. The tsar was a convinced 'Westerner'. Influences in his partly Germanic entourage may have played a part. It is possible also that he was more firmly committed to a policy of perestroika than is sometimes believed. Lastly the reform process may have developed a momentum of its own. Major reforms like those of the law courts and of local government were, in 1863–4, still in process of elaboration.

However, the Polish rising, coinciding as it did with the student movement and various manifestations of radical extremism, profoundly affected public opinion. That part of it which carried most weight with the government renounced its liberal attitudes and turned decisively against the remaining reformers. Among those who changed their earlier stance were the Moscow law professor K. P. Pobedonostsev, the journalist Mikhail Katkov, and the landowner Count Dimitry Tolstoy, future Minister of Education and the Interior. Feodor Dostoyevsky gave up his utopian socialism. The Polish rising at the same time provoked a nationalist backlash. The Polonophile Aleksandr Gertsen was replaced as leader of opinion by Mikhail Katkov, the proponent and spokesman of militant Great Russian chauvinism.

For a while the tsar continued to ignore the rising nationalist, reactionary and anti-nihilist tide. A dramatic event, however, led him to modify his views. On 4 April 1866 while taking his daily stroll in the Winter Garden in St Petersburg, he was fired on at point-blank range and saved only by the presence of mind of a passing *muzhik*. The would-be assassin, Dimitry Karakozov, was an ex-student of 25 originating in the lesser gentry. He had made the attempt on his own initiative against the advice of the small group of student revolutionaries to which he belonged.[2] In due course, Karakozov was hanged. Thirty-four members of illegal circles suffered lesser penalties.

This, the first attempt at regicide since the murder of Paul I in 1801, created a furore. Many were horrified. The following year moreover, during a visit to the Paris World Exhibition, the tsar was fired on again, this time by a Polish émigré. The nationality of the would-be assassin merely intensified Russian indignation. Two attempted assassinations within the space of two years understandably alarmed the tsar. Immediately following the first he reinforced the security apparatus. A reactionary general now replaced a liberal as head of the St Petersburg police. Peter Shuvalov, an intelligent aristocrat of reactionary views, joined the circle of the tsar's confidants as head of the Third Division.

A special Commission set up to investigate the background to Karakozov's crime reported that students were prominent among members of revolutionary circles. This the commission attributed to the state of educational institutions. At every level, it claimed, teachers were politically unreliable. Insubordination was rife in schools and universities. The younger generation was steeped in atheism, materialism and socialism, propagated not only by teachers but also by radical publicists and writers. To remedy the situation the Procurator of the Holy Synod, Count Dimitry Tolstoy, was appointed Minister of Education.

In the face of determined opposition from liberal-minded bureaucrats entrenched in the State Council, Tolstoy, urged on by Katkov, then set out to reform Russian education. It was held by conservatives that the prevailing 'harmful' spirit resulted from the study of science which inculcated a superficial and materialistic outlook. Equally dangerous was the liberal approach to the teaching of Russian history and literature. Conservatives sought to remedy the 'bad spirit' which was especially prevalent in secondary schools, through the discipline supposedly generated by the study of ancient languages and mathematics. In accordance with these views, the teaching of science was banished from grammar schools and that of other 'suspect' subjects reduced. Instead, classics, with a heavy emphasis on grammar, were given pride of place. Moreover, teachers were turned into police informers, obliged to submit reports on the views and conduct of their charges. Under the mask of strict discipline, hypocrisy, time-serving and denunciation flourished. It was a system designed to breed radicals. Students were expelled from schools and universities for trivial breaches of discipline. Thousands failed to pass the stiff examinations in the classics and had to leave without a diploma. Expelled or relegated students would soon constitute the core of active revolutionaries. Even an arch-conservative publicist noted that while Tolstoy had created dozens, even hundreds of new gymnasia, his system had turned them into hotbeds of political subversion. From this time onwards can be dated the irrevocable alienation from the régime of a large part of Russian educated youth and of the adult intelligentsia recruited from its midst. In a major area of Russian life, the experiment in liberal autocracy and glasnost had proved a failure.

*   *   *

However, the post-Karakozov purge did not wholly end perestroika. Reutern, who held the finance portfolio from 1862 to 1878 was responsible for a number of technical innovations such as the production and publication of a consolidated budget (replacing separate balance sheets prepared by various agencies), the creation of a single treasury and the introduction of a system of centralized accounting and auditing. He also struggled valiantly to balance the books and to stabilize the value of the inconvertible paper ruble. The desired convertibility and adoption of a gold standard, however, proved hopelessly beyond his reach. One major strand of Reutern's economic policy was the promotion of railway construction by private companies through concessions and guarantees of minimum interest on capital invested. Capital was provided by both Russian and foreign bankers. In this field, at least, some results were achieved. During Reutern's tenure of office, the Russian network grew from some 2,200 to around 14,200 miles. Though modest in relation to the size of the empire, and though the railway companies were, in general, inefficiently managed, wasteful and often dishonestly run, their construction yet marked the beginnings of an industrial infrastructure. If the production of steel stagnated, coal output under Reutern rose from 21.1 to 154 million *pud* (one *pud* roughly equals 36lb or 16.3kg). The value of imports quadrupled over the period, that of exports rose from 180 to 630 million rubles. The most Reutern could achieve however was to repair some of the financial damage caused by the Crimean War and to pave the way for what would become Russia's economic take-off.

At the Ministry of War, meanwhile, Dimitry Miliutin was overseeing the reconstruction of the Russian armed forces. Among his early achievements was the abolition, in 1863, for both soldiers and civilians of the more barbarous kinds of punishment. Military service was reduced from 20 years under Nikolai I (a 'life sentence') to 16. The Military Code was humanized. Procedures of courts martial were brought into line with those established for the civil courts by the statute of 1864.

Nowhere, however, was the new spirit more conspicuous than in the training of future officers. The old Cadet Corps, wedded to routine and formalism, to parade ground and ceremonial drill, were abolished. They were replaced by gymnasia offering instruction similar to that provided by their civilian counterparts, supplemented by some military training. Having acquired a degree of general education, pupils would then attend officer-cadet schools for specialist instruction in their chosen branch of the service. The new officers would pass out better educated and technically trained than their predecessors. Nor did the new educational spirit stop at future officers; under the influence of Miliutin, a determined effort was made to eradicate illiteracy among recruits.

Hand in hand with these changes went reforms in the technical sphere. Among the more important was a decentralization of the top heavy military administration by the establishment of military districts which enjoyed a degree of autonomy. The status of the General Staff was raised. In 1865, the post of Chief of the General Staff was created. Overdue reforms were introduced in the commissariat and medical services. Military engineering was improved, the construction of strategic railways speeded up. The obsolescent weapons of the Crimean War were gradually replaced by more up-to-date ones, but in this Miliutin was hampered by severe financial constraints. In consequence, re-equipment of the Russian infantry was characteristically piecemeal with weapons of different types (mainly American).

Miliutin's major achievement however was the introduction of a 'revolutionary' system of conscription. Hitherto, liability to military service had been confined to the tax-paying orders: serfs and members of the lower middle class. From the moment of his appointment Miliutin had been determined to abolish this system which he considered incompatible with the liberation of the serfs. In 1863 a mixed commission charged with preparing a new statute on military service was set up. Stiff opposition from vested interests (the nobility and the merchant class) who defended their traditional exemptions impeded progress. Ministerial colleagues led the opposition to Miliutin's proposals. Then following Karakozov's assassination attempt, the proposed reform was shelved.

The German victory over France in 1870–1 altered the situation. Miliutin prefaced a new memorandum on military service with the brave declaration that the defence of the fatherland formed 'the sacred duty of *every* Russian citizen'. The actual call-up of the annual contingent of recruits should, he proposed, be effected by ballot. Only those unfit for service would be exempt, but temporary deferment might be granted on compassionate grounds or in the interest of the national economy. Substitution and exemption by purchase would disappear. Of the 15 years' service, six would be spent with the colours, the rest in the reserve. The overall objective, following the Prussian model, was to combine a relatively small peacetime army with ample reserves for emergencies. While many *zemstvo* assemblies, some municipal gatherings and even a few assemblies of the nobility presented addresses welcoming Miliutin's proposals and while the tsar sanctioned the underlying principles, opposition rallied under the leadership of a respected military figure, Field Marshal Bariatinsky. As the law implementing the reforms was passing through its legislative stages, there were repeated attempts to exempt a variety of categories. But the tsar backed his minister and on 1 January 1874, the new statute received his formal assent. 'Under present legislation,' the preamble declared,

the duty of military service falls exclusively on the lower class of town dwellers and on the peasants. A significant section of the Russian people are exempt from a duty which should be equally sacred for all. Such an order of things, which came into being in different circumstances, no longer accords with the changed conditions of national life; nor does it satisfy our military needs. Recent events have shown that the strength of armies is based not only on the number of soldiers but on their moral and intellectual qualities. These attain their highest development where the defence of the fatherland has become the common concern of the whole people and where all, without exception and without distinction of calling or estate, combine in this sacred task.

The new law was designed to apply these principles.

Two features relating to the conscription statute are significant. Its spirit, expressed in the preamble, swept away traditional class privileges in a revolutionary way. 'The new method of conscription', Florinsky considers, 'was a step towards social equality, even though shorter terms of service for holders of diplomas favoured propertied groups ... Strange as this may seem, it was in the army ... that Russian democracy scored one of its first modest, yet real successes.'[3] Secondly, like liberation with land, the statute of 1874 democratizing the Russian army could never have passed into law without the determined support of the tsar's autocratic power or indeed the German victory at Sedan. Even during the post-Karakozov reaction, the tsar was ultimately prepared to support his radical reforming minister against the conservative opposition.

The third (surviving) minister of liberal inclinations was Aleksandr Gorchakov. Appointed after the Crimean War, he continued to direct foreign policy nominally until 1882, effectively until the Congress of Berlin in 1878. He was thus the tsar's chief adviser during a period of dramatic changes on the international scene. The Crimean War had revealed both Russia's military shortcomings and her diplomatic isolation. The old European order based on co-operation between Russia and the Habsburg Monarchy – so effective during 1848–9 – had collapsed. Its dissolution would provide the opportunity first for Cavour's Piedmont and then for Bismarck's Prussia to realize long-cherished national and dynastic ambitions at Austria's expense.

Overall the after-effects of the Crimean War combined with the preoccupation with domestic change forced upon Russia a policy of abstention in international affairs, and during this time the situation changed to her disadvantage. Neither in economic nor in military terms could she hope to match the mighty German empire which had emerged. Germany's alliance with Austro-Hungary in 1879 was a further blow, obstructing as it did Russian ambitions in the Balkans. England was hostile, France weakened by defeat and internal turmoil. Russia thus faced an uncertain international future, her isolation concealed only imperfectly by residual Russo-German dynastic solidarity.

*   *   *

The Russian political system developed after 1866 in a number of ways, being now marked by internal strains and divisions. On one side stood the surviving reformers in government and the bureaucratic and gentry partisans of the reforms, with Dimitry Miliutin prominent among them. They enjoyed the support of a number of journalists and publicists, and their papers. Opposed to them stood the serried ranks of nationalist conservatives. A powerful conservative, indeed reactionary, body of opinion opposed to reform and to the new institutions it had created was coming into existence. Perestroika had split the Russian ruling and official classes from top to bottom, a split never to be fully healed.

In the face of this division, Aleksandr II remained true to the principles imbibed in his youth from his teacher Speransky; to rule with a coalition government.[4] A majority of conservatives (both ideologues and 'policemen') had to co-exist with a minority of residual reformers and modernizers. Each represented a different aspect of government policy. On one side stood the protagonists of law and order, on the other those of glasnost and the spirit of the Great Reforms. Inevitably, the results failed to satisfy either group. The new judicial institutions could not be introduced smoothly, let alone operate satisfactorily, under a Pahlen, nor *zemstvo* institutions under a Timashev. Neither could education flourish under the régime of Tolstoy and Katkov. On the other hand, the reforming spirit notably in the State Council remained sufficiently strong to prevent a return to naked reaction. The outcome was something like an undeclared civil war in the bureaucracy, in public opinion and indeed within the imperial family itself. It is difficult to say how far this dualism was the result of deliberate strategy adopted by Aleksandr II of balancing the rival factions while, like Gorbachev, he stood, as he imagined, above the fray. However, given previous domestic developments and the imperatives of the international situation, dualism and ambiguity in government were arguably dictated by necessity. What was emerging was a limitation of the sphere of reform without its complete abandonment.

It was at this point that a new and somewhat fortuitous development supervened. Aleksandr II was beginning to age prematurely. He had always been a womanizer. Then during 1865, at the age of 47, he fell passionately and romantically under the spell of a girl of 22 who was, by all accounts, not unduly prepossessing. Catherine Dolgoruky came from an old aristocratic family – an earlier mistress of the tsar had been a distant relative. After almost two years of being wooed, Catherine finally yielded to her suitor's importunities in the summer of 1866. When doing so, however, she obtained (or exacted) a solemn promise. 'To-day, alas,' the tsar was reported to have told her, 'I am not free; but, at the first opportunity, I shall marry you; for from now and for ever I regard you as my wife before God.'[5] Henceforth, several times a week, Catherine Dolgoruky would secretly visit the Winter Palace. In 1872 a son was born, to be followed by three further children, to all of whom the aging tsar was sincerely devoted.

The emperor's attachment had serious consequences. It gave offence to members of the imperial family starting with the empress and the morally straight-laced tsarevich. Though outward appearances were preserved, if with increasing difficulty, the liaison could not be kept a secret. It scandalized the religious elements in St Petersburg society, and much sympathy was felt for the pious and ailing empress. In human terms, the besotted tsar and his second family soon found themselves almost completely isolated.

What matters in the present context is the fact that the liaison came to acquire political overtones. In the face of social ostracism, Catherine Dolgoruky began to gather around herself a small coterie of people willing to accept her. Her salon gradually came to be frequented by men of liberal disposition and tolerant morality. With the anticipated demise of the empress, Catherine Dolgoruky was expected to succeed her. Catherine and her entourage attracted the bitter hatred of a rival coterie gathered around the heir-apparent. Its members, under the aegis of Pobedonostsev, looked forward to a reign of impeccable conservatism, probity and morality. The personal detestation felt for each other by the two principal actors in the drama, Catherine Dolgoruky and Aleksandr Aleksandrovich, thus had a significant ideological dimension. The tsar's personal behaviour brought him discredit and also divided both court and society.

The effects on Aleksandr II of his personal problems and growing isolation were both physical and psychological. The need to preserve appearances by commuting between his two families involved increasing physical strain, compounded during the late 1870s by problems of security in the face of a growing terrorist threat. The strains of the situation contributed not a little to the emperor's physical decline, while also distracting him from important affairs of state.[6] As an autocrat, he should have been able to give his undivided attention to urgent public matters. Instead, he was increasingly withdrawing into private life.

Psychologically, the strain had produced discouragement and disillusion. In the face of many problems Aleksandr II, never entirely self-assured, had developed a growing sense of uncertainty. His undoubted good intentions, vague liberalism and desire for modernization had not borne the desired fruit. Instead of peaceful progress, perestroika had produced widespread discontent. This had helped to develop in the 'Tsar Liberator' a deep-seated sense of grievance. He was beginning to complain of ingratitude. When told that somebody had spoken ill of him, he was credited with having observed, 'Strange, I don't remember ever having done him a kindness; why then should he hate me?' Asked if that was really his opinion of people, he replied: 'Yes, that is what I have learnt in the bitter school of experience; all I have to do to make an enemy is to do someone a favour.'[7]

* * *

While the 'Autocrat of All Russia' was slowly losing his grip, two very different dangers were looming on the horizon. During the late 1860s and early 1870s, radical leaders had revived the slogan 'To the People!' first coined by Aleksandr Gertsen. After the failure of a campaign to convert peasants and workers to socialism by personal contacts and propaganda, the revolutionaries decided to create an effective centralized organization, 'Land and Liberty'.

Trials of revolutionaries during 1877–8 produced a cause célèbre. In January 1878 a revolutionary, Vera Zasulich, had shot and severely wounded General Trepov, the St Petersburg chief of police. Amidst public excitement the jury, at her trial in March, returned a 'not guilty' verdict. Frenetic applause resounded from the packed gallery. It was a slap in the face for the government. Parts of the public, including generals and high officials, were siding with the revolutionaries. A second danger meanwhile was developing, following the declaration of war by Serbia and Montenegro on Turkey in 1876. Russian opinion was in a ferment. Soon the stream of Russian volunteers, described at the end of Tolstoy's *Anna Karenina*, was on its way to the Balkans – with semi-official blessing. Their departure was a challenge to the tsar's authority.

Adjured by Reutern not to place in jeopardy such modest fiscal progress as had been achieved, Aleksandr II tried to resist the public clamour for intervention. By the autumn, foreign observers were doubting the tsar's ability to resist the public agitation. Backed by a handful of moderate ministers, he had to confront the Orthodox Church, linked in unholy alliance with Moscow old-believer millionaires, the empress and her coterie of pious aristocratic ladies, assorted military adventurers, the tsarevich and his following, and the greater part of the Russian press led by the indefatigable Katkov and the able publicist Ivan Aksakov. By the autumn of 1876, however, the interventionist agitation appeared to be subsiding.

It was against this background that the tsar called a conference of his closest advisers at his summer residence in Livadia in the Crimea. Apart from the near-senile Gorchakov, all present favoured a 'national' policy from which the possibility of war was not excluded. The tsar agreed, probably against his own better judgement, to a partial mobilization. Two grand-dukes were appointed commanders-in-chief respectively of the Danubian and Caucasus armies. When a proposal agreed by the powers was rejected by Turkey, an imperial manifesto of 24 April 1877 informed the Russian people that the country was at war.

The ensuing campaigns brought the Russians a string of disappointments. When Turkish resistance finally collapsed and an armistice was concluded (January 1878) it was already too late. British warships were anchored in the Bosphorus. England and Austria were assuming a threatening posture, and nothing beyond a promise of benevolent neutrality could be extracted from Bismarck. The danger of a renewed hostile coalition loomed, a prospect Russia could not contemplate. She therefore had to consent to a revision of the treaty previously imposed on the Turks at St Stefano. This was effected later in 1878 at the Congress of Berlin. Though it allowed Russia modest territorial gains, the new treaty and the manner of its imposition caused bitter disappointment in St Petersburg.

Heady Pan-Slav exaltation was followed by a sober disillusionment. The Russian armies had won little glory. The diplomatic constellation, unfavourable to Russia from the start, threatened to become near hopeless when, in 1879, the Russian government learned of the Austro-German Dual Alliance. Russian finances had suffered throughout the war and foreseeing this, Reutern had resigned in despair. Despite considerable expense in blood and treasure, Russia had achieved little for the Slav brethren. Much of the blame for these failures lay with members of the imperial family, not least the incompetent Grand-Duke Nikolai. Endemic corruption, soon to emerge in public, had been rampant as usual in the commissariat and medical departments and parallels with the Crimean War were disturbing.

Following the disappointing outcome of the Turkish War, three separate developments combined to produce a domestic crisis. The least important of these was the tussle between the rival coteries of Catherine Dolgoruky and the tsarevich, shortly to reach a climax with the anticipated death of the empress. A bitter struggle for control and, by implication, for the succession was in prospect. The centre of power was visibly weakening.

The second element consisted of the after-effects of the undistinguished war and unsatisfactory peace. Grave shortcomings had been revealed in both military and diplomatic performance under an incompetent army commander and a superannuated minister of foreign affairs. The 'brave new world' of Aleksandr's perestroika, compromised by the reaction after 1866, had now been further tarnished. Anger and a sense of helplessness were weakening traditional autocratic loyalties.

The third strand was the radicalization and centralization of the revolutionary movement with an emerging threat of revolutionary terrorism. Apart from the technical security aspects, there was also the growing alienation from the government of what was described as the 'educated public'. Aleksander had ceased to be the once beloved 'Tsar Liberator'.

NOTES

1. W. E. Mosse: *Alexander II and the Modernization of Russia* (London, 1958; R/pb, London, 1992), p 128.
2. 'The so-called Nikolai Ishutin group, which had met in Moscow since 1863, was impregnated with extreme radicalism, held that "all reforms" were futile, and devised daring, though childish, schemes for social revolution and the overthrow of the government.' Michael T. Florinsky: *Russia* (New York, 1955), vol II, p 1075.
3. *Ibid*, Vol II, p 909.
4. In the view of Lincoln, the tsar 'regarded it as his function as an autocrat to act as a mediating force between those groups which called for change and those which argued for preserving the existing order, a notion which the elder statesman M. M. Speransky had instilled in him during his student years. In order to preserve his autocratic power, Alexander sought to balance these forces in the Russian political arena and still work towards the goal of gradual and moderate change' (W. Bruce Lincoln: *Nikolai Miliutin: An Enlightened Russian Bureaucrat of the 19th Century* (Newtonville, MA, 1977), p 80). This reads almost like an account of the tactics adopted with indifferent success by Mikhail Gorbachev as President of the Soviet Union.
5. Maurice Paléologue: *The Tragic Romance of Alexander II of Russia*, translated from the French (London, Hutchinson, n. d.), p 49.
6. People in St Petersburg blamed Catherine Dolgoruky for the tsar's decline. 'She was distracting the sovereign from his imperial duties; her voluptuousness was enervating him: she was sapping all his vigour and all resolution . . . The hollow cheeks, the bowed figure, the uncertain gesture, the asthmatic breathing, the whole worn-out body – this was what she had brought him to' (Paléologue, *The Tragic Romance*, p 124). The description was no doubt highly coloured and exaggerated. The German ambassador, almost a personal friend, noted that the tsar's distrust of and contempt for people, both justified by his experiences, were increasing with the years (Hans Lothar von Schweinitz: *Denkwürdigkeiten des Botschafters General von Schweinitz*, Berlin, 1927, vol II, p 94). He would later refer to Aleksandr's personality change after the Turkish war and through his fatal liaison. He had lost his dignity and self-respect (*ibid*, p 152).
7. Mosse: *Alexander II*, p 163.

Part III

Loris-Melikov

5

The First Crisis of the Régime and the Failure of 'Liberal' Bureaucracy

Vera Zasulich's assassination attempt on General Trepov, unlike those on the tsar of 1866–7, would not remain an isolated incident. It became in fact the harbinger of a whole series of attacks on senior officials. The government could do little to stem the terrorist tide.[1] Following a further attempt on the tsar's life, the Minister of the Interior and Miliutin prepared a plan for establishing temporary military governors-general in the two capitals and other large cities and for enforcement of martial law. Among the first governors-general to be appointed was Count Loris-Melikov in Kharkov, a recent war hero. As governor-general, Loris-Melikov pursued a distinctive policy. While no less severe than his fellows, he held the opinion that repression alone was insufficient. There must be a constructive counterpart in the shape of a redress of local grievances. The overall goal of restoring tranquillity, he wrote, could be attained only if the governors-general were in contact with representatives of local interests (the *zemstvo* boards, marshals of the nobility and town mayors), learned of local needs, acted effectively on lawful petitions on them and generally rendered support (to local interests) as circumstances might require. Repression must be progressively reduced. Punitive measures would be effective only so long as society was willing to tolerate them. Prolonged use of such measures would diminish their salutary effect. 'The clever equivocal policy of Loris-Melikov and several of his semi-liberal pronouncements' a revolution-ary publication lamented, 'calmed an agitated society and won over public opinion.'[2]

Loris gained positive opinion for his energy in combating the outbreak of an epidemic – rumour spoke of the bubonic plague – in the region of Astrakhan. The government, in alarm, had instructed him to take charge, and to adopt all necessary measures. Within six weeks, he was able to report that thanks to his 'sanitary measures', the epidemic was over and the region again healthy. His decisiveness and success impressed both the tsar and those in St Petersburg. Meanwhile, after an attempt by terrorists to blow up the Winter Palace in St Petersburg, governing circles felt a need for new and decisive measures. Katkov, in an editorial, called for a civilian dictatorship.

On 9 February 1879 the tsar duly announced the setting up of a Supreme Administrative Commission to be headed by Loris-Melikov. Loris, according to Dimitry Miliutin, 'understood his role to be not only that of chairman of an investigative commission, but of a dictator to whom all ministers, all other officials were subordinate'.[3] Moreover, it was he who would choose his colleagues on the commission.

The conferment on Loris of what amounted to dictatorial powers proved a shrewd political move. On the one hand, it met the wishes of the Right for a total centralization of authority. On the other, the key appointment had gone not to a candidate of the Right, but to a pseudo-liberal military man. It is not difficult to see in the choice of Loris the hand of Catherine Dolgoruky, whose salon he had for some time frequented. The new 'dictator' would be a partisan of the reformist bureaucracy. Was this a subtle policy decision of the emperor or simply another attempt to balance the rival forces of in this case the tsarevich and the princess?[4]

Besides a number of high officials, Loris chose as his colleagues on the commission two generals and two intimates of the tsarevich, one being K. P. Pobedonostsev. Concurrently with the setting up of the commission, changes took place in the government. Then, while the commission was preoccupied with matters of security, ministers in accordance with Loris's binary policy began to discuss the possibility of resuming and supplementing the Great Reforms.

Two separate interests were involved. Loris, as he had done in Kharkov, felt the need to win over to the side of the government the broad spectrum of liberal and reforming opinion. Within days of the setting up of the commission, he explained his intentions to the inhabitants of St Petersburg. Some practical measures followed. A number of prisoners were released. Censorship was relaxed. Some restrictions on *zemstvo* activities were lifted. The oppressive salt tax was abolished. The fight against subversion became less obtrusive. The perceived start of a thaw or spring dubbed the 'Dictatorship of the Heart' was greeted with joy by a large part of the public. Early in May, the German ambassador could report to his government that the new administration had secured a relaxation of tension, however ephemeral.

The second motive power behind the 'new course' lay in the ambitions of Catherine Dolgoruky. In May 1880, the long-suffering empress finally breathed her last. Six weeks later the tsar, with Loris and Miliutin as official witnesses, made the princess his morganatic wife. Their children were legitimized and in December, Catherine was given the style of princess Yurievskaya (the family name of the Romanovs). She was installed in the Winter Palace and presented formally in society as the emperor's consort. It was now her wish to exchange her morganatic status for that of empress of all Russia. The new ministers appointed with her blessing and notably Loris, were sympathetic. To neutralize opposition as far as possible, the tsar, the princess and Loris sought to win the support of liberal opinion by a striking political gesture.[5] The occasion should be either Aleksandr's silver jubilee or Catherine's coronation as empress. What was proposed was a modest involvement of elected representatives in the preparation of new laws. This must be sufficient to impress liberal opinion without, however, provoking the outright opposition of the tsarevich and his supporters. Indeed Aleksandr II was determined to carry the heir-presumptive with him.

The idea of involving elected representatives of provincial *zemstva* in the central legislative processes went back to the reform period of the sixties. Both Valuev and Grand-Duke Konstantin had then drawn up plans which, however, were coldly received by the tsar. In the second half of 1879, liberal bureaucrats, had once more begun to canvass these proposals. Aleksandr, also, had shown an interest. He told his brother 'that he would like to show Russia a sign of his trust on the twenty-fifth anniversary of his accession and to take a new and important step towards the completion of state reforms. He would like to grant society a greater voice in the discussion of important affairs.'[6]

Action followed rapidly. In accordance with time-honoured practice, a Special Conference was set up, to be chaired by the grand-duke. In rapid succession, four meetings, the first presided over by the tsar himself, were held. Owing to the opposition of the tsarevich, the outcome was negative. However, the idea of some modest institutional changes was widely popular among both liberal-minded officials and members of the higher intelligentsia. 'What I hear . . . from highly placed and learned men', Pobedonostsev lamented, 'makes me sick, as if I were in the company of half-wits or perverted apes. I hear everywhere the trite, deceitful and accursed word – constitution. This word, I fear, has made its way into high circles and is taking root.'[7] And, from the opposite end of the official spectrum Miliutin, in June 1879, after returning from the Crimea, noted in his diary: 'I found a strange mood in St Petersburg; in the highest spheres of government there is talk of the need for radical reform, even the word 'constitution' is heard. No one believes in the permanence of the existing order of things.'[8]

It was against this background that Loris, having survived an attempt on his life, persisted in his policy of pacification. Repersssion gradually gave way to cautious reform. From February 1880, overt acts of terrorism ceased. In July Loris persuaded the tsar to abolish the Supreme Administrative Commission and with it his own dictatorship. Instead, he was appointed Minister of the Interior and Chief of Gendarmes; in effect Prime Minister. In a memorandum submitted to the tsar on 28 January 1881, Loris drew attention to his original brief enjoining the 'utmost possible satisfaction of lawful requirements and the needs of the people'. The main task now remaining was, in his view, the execution of a programme designed to reduce the basis for the spread of subversive doctrines. Loris opined that the healthier situation which had developed must be utilized 'for the further development of order'. To complete the Great Reforms, a number of projects had been prepared in the central institutions. However, while recent senatorial revisions had provided useful data, such information was insufficient without the practical knowledge of persons closely acquainted with local conditions and requirements. Representatives of local society must be brought into the discussion of new legislative measures. It was the participation of precisely this group of individuals which would be required in the future struggle against sedition. There could be no question of the introduction in Russia of parliamentary institutions. Nor was it intended to return to the antiquated *zemsky sobor* (the pipe dream of the Slavophils). Instead, Loris recommended the setting up of temporary preparatory commissions (similar in character to the Editing Commissions of 1858). Of these, there would be two, one admininstrative, for the discussion of measures within the ambit of the Ministry of the Interior, the second for matters of finance. Each would be divided into subcommittees or sections. The administrative commission would concern itself more particularly with the reform of local government and with measures to improve the rural order created by the emancipation statutes.

The commissions would be staffed by officials and experts selected by the emperor, with representatives of *zemstva* and towns joining in the deliberations. Senior officials would take the chair. In fact, the proposed commissions would differ little from the bureaucratic bodies which had traditionally discussed major legislative projects. Drafts would be prepared 'within the limits set by His Majesty's will' and no legislative projects would be embarked upon without 'His Majesty's orders'. Thus the tsar's autocratic power would remain unimpaired. Indeed, the only real innovations would be participation in discussions of 'wise men' chosen by *zemstva* and towns, and the ongoing nature of the commissions.

Drafts prepared by the two commissions, would be reviewed by a general commission. This would consist of members of the preparatory commissions supplemented by elected representatives from provinces with *zemstvo* institutions, and from some major cities; two from each province or city. In provinces without *zemstva*, local officials would select deputies. The commission would sit for not more than two months in each year. Any draft project elaborated by the commission would then be submitted to the State Council together with the comments of the relevant ministry. So far, the proposal was almost conventional but then, greatly daring, Loris added a further tentative suggestion. 'In order to lighten the workload of the State Council in this area, perhaps Your Majesty will decide to add ten to fifteen new voting members, representatives of public bodies who possess special knowledge, experience and outstanding talents.' The mode of selection of such members was left prudently open.

Aware of the slender chance of securing acceptance of even these relatively modest proposals, Loris stressed that the role of the new bodies would be purely advisory. 'This system of the preliminary analysis of crucial questions connected with the national interest has already proved its practical value and has nothing in common with the western constitutional forms. The sovereign retains the universal and exclusive right of legislative initiative and the right to set limits on proposals in whatever way he sees fit.' Legislation would be prepared by officials with the assistance of a few non-officials, well known to the authorities. Elected representatives of public institutions would join only in the later stages.

Loris assumed that the preparatory commissions would be ready to start work by the autumn of 1881. The general commission might then be convened early in 1882. In the conclusion – no doubt in the hope of persuading the tsar – Loris added a warning, indeed an implicit threat. 'I will permit myself to state before Your Majesty', he declared, 'my profound conviction that failure to satisfy at the present time the expectations set out above, will lead, unavoidably, if not to public disillusionment at any rate to apathy in public affairs; as shown by the sad experience of recent years, such apathy constitutes the most fertile soil for anarchist propaganda.'[9]

Such was the project, variously described as an 'innocuous scheme', as the Loris-Melikov 'constitution', or as the germ which 'under certain conditions . . . might have been a step toward a constitution – a frail constitution that nevertheless might have promoted a certain invigoration of Russian political life and, eventually, the formation of bourgeois political parties.'[10] The latter view, it would appear, was shared by Lenin and, at the opposite end of the political spectrum, Pobedonostsev. A prominent St Petersburg journalist who knew Loris well considered that while personally favouring constitutional development, Loris had sought to minimize the impact of his proposals to make them less unpalatable to the tsarevich.

Aleksandr II acted promptly. On 5 February 1881, he chaired a meeting of the customary informal council. Though Miliutin was unaccountably absent, the liberals prevailed. The proposals were approved in broad outline. A drafting committee would work out the details. These, eventually, were approved with some restrictive modifications.

Rumours of what was in the air had, not surprisingly, leaked out. Among those registering opposition was the German emperor who, in a personal letter, urged his nephew the tsar to abandon the proposal. He suggested instead that should matters reach a point where concessions could no longer be avoided, making some form of representation a political necessity, popular representation should be kept to a minimum and all real power retained by the government. Undeterred by this unsolicited advice, the tsar approved the committee's recommendations on 17 February. A draft proclamation announcing the reforms was drawn up, and a meeting of the Council of Ministers was convened for the afternoon of 4 March to give its final approval. By the afternoon of 1 March, however, Aleksandr II, the 'Tsar Liberator' had fallen victim to the terrorists' bombs.[11]

There is little agreement about the significance of the Melikov reforms. From widely differing standpoints the tsarevich and Pobedonostsev; Wilhelm I and Bismarck; the surviving members of the People's Will and Lenin regarded them as weighty: a first cautious step, modifying autocracy with the addition of a modest element of popular representation.[12] They would in fact continue the process initiated with the introduction of the *zemstva*. Against this, however, it has been pointed out that the proposed elective component, consultative in character, was neither significant nor entirely novel. Whether the implementation of the reform might in fact have proved a first step towards the introduction in Russia of a pseudo-constitutional régime on the Prusso-German model must remain a matter for conjecture. Lenin at any rate believed in the possibility. So did Pobedonostsev, the future Aleksandr III, Wilhelm I and Bismarck. Perhaps the most judicious assessment is that of the soviet historian P. A. Zaionchkovsky, the leading expert on the events described. According to Zaionchkovsky, the policies outlined by Loris embodied a wide-ranging programme of economic and administrative reforms, a genuine perestroika. The proposal to involve public figures in the legislative process signalled an attempt by the government to broaden the social basis of its support. However, even such modest proposals encountered strong opposition in ruling circles and secured the tsar's approval only in a diluted form. The reforms, bourgeois in nature, were objectively progressive. They were designed to 'soften the feudal features of the system of state administration'.

Taken *as a whole*, the reform package put forward by Loris and his liberal colleagues promised a significant extension of the Great Reforms and a reversal of the reactionary policies pursued since 1866. A decade of reform under the aegis of Loris might well have altered the face of Russia as the earlier Great Reforms had done. An organic evolution of the autocratic/bureaucratic régime towards a form of pseudo-constitutionalism was not, at this point, an impossibility.

What is puzzling is the attitude of the tsar. While receptive to the projects of Valuev and Grand-Duke Konstantin the previous year, he had speedily dropped them in the face of conservative opposition. However, when first presented with the Melikov programme, he had lent it cautious support. Then, when some procrastination would have been understandable, he had actually forced the pace. Why, it may be asked, was the tsar prepared to resume a policy of reform? Aleksandr II was far from being a liberal, though he could be described as a modernizer and, within certain limits a Westernizer. He was convinced of the need to preserve autocratic authority for the introduction of necessary reforms that could not otherwise be realized, owing to the opposition of vested interests and bureaucratic obstruction. Perestroika, in whatever form (other than by revolution) was unlikely to be achieved in any way other than by the employment of the autocratic power. Was the tsar then convinced of the rightness of Loris's political strategy, with its mixture of repression of terrorism and concession to liberal opinion? It is certain that, for the best part of a year there had been no overt terrorist attacks. Aleksandr II, therefore, may well have felt personally reassured by the seeming effectiveness of the 'Loris-Melikov system'. No less significant was the fact that Loris and his liberal colleagues enjoyed the firm backing of the Princess Yurievskaya. Parts of the proposed perestroika had become associated with plans for her proclamation as empress. What is certain is that the reform programme was not a direct response to the terrorism of the People's Will. Indirectly, of course, Loris's major aim was to wean liberal opinion from its passive support of terrorism. At any rate, this was the argument used by the reformers to persuade reluctant conservatives. However, while with some protagonists, such tactical considerations may have predominated, this was not the case with liberals like Dimitry Miliutin or Abaza. Loris himself may have believed in constitutional progress, and such was the case also with the Grand-Duke Konstantin. The real views of Valuev remain unclear. Others were guided by considerations of self-interest involving imperial favour or career prospects under the tsarevich.

It would appear that, with the unofficial 'premiership' of Loris-Melikov, liberal bureaucrats gained the ascendant in the central administration. Despite his misgivings and occasional vacillations they were able, with the support of the princess, to carry the tsar with them. While Pobedonostsev and the tsarevich sulked, such conservatives as remained in government were disorganized and incapable of resistance. Thus, while the 'Loris-Melikov system' was always precarious, resting as it did on the survival of the emperor and the continued influence of the princess, there was no inherent reason why it should not have continued for a number of years.

*   *   *

On 8 March, a week after the murder of his father, the new tsar, Aleksandr III chaired a meeting of the Council of Ministers to consider the future of the Melikov reforms. 'I give you advance notice,' he announced, 'that the question has not been decided yet, since my late father also wanted the Council of Ministers to examine these proposals before their final confirmation.' Indeed, the new tsar appeared, at this point, to be undecided. His brother, the Grand-Duke Sergei, had warned Pobedonostsev two days earlier 'that His Majesty might go along with Loris-Melikov'. Pobedonostsev for his part, adjured his erstwhile pupil to reject the proposals and to dismiss Loris.

> If they sing you the old siren song . . . that You should continue in the liberal course, that You must bow before so-called public opinion – for God's sake, Your Majesty, don't believe them, don't listen. This would be disaster, disaster for You and for Russia . . . The mindless malefactors who killed Your father will not be satisfied by any concessions, they will merely become more cruel. Once the evil seed has been sown one cannot destroy it except by iron and blood . . . Pardon my frankness. Do not leave Loris-Melikov. I do not trust him. He is a trickster and may still continue to play his *double game*. If You surrender Yourself into his hands, he will lead You and Russia to disaster. He only knows how to introduce liberal projects and conduct intrigues. He is not a Russian patriot. For God's sake, Your Majesty, watch out that he does not win Your favour and don't waste time.[13]

Battle was joined in the Council of Ministers (8 March). Loris, at the tsar's invitation, read his memorandum of 28 January, the draft proclamation sanctioned by Aleksandr II and a revised version, prepared after his assassination. In the debate which followed, Pobedonostsev indulged in a long and emotional tirade. 'I find myself', he declaimed, 'not only in confusion, but in despair. As in former times, before the fall of Poland, they said *"finis Poloniae"* so we are almost compelled to say *"finis Russiae."* Thinking about the plan proposed for Your approval makes one's heart sick. The plan sounds deceitful; I will say more it breathes deceit.'[14] The project, Pobedonostsev asserted, heralded the introduction of a constitution of the Western European type. Such constitutions gave rise to every injustice, and every intrigue. Russia was strong because of her autocracy, the unbreakable union of tsar and people. Pobedonostsev then launched into a violent attack on the reforms of the 1860s, more particularly the *zemstva* and the judicial statute (which he had himself helped to draft). And then, in a climax of demagogy:

> And when, your Majesty, do they propose that you found on foreign models a new parliament? Now, only a few days after that nefarious deed when, on the other side of the Neva, the remains of the benevolent Russian tsar so harried during his life, are not yet interred ... At such a terrible time, Your Majesty should not think about founding a new parliament, in which corrupting speeches will be pronounced, rather, one should think of action. You must act.[15]

In Pobedonostsev's impassioned view, the entire policy of reform of the late emperor had been nothing but a 'criminal mistake'. Nine speakers nevertheless supported the project, while Pobedonostsev, found three allies. Three others refused to commit themselves pending further discussions. No decision was taken.

Although Aleksandr III did not express an opinion, evidence suggests that he predictably favoured the views of his old tutor. However, he may well have been frightened and had not yet found his bearings. He, therefore, opted for a policy of delay. The liberals, meanwhile, differed in their assessment. While Loris-Melikov was depressed, the usually sanguine Grand-Duke Konstantin professed optimism. Miliutin also remained quietly hopeful.

In fact, matters hung in the balance for weeks while a fight to the finish was waged between Pobedonostsev and his supporters, and the liberal triumvirate of Loris, Abaza and Miliutin. Slowly, however, the scales were tilting against the Liberals. On 9 April, the Austrian ambassador reported to his government that the recently all-powerful Loris was heading for a fall; '... although he is still Minister of the Interior, he has had the rug pulled from under him. He has lost authority and this paralyses that vital institution the Ministry of the Interior where nothing has been done for several weeks.'[16] New stars were in the ascendant. On 16 March, Miliutin recorded in his diary that he had discussed the current situation in absolute secrecy with Loris-Melikov. They had decided to adopt a waiting posture until it should become clear which path the emperor would choose.

The final dénouement, however, was slow in coming. On 21 April, the tsar chaired a further meeting of the Council of Ministers. Loris, supported by Miliutin, once more developed his programme. Four colleagues gave their support. Pobedonostsev, who spoke last, was uncharacteristically moderate. The tsar finally instructed ministers to settle the most contentious issues to be discussed at the next meeting. Members of the liberal group once more came away hopeful. They were in error. On that very day Aleksandr III told Pobedonostsev: 'To-day's meeting made a sad impression on me. Loris, Miliutin and Abaza resolutely continue the same policy and they want, by one means or another, to lead us to representative government. Until I am convinced that this is necessary for Russia's welfare, it will not happen; I will not permit it.' 'It is strange', he added, 'to listen to intelligent people, who can talk *seriously* about a representative element in Russia, and recite the formulas that they read in our scandal sheets and hear from bureaucratic liberals.'[17] The tsar had made up his mind.

Why did Aleksandr III, after earlier hesitation, finally come down on the side of reaction? Zaionchkovsky considers that the decision was influenced by an optimistic report about the weakness of the residual terrorist organization. Intimidated earlier by the boasts and threats of arrested terrorists, he had now begun to feel relatively secure. 'The young tsar's political outlook', Zaionchkovsky considers, 'was very clearly defined and as soon as the fear began to lift, he began to clarify his position.'[18]

Pobedonostsev finally saw his chance. In a long note of 23 April he urged the tsar to put an end to uncertainty by an unambiguous and firm proclamation to his people. Such a declaration he claimed, would 'embolden all loyal and well-intentioned citizens'. Two days later, he reiterated his plea. 'The state of indecision', he wrote, 'cannot continue, this would be fatal . . . You must speak out. I am sitting for the second day trying to draft a manifesto with the advice of count S. G. Stroganov and I shall send it for your perusal.'[19] On 26 April, the draft was duly submitted. 'In my opinion,' Pobedonostsev observed, 'this draft meets the need of the present time. Russia awaits this manifesto and will accept it with delight . . . Please notice that the manifesto deliberately expresses a firm resolve to preserve autocratic power.'[20] However, Pobedonostsev was still uncertain. 'If Your Majesty really has the firm intention, not to permit the creation of institutions that are senseless and damaging to Russia,' he pleaded, 'then I pray You not to hesitate to announce Your intention publicly.' On 27 April, the tsar replied: 'I approve the draft manifesto wholeheartedly. Meet me tomorrow at 2 p.m. to talk in more detail.' Pobedonostsev had won.[21]

On the evening of 28 April, ministers were informed by a colleague of the impending manifesto. Pobedonostsev admitted authorship. Loris-Melikov, Miliutin and Abaza expressed their indignation and announced their intention of resigning. The manifesto was published the following day: 'In the midst of Our great grief,' it declared in the unctuous language of the Procurator, 'the voice of God bids Us to stand firmly for government relying on God's design, with faith in the truth of autocratic power, which We are called to affirm and preserve in the national interest.'[22] It would be the basic object of the reign to preserve the purity of the principles of autocracy. In the view of Miliutin, it was reaction under the banner of nationality and orthodoxy.

The inevitable change of government followed. On 29 April Loris-Melikov tendered his resignation. The following day, Abaza followed suit. Miliutin, for reasons of courtesy, delayed until 12 May. The princess, shortly after the funeral of Aleksandr II, left Russia with her family. The men of the new reign took over.[23] A purge in the higher bureaucratic echelons followed. The age of the Great Reforms had followed its originator to the grave.

Thus terrorists and Pobedonostsev in unholy alliance had defeated the liberal bureaucrats. Possibilities of peaceful constitutional evolution had been foreclosed. The age of counter-reform, the negation of perestroika, had begun, at any rate in the political sphere. With the failure of Loris, the last chance had been lost for a peaceful *political* perestroika.

Two aspects of the long, drawn-out crisis are worth noting. One is the strength of liberal bureaucracy. With the hesitant support of Aleksandr II, the Miliutin brothers had not only pioneered a major perestroika but had formed what could almost be considered a party of liberal and reforming bureaucrats. Their efforts had foundered in the end, due to a second notable influence, the autocratic power. Indeed the way in which the last fateful conflict had been resolved revealed the central role in the Russian system of the autocratic ruler. The decision on the overall direction of policy had been his and his alone. The tsar's inclinations and idiosyncrasies were decisive. And, as often as not, the ruler could be influenced, indeed manipulated whether by a Konstantin Nikolayevich, a Peter Shuvalov, a Yurievskaya or a Pobedonostsev. It was an aspect characteristic of personal rule.

It was the conjunction of several factors which had first made possible, and then finally frustrated Loris-Melikov's abortive perestroika. One factor was the tenacity of liberal bureaucracy embodied in the persons of Dimitry Miliutin and Loris-Melikov. They had owed their opportunity to the fortuitous support of the Princess Yurievskaya and her influence over the tsar – as well as to her ambitions for herself and her family. The decisive influence was, however, that of the autocrat. The adoption of the reform programme was possible only to the extent that it enjoyed the emperor's support. As in the case of the Great Reforms, which Loris wished to complete, the success of his perestroika would depend on the co-operation of the tsar and reforming bureaucrats. A further influence, to some extent a passive one, was public opinion. It was this which Loris was trying to conciliate. The public's support, it was hoped, would help to sustain the liberal bureaucrats in their uphill struggle with entrenched conservatism. The terrorists of the People's Will also played a part in the genesis and subsequent fortunes of the 'Melikov constitution'. Loris owed his position and the confidence he inspired in Aleksandr II to his sophisticated and seemingly successful methods – combining firmness with discretion – in dealing with the terrorists. His strategy had appeared to bear fruit.

The Melikov project initially benefited and then suffered from a number of fortuitous factors. One is the relationship of Aleksandr II and the princess. It was the latter's isolated position in St Petersburg society which made her salon a haven for liberal bureaucrats. It was her influence over the tsar which enabled this liberal coterie to become for a time 'the government'. It was, at the same time, the private situation of the tsar which contributed not a little to the hostility of the tsarevich. The rift in the imperial family under the impact of the reform programme contributed to the formation of two proto-parties in the highest echelons of government. The projected perestroika became a divisive influence. Ideological differences were profound and irreconcilable.

Another fortuitous factor was timing. There is no suggestion that the murder of Aleksandr II was connected with the impending reforms. Yet had Aleksandr II died three days later, the reform might already have become irreversible. Ministers were certain to approve the proclamation. Had it been promulgated expeditiously it would have been impossible to withdraw it. However grudging its execution under the new ruler, its implementation would have advanced the process begun with the institution of the *zemstva*. Pobedonostsev's fears of creeping constitutionalism were, almost certainly, justified. It is no accident that, from a different perspective, Lenin reached a similar conclusion. Had the proclamation been issued by the time of his accession, the insecure and wavering Aleksandr III seems certain to have resigned himself to the changes.

A final fortuitous factor was the weakness and quiescence of what was left of the People's Will during the critical weeks while the fate of the 'Melikov constitution' hung in the balance. It was this which may have given Aleksandr III the self-assurance which made Loris and the liberals expendable. If the residual terrorists were indeed as weak as a police report suggested – and as in fact they were – repression rather than concession would suggest itself to the new tsar as the preferable alternative.

What was not perhaps understood at the time and would become apparent only in retrospect was that, with the failure of the Melikov programme, Russia lost her last chance of organic constitutional development. Although new factors would come into play, it could yet be argued that, with the triumph of Pobedonostsev, Russia was set on the road to revolution. The chance offered by Loris and his policies would not recur. His spiritual successor, Stolypin, would have to operate his perestroika in different circumstances.

Loris-Melikov's reform programme, like Aleksandr II's Great Reforms which it was intended to supplement and complete, had been broadly based. While the early emphasis had been on institutional reforms, these were intended to facilitate necessary economic and social changes more particularly in rural life. The operation alike of peasant institutions and *zemstva* was to have been reviewed with the aid of local representatives familiar with the needs of their constituents. Legislation to remedy defects in the operation of new institutions would have been prepared. A 'small *zemstvo* unit' was likely to have been introduced. Local self-government might have been encouraged at the expense of bureaucratic centralization. Moreover, the Melikov policies with their concessions to liberal opinion were certain to extend the area of glasnost. They might have strengthened and protected civil rights following the anticipated defeat of terrorism. In Loris's 'new order', liberal opinion might have had an important part to play. A degree of harmony between government and public might have been achieved. There might have been a 'St Petersburg Spring'.

NOTES

1. For the following see P. A. Zaionchkovsky: *Krizis samoderzhaviia na rubezhe 1870–1880–x godov* (Moscow, 1964; published in English as Gary M. Hamburg, ed: *The Russian Autocracy in Crisis 1878–1882*, Gulf Breeze, FL, 1979). See also P. A. Zaionchkovsky: *Rossiiskoye samoderzhavie v kontse XIX stoletiia* (Moscow, 1970; published in English as David R.

Jones, ed: *The Russian Autocracy under Alexander III*, Gulf Breeze, FL, 1976). These are the two classic studies of Russian politics between 1878 and 1894.

2. Zaionchkovsky: *Crisis*, p 57.
3. *Ibid*, pp 57ff.
4. *Ibid*, pp 181ff.
5. The role of Catherine Dolgoruky is described by Zaionchkovsky: 'Evidently, Loris-Melikov often exploited Yurievskaya's favourable disposition in order to exert pressure on the weak-willed emperor. Slow and uneducated, Yurievskaya nevertheless possessed a much stronger character than her morganatic spouse. Deeply in love with his young wife, the aged Alexander II humbly acceded to her wishes. D. A. Miliutin wrote in his diary in 1881: "The late tsar was completely in the hands of Princess Yurievskaya . . ."' (Zaionchkovsky: *Crisis*, p 147).
6. *Ibid*, p 84.
7. Michael T. Florinsky: *Russia* (New York, 1955), p 1089.
8. Zaionchkovsky: *Crisis*, p 79.
9. *Ibid*, pp 183–4.
10. *Ibid*, p 184. 'According to V. I. Lenin, "the realization of the Melikov project *might* under certain conditions have been a step towards a constitution, but it might also not have been: Everything depended on which would be stronger – the pressure of the revolutionary party and of liberal society, or the resistance of the very powerful, coherent and unscrupulous party of unwavering adherents of the autocracy"' (Zaionchkovsky: *Crisis*, p 182).
11. The assassination of Aleksander II was unrelated to the proposed constitutional changes.
12. For Wilhelm I's advice to the tsar see Zaionchkovsky: *Crisis*, p 186. Under the impact of the assassination of Aleksander II the German emperor, while still advising extreme caution, accepted the advantage of summoning popular representatives (Zaionchkovsky: *Crisis*, p 206).
13. Zaionchkovsky: *Crisis*, p 205f.
14. *Ibid*, p 208.
15. *Ibid*.
16. *Ibid*, p 212.
17. *Ibid*, p 232.
18. *Ibid*, p 233. And again, the tsar 'gradually was losing the fear that had gripped him the whole month of March' (*Ibid*, p 222).
19. *Ibid*, p 234.
20. *Ibid*, p 235
21. *Ibid*.
22. *Ibid*, p 237.
23. For a description of Aleksandr III and the personalities of the Great Reaction, see 'Alexander III and His Advisers' in Zaionchkovsky: *The Russian Autocracy under Alexander III*, pp 14–41 – indispensable and absorbing reading.

6

Interlude: The Great Reaction

In a study of perestroika and glasnost the next phase, that of the Great Reaction, needs only to be considered briefly. It contained little of either but brought, instead, a 'deep freeze', a profound illiberal reaction against both. It did, however, create some of the preconditions for the next attempt at perestroika, that associated with the name of Sergei Witte. An otherwise arid period produced developments which would have a bearing on Witte's perestroika.

Among the changes was the dramatic realignment of Russian foreign policy culminating in the Franco-Russian alliance. Russian policy directed by Aleksandr III with assistance from Giers, his Germanophile Minister of Foreign Affairs, had been, during the early years of the Reaction, one of alignment with Germany and Austria-Hungary. Giers, an admirer of Bismarck, considered close relations with Germany essential for Russian interests. The tsar held them to be at any rate opportune for the time being. An alliance of conservative monarchies appeared as an instrument of stability. It also enabled Russia to escape the isolation experienced at the time of the Berlin Congress.

Problems arose, however, when the Russians clashed in the Balkans with Austria-Hungary, Bismarck's partner in the Dual Alliance. Bismarck, claiming to act as the 'honest broker', effectively prevented Russia from attaining her objectives. The result was a virulent campaign during the course of 1886 by Katkov against Britain, Austria-Hungary, Germany and the Germanophile policy of Giers.

When the treaty linking the three conservative monarchies ran out in 1887, Giers and Bismarck, with the blessing of Aleksandr III, negotiated a secret agreement known to history as the Re-Insurance

Treaty. It was a defensive pact, protecting each country against having to fight two major powers single-handed. Bismarck also promised diplomatic support for Russian policy in the Balkans in return for a guarantee of Russian neutrality in the event of a Franco-German war. The treaty would operate in the first instance for a period of three years. However, during the operation of the treaty, serious differences arose between Russia and Germany over commercial and financial matters. At the same time, the German government felt disquiet at the evident eclipse of Giers. In 1888 the widely respected German emperor Wilhelm I died to be succeeded, after a brief interregnum, by his grandson Wilhelm II. For the latter, the tsar felt nothing but contempt. In 1890, in the middle of negotiations for the renewal of the Re-Insurance Treaty, Bismarck fell from power. His successor allowed himself to be persuaded – and convinced the new German emperor of the fact – that the Russo-German treaty conflicted with the recently renewed Triple Alliance of Germany, Austria and Italy. On 15 March 1890 – a fateful date in Russian, European, indeed world history – the German ambassador in St Petersburg was instructed to inform his Russian counterpart that the treaty would not be renewed. While Giers was distressed at the news, the tsar professed himself satisfied. The conservative phase of Russian foreign policy was at an end.

For several years already, autocratic Russia had been drawing closer to republican France. Katkov, since 1886, had pleaded for a *rapprochement* of the two countries. He had found an echo in French nationalist circles. In 1887 Paul Déroulède, president of the *Ligue des Patriotes* had attended Katkov's funeral in Moscow. On his return journey, in St Petersburg, he had been guest at a dinner organized in his honour by Russian journalists. There, in the name of the French people, he had toasted a Franco-Russian alliance which, he claimed, already existed despite official opposition. Déroulède had been received by Vyshnegradsky, the Minister of Finance, who waxed lyrical about a union of Russian power and French capital, an alliance of two great nations that would guarantee France's external security. Déroulède, on his return, opened a press campaign extolling the state of Russia's finances and her great potential wealth. In December 1887, a major Russian gold loan at 4 per cent interest was successfully floated on the Paris *Bourse*.

Shortly before this, as a reprisal for measures against landowners of foreign nationality in Russia's border provinces, Bismarck foolishly prohibited the *Reichsbank* from accepting Russian securities as a collateral for loans. The prohibition resulted in a steadily increasing sale of Russian values on the Paris *Bourse*. 'He is not a good Frenchman', the saying went, 'who has not deposited a packet of

Russian bonds with his banker or solicitor.' Between the end of 1888 and early 1890, the Russian government floated four substantial loans in France. It also placed a large order for infantry weapons with French firms. There was thus a strong financial background to the *rapprochement* of the two countries.

The *rapprochement* then spread to official circles. In May 1890, the French Prime Minister and his Minister of War received a Russian grand-duke. Both expressed a hope for future Russo-French military co-operation. It was therefore in an atmosphere of mutal goodwill that in the summer of 1891 a French naval squadron paid an official call to Kronstadt. Aleksandr III, on a visit to the French flagship caused amazement by listening, standing and bare-headed, to the strains of the *Marseillaise*.

Political negotiations ensued. On 15 August 1891, in an exchange of notes, the two governments agreed on mutual consultations in the event of a threat to peace. They would co-ordinate measures to be adopted 'immediately and simultaneously'. On 5 August 1892, the agreement was supplemented by a military convention. Were France to be attacked by Germany or by Italy assisted by Germany, Russia would mobilize all available forces in her support. Were Russia to be attacked by Germany, or by Austria-Hungary supported by Germany, France would act in a similar manner. Were the Triple Alliance or any of its members to mobilize, Russia and France would in turn mobilize forces of respectively 7–800,000 and 1,300,000 men. Despite opposition from Giers, the convention was ratified by the two governments at the end of 1893. A fateful diplomatic revolution had been accomplished. More particularly in its financial aspects, the new alliance would profoundly affect Russia's attempt at perestroika. Its outcome, as a result of the alliance, had been an important concern of both countries.

A second change destined to have far-reaching consequences was the accession in 1894 of a new tsar. Unlike his imposing father, Nikolai II was 'puny' and delicate. He was also weak, indecisive and shifty. He was easily influenced by others and little fitted by temperament for the exercise of absolute power. It is ironic that under such a ruler Russia should nevertheless have taken substantial strides towards the creation of a new order. Almost against the tsar's tastes and predilections Russia, under his rule, would undergo a major transformation.

The first signs of an approaching perestroika already appeared in the financial sphere before the accession of Nikolai II. To understand their nature, it is necessary to consider the major problem confronting successive Russian ministers of finance.[1] It was a problem inextricably linked to Russia's unique position as, at the same time a great power and an economically underdevelopd country. It has been stated as follows:

> Ever since Russia had attained the status of a great power in the eighteenth century the military requirements for the maintenance of that position imposed on the Russian treasury a task of a magnitude disproportionate to the largely natural economy of the country and the poverty of its people. This imbalance led to chronic budgetary deficits, despite increased taxation, and recourse to the printing press and foreign loans.

Specifically 'the financial strain imposed by an active foreign policy was frequently reflected in inflation and the squeezing out of circulation of metallic currency.'[2]

Repeatedly during military campaigns – the wars of Catherine II, the campaigns of Aleksandr I against Napoleon, the Crimean War and the Russo-Turkish War of 1877 – the Russian government had financed military operations by printing paper rubles. The Turkish War alone had swallowed over 1,000 million paper rubles. Each new war had brought to nought such progress towards stabilizing the currency as had been achieved during the preceding period of peace. War expenditure had nullified the currency reform of Count G. F. Kankrin under Nikolai I (1839–43) and the progress made in the reign of Aleksandr II between 1868 and 1875 under M. K. Reutern. The cost of an active foreign policy had been high.

> In the long run an active foreign policy not only affected Russia's finances but tended indirectly to perpetuate the backwardness of her economy, as all potential savings were skimmed off by taxation and absorbed by the budget for military and other mainly unproductive expenditure. When defeat brought home the realisation that to maintain her international status she must increase the productivity of her economy, the process of modernisation was conditioned by the legacy of the past. Among the outstanding features of this legacy was the depreciated, unstable and inconvertible paper currency.[3]

During the decade 1879–88 average depreciation of the ruble had been around 38 per cent. Even more damaging had been fluctuations in its value, in some years within a range of over 30 per cent. Apart from its effects on Russia's economic life and international credit, the state of the currency had weakened her international position in 1877. Ten years later, it had made her vulnerable to German pressure. The principal market for speculation in paper rubles was located in Berlin.

Clearly, the parlous state of the Russian currency and its effect on the country's international position pointed to two prime necessities: the preservation of peace at almost any price, a need which Aleksandr III had well understood, and stabilization of the currency, if possible leading up to full convertibility, on the basis of an internationally acceptable bullion cover. The political implications of the state of the currency and of a possible currency reform had formed a frequent topic of discussion in St Petersburg circles.

Several attempts at financial reform, including those of Kankrin and Reutern, had foundered on the overriding need to finance military operations. Reformers had, moreover, encountered a further obstacle. Conversion of the fluctuating paper ruble into a 'respectable' currency would, inevitably, involve a measure of devaluation. This had been consistently opposed by the State Council, the senior advisory body on legislative matters. Thus it had vetoed a proposal by Reutern to legalize business transactions in gold at the rate of the day, which would have introduced something like a binary system and given official recognition to the premium on gold.

The first finance minister of the Reaction (1882–6) N. K. Bunge, a former professor of economics, had at first tried to improve the situation by withdrawing from circulation part of the paper notes issued to pay for the Turkish War. This had soon proved impracticable. Population growth and increasing commercial demands had necessitated maintaining the supply of paper money. Bunge then tried to revive Reutern's expedient of permitting transactions in gold at the current price. It had again been torpedoed by the State Council. Bunge then concluded that the only hope of a stable currency lay in a general strengthening of the economy in both its agricultural and industrial sectors. This he sought to achieve by reducing the tax burden on the peasantry, by providing capital for agriculture through the Nobles' and Peasants' Land Banks and by raising import duties to stimulate industrial development. However, these were long-term policies and meanwhile, tax relief for the peasantry reduced government revenue. Some new taxes, mainly indirect, failed to make good the deficiency. It proved impossible to balance the books. During 1881–6, 32 per cent of average annual expenditure was swallowed up by the military and almost 30 per cent by servicing a debt which since the Turkish War had grown by 50 per cent. The budgetary deficit could only be covered by borrowing abroad. This made it imperative to improve Russia's balance of trade. Bunge, while achieving some reduction of imports, failed to bring about a significant growth of exports from the agricultural sector. Grain prices were falling while Russia was experiencing a succession of poor harvests. Political crises in 1885 and 1886 depressed the value of Russian securities abroad.

The paper ruble fell to its lowest ever level. In 1887, faced with the failure of his policies, Bunge resigned.

His successor was a man of a different stamp. Like Bunge, he was a former professor, this time, however, of mechanical engineering at the prestigious Technological Institute of St Petersburg. I. A. Vyshnegradsky, an authority on engineering education, had combined headship of the institute with a directorship of the South Western Railway Company. Not only was he an engineer but also a successful man of affairs, a skilful operator on the stock exchange. With him, for the first time, a capitalist had entered the charmed circle of the high bureaucracy, ironically put in place by Meshchersky, the leading champion of gentry interests.

Conscious of the need for a radical economic perestroika, Vyshnegradsky understood that this presupposed currency reform. As a first step, he proposed to stabilize the paper ruble at its existing level, which he hoped to achieve either by permitting transactions in gold or by accumulating a substantial gold reserve. The first course, once more, was blocked by the State Council. Vyshnegradsky therefore, was obliged to pursue the second. To achieve a favourable balance of payments, to expand exports and keep down imports and expenditures abroad, to attract gold into the country and to direct it into the treasury became the overriding objectives of his policy. It seems hardly necessary to draw attention to contemporary parallels. In his endeavours, Vyshnegradsky was favoured by fortune. Good harvests in 1887 and 1888 raised Russian grain exports to the highest level of the century. European demand for wheat was high at a time when American deliveries were falling off. Buoyant exports were further stimulated by the introduction of differential freight tariffs on the largely state-controlled railways, used to facilitate grain exports from remote areas, and by the ruthless collection of tax-arrears, forcing peasants to sell a maximum of grain.

In 1891, Vyshnegradsky introduced a consolidated tariff designed at the same time to reduce imports and raise revenue. The result of his measures was a greatly improved balance of trade. Under Bunge, this had averaged 68 million rubles annually, during Vyshnegradsky's administration it reached an annual average of 311.2 million. Moreover, in the favourable political climate created by the run-up to the French alliance, Vyshnegradsky was able to draw on French financial resources. Skilful conversion operations on the Paris *Bourse* enabled him to effect an annual saving of 12.5 million gold rubles on the servicing of Russia's foreign debt. At the same time, he was chary of raising new loans abroad, relying instead on the growing internal resources created in part by Bunge's encouragement of savings banks.

The gold reserves of the State Bank were augmented by other

means. Parts of its resources and of the treasury reserves were used for the purchase of gold bills from Russian exporters, as were increased revenues from indirect taxation, state-owned railways and from state lands and forests. Domestic output of gold was boosted. As a result of these measures, Russia's gold reserve at the beginning of 1893 stood at 581 million rubles. Under Vyshnegradsky's administration, it had increased by 281.5 million.

Yet the state of the currency remained parlous, due largely to speculation in paper rubles on the Berlin exchange. In part, this was the result of political circumstances. Vyshnegradsky also on occasion encouraged a depreciation of the ruble to stimulate Russian exports. Russian banks and exporters in their turn had an interest in low exchange rates. Then, 'His Majesty the Harvest' intervened. Complete or partial crop failures in 1891 led to famine conditions in some 20 provinces. The following year, a cholera epidemic broke out. With the alleged comment 'we ourselves will not eat, but we shall export', Vyshnegradsky insisted that the level of exports must be maintained. He was blamed for having contributed to rural distress by his policy of raising taxes on articles of peasant consumption and by his forcing of exports. While scholars differ about the extent to which Vyshnegradsky's policies contributed to the pauperization of the peasantry, he unquestionably increased the peasants' tax burden and neglected agriculture, Russia's basic industry. In general, concentrating as he did on fiscal expedients, he did little to develop the economic resources of the empire, and merely exploited those already existing. The famine of 1891–2, it is claimed, seemed to indicate that the limit of endurance had been reached. Its fiscal effects were close to catastrophic. Grain exports ceased and tax receipts fell, while famine relief cost the exchequer close on 150 million rubles. Much of the relief, moreover, was misdirected contributing to the discredit of officialdom. Nor was it only the peasants who suffered under Vyshnegradsky. Gentry landowners also had cause for complaint. High tariffs on imported agricultural machinery forced them to buy domestic products of inferior quality. Moreover, Vyshnegradsky had, for good fiscal reasons, been sparing in his subsidies to impecunious petitioners.

At the height of the crisis (1892), Vyshnegradsky suffered a stroke and resigned. The advance in Russia's financial position achieved under his administration would form an important stepping stone on the road to a sound Russian currency. However, in a poor country like Russia, the result was bought at a heavy price. 'The peasant economy', an official report claimed, had come to a full collapse and ruin, from which it would not recover in several years even with good harvests.

NOTES

1. For a lucid account of the financial problems and the attempts of successive ministers to tackle them, see 'Russian financial policy and the gold standard at the end of the nineteenth century', in Olga Crisp: *Studies in the Russian Economy before 1914* (London, 1976), pp 96–110, reprinted from the *Economic History Review*, 2nd Series, vol VI (1953).
2. Crisp: *Studies* (London, 1976), p 96.
3. *Ibid*, p 97.

Part IV

Perestroika in the Age of Imperialism

7

Witte's First Perestroika

It was a mixed legacy which had fallen to the lot of Vyshnegradsky's successor. The tsar's choice, once more guided by Meshchersky, had fallen on Sergei Witte, the fast-rising star in the St Petersburg bureaucratic firmament.[1] Witte's career – like that of his predecessor – had been an unconventional one for a leading tsarist official. A university student of mathematics, Witte had made his career in the railway service, first as business manager and subsequently as an executive director of the (privately owned) South Western Railway Company. In 1889 Vyshnegradsky – they had for a time been colleagues – invited him to set up a railway department in the Ministry of Finance with a remit to introduce a unified freight tariff and to make the railways serve economic development. Although transfer from the private sector to state service involved a large drop in salary, Witte accepted this in deference to the tsar's personally expressed wishes.

As head of the Railway Department, Witte proved an outstanding success. Within a year, he was charged with representing his ministry in that of communications. There he was given the congenial task of directing the construction of the Siberian Railway. He had long favoured the undertaking while Vyshnegradsky, preoccupied with the likely effect on Russian credit, hung back. Witte also succeeded in reducing the chaos on the Russian railways in the aftermath of the great famine. In the summer of 1892, he dealt fearlessly with a cholera outbreak in one of the Volga provinces. That assignment completed, he was appointed Vyshnegradsky's successor as the Minister of Finance. His rise in the St Petersburg bureaucracy, measured in terms of Peter the Great's venerable Table of Ranks, had been meteoric and had not endeared him in bureaucratic circles.

In St Petersburg society, Witte, a rude provincial lacking in refinement of manners and with a pronounced Ukrainian accent that would, according to circumstances be a source of merriment or derision, was a complete outsider. Though descended on his mother's side from a respectable family of soldiers and bureaucrats, his paternal grandfather had been a German (Witte would later claim Dutch) agronomist. What made Witte 'impossible' in polite society was his (second) marriage, early in his St Petersburg career, to a divorcee of Jewish origin and shady antecedents whom he had to all intents and purposes 'bought' from her previous husband. Mathilde Witte soon revealed some unattractive qualities, among them an excessive and unscrupulous cupidity and overweening social ambition. The Wittes, in consequence, could be received neither at court nor in polite society.

Though Witte had been able to establish cordial relations with Aleksandr III, himself something of a rough diamond, he could never hit it off with the fastidious, refined and soft-spoken Nikolai II. Witte, with his huge person and loud voice – he was sometimes compared to a bear – enjoyed the kind of physical ascendancy the new tsar, delicate and small in stature, resented. It goes without saying that Aleksandra Feodorovna, determined to see her husband play the unsuitable role of 'the master' became Witte's bitter and, in the end, implacable enemy. Witte's position following the death of his venerated patron Aleksandr III, would always remain, to a degree, precarious. Of Nikolai II, Witte in his memoirs would one day paint a less than flattering picture.

Despite many disadvantages Witte would, with skill and lack of scruple, make his way amidst the bureaucratic, political and social pitfalls of St Petersburg. If he had numerous enemies, he also had influential patrons. His early rise he owed, besides Aleksandr III and Vyshnegradsky (against whom he is said eventually to have intrigued) to the unflagging support of Meshchersky, the *éminence grise* of two emperors whose salon Witte frequented for a time. (He would for good reason play this down later in his memoirs.) He subsequently retained the prince's goodwill by subsidies for his journal *Grazhdanin* and by the occasional provision of minor jobs for one or other of his minions. Early in his bureaucratic career also, Witte struck a bargain with Pobedonostsev, whose world view he partly shared. In return for the Procurator's political support, he would provide funds for the parish schools so dear to Pobedonostsev's heart. A patron of a different kind was the still influential dowager-empress who continued the goodwill shown to Witte by the late emperor. Beyond this, Witte had to depend on chance alliances with ministerial colleagues to gain acceptance for his policies as circumstances required. Moreover,

Witte was able to build up a clientèle, composed in part of former railway men.[2] The eccentric prince Khilkov, a railway engineer, would soon become Minister of Communications. Senior positions in the Ministry of Finance were filled by Witte's cronies often recruited from the ranks of railway administrators in the South. Witte in fact had a power base which, in the end, would help to keep him in office until 1903. Many who disliked his arrogance and overbearing manner yet recognized his talents and some even considered him indispensable. His policy of economic modernization found support also among wider sections of the Russian public. Among his partisans was S. M. v. Propper, owner-editor of the influential Exchange Gazette (*Birzhevye Vedomosti*).

I

When Witte assumed responsibility for the management of her financial and commercial affairs, Russia was still an underdeveloped country. During the Crimean War, for want of a railway link with the south, the garrison of beleaguered Sevastopol had to be provisioned by convoys of ox carts and the wounded evacuated in a similar manner.[3] Until 1855 Russia's railway network totalled 1,045 km (653 miles). There were practically no metalled roads. When, at the end of the 1860s Russia's 'steel-king', the British entrepreneur John Hughes, started the first south Russian steel works using mineral fuel, the obstacles he had to overcome were formidable. Materials and implements had to be shipped from England through the port of Taganrog and then carted hundreds of *versts* across trackless steppe (one *verst* equals two-thirds of a mile). He had to find unskilled Russian labour – the skilled craftsmen were imported from Great Britain – and to house them on the empty plain. Until the end of the 1870s, materials for the Russian railways consisted almost entirely of duty-free imports from abroad.

Similarly, before the brothers Nobel began their work in the mid-1870s, the production of oil in the Apcheron peninsula (Baku) was of the most primitive. All naphtha fountains and boreholes taken together produced a mere 8,000 tons of petrol a year. These were transported on two-wheeled carts in skin bags or wooden barrels. In 1876, the Nobels, following the example of Pennsylvania, laid the first pipeline in the Old World (13 km/8 miles in length). The first iron tanker-waggons were built in 1877. Whereas in 1860 the USA produced 70,000 tons of petrol and Russia 1,300 tons, in 1885 the USA produced 3.12 million and Russia already 2 million. In 1900 the Russian output exceeded that of the USA by 1.7 million tons. In 1901 with 12.17 million tons, Russia would be well ahead of the USA with 9.92 million. She became, thanks largely to the Nobels, the world's leading oil producer.[4]

II

Witte's perestroika, unlike the policies of his predecessors, was based on a coherent economic and indeed political philosophy of national development. Its object, in the broadest terms – the contemporary parallels are obvious – was to develop Russia's vast untapped resources and to create an industrial base for the fulfilment of her world mission and national destiny. By the time he entered government service Witte had become a disciple of the German economist Friedrich List who, in his writings, had stressed the link between economic strength and political influence:

> Poor, weak and uncivilized countries [List had written] have not infrequently attained power and wealth by a judicious commercial system, whilst others have sunk from a high rank for want of such a system; nations have even lost their independence and their political existence because their commercial policy had not aided the development and the consolidation of their nationality.[5]

Economic development, more particularly for underdeveloped countries, was a necessary precondition of political power. 'The more rapidly the genius of discovery and industrial improvement as well as of social and political progress advances, the more rapidly is the distance between stationary nations and those which are progressive increased and the greater is the peril of remaining behind.'

It was a view echoed by Witte who, in a report to the tsar in 1900 warned of the political implications of economic backwardness: 'It is possible that the slow growth of our industries will endanger the fulfilment of the great political tasks of the monarchy. Our economic backwardness may lead to policital and cultural backwardness as well.'[6] Fusing nationalism and industrialization, List had urged the promotion of native industry by a high protective wall. The development of industry would, in turn, stimulate agricultural growth.

> Production renders consumption possible, and the desire of consuming excites production. A purely agricultural country depends for its consumption on the condition of foreign countries and when that is not favourable to it, the production excited by the desire of consuming increases. But in a nation uniting in its

territory both manufacturing and agricultural industry, their reciprocal influence does not cease and the increase of production proceeds on both sides and so also does that of capital.

Such was the gospel Witte had made his own and which in a lengthy pamphlet on Friedrich List published in 1889 he had tried to popularize in Russia.[7]

Witte considered List's doctrine particularly apposite to the case of Russia with its boundless reserves of cheap labour and unexploited raw materials. In a secret memorandum submitted to Nikolai II in March 1899, he applied List's philosophy to the Russian situation. Russia, he wrote,

> remains even at the present essentially an agricultural country. It pays for all its obligations to foreigners by exporting raw materials chiefly of an agricultural nature, principally grain. It meets its demands for finished products by imports from abroad. The economic relations of Russia with western Europe are fully comparable to the relation of colonial countries with their metropolises . . . [Russia] was, and to a considerable extent still is such a hospitable colony for all industrial developed states, generously providing them with cheap products of her soil and buying dearly the products of their labour.[8]

There was, however, a radical difference between Russia and a colony:

> Russia is an independent and strong power. She has the right and the strength not to want to be the eternal handmaiden of states which are more developed economically . . . She is proud of her great might, by which she jealously guards not only the political but also the economic independence of her empire. She wants to be a metropolis herself.[9]

The protective system, attacked by critics as inimical to the national welfare would, on the contrary, promote that welfare – at least in the longer term:

> National labour, which at present is intensively employed only for a short agricultural season, will find full application and consequently become more productive. That in turn will increase the wages of the entire working population; and that again will cause an improvement of the physical and spiritual energy of the people. The welfare of Your Empire is based on national labour. The increase of its productivity and the discovery of new fields

for Russian enterprise will always serve as the most reliable way for making the entire nation more prosperous.[10]

The policy, Witte admitted, required heavy sacrifices, but these would in future be amply rewarded:

Even the most beneficial measures of the government in the realm of economic policy during the first years of their operation often seem to impose a hardship on the population ... Years, even decades must pass before the sacrifices can bear fruit. Wise statesmanship requires, then, that these difficult years be suffered patiently as the experience of other peoples shows that the sacrifices demanded by the coherent and steadfast adherence to a firm and just economic system are always rewarded a hundred fold.[11]

There must, Witte pleaded, be no stop-go policy:

It would be extremely harmful from the government viewpoint to repudiate the protective system before those industries had been securely established for whose creation whole generations had paid by a high tariff ... one should throw one's weight in favour of the system already existing, for which the people bore such heavy sacrifices and to which the country's economy is already adapted ... The results of state policy in economic matters are the work of decades, and the most harmful of all commercial and industrial systems is that which is inconstant and wavering.[12]

Witte then turned to a major feature of his system, under fire from Russian nationalists, the reliance on foreign investment.[13] While admitting its drawbacks, he stressed its advantages, indeed its indispensability:

The influx of foreign capital is ... the sole means by which our industry can speedily furnish our country with abundant and cheap goods. Each new wave of capital swept in from abroad, knocks down the immoderately high level of profits to which our monopolistic entrepreneurs are accustomed and forces them to seek compensation in technical improvements, which, in turn, will lead to price reductions ... the influx of foreign capital is disadvantageous primarily to entrepreneurs, who are harmed by any kind of competition.[14]

In any case, Witte continued, the amount of foreign capital involved had been exaggerated. In 1896, 22 foreign companies had been formed with a capital of 80 million rubles. Even if foreign capital invested in Russian companies was added (12 million in 1896, 22 million in 1897), the total did not exceed one-third of the total capital invested in joint stock companies in these years. Russian capital was, by preference, invested in personal enterprises or family partnerships. Of all capital invested annually in Russian industry, the foreign share constituted no more than one-fifth or one-sixth. True, the impact of foreign capital was disproportionate to its amount but that, according to Witte, was an advantage. 'Foreign capital, five times smaller than Russian, is nonetheless more visible, it rouses attention because it carries with it better knowledge, more experience and more initiative. But it deposits these cultural forces in Russia and with that we really cannot find fault.'[15] Which was better, he pursued, 'to import finished goods, or to draw from abroad foreign capital, which enables our Russian productive forces to manufacture them here at home?' Foreign capital attracted into Russia by higher than its domestic interest rates would end by reducing dividends. It would also promote native capital formation. Indeed, it was a necessity. 'Considering the fact that the influx of foreign capital is the chief means for Russia in her present economic condition to speed up the accumulation of native capital, one should wish that our legislation concerning foreigners might be simplified.'[16] Only a disintegrating nation had cause to fear foreign enslavement. Russia, however, was not China. Any obstructions placed in the way of foreign capital would merely delay the establishment of a mature and all-powerful industry.

In terms which have a strong contemporary ring Witte in his first 'Most Respectful Budget Report' (1893) outlined his entrepreneurial [market] philosophy, the 'kindling of a healthy spirit of enterprise':

> Our fatherland [he wrote] overflows with all kinds of natural riches, but has not yet utilized these riches to any degree desirable for the increase of its wealth. Financial policy should not fail to pay attention to the undesirable effects of excessive thrift in meeting the growing demands but, on the contrary, should give reasonable assistance to the development of productive forces of the country.[17]

Such a policy should show better results also in regard to government finances. It should raise not only the welfare of the population but also its paying power thus increasing the sources of government revenue. In order to attain these ends '*one must above all aim at removing the unfavourable conditions which cramp the economic development of the country and at kindling a healthy spirit of enterprise* [underlined in original] in accordance with the natural conditions and demands of our national industries'.[18] The desired result, Witte considered, could at this point in time be achieved best by expanding the railways and heavy industry: industrialization. This would also promote private initiative. The new wealth created by active entrepreneurs would find its way back into the treasury and free it from its chronic embarrassment.

The economic system pursued since the days of Aleksandr III, Witte argued, had, as its starting point and cornerstone the protective tariff of 1891. 'That protective system has for its aim the creation of a Russian national industry, which would contribute to the growth of our economic and consequently also our political independence and would make possible more favourable terms for both international and domestic trade.' The task, demanding great sacrifices from the population had, in some respects, already been accomplished. Russia now had an industry of vast size. The interests of her entire economy were closely tied to its future. Industry had not yet, however, reached such an extent or state of technical perfection as to furnish the people with an abundance of cheap goods. Its services cost the country too dearly and these excessive costs had a destructive influence on the welfare of the population, particularly the part engaged in agriculture. This, Witte opined, could not be sustained much longer. The competition of foreign capital would help Russian enterprise to promote native industry and speed up the accumulation of native capital. As Russian industries grew with the help of foreign investment, it would become possible 'gradually and in strict accordance with the course of our industrial development' to lower tariffs.

> If we carry our commercial and industrial systems, begun in the reign of Aleksandr III consistently to the end, then Russia will at last come of age economically. Then her prosperity, her trade and finance, will be based on two reliable pillars, agriculture and industry; and the relations between them, profitable to both, will be the chief motive-power in our economy. Russia will move closer to that goal with the help of foreign capital which, anyway, is required to make the protective tariff of 1891 effective.[19]

The economic policy the Russian government had followed for the last eight years, Witte maintained, had been a carefully planned system in which all the parts were inseparably inter-connected.

Witte's nationalist policy of economic development was embedded in an ideology of fashionable economic (as well as cultural and political) imperialism. To this, Witte gave a broad philosophical, roughly Slavophile interpretation:

Standing on the confines of two such different worlds [Western Europe and Asia], in close contact with each of them, Russia nonetheless represents a world apart. Her independent place in the family of peoples and her special role in world history are determined both by her geographical position and, in particular, by the original character of her political and cultural development, a development which has been achieved through the living interaction and harmonious combination of elements that have manifested their full creative power only in Russia. These elements are: first, Orthodoxy . . .; secondly, Autocracy . . .; thirdly, the Russian national spirit . . . It is on these bases that the whole edifice of Russian power has been built up, and it is therefore impossible for Russia to be fused with the West. At the same time, she has long since appeared among Asiatic peoples as the bearer of the Christian ideal, striving to spread among them the principles of Christian enlightenment . . . in the Asiatic East, Russia has long since taken upon herself the mission of cultural enlightenment in the spirit of those principles which have given a special character to her own development.[20]

The underlying reality, was more prosaic. Asia for Witte was first and foremost a market for Russian textiles. Russia's 'present losses in the European trade', he explained, could, once her products had become cheaper, be converted into profits in the Asiatic trade. It was pleasing to observe a noticeable increase of Russian exports to Persia, Bokhara, Central Asia and China. These exports, worth three and a half million rubles over the past decade, had now risen to twelve million. If such figures were still relatively modest, they yet held out the promise of better things to come.[21]

III

In the practical application of his economic theories, Witte would be responsible for three notable achievements; currency stabilization, construction of the Siberian Railway and attendant industrialization, and commercial penetration in the Far East. Each of these will now be considered in turn.

Persuaded that only an influx of foreign capital could accelerate Russia's still sluggish economic development, Witte attached a central importance to Russian credit abroad. A wildly fluctuating currency would deter foreign investors. Consequently from the start, Witte took steps to curb currency speculation both domestic and foreign. In 1894 he mounted a spectacular coup on the Berlin stock exchange which resulted in currency speculators getting their fingers burnt. From this moment, foreign speculation on the ruble diminished dramatically. Simultaneously, the Russian State Bank, by means of transactions in gold bills was keeping the exchange rate of the paper ruble within fixed limits.

With currency stabilization largely achieved, Witte turned his attention to convertibility. He inherited from his predecessor a bullion reserve of 335 million rubles which, by the end of 1896, had grown to 500 million. A loan of 100 million rubles had been raised in Paris at the low rate of three per cent. A further 65 million worth of gold had been bought in the open market. Heavy taxation, heavy grain exports and revenue from customs dues had still further swelled the reserves and put the finances of the empire on a relatively sound footing. In these conditions, the State Council at long last dropped its longstanding objections to the legalization of gold transactions at the rate of the day. The halfway measure, however, failed to achieve its object owing to public lack of confidence.

Any attempt to establish full convertibility inevitably involved an element of devaluation. Though approved by the Finance Committee responsible for supervising state credit operations, the proposals again ran into opposition in the State Council. While some members objected to the devaluation, others expressed misgivings about foreign loans and the resulting interest charges. With the balance of trade uncertain, there might again be an outflow of gold. By the autumn of 1896 it was clear that Witte's measure would be rejected. With Russia's credit abroad suffering by the delays, Witte was able to persuade Nikolai II to use his autocratic power. At the beginning of 1897 a meeting of an enlarged Finance Committee chaired by the tsar authorized the minting of gold coins of five and ten rubles. These would form the basis of the reformed currency. By-passing the State Council and over the protest of its president at the method adopted, Nikolai promulgated the decision by imperial *ukaz*. Presently, again by use of imperial prerogative, the ruble was made fully convertible. The paper ruble henceforth would be exchangeable against gold at a fixed rate of 1.5:1. Not however until the summer of 1899 would a new monetary statute consolidating earlier piecemeal arrangements be finally promulgated with State Council approval. Stringent requirements regarding gold coverage of any paper issue ensured foreign confidence in the new currency. The amount of paper in circulation dropped rapidly. When Witte left office in 1903, 552 million paper rubles in circulation were backed by a gold reserve of 725 million. While one of his associates hailed the reform as among the most significant steps of cultural progress in our fatherland Witte himself, without false modesty, would later describe it as 'one of the greatest successes in the peaceful cultural development of mankind'.

IV

The stabilization of the ruble and the consequent enhancement of Russia's credit abroad were for Witte a means to an end, the development of Russia's industrial potential. In this, railway construction had a key role to play. Its centrepiece was the Trans-Siberian Railway. Begun before Witte became Minister of Finance, the railway was crucial to his vision of linking Russia and the Far East in an intensified exchange of goods. The new line, when completed, would shorten the transit between the two by almost three weeks. It ranked among the developments that 'usher in new epochs in the history of nations and not infrequently bring about radical changes in established economic relations between states'.[22] Russia, it was hoped would drive the British from Chinese markets and inaugurate close Russo-Chinese relations. A new solidarity of interests would develop with the United States. Assisted by Russian industry the railway would promote the development of the vast resources of Siberia which would become a market for Russian goods. Witte anticipated optimistically that the new line would soon be operating at a profit and enable the government to recoup its initial outlay.

The poverty of the Russian exchequer meant that the Trans-Siberian could be no more than an economy railway. Safety standards on the European section had to be relaxed. The rails were unusually light, curves sharp and gradients steep. The road-bed was narrow. Only three trains a day could pass along the line in either direction – at low speeds. To shorten the route, major centres of population were by-passed. What emerged from the gigantic undertaking – not to be finally completed until 1905 – was only a 'poor man's railway'.

The Siberian railway was only part of an extensive construction programme. With the principal lines already completed, new operations took the form of doubling track, shortening connections and constructing branch lines. Two-thirds of the activities were located west and south of the Urals. Between 1896 and 1902 some 1,250 miles of new track were annually opened to traffic. At its peak in 1899, the figure reached 3,125 miles. Altogether between 1891 and 1902, the railway network increased by some 17,000 miles, almost 5,400 in Asiatic Russia.

In general, while the construction of the more profitable lines was left to private initiative, the state assumed direct responsibility for building those with poor prospects. Also in doubtful cases, the government would guarantee a minimum return on railway bonds and sometimes company stock; guarantees which were in fact frequently invoked. Witte also bought up a number of privately owned railway companies at high prices in order to encourage Russian entrepreneurship. Altogether between 1893 and 1900 the government invested in the railway industry 2,226.6 million rubles of new capital, an average of 278.3 million per year. By the end of Witte's administration almost two-thirds of the Russian network would be state-owned and managed. The state would regulate the crucial freight tariffs. The railways, no longer directed solely for profit, had become an instrument of state policy both economic and military-strategic.

A major spin-off of railway construction, apart from a general quickening of economic life, was the vast market it provided for the products of nascent heavy industry. Already in 1885 before Witte's arrival in St Petersburg, the so-called 'Catherine Railway' had been completed. Covering a distance of some 200 miles, it linked the iron ore deposits of Krivoi Rog in the Dnieper bend to the coal mines of the Donets basin further to the east. It laid the foundations for the development of industry in the Donbas. From 1887 onwards, with coal output from the Donets mines rising rapidly, blast-furnaces and rolling mills had almost literally been shooting out of the ground. The capital flowing in from Russia's French ally played a leading part.

The railway construction promoted by Witte added a powerful impetus. Until building activities peaked in 1899, the demand for a variety of materials would be almost limitless. Witte, besides facilitating the influx of French capital, would provide long-term orders sometimes including an element of subsidy through bonuses or even direct payments. His ministry ensured that government orders went exclusively to domestic producers. The Siberian Railway not only used Russian materials but also home-built rolling stock. According to one estimate, the government, in the 1890s purchased railway materials worth 116 million rubles. Between 1893 and 1899, it has been estimated, railway construction provided 37 per cent of the total market for pig iron. Again, whereas in the 1870s Russian production had met 41 per cent of domestic demand, that figure, for the decade after 1890 would rise to 73 per cent.

Output figures tell the tale of industrial expansion.[23] Coal production in the Donbas rose from 125 million *pud* in 1887 to 240 million in 1893 and 562 million six years later. Figures for cast iron for the same dates jumped from 4.2 million *pud* to 20 million and then to 82.6 million. Production of iron and steel rose from 3.3 to 17.8 million, and then to 61.8 million *pud*. Output between 1887 and 1899 more than doubled even in the old charcoal-based iron industry of the Urals with its slower rates of growth. Other industries not connected with the railways, notably oil and sugar also showed spectacular advances.

The quickening of economic life was reflected also in the amount of capital invested in new joint stock companies. From 24.2 million rubles in 1887, this rose to 61 million in 1893, to reach a peak of 431 million in 1899. It was foreign capital, mainly French and Belgian in mining and metallurgy, British in oil and gold, German in the electrical industry. With it came the technical know-how and management skills of the advanced industrial countries.

The overall results of Witte's policies are reflected in the figures assembled by one authority. According to this, between 1890 and 1900 the number of factories and works increased from 32,254 to 38,141. During the same period, the value of output rose from 1,502 million rubles to 3,439 million. Lastly the industrial workforce (excluding cottage industries employing only manual labour and enterprises employing less than 50 workers) jumped from 1,424,800 to 2,373,400. Even if the figures are only approximate, they are nevertheless indicative of the industrial take-off set in motion by Witte's perestroika.

In a report to the tsar, 'On the Condition of our Industry' (1900), Witte nonetheless took a sober view of the results achieved so far.

In the speed and force of this expansion [he wrote] Russia stands ahead of all foreign countries that are economically developed. And there is no doubt that a country which showed itself able to increase its mining and manufacturing industry more than three-fold within two decades certainly contains in itself a rich store of internal resources for further development.

Nevertheless, Witte continued, Russian industry remained comparatively backward:

No matter how great the results so far, in relation to the needs of the country and in comparison with foreign countries our industry is still very backward.

As evidence of this, Witte cited per capita consumption of items like coal, iron and cotton in Western countries and in Russia, and the fact that Russia remained predominantly an agricultural country subject to the vagaries of its climate.

On the eve of World War I, Russia was, in effect, far from having 'caught up' with the more advanced industrial nations. In 1913, her industrial production still lagged well behind theirs:

The industrial output of major countries in 1913 (in million tons)

	Pig iron	Steel	Coal
Russia	4.8	5.2	36.0
USA	30.9	31.3	509.0
United Kingdom	10.3	7.7	287.0
Germany	19.3	18.3	190.0*
France	5.2	4.7	40.8

* if brown coal (lignite) is included, 277.

Source: B. H. Sumner: *Survey of Russian History*, 2nd edn (London, 1946), p. 362.

The respective shares of world markets at the end of the nineteenth century tell a similar story: Great Britain: 20 per cent of commercial turnover; Germany: 11 per cent; United States: 10 per cent; France: 8 per cent; Holland: 7 per cent; Russia: 6 per cent; Austria: 5 per cent; Belgium: 5 per cent.[24]

V

A by-product of railway construction was, besides the opening of a swathe of territory across Siberia, the promotion of Russian economic interests in the Far East. From the start, in urging the construction of the line, Witte saw it as opening up new markets for Russian textiles and, to a lesser extent, metal goods. There was also the political object of strengthening Russian influence in a region in which other powers, notably Britain and Japan, were evincing a growing interest. What was at stake was the future fate of Northern China, of Manchuria and of Korea. Witte intended to secure for Russia the lion's share of the booty – if at all possible through peaceful commercial penetration.

Witte's opportunity came in 1895 after Japan's defeat of China. In June of that year, the Russian government with funds provided by French and Russian banks guaranteed a Chinese loan of 400 million francs to enable China to pay her war indemnity. In December, with the bulk of the capital once again provided by French sources, a Russo-Chinese bank was set up, headed by a leading protagonist of Russian expansion in the Far East. On its board sat prominent officials of Witte's ministry. The foundations had been laid for imperialist expansion financed by Russia's French ally.

Under the aegis of Witte, and aided by an extensive injection of French capital, Russia then embarked on a policy of peaceful penetration of Manchuria. In 1896, the Russian government secured from the Chinese an 80-year concession for a railway line across Manchuria to be known as the Chinese Eastern Railway. A strip of territory on either side of the line was placed at Witte's disposal to be policed by armed Russians under the control of the Ministry of Finance. In 1898, Russia obtained from China the lease of Port Arthur and Dairen on the Liaotung Peninsula for a period of 25 years. She was also granted a concession for the construction of a South Manchurian railway to be financed by the Russo-Chinese Bank (again with largely French capital). Finally, in 1900 Russia improved the shining occasion of the Boxer Rebellion to occupy the chief cities of Manchuria. It was to prove the high watermark of Russian influence.

Meanwhile, Russia was beginning to extend her tentacles also to Korea. It was at this point that other powers took alarm. Japan in particular demanded compensation in Korea for the Russian advance in Manchuria which the Russian government refused. Instead, an unofficial group of highly connected adventurers, the so-called 'Bezobrazov clique' (named after its leading member) induced the tsar, with the lure of vast profits, to join in the exploitation of its timber concessions on the Yalu river in North Korea.

Witte and his ally, the Foreign Minister, Count Lamsdorff, tried to oppose the adventurism of the Bezobrazov clique. While Witte wished to avoid war with Japan at all cost, his arch-rival Plehve on the contrary favoured a 'little victorious war' to stem the rising tide of disorder. After a visit to the Far East late in 1902, Witte earnestly warned the tsar against supporting Bezobrazov's 'misconceived' schemes. The warning fell on deaf ears. It annoyed the tsar and merely contributed to Witte's downfall the following year. Instead, Nikolai set up a Vice-Royalty of the Far East under Admiral E. I. Alekseyev, a crony of Bezobrazov's and widely believed to be an illegitimate son of Aleksandr II. He was placed directly under the tsar's orders, by-passing Witte and Lamsdorff.

Already early in 1902, Japan had reacted to Russia's refusal of a deal over Manchuria and Korea by concluding an alliance with Great Britain. Under it, Britain had recognized Japan's preponderant interest in Korea. She promised benevolent neutrality should Japan become involved in war with Russia. Should Russia then be joined by a second power, an unlikely contingency, Britain would come to Japan's assistance. What Witte and Lamsdorff had been striving hard to avoid – they had been prepared throughout to leave Korea to the Japanese – had come to pass. Thanks to the greed and irresponsibility of the tsar (and some associated grand-dukes) and the scheming calculations of Plehve, the St Petersburg 'hawks' had scored a fateful victory. Witte's cautious imperialist policy of slow commercial penetration lay in ruins.

VI

In the process of carrying out his perestroika, Witte acquired a unique position among Russian ministers. Through his control of the purse strings he was able to force his colleagues to submit for his approval any project requiring a financial outlay. Any who failed to do so he would savage in the State Council. Furthermore, a flood of polemical memoranda and pamphlets defending his policies and attacking those of his political opponents, poured forth from the pens of journalists and publicists either employed on his staff or placed by him on the boards of private companies. By these and other means Witte, credited with an unrivalled gift for intrigue, was able to exercise a measure of control over a number of his fellow ministers. These included the Ministers of Communications and of State Domains and Agriculture, as well as two successive ministers of the interior. Witte's influence extended also to the Ministry of Marine. During the tenure of Count V. N. Lamsdorff from 1900 onwards his voice was also given a hearing at the Ministry of Foreign Affairs. In effect, by a variety of means, Witte had secured a position resembling that of an unofficial premier.

Characteristic was the manner in which Witte helped to bring about the dismissal in 1899 of I. L. Goremykin from the Ministry of the Interior. Goremykin, in 1898, had submitted to the State Council a project for the introduction of *zemstva* in some western and south-western provinces which had hitherto been deprived of them because many local landowners were Poles. Only the habit of self-government, Goremykin had argued, could develop a people's capacity for organization and self-assertion. Bureaucratic tutelage on the other hand, created nothing but depersonalized and disunited crowds of people, mere human atoms. In no circumstances could *zemstva* lead to Western style parliamentary institutions. With her vast spaces, Russia was in fact a country predestined for local self-government.

Goremykin's plea for a policy of cautious decentralization and debureaucratization infuriated Witte. He resented the *zemstva*'s rating powers, and in 1895 assumed control of their funds on the pretext of preventing mismanagement. They also dared to criticize his economic policies. In 1895 some progressive *zemstvo* members asked for a reduction of freight tariffs and for a lowering of the tariff barriers in the interests of agricultural producers. Others were critical of the currency reform.

Witte objected to the *zemstva* also on broader political grounds. His views were set out in a memorandum written by one of his acolytes and submitted by him to the tsar in 1899. (It was later published as *Samoderzhavie i Zemstvo*.) Russia, Witte argued, was by historic tradition a country of rigid administrative centralization. It had invariably

been a progressive bureaucracy which had taken the lead in modernization and had thereby made Russia a great power. *Zemstva*, on the
other hand, were costly and inefficient, more particularly in their
financial management. Some of their functions should therefore be
transferred to the state. There was a need for administrative uniformity and for a congruence of central government and local administration. 'Whoever is master of the government must also be master of
the administration.' What Russia needed was a strong legal framework
established by a progressive bureaucracy within which there would be
room for 'the broadest possible development of lawful private enterprise' and for 'the development of personal and social initiative with
freedom of speech and thought'. A good government, moreover,
would listen to public opinion. His own ministry, Witte asserted, had
'always listened to public opinion and let the public take an interest in
its activities'. This form of centralized 'enlightened absolutism'
appeared to Witte (almost certainly rightly) as the administrative
framework best suited to industrialization. It was capable, he maintained, of removing expeditiously 'all the unfavourable conditions
which hampered the economic development of the country'. It would
be the instrument for creating a healthy spirit of enterprise, for
developing the country's natural resources.

In the event, Witte won his argument against Goremykin by
convincing the tsar that *zemstva* contained within them the seeds of
constitutional government. Goremykin was obliged to go. He was
succeeded by Sipyagin, a landowner of reactionary cut (a believer in
autocracy *sans phrase*: autocratic infallibility) and one of Witte's
political allies. With Goremykin eliminated, Witte was able to reduce
still further the *zemstva*'s financial competence. No more than Nikolai
Miliutin, another enlightened bureaucrat, would Witte brook the
competition of local interests. In his view, it was reform-minded
bureaucrats, not least himself, who alone knew what was best for
Russia. It was the task of the autocratic power to secure the implementation of their policies and to overrule any opposition. Enlightened absolutism, as personified by Aleksandr III, was Witte's political
ideal.

VII

But Witte began to stand increasingly in need of the autocratic support
on which his bureaucratic career had rested from the start. Criticism
of both the man and his policies was rising fast and came from several
quarters. Many took exception to his personal arrogance. One who
knew him well and admired his achievements described the effect of

his seeming success on his character and behaviour. Witte, he observed, would no longer admit that he might be fallible. Whatever he undertook was, in his own view, superb and designed to ensure the salvation of Russia. Whatever was done by others who had failed to heed his advice or, indeed, to secure his prior approval, was faulty, foolish and pernicious and called forth his fierce opposition. In political in-fighting Witte was unscrupulous. Senior St Petersburg bureaucrats never forgave his irregular career and meteoric rise. Nor could they approve his high-handed procedures. The way in which the State Council had been by-passed in the currency reform in 1897 was a case in point. In the wake of the Great Reforms, quasi-constitutional or at any rate legalistic attitudes gained currency in the higher echelons of officialdom. Polovtsev, secretary of the State Council, confided to his diary the views of its members on the manner of introducing the reform. As an autocrat, they conceded, the tsar of course had the right to issue any order he pleased. But where then lay the difference, a distinction current at least since the days of Mikhail Speransky, between monarchic government and Asiatic despotism? Whereas the monarch observed the country's laws (conventions would perhaps be a better term), the despot disregarded and destroyed them. To advise the tsar to follow such a course was to lead him down the road trodden by Paul I, who had been assassinated in 1801.

While Witte was thus detested by the bulk of St Petersburg officialdom, he was not received in 'Society', and nor was his grasping divorcee wife. Representatives of gentry interests were protesting with some justification against the one-sided preference given in the allocation of resources to industry and commerce. Moreover, the bureaucratic gentry opposition to Witte and his perestroika had found a prominent leader. Born the son of a tenant farmer in 1846, Wilhelm Plehve, had been baptized a Lutheran. When his father became steward of an estate in Russian Poland, he had embraced Roman Catholicism and changed his name to Vaclav. When Plehve senior ended his peregrinations in a province of Central Russia, Plehve joined the Orthodox Church and became Viacheslav. On completing his law studies at St Petersburg university, he entered the Ministry of Justice. His bureaucratic career was spectacular. The year 1881 saw him at the head of the state police where his skilful investigation of the murder of Aleksandr II and prompt liquidation of the residual People's Will attracted the attention of Aleksandr III. Plehve became deputy minister in 1884, and Imperial State Secretary (head of the Imperial Chancellery) ten years later. After 1899, as Secretary of State for Finland, he earned the undying hatred of the native population by the brutal policy of Russification carried out under his direction. In 1902, he succeeded the murdered Sipyagin as Minister of the Interior.

The story went the rounds that in 1899 following the dismissal of Goremykin, the tsar had consulted Pobedonostsev on the choice of a successor. Cynically, the Procurator was said to have replied that there were two possible candidates, the first, Sipyagin, a fool, the second, Plehve, a villain. After the 'fool', a friend and ally of Witte's, came the turn of the 'villain', Witte's arch-enemy.

In Plehve, intelligence and shrewdness were matched by an utter lack of scruple in the choice of means. He was motivated by an implacable hatred not only for revolutionaries and nihilists, but also for any manifestations of liberalism, not least the *zemstva*; for all minorities – Finns, Poles, Armenians, Jews and Ukrainians, all of whom he persecuted. Positively, Plehve professed ultra-conservative views and a devotion to autocracy. In contradistinction to Witte, he claimed to see in the landed gentry not only the traditional support of the throne but the sole basis for its survival. Accordingly he made himself the spokesman of agricultural interests in general and of the landed gentry's (to which he did not himself belong) in particular. The personal rivalry of Plehve and Witte reflected a fundamental clash of views on economic and social policies. While in the early years of his administration Witte's approach had enjoyed an unchallenged ascendancy, the state of Russian agriculture in the later 1890s lent increasing weight to the criticism of the agrarians. The deplorable state of Russian farming became the Achilles heel of the 'Witte system'.

VIII

Several good harvests in the 1880s with correspondingly low grain prices, were followed by mediocre ones broken by the disastrous crop failure of 1891. The harvest of 1897 was again disappointing while 1898 saw a partial crop failure mainly in the eastern central provinces. The result was widespread hunger accompanied by the spread of scurvy. After a tour of famine-stricken areas in the spring of 1899 two German observers in a report published the following year under the title of *Starving Russia* drew a harrowing picture of rural distress.[25] After years of observing two villages in the province of Voronezh, a *zemstvo* doctor compiled a report entitled *The Dying Village*.[26] Tolstoy, in *Resurrection* (published in 1899) reached the startling conclusion (contradicted however by statistical evidence) that the rural population was dying out. The year 1901 saw a further crop failure. Widespread undernourishment and ill health aggravated by deficient hygiene were now the common lot of the Russian peasantry. A partial crop failure might spell disaster.

Landed gentry, notably the middle and poorest strata, as well as peasants had suffered. One indicator of the state of gentry farming is the loss of land mainly to merchants and a small peasant minority. Gentry landholding, between 1861 and 1887 shrunk from 77.8 to 65.3 million desyatins (a desyatin equals 2.7 acres or 1.092 hectares). Between 1887 and 1905 it dropped further – and at an accelerating rate – to 49.9 million desyatins. The rise in mortgage debts piled up by noble landowners tells a similar story. Small wonder that those who saw the 'premier estate' as the very backbone of the imperial régime should utter cries of alarm.

It was the condition of the peasantry however which was causing the most immediate concern. While in many regions peasants still managed to pay their redemption dues, elsewhere they were falling into unrecoverable debt. In 1899, total arrears exceeded the amounts paid. As early as 1897, the State Controller warned of exhaustion of the rural population's 'paying powers' in the central provinces. Nikolai II had commented in the margin of his report: 'It seems so to me too.' In the spring of 1898 the Committee of Ministers discussed the declining 'paying powers' of the rural population. 'The impoverishment of the Centre' became a stock phrase both in government and bureaucratic circles and in public press discussion.

How far, it may be asked, could Witte's policies be held responsible for the sorry state of Russian agriculture? Clearly, they could not be blamed for the vagaries of the Russian climate. Nor were they responsible for primitive farming methods and abysmally low productivity. Deficiencies of the transport system were only partly within the control of government. Nor yet could the authorities prevent the population explosion which increased the population of the empire from 71.3 million in 1861 to 134.8 million in 1901. Between 1883 and 1892 alone, the rural population increased by 16 per cent, during the following decade by a further 13 per cent. Neither could the government be held accountable for the resulting shrinkage in the average holding of allotment land per household, something over 5 desyatins in 1860, to 3.5 in 1880 and a mere 2.6 in 1900 (the sources disagree as to the exact figures). Nor yet, except perhaps through the forcing of grain exports, did the government cause the collapse of grain prices in world markets from 1.44 rubles a *pud* of wheat in 1871 to 0.74 rubles in 1896 and from 0.78 to 0.54 rubles for a *pud* of rye.

Lastly Witte's policies, except for sins of omission, could hardly be held responsible for the operation of longer-term causes aggravating the effects of the periodic droughts and progressively reducing productivity: widespread deforestation, lack of fertilizer, widespread strip farming, primitive crop rotation, over-cropping and disastrous soil erosion. As a government committee set up to investigate the causes of the exhaustion of the central provinces (for a variety of reasons, these causes operated less on the periphery of the empire), reported:

> Since the Emancipation, the woods have been cut down (owing to the extension of cultivation), the streams have become shallow or have disappeared, drifting sands have invaded the fields, the meadows have been ploughed up, the fields have broken up into ravines and instead of once fertile lands, gullies, water-courses, landslips, even precipices, have made their appearance: the land has lost fertility, its productivity has fallen, the natural wealth is exhausted and the people are impoverished.[27]

All this had appeared well before the days of Vyshnegradsky and Witte, though perhaps accelerating under their administrations.

Beyond any doubt, the policies pursued by the two ministers seriously aggravated the problems of Russian agriculture. In the first place, Witte singlemindedly channelled the scarce resources of the Russian Exchequer into non-agricultural projects, notably the Siberian railway. With sensible economic justification, he cut down assistance to impoverished and/or importunate landowners. In 1897, he set his face against a subsidy of 35 million rubles recommended by a Special Conference on the Needs of the Landed Nobility. Chaired by a former Minister of the Interior, its business was conducted by the then head of the Imperial Chancellery, V. K. Plehve. In refusing to subsidize the gentry, Witte argued that peasant welfare, on which the prosperity of the gentry also depended, must have priority. His concern was for the condition of the whole people, not for that of a selfish and privileged minority.

No less serious was the contribution of the 'Witte System' to the plight of the peasantry. On top of excessive redemption payments, increased taxation on articles of peasant consumption, imposed for fiscal and commercial reasons by Vyshnegradsky and Witte, aggravated the condition of the rural masses. While the impact of indirect taxation has been disputed, there is incontrovertible evidence that it increased the peasants' burden. True there had been a significant reduction of the tax load under Bunge, but this was more than offset by his successors. Revenue from the excise duty on vodka, borne largely by the peasantry, had risen from 225 million rubles in 1881 to 310 million in 1899. Income from excise duties on other articles of common peasant consumption – tobacco, sugar and kerosene – rose from 16.5 to 139.5 million rubles during the same period.[28] Witte ingenuously claimed that indirect taxes were paid voluntarily and reflected fairly the purchasing powers of the population. A close observer of rural life, however, saw matters in a different light. He wrote:

> . . . if in winter you do not want to sleep for 17 hours a day – pay excise on matches and kerosene, if you want to smoke – pay excise on matches and tobacco; if you want to imbibe a glass of vodka – pay fifteen times its actual value[29]; if you want to plough with a metal plough – pay the customs duty on iron etc. etc. In general, wherever the rural inhabitant turns, everywhere he feels that they take from him, take, take, take.[30]

Heavy import duties on raw cotton augmenting the price of textiles might have been added to the list.

Whatever the relative weight of indirect taxation,[31] there is no question about the increase in the overall tax burden on the peasantry – and, indeed on town dwellers – which resulted from the post-Bunge perestroika. As the liberal leader Paul Miliukov would presently tell an American audience:

> If the Russian peasant has no time to work for himself; if he is fatally underfed and underclothed; if he needs money badly, it is first and foremost because he is compelled to perform his function as a tax payer. He does his best to pay his taxes; and if, in spite of all his exertion, he accumulates arrears upon arrears, it is not because he will not, but because he cannot pay.[32]

Between 1883 and 1892, Miliukov claimed, population grew by 16 per cent and taxation by 29 per cent. Between 1893 and 1902, the respective figures had been 13 per cent and 49 per cent. Whereas between 1871 and 1880 every desyatin of peasant land had owed the exchequer the equivalent of 19 cents, between 1881 and 1890 the average was 24 cents, and between 1891 and 1900 it rose to 54 cents. Ordinarily, Miliukov added, the authorities collected taxes by compulsory sales before allowing arrears to accumulate. Thus, Miliukov concluded, 'the peasantry is reduced to a state of chronic insolvency, and finally grows quite apathetic'.

In fact the 'Witte System' not only failed to alleviate the now chronic plight of Russian farming but helped to intensify it by tightening the fiscal screw to a point at which it had become counterproductive. Between 1893 and 1900 not only had the exchequer lost 314 million rubles by the remission of tax arrears, it was obliged to disburse another 275 million in famine relief. It was mainly the rural population which had to pay the price of Witte's perestroika. In a poor and underdeveloped country like Russia, one moreover with a swollen military budget, there was no other road to modernization. Foreign investment, an indispensable element, was available on reasonable terms only to a country with a stable currency and balanced budget. As in their different ways the experiences of Bunge and Vyshnegradsky had shown, foreign investment could be achieved in Russia only by heavy taxation of the rural classes resulting in the forced sale and export of grain. Even if the 'Witte System' was neither the sole nor perhaps the prime cause of the agricultural crisis, it therefore did much to aggravate it. The social cost of Witte's perestroika, borne largely by the rural population, was a heavy one. There was force in the arguments of Witte's opponents, even if they felt more deeply the grievance of the landowners than those of the peasantry. The desperate state of Russian agriculture in any case served as a welcome stick with which to beat an increasingly unpopular minister.

IX

The partial failure of the harvest in 1897 finally alerted Witte to the need to confront the crisis in the central provinces. In the spring of 1898 during a special meeting of the Council of Ministers on the declining 'paying powers' of the rural population, Witte blamed 'the economic disorganization of the peasant population'. The remedy, he considered, lay in giving the peasant full title to his land, a code term for decollectivization, the abolition of the land commune with its repartitional tenure. In a letter to the tsar some months later, he again advocated an unshackling of the peasantry, encouragement of peasant initiative and the provision of opportunities for individual peasant families to improve their lot. Too many different authorities, he claimed, meddled in peasant affairs. Corporal punishment still inflicted by peasant courts was degrading. Peasants did not own their land. The collective responsibility for the payment of taxes was an ever-present element of insecurity. Only a healthy peasantry, Witte concluded – anticipating the views of Stolypin – could form the backbone of a strong Russia. Witte therefore proposed the setting up of a special conference of senior officials to work out detailed proposals. The suggestion, however, fell on deaf ears. Fellow ministers were either hostile like Goremykin or indifferent like Pobedonostsev. The tsar himself procrastinated, unsure about the issue of privatization. Nor was it certain that even Witte himself was ready to pay the inevitable financial price of agrarian reform. It would take the crop failure of 1901 and the subsequent peasant disorders finally to put the peasant question belatedly on the agenda.

The reasons for official dilatoriness are not hard to discover. At one level, there was the general policy of drift that characterized the first decade of Nikolai II. The only exception to a general passivity of central government was, in fact, Witte's energetic activities. It was precisely his measures, however, which helped to delay government intervention in the affairs of the central provinces. No rural programme was likely to be implemented without massive government expenditure. In the interest of his industrial policy, however, Witte was determined to avoid such expenditure. He was unwilling to subsidize gentry landowners, who were parasites in his view. Only with extreme reluctance, did he consent to reduce interest from 4 per cent to 3.5 per cent on existing mortgages from the State Land Bank. As regards peasant distress, all Witte was prepared to do was to fork out substantial sums to relieve acute starvation. At the same time, he begrudged every ruble spent by *zemstva* on the general improvement of rural conditions. By reducing the financial autonomy of the *zemstva* (in tandem with his enemy Plehve, if for different reasons), he was impeding what was arguably the most promising approach to improving the peasants' lot.

Beyond such fiscal and economic considerations lay the fact that the peasantry did not as yet appear to constitute a social or political threat. By and large, the peasants remained quiescent from a mixture of residual monarchical loyalty, ignorance, apathy, fatalism, hunger and the inability to organize over great distances. Among them, if seriously and hopefully exaggerated by Lenin and others, there existed substantial and growing divisions between the village poor, subsistence middle peasants and relatively prosperous *kulaks*. In some areas, these divisions might be aggravated by ethnic differences. As a result, in spite of periodic incidents or disorders resulting mainly from local grievances, the new *Pugachevshchina*, dreaded by landowners and officials, never materialized. The immense land-hunger of the rapidly increasing rural population might indeed with time pose a threat to the established social order. But while tensions were growing, there was as yet little indication that they might one day endanger the status quo.

What did alarm government circles was a different aspect of the situation. The famines and epidemics periodically afflicting the interior which, despite an almost total lack of glasnost could not be entirely concealed, had a twofold adverse effect. In the first place, they afforded *obshchestvennost*, the educated public, just grounds for pillorying the inefficiency, callousness, secretiveness and corruption of officialdom. At the same time they provided opportunities for demonstrating the greater effectiveness and more caring attitudes of local and voluntary bodies and their agents. The relatively effective relief efforts of a generous and concerned Russian public constituted, in the eyes of many, a standing reproach to the slow, clumsy, unfeeling and suspicious agents of central government.

The contrast between the relief efforts of officialdom and those of the public would help to undermine in the public at large whatever faith was left in government. The prestigious spokesman for the moral majority was none other than the glory of Russian letters, Count Leo Tolstoy. *Resurrection*, his comment on the Witte era (though not on Witte's policies), had the distinction of combining literary merit with powerful social and, in as far as was possible, political protest in the style of Émile Zola. It was a manifesto of the socially conscious and morally sensitive opposition. It is unlikely, however, that such manifestations greatly affected Witte. His industrial policies would, he confidently expected, eventually help to raise the living standards of the Russian *muzhik*, hopefully even to Prusso-German levels. The road to greater welfare for the mass of the Russian people, who were not anyway his most immediate concern, lay in the determined execution of his industrial policies.

More serious in Witte's eyes and a possible spur to state intervention, would be the impact of the crisis abroad. Foreigners would learn about Russian backwardness, underdevelopment, poverty, lack of culture and elementary hygiene, corruption and the arrogant and selfish insensitivity of petty local officialdom. In particular, it was undesirable that the French public and government should discover the realities behind the imposing facade of budget surpluses, the convertible ruble, the glowing annual reports of Witte's ministry and the impressive statistics of industrial and commercial growth. Moreover, a wider Russian public was distressed at the impression created abroad by reports of Russian conditions from occasional Western travellers. So far as Witte was concerned, if foreign investment and loans continued to flow, the plight of the peasantry was of secondary importance. His policies would continue essentially unchanged.

* * *

The chronic agriculture crisis in the central provinces coincided, unfortunately for Witte, with another affecting Russia's developing industries. His industrial perestroika was shown to have an Achilles heel. Among the consequences of rapid industrialization (with the significant participation of foreign capital) had been a growing Russian dependence on world economic trends. When, between 1899 and 1903, the European economy experienced a sharp if short-lived recession, Russia was also affected. The situation was aggravated by the fact that, with the approaching completion of the Siberian railway, long-term government orders to heavy industry were declining. For a number of years it would suffer from over-capacity. In August 1899 the State Bank's discount rate rose sharply and share prices declined. Two large firms owning railway lines and factories became insolvent. In 1900 prices for industrial products began to fall and would continue to do so until 1902. Pig iron, which in mid-1900 had sold for 70–80 kopeks a *pud*, fetched only 45–48 by the end of the year. The price of Donets coal fell from 9–10 kopeks a *pud* early in 1900 to 6–7 kopeks at the end of 1902. Crude oil prices dropped from 17–18 kopeks in 1900 to 4–6 kopeks early in 1902. The fall in prices brought a reduction in output. That of pig iron fell from 172.8 million *pud* in 1901 to 156.5 in 1902 and to 149.5 *pud* in 1903. The metallurgical industry of the south, Witte's favourite child, was hard hit, with some weaker firms going into liquidation and capital becoming concentrated in larger ones. The recession marked a major, if temporary, set-back to Witte's industrial hopes. It was, like the agricultural crisis, grist to the mill of his critics.

The industrial recession drew increasing attention also to a longer term by-product of Witte's perestroika, the growth of an industrial working class. The Russian proletariat, emerging progressively from within a larger workforce of factory peasants, remained small in numbers compared to the mass of the peasantry. An economist, on the basis of official statistics, arrived at a figure of around 2.2 million in 1896. By the end of the century, he considers, the true figure may have been nearer three million. While 550,000 were working in the textile industry and another 500,000 in metallurgy, 400,000 were employed on the railways.[33] A significant feature of the growing proletariat was its concentration in and around St Petersburg, in the central industrial region around Moscow, in the Donbas, the Caucasus and parts of Poland and the Urals. A further aspect of concentration was that many workers were employed in what, by European standards, were large enterprises.

Living and working conditions of the still small but growing proletariat, while showing some variations, generally resembled those of workers anywhere during early industrialization: long hours, low wages, bad housing, attempts to impose factory discipline, rough treatment by managers, abuses like the truck system, excessive fines and irregular payment of wages. The recession would add new grievances: short-time working, wage cutting, redundancies and unemployment. The inevitable consequence of workers' grievances were periodic strikes, mainly in the textile industry, and the beginnings of a rudimentary labour movement. This took at first the form of small, illegal and often ephemeral unions, usually with the active participation of revolutionary intellectuals. After earlier outbreaks notably in 1878–9 and again in 1885, 1896 saw a major strike in the

St Petersburg cotton mills. Some 35,000 mill hands in several enterprises downed tools and stayed out for almost a month. They came out again in 1897, claiming that the management had reneged on earlier undertakings. Their demands, mainly of an economic nature, were met in part. The strike attracted wide attention not only for its scale, but also for its duration and for the degree of organization involved. It was, in some respects, a novel phenomenon for Russia. During the late 1890s, moreover, new regions and industries were affected by strikes.

In 1901, during a strike at the Obukhov metalworks in St Petersburg, armed workers resisted a police attempt to occupy their factory. In November 1902 a strike in the railway workshops of the capital spread rapidly to nearly every industrial enterprise. Speakers were demanding not only higher wages and a nine-hour working day but also an end to autocracy. The disturbances, quelled by military force, were followed by numerous arrests. In March 1903 a strike of miners at Zlatoust in the Urals provoked riots during which, on orders of the provincial governor, troops fired on unarmed strikers. There were casualties. Three months later, strikes erupted all over southern Russia culminating in a general strike by some 250,000 workers. Their demands included higher wages, shorter working hours and the legalization of trade unions. Social Democratic speakers were calling for the convocation of a constituent assembly. Ironically, the strike was set off by the activities of a 'yellow', apolitical union sponsored by the Ministry of the Interior but infiltrated by revolutionaries. The union was promptly disbanded.

Overall, the Russian government met the nascent workers' movement with a mixture of concessions, among them Witte's Factory Act of 1897, and repression in the form of arrests and punishment of unofficial union organizers and strike leaders. Its attitude towards the workers and their demands was in fact ambivalent. There existed a wish, particularly in the Ministry of the Interior and inspired mainly by concern for security and public order, that legitimate economic grievances should be redressed. Witte similarly desired an improvement of working conditions but, in the interest of employers and foreign investors, also felt impelled to protect the interests of management. The two ministries clashed over the formation of 'yellow unions' by Zubatov, head of the Moscow *Okhrana*. Matters came to a head, when the union, with substantial workers' support, began to organize economic strikes in foreign-owned factories. When the French government protested, Witte found himself in a quandary.

A further bone of contention, this time between the factory owners championed by Witte and the agents of the Ministry of the Interior, concerned the role of the police in industrial relations. Whereas employers preferred police detachments to stand by outside factories in case of need, the police authorities supported by the Ministry of the Interior wished to station them within the factory precincts to facilitate surveillance. Yet another source of friction involved control of the Factory Inspectorate, an agency originally of Witte's Ministry of Finance. Following bitter wrangles, a compromise was reached under which the unfortunate inspectors (of whom there were in any case too few), remained under Witte's overall control but were made answerable in an ill-defined manner to local agents of the Ministry of the Interior.

Government policies towards the workers thus evolved from a constant tug of war between the two most powerful ministries. Where Witte saw labour relations under the twin aspects of industrial growth and foreign investment, Plehve's policemen gave priority to the maintenance of public order and the fight against subversion. Even where the two objectives might appear to be complementary, there was disagreement about methods. The clash between Witte and Plehve, not least in the sphere of labour policy, reflects the fundamental ambiguity of the attempt to carry through an economic perestroika within the framework of a police state.

Although the workers' movement was contained with comparative ease, it nonetheless increased Witte's vulnerability. Up to the 1880s at least, conservative and nationalist Russians had prided themselves on the fact that, unlike the 'rotten' West, Russia had produced no proletariat. This had been seen as a distinctive and positive feature of the Russian social system rather than as an expression of economic underdevelopment. Now the illusion was shattered and Witte's perestroika was held largely responsible. Working class unrest not only laid Witte open to criticism but was designed also to alarm Nikolai II with his vaguely paternalistic views of relations between the autocrat and his people. The strike wave of 1902–3 lent some force to widespread criticism of over-rapid industrialization. The 'Witte System' – like Gorbachev's perestroika – could quite convincingly be held responsible for undermining (partly imaginary) social stability and order.

X

Witte's relations with the imperial couple had never been easy. His brusque manner, loud voice and overbearing personality were, as already indicated, uncongenial to the gentle, soft-spoken, indeed 'feline' tsar. The tsaritsa in her turn deeply resented anyone's influence but her own over the decisions of her pliable husband. However, from loyalty to the memory of his father, from deference to

his mother the dowager-empress and also through a grudging realization of Witte's talents and achievements, Nikolai II had for years
swallowed his aversion. As late as 1899 and 1900 he appointed two
ministers largely of Witte's choosing, Sipyagin and Lamsdorff. At the
same time, however, he lent a willing ear to Witte's numerous critics.
Moreover, his confidence in Witte could not but be shaken by the
onset of the economic crisis superimposed on the chronic plight of
Russian agriculture and against a background of growing unrest.
When, in 1902, Plehve replaced the murdered Sipyagin, the writing
was on the wall.

Still Nikolai II was loth to part with the only minister to enjoy an
international reputation; a reputation, moreover, which formed the
base of Russia's international credit. However, Witte's opposition to
the Yalu venture and to over-expansion in the East generally, together
with the south-Russian strikes finally convinced the tsar the time for a
change of ministers had come. Characteristically, Nikolai gained the
necessary self-assurance for the deed through a deeply spiritual
experience. In July 1903, largely at the behest of the empress, he led
a pilgrimage to a monastery south of Nizhni-Novgorod ostensibly for
the canonization of a recently deceased ascetic monk. Its true purpose
inspired by the tsaritsa was to gain, through the intercession of the
new saint, the fulfilment of her dearest wish – the birth of a belated
son and heir.[34] Nikolai was joined in his pilgrimage by members of his
family, the Court, high officials (including Plehve, who offered a
moving spectacle of the deepest hypocrisy) and an estimated 300,000
of his subjects.

From a number of more or less bizarre ceremonies, including by all
accounts a naked bath by the empress at night in a pool associated
with the 'holy man', the emperor emerged consoled and spiritually
refreshed. The pilgrimage, an undoubted popular success, was for
him a deep spiritual experience, a communion between the autocrat
and his people: many cripples and sick people had received his
blessing.

Immediately following his return, Nikolai II felt ready to 'take the
bull by the horns'. It was then he appointed Alekseyev Viceroy of the
Far East, thus ending Witte's long control over Manchurian affairs.
On 15 August, after a meeting of the Committee on Peasant Affairs
at which he had shown himself unusually gracious, the tsar asked
Witte to bring the Governor of the State Bank with him for his routine
weekly report the next day. During the report, while von Pleske, an
ailing nonentity, waited in the antechamber, the tsar once again
showed unusual amiability. Having ended the interview by enquiring
after Witte's health and urging him not to wear himself out, he
accompanied him to the door. As Witte was on the point of leaving,

the tsar called after him: 'By the way, I forgot to congratulate you, Sergei Iulyevich, I have appointed you chairman of the committee of ministers.' It was Witte's notice of dismissal. The new post was a mainly honorific one. Witte, understandably, was furious. 'I swear by all that I hold dearest, by my wife and by my daughter,' he told a confidant some days later, 'that I will never forget this.' And remember it he did as he would show years later in his memoirs with their highly critical appraisal of Nikolai II.

NOTES

1. For Witte's career and achievement, see especially Theodore H. Von Laue: *Sergei Witte and the Industrialization of Russia* (New York, 1973).
2. In 1904 a critic of Witte's new order would complain of '. . . people who occupy a high position, but who are little more than jumped-up railway station baggage checkers, who try at every turn to put down one who requires something of them if he is not of their kind, but comes of decent society' (quoted in D. M. O'Flaherty: *Tsarism and the Politics of Publicity 1865–1881*, unpublished PhD thesis, pp 46–7).
3. For the following see Werner Keller: *Ost minus West null*, (München-Zürich, 1960), pp 204–8 (translated into English as *Are the Russians Ten Feet Tall?*).
4. *Ibid*, pp 208–9.
5. Friedrich List: *The National System of Political Economy* (1841), quoted in Theodore H. Von Laue: *Sergei Witte and the Industrialization of Russia* (New York, 1973), pp 60–1.
6. Laue: *Sergei Witte*, p 56.
7. Laue: 'A Secret Memorandum of Sergei Witte on the Industrialization of Imperial Russia', in *The Journal of Modern History*, vol XXVI (1954), No 1, pp 60–75.
8. *Ibid*.
9. *Ibid*.
10. *Ibid*.
11. *Ibid*.
12. *Ibid*.
13. For details of the extent of French investment in Russia, see Olga Crisp: *Studies in the Russian Economy before 1914* (London, 1976), pp 159–216. In Russia's current perestroika the place of France seems likely to be taken by Germany, again with political implications.
14. Laue: 'Memorandum'.
15. *Ibid*.
16. *Ibid*.
17. *Ibid*.
18. *Ibid*.
19. *Ibid*.
20. *Ibid*.

21. *Ibid.*
22. Laue: *Sergei Witte*, p 82.
23. For comprehensive statistics of Russian trade, finance and industry in 1800–1914, see the Appendix to P. A. Khromov: *Ekonomicheskoye razvitie Rossii v XIX–XX vekakh* (Moscow, 1950), pp 434–545.
24. Gregor Alexinsky: *Modern Russia*, English translation (London and Leipzig, 1913), p 98.
25. C. Lehmann und Parvus: *Das hungernde Russland* (Stuttgart, 1900), an informative, if tendentious, account of the miserable conditions of the peasantry during the 1898 famine in the Volga provinces.
26. It is summarized in John Maynard: *The Russian Peasant and Other Studies* (New York, 1962), pp 62–8.
27. Maynard: *Russian Peasant*, pp 68–9.
28. Figures in Khromov: *Razvitie*, pp 498 and 502.
29. Witte had raised the excise duty on vodka from nine to 15 kopeks per degree proof. Under the state monopoly he introduced, vodka provided one-third of total state revenue.
30. L. Martov, P. Maslov and A. Potresov, eds: *Obshchestvennoye dvizhenie v Rossii v nachale XX veka* (St Petersburg, 1909–10), vol I, p 158.
31. See Crisp: *Russian Economy*, p 27.
32. Paul Miliukov: *Russia and Its Crisis* (New York, 1962), p 323.
33. According to another computation, the average annual number of workers employed between 1890 and 1900 in 50 provinces of European Russia was 1,638,000. The total for 1900 for the whole empire is given as approaching 2.2 million.
34. The imperial couple had produced four daughters, but since 1797 women had been debarred from the Russian throne. The empress was determined to leave no stone unturned to prevent the succession from passing to the Grand-Duke Mikhail, the tsar's younger brother. This had appeared a distinct possibility when Nikolai suffered an attack of typhoid.

8

Witte's First Perestroika: an Appraisal

I

Was Nikolai II wise in dispensing with the services of his ablest minister? After a brief interregnum, Witte would be replaced by his deputy Kokovtsev who, cast in a duller bureaucratic mould, would continue Witte's policies. As regards Witte's opposition to risky adventures in the Far East (probably the major cause of his downfall), he would be proved right within the year. With his relatively cautious Eastern policy, he would almost certainly have reached an accommodation with Japan and avoided looming disasters. That the tsar finally came down on the side of Witte's opponents is, however, understandable. Plehve not only backed the Bezobrazov adventure but also appeared indispensable in view of the domestic situation. Moreover the tsar, in yielding to the anti-Witte lobby, was following his natural inclinations. The number of individuals benefiting from Witte's perestroika – as is the case with Gorbachev's – had been relatively small while its social cost had been a high one.

In fact, the results of Witte's first perestroika were finely balanced. There is no question about his achievements in regard to railway construction, financial management, the improvement of Russian credit abroad, the extension of Russia's Asiatic interests, the development of industry and commerce, and the promotion of technical and commercial education. Strings of statistics bear witness to the material success of Witte's policies.

Yet, seen in a wider context, Witte's achievements were laying up trouble for the future. Russia's problems sprang mainly from her poverty combined with heavy military expenditure. Economic modernization, from which the great mass of the Russian people derived little immediate benefit, had to be paid for. The cost, both financial and social was high. Foreign loans and foreign investment had their price, railway construction required heavy subsidies. Social cost was transformed into fiscal through the need for famine relief. The price of perestroika was paid by an impoverished population in the shape of high taxation and high customs duties. The main cost of Witte's perestroika fell necessarily on the peasant masses. Under Vyshnegradsky and Witte, the tax screw was tightened to the limit of endurance. The price exacted was chronic malnutrition and occasional starvation for hundreds of thousands. Industrialization in a country as poor as Russia, could, at this stage in her development, be achieved only at the expense of popular welfare. Witte's argument that in the end the mass of the people would benefit through cheaper and more plentiful consumer goods has a hollow ring. It contained a large element of wishful thinking and whistling in the dark. Industrialization, in developing countries like Russia, was based primarily on the development of heavy industry largely for military purposes and was not geared to the production of consumer goods. While the provision of agricultural machinery might increase the productivity and hence the prosperity of agriculture, the protective tariff of 1891 greatly increased its cost. Primitive methods of peasant farming and landholding as well as cost necessarily confined its use to gentry estates. What good, on the other hand, were railways carrying away their grain for export to distant destinations to the hungry rural masses of the central provinces?

Additional employment opportunities in the growing industries, when measured against the steadily escalating numbers of the rural under-employed, were small. Migration to Siberia encouraged by the government and facilitated by the new railways could reduce population pressure only to a limited extent. Only areas bordering the railways could be colonized. Many of the migrants in any case preferred to trek on foot.

Next to the peasants, it was the workers in industry who bore the brunt of perestroika. Witte, logically from his point of view, repeatedly drew attention to the abundance of cheap labour as one of Russia's greatest assets. Her industrial development, in effect, was based on the exploitation of cheap labour, whether in factory or cottage industry. It was labour often subsidized by the villages in the form of allotments which gave absent factory workers a minimum of social security in case of illness, disablement or old age. However, if Russian labour was abundant and cheap, it was also of low productivity. Higher wages in much of Russian industry would have priced its products out of limited markets. Even if an 'aristocracy of labour' employed in the large metallurgical enterprises of St Petersburg or the textile mills of the Narva district with their British connections, could achieve tolerable living conditions, the rest of the labour force could not. Poverty and ill health aggravated by the wholesale consumption of vodka were widespread, the barracks or tenements in which especially seasonal workers were housed, appalling.

Belated factory legislation, did little to shorten working hours or ensure even minimal safety standards. The police stood by ready to protect the interests of owners and management. Workers, on the other hand, had no protection against wage cutting or unemployment in conditions of recession or, alternatively, against a lengthening of working hours. Independent trade unions were illegal and remained weak and localized. Strikes were outlawed, their leaders subject to dismissal and blacklisting. Social and educational facilities provided by short-lived 'yellow' unions were appreciated. Factory workers, in short, shared with the peasantry the cost of Witte's perestroika based on the abundance of cheap labour.

The landowning gentry were also among the losers. Had greater subsidies been available to them, this might at any rate have slowed down the shrinkage of their estates. For them, however, Witte had neither sympathy nor cash. Again they regularly complained that the tariff of 1891 raised the price of agricultural machinery, both imported and home-produced. Yet, even though penalized, landowners still escaped their fair share of the burden. Ever since the days of Bunge the weight of direct taxation had been shifting from agriculture to industry and commerce. Under Witte, while the relative proportion of revenue from commercial and industrial sources had risen, that of the land tax had declined. It is at the same time debatable how far this had benefited individual landowners, who also bore a substantial share of the *zemstvo* rates. Except for a small but growing entrepreneurial or investing class which Witte did his best to nurture, it is doubtful whether any part of the population gained in well-being as a result of his perestroika.

The policy of rapid industrialization pursued by Witte raised also more fundamental questions. While earlier industrial activity (notably in textiles) had developed spontaneously, Witte's new metallurgical industries were mainly state-induced. The government helped to bring them into existence and to keep them alive by high protective tariffs. It provided vast subsidies both direct and indirect as well as providing markets for their products. Arguably, the new industries had been grafted artificially on to a slowly evolving native structure integrated into the rural economy. Witte's creations had little connection with the transactions at the traditional Russian fairs, notably the vast one held annually at Nizhni Novgorod. The 'Witte System' effectively left Russia with two imperfectly integrated economic sectors; a native one evolving from agricultural society, and a largely imported one relying on foreign capital and expertise.

At Witte's dismissal in 1903, the future of the 'modern' sector appeared problematic. Would it, in time, become integrated with the native economy, or would it wither away as some earlier state-induced industries had done? The demand for railway materials was finite, the market for other products limited. The armaments industry would be pitted against often superior imports; nor were its markets unlimited. Finally, the progress of the 'Witte industries' would require continued state support. Could such support be relied on following Witte's dismissal? Might there not be a return to investment in agriculture? And would foreign, mainly French, investment continue in the face of Russia's domestic problems and a possible realignment of her foreign policy? How would the reformed currency stand up to the strains of war? The question marks hanging over the future of Witte's creations were legion.

Witte's innovations also raised questions about the relation between economic modernization and its political framework. As has been seen, Witte was a believer in autocracy as practised by Aleksandr III. Necessary reforms, in his view, could be introduced only by enlightened bureaucrats with the support of the autocratic power. Russian experience from the emancipation of the serfs to the introduction of the gold standard appeared to support this view. Absolute power, in effect, seemed to be a prerequisite of perestroika as the only means for overcoming opposition and obstruction from traditionalists, vested interests and ideological critics. A further obstacle which only a determined use of power could partially neutralize lay in bureaucratic *oblomovshchina*, the desire of officials at all levels for an easy, lazy life and for avoiding the effort required by innovation. Again, no effective reform appeared possible without the existence of an arbiter to adjudicate between conflicting claims, interests and personalities. Without a determined decision-maker, any major reform would be paralysed by prolonged infighting, conflicts of interest, endless committees, conferences and intrigues. A radical innovator in the economic sphere, therefore, Witte was an authoritarian in his political views. Moreover, such views were an essential prerequisite for an economic reformer under rulers like Aleksandr III and Nikolai II. Without an impeccable autocratism, a Witte under either tsar would have been unthinkable. Even had Witte not been a believing autocratist, and he may well have been, the profession of strictly conservative principles was a necessary precondition of his ministerial career.

On a more mundane level, the success of Witte's policies would require domestic stability and order. This was needed above all to reassure foreign investors. It was necessary also to secure his own tenure. The steady deterioration of the security situation, more particularly after 1901, was in fact slowly undermining his position. It also had the political disadvantage of strengthening Plehve and his 'law and order' men.

Witte, for a variety of reasons, was therefore committed to the political status quo of the Reaction. He tried to restrict the role of the *zemstva* because of his own political conviction and because they represented rival spending authorities.[1] The *zemstva* were, whether actually or potentially, agents of a rival form of modernization with political overtones. Their philosophy ran counter to Witte's bureaucratic and centralist, indeed dictatorial, instincts. In many respects Witte was thus at this time politically a true representative of the Reaction. His policy of economic modernization had to be conducted within a strictly conservative framework.

What separated Witte from the conservatives, besides his anti-gentry bias, was that, for practical rather than humanitarian reasons he was opposed to the more severe measures of discrimination directed against Jews. His attitude in this regard was purely utilitarian. Jews or men of Jewish origin were prominent among railway entrepreneurs (including Witte's former chief on the southwestern railway, I. S. Bliokh), among directors of joint-stock banks and indeed on the wider commercial scene. An article published in 1898 claimed that of 421 merchants of the First and Second Guilds listed for St Petersburg in 1896, 18 per cent were Jewish. In Moscow, no fewer than 37 per cent of those entitled to vote in the First Guild were Jews. Witte, in short, could not afford to alienate so important a capitalist group. Neither was he prepared to endanger transactions abroad where some Jewish bankers were showing a measure of solidarity with their persecuted Russian brethren. In practice, all Witte did was to encourage a handful of wealthy Jewish capitalists. Except for concern at adverse publicity abroad caused by Russian pogroms, the fate of the Jewish millions in the Pale of Settlement left him cold.

Witte was therefore able to combine an impeccably conservative political stance with innovative economic policies. But was a successful perestroika without glasnost a practical possibility? Were perestroika and glasnost separable? To Witte it appeared so and was, indeed, a practical necessity. Economic development, as his experience under Aleksandr III seemed to suggest, was compatible with reactionary policies under an authoritarian system of government. Industrial and commercial progress had coexisted with government devoid of glasnost or freedom. Entrepreneurial enterprise, while requiring the stimulus of state aid, did not stand in need of constitutional or elective government or political participation. And yet, the question remains whether, for any length of time, economic progress could be divorced wholly from political. Could Russia continue to industrialize without accompanying political change? How far would sustained entrepreneurial initiative and expansion require a degree of political freedom? How long would a growing modern sector in the economy remain compatible with a political system based on autocracy and bureaucracy? Witte for one, under the influence of a quasi-Marxian analysis, appears to have held the view that at some stage political change must necessarily follow economic. And indeed, during his last years in office, it was becoming increasingly doubtful whether the weakening system of the Reaction could long withstand the forces, in part conjured up by Witte's activities, which were now pressing for a measure also of political change.

II

From the point of view of the tsarist régime, the effects of Witte's perestroika were mixed. On the one hand, it partially modernized the empire's network of communications, strengthened its industrial and commercial structures, improved its finances, encouraged native entrepreneurship and promoted the spread of modern capitalist attitudes. In doing this it helped to safeguard Russia's place among the powers. It did so, moreover, without political upheaval if not without social unrest. On the negative side, it contributed to a lowering of living standards for the mass of the population. It accelerated the decline of the traditional ruling class. Tensions between the modern and traditional sectors of Russian society were intensified. Some of the consequences, as expressed in the rival Far Eastern policies respectively of Witte and Plehve would emerge within months of Witte's downfall. The subsequent course of events raises, at least speculatively, the question of possible alternatives to the 'Witte System'.

In the first place did there exist for Russia, as both conservative, Slavophil and populist romantics including Leo Tolstoy fondly imagined, a non-industrial option? Could tsarist Russia have developed, as countries like India or China have done until comparatively recently, on the basis of peasant agriculture and cottage industry? There is little doubt that this might have been a possible path of development. However, particularly in view of the demographic explosion, this was likely to have proved a path beset with grinding and perhaps increasing poverty. The mass of the population would have benefited little. Moreover and perhaps more importantly, at least in the eyes of the Russian ruling class, such a course would inevitably, have spelt the end of Russian power. Modern warfare required strategic railways, state of the art artillery, rifles and shells, up-to-date means of communication. Before long, motorized transport and aviation would come into their own. Under a non-industrial policy (or, at least, one oriented away from heavy industry), the bulk of military hardware would have to be imported resulting in a complete dependence upon the foreigner. A purely agricultural economy, moreover, with only *kustar* industries to back it could hardly bear the cost of such imports. Adoption of a non-industrial option would have turned Russia, of necessity, into either a French or a German dependency, a fate she would in any case only partially escape. Without Witte's perestroika such dependence was likely to have become total. Given Germany's century-old *Drang nach Osten* Russia would have stood in danger of losing her independence.

In addition, the non-industrial option would in all probability involve a retreat into 'splendid isolation', a partial withdrawal from Europe and the jettisoning of Westernization as pursued since the seventeenth century. The non-industrial option would, at the same time, be an Asiatic one. This was a choice from which the bulk of the Westernized ruling class with its liking for Western culture and Western comforts recoiled. The cult of *samobytnost*, the innate Russian 'being' propagated by Dostoyevsky (and to which Alexander Solzhenytsin is no stranger), was little more than an intellectual affectation, an esoteric expression of nationalist romanticism cultivated by some writers and intellectuals. Westernization on the other hand, was an elemental and probably irresistible force. For these reasons the non-industrial option could be seriously entertained only by the starry-eyed and the muddle-headed. It was never a serious alternative.

There remained the question of the pace of industrial development. Some among Witte's critics, while not rejecting industrialization *a limine* and indeed regretfully admitting its necessity, argued that by needlessly forcing the pace he produced unnecessary negative manifestations. Some of the evils resulting from over-rapid change could, at the very least have been mitigated.

Neither Vyshnegradsky however, nor Witte were given to gradualism. Witte was convinced that only shock therapy could produce results in the face of widespread sloth and apathy. Again, Witte explained to the tsar that (as with Yeltsin's price rises) the Russian people could bear the hardships associated with his perestroika for only a limited period of time. Speed, therefore, appeared to be of the essence. With a slower rate of industrialization moreover, the gap between Russia and the more advanced nations, most notably imperial Germany, would have widened inexorably. The prime object of perestroika, the preservation of Russia's international position would have been jeopardized. For Witte at any rate, gradualism was not a viable option.

A third choice, that of a different type of industrialization geared predominantly to the production of consumer goods and possibly *zemstvo*-based, a choice that might have commended itself to Bunge, was impracticable for several of the reasons that ruled out the other alternatives. It would fail to sustain Russia's international standing and the preservation of her independence. It was also economically unviable. All materials for the construction of essential railways would have to be imported which would play havoc with the balance of trade. Foreign investment, partly strategic or political in purpose, would dry up. Last but not least, given Russian poverty and the existence of well-established cottage industries with a recognized marketing system, it would take a long time to develop a domestic market for industrially produced consumer goods. Small industrial enterprises geared to their production would, with few exceptions, for a long time remain unprofitable. Consumer-oriented industrialization was therefore not a viable alternative. Witte's path was almost certainly the only practicable route to economic modernization.

III

It is instructive to compare and contrast Witte's industrial policies with those of the next industrial perestroika associated with the name of Stalin.[2] While this is not the place to develop the comparison in detail, some similarities and differences may be pointed out. In each case, the policy adopted was one of economic modernization within a repressive political system. In each case, industrialization was directed from the centre by a government with almost unlimited power. Each of the perestroikas was pursued at heavy social cost expended by the mass of the population. Each also was closely related to the international constellation. The object of industrialization in the case of Stalin and perhaps in that of Aleksandr III and Witte also, was to prepare the Russian state to confront a perceived German threat. In Witte's case at least, it was designed also to further Russian expansionism in the Far East. It could be said that Russian poverty and inherent inertia, the overriding urge to maintain great power status, the perceived foreign threat and the need for a strong centralized government to meet it, were constants of the Russian situation.

At the same time, the differences were perhaps more important than the similarities. Witte was, of course, no Stalin, and his methods bear no comparison with those of the 'man of steel'. Where Witte (and Vyshnegradsky before him) would employ financial expedients and inducements to achieve his objectives, Stalin would, where it appeared necessary, resort to coercion. There were, in particular, great differences in their agricultural policies. Whereas Witte would seek to

finance his industrial policies through taxation and the determined
export of grain, Stalin sought to achieve similar results through the
twin policies of collectivization and mechanization of farming,
reinforced by forced requisitioning of grain in the guise of taxation.
Whereas Witte came to contemplate privatization as a means of raising
agricultural productivity, Stalin, with the same object in view, moved
instead in the opposite direction. In this respect, the practical considerations apart, Witte and Stalin may also have started from different
ideological positions.

This, to some extent, can also be seen in the industrial sphere.
Witte, with the state as a necessary partner, on the whole encouraged
private enterprise. Stalin, in liquidating the NEP, moved again in the
opposite direction. Even if the activities of Witte's ministry were by no
means unplanned, they do not bear comparison with Stalin's rigid
command economy. In these respects – there may be others – the
differences between the two attempts at perestroika are perhaps more
significant than the similarities. Yet one basic feature, perestroika with
little glasnost, rapid economic change introduced from above under a
repressive political régime, if different in degree, is in fact common to
both. The 'Witte System' and the 'Stalin Revolution' in this respect at
least represent comparable variants of economic modernization, and
arguably the most effective ones at that.

Witte, in fact, was obliged to pursue his policies within a predeter-
mined political framework which he was unable to change or modify
even had he desired to do so. Indeed he encountered the greatest
difficulty in manipulating the political system even on matters crucial
to his economic programme. Within the constraints imposed by
autocracy he was able, thanks to the confidence and esteem of
Aleksandr III and the less assured support of his son, to operate with
considerable effect and lasting results. His was a major share in
initiating Russia's industrial take-off. The problems created in the
process were an inevitable concomitant, as were the sufferings
imposed on the Russian population. In the face of imperialist rivalries,
the need for rapid modernization, in the first place through railway
construction, appeared in the eyes of the Russian government incontrovertible. Witte was the man with the required energy, experience
and vision to carry through the necessary policies. The need for his
measures was widely, if by no means universally or enthusiastically,
conceded. Perestroika was seen as an ineluctable necessity. What
proved fatal to Witte's 'first' bureaucratic career was his loss of control
over the conduct of foreign policy, combined with the alienation of
Nikolai II and his entourage. Here the dangers of an autocratic system
headed by a Nikolai II stood glaringly revealed. Shady adventurers
were allowed to shape policy over the heads of responsible advisers.

With perestroika, Witte's eclipse was only loosely connected. The approaching Japanese debacle and its consequences were of course concealed from the beholders. However, the fact that recession and growing unrest were directing Russia towards a crisis had, by 1901, become apparent and was commented on by some perceptive contemporaries.

NOTES

1. It is suggested that the *zemstva* had been raising their rates dramatically to force a change in Witte's policies.
2. 'Impatient to make Russia strong, he [Witte] was a forerunner of Stalin rather than a contemporary of Nikolai II. His work revealed the basic problems which have haunted Russia ever since.' Theodore H. Von Laue: *Why Lenin? Why Stalin?* (Philadelphia and New York, 1964), p 52.

9

Interim Balance

At Witte's dismissal in 1903, 47 years – little more than the lifespan of one generation – had elapsed since the end of the Crimean War. During the interval, Russia's rulers had transformed the economy, patchily modernized administration and government and, largely as an unplanned by-product, modified the structure of Russian society. The initiative for the changes had come mainly from the centre, the modernizing section of the high bureaucracy, in indispensable alliance with the autocratic power. At the same time, however, some basic aspects of the régime and of Russian society had undergone little change. Forces of conservatism, of inertia, and not least of self-interest were strong and consistently obstructed or distorted perestroika, even where they could not wholly prevent it. Again, Russia's overall poverty set limits to possible achievement.

There emerged in Russia, as indeed can be observed in contemporary underdeveloped countries, a distinctive dialectic of change. So far as government was concerned, the dialectic related (in the terms popularized by Arnold Toynbee) to a mechanism of 'challenge and response'. Challenge, in the main, came from the outside. Internal challenges, whether from peasants or workers, intelligentsia or critical gentry, were confined to a secondary place except perhaps during the brief peak of terrorist activity of the People's Will. The first challenge to the established order was the war in the Crimea. The response to the shock of Sevastopol had barely worked itself out when a new challenge emerged in the shape of the Prusso-German defeat of France. International rivalries sharpened, forcing Russia to compete for membership in a league for which she was barely qualified. The response to the Crimean challenge were the Great Reforms of

Aleksandr II; the German challenge produced the 'Witte System' and the French alliance. Both encountered the sometimes bitter if understandable resistance of conservative forces and interests. The response to the next challenge, that of the People's Will instead turned out to be the Great Reaction. The three responses effectively shaped the character of the period.

Throughout all changes Russia's basic institutions, autocracy and bureaucracy, remained untouched. The tsar continued to appoint and dismiss his ministers who were answerable to him alone. On important occasions, he personally presided over meetings of the Council of Ministers. There was no trace of ministerial solidarity – let alone collective responsibility. No Russian minister could resign, at least in theory – he was expected instead to await dismissal or the gracious permission to quit. No major policy initiative was possible without explicit imperial sanction. The tsar himself was answerable to no one. His official responsibility 'to God and to his conscience' was inevitably something of a euphemism. He continued to exercise supreme command over the armed forces and, through the Procurator of the Holy Synod, over the subservient Orthodox episcopate. The conduct of foreign affairs remained his personal prerogative. Not merely in constitutional theory but to a large extent in practice, the vast empire was ruled, in the last resort, by a single man and by those whose advice he chose to take. In this regard, there had been no change whatever.

Beneath the tsar, at the top of the bureaucratic ladder, his principal executive officers were in an anomalous position. In relation to their master, they enjoyed neither status nor authority. They held office during his good pleasure. Chance alliances apart, they were not bound to their colleagues. Successive autocrats indeed watched their rivalries without displeasure. At the same time, while powerless in relation to the emperor and isolated among their peers, individual ministers ruled – all but autocratically – over vast bureaucratic hierarchies extending from their St Petersburg offices to the remotest corners of the empire. To their subordinates, whose fate and careers depended on their goodwill, these were awe-inspiring personages. Ever since the days of Nikolai I hierarchical subordination had been emphasized by the rule that on all formal occasions officials, from the all-powerful minister downwards, must present themselves in civil service uniform. The keynote of the bureaucratic systems lay in subordination to superiors. No official, moreover, could be prosecuted for any misdemeanour however grave, without his superior's explicit permission.

That at least superficial ideological conformity in these conditions was the norm goes without saying. Reforming and even liberal attitudes were in the ascendant during the Great Reforms and were at any rate tolerated within the Witte empire. They also found something of a refuge within the State Council, whose usually superannuated members no longer had careers to make, often bore the imprint of the Great Reforms and were without superiors in the bureaucratic hierarchy. Their annual reappointment by the tsar was normally a matter of routine. In 1903 all this was much as it had been some 40 years before.

Nor had there been any change in the role of provincial governors. These satraps, officially the tsar's representatives on the spot though notionally subject to the intermediate authority of the Minister of the Interior, enjoyed in their bailiwicks almost unfettered powers. Control over them was exercised through so-called 'Senatorial revisions' or inspections which, though sometimes thorough, were intermittent and infrequent. Slightly more effective was the informal social control of the local nobility and its marshals. Such controls, however, were minimized by the fact that, as a matter of policy, the Ministry of the Interior rotated provincial governors at frequent intervals. This greatly reduced the possibility of local influences acquiring an undue weight. Moreover, the arbitrary powers of governors were further increased during the anti-terrorist campaign. Governors then acquired wide discretionary powers all too easily abused. The major constraint, perhaps, came from the terrorists.

A last unchanged aspect of the system was the relationship between *chinovniks* (bureaucrats) and the Russian public. In general a member of the public, unless an aristocrat or exceptionally well-connected had no effective recourse against the most arbitrary proceedings of even middle-ranking officials. At the lowest level, orders of the local police captain had to be obeyed without question by everyone except the local 'big wig'. Complaints against official arbitrariness could be lodged with a superior, a lengthy, frustrating and usually fruitless operation. As regards action in the courts, permission to prosecute might be refused. If granted, judges might be loth to take cognizance of official misdemeanours. Attempts by aggrieved parties to have resort to publicity, glasnost would as likely as not be frustrated by the censors. So long as an official retained the goodwill of his immediate superior, not infrequently his partner in crime, he could operate with near impunity. A mere subject could look for little redress. Moreover, in spite of attempts notably by Aleksandr II to fight endemic corruption, bureaucratic abuses of various kinds proved ineradicable. At best, they were driven underground. Officials were poorly paid and at the same time exercised extensive and virtually uncontrolled powers. The tsar and his ministers depended on *chinovniks* for the execution of their orders and could ill afford to alienate these indispensable agents. Indeed for their own self-preservation, they were forced to increase those agents' arbitrary powers. They had had little choice other than to condone their misdeeds. If anything, officialdom became more powerful and arbitrary under Plehve than it had been in the days of Nikolai Miliutin.

The basic structure of state power, subsumed by Russian publicists and historians under the term of *vlast*, (a compound of power, state and authority) had thus undergone little change since the Crimean War. The autocratic tsar enjoyed the plenitude of power, delegated in part to the occupants of ministerial office, in part to provincial satraps. Outside these, some senior police officials and some military commanders, no one in the Russian empire possessed effective executive power. Beyond official state power moreover lay the extra-legal realm of the 'dark-forces' – those having the ear of the autocrat without the exercise of official function or official responsibility.

I

However little had changed over these years in the structure and methods of government, there had taken place under the impact of perestroika, profound if barely perceptible changes, particularly in the social sphere. Longer-term and gradual in their impact, these are difficult to measure or to assess. Yet about their occurrence, there can be little doubt.

Under the impact of perestroika a new social force emerged described by Russian publicists and social historians by the term *obshchestvennost* inadequately translatable either as 'educated public' or 'society'. *Obshchestvennost*[1] embraced, broadly, people with a higher education not employed in the state service. While the term was a fluid one it included members of the rapidly growing professions, the liberal segment of the gentry grouped around the *zemstva*, a small but growing commercial bourgeoisie and, arguably, the Third Element of *zemstvo* employees. To these may be added members of the 'free professions'; writers and artists together with those of the old intelligentsia, the so-called 'men of the forties' and their successors. While a rudimentary *obshchestvennost* predated the Great Reforms, its numbers and weight grew considerably under the impact of perestroika. The census of 1897 recorded that in the whole of the empire there were some 100,000 people with a higher education. If those with a completed secondary education are added, and many of these could be included in *obshchestvennost*, the numbers would be considerably greater. It is worth discussing briefly some major components of the new social formation, product of the changes Russian society had undergone since the Crimean debacle.

One major change resulting from the Great Reforms was the new status acquired by the law and its practitioners. The Statute of 1864, modernizing and Westernizing the archaic legal system, produced several important effects. One was the gradual increase in the number of people with legal training and outlook. The reforms brought an unprecedented expansion of the law faculties and the numbers of their students, notably in the universities of the two capitals. In the new courts, the traditional pettifogging attorney and his written procedures was replaced by the oral pleading of a Western-style advocate. The creation of an organized Bar raised the self-assurance and status of the profession. Judges meanwhile gained a measure of independence from the executive.

Individually, and to a lesser extent also collectively, practitioners of the law were, by definition, articulate. At the same time their very occupation made them in some respects public figures. Whether as senators, judges, advocates (particularly in political cases), or as simple justices of the peace, they enjoyed both social prestige and a degree of independence. Though many made their careers in the state service and as procurators (prosecutors or investigating magistrates were absorbed into the bureaucracy), others either stood outside it as free professionals or occupied within it a distinctive position as senators or members of the State Council. While some occupied prestigious academic positions, others were linked by professional ties to the world of commerce. The quickening pace of commercial activity steadily increased the demand for their services. Members of gentry families like Fedor Rodichev of Tver or Boris Chicherin made legal studies the basis of political careers. Overall, the professional scope and demand for the services of men trained in the law increased significantly after the judicial reforms. Supply was beginning to catch up with demand. The legal profession which, after spawning Pobedonostsev would one day also produce a Kerensky, became during these years one of the pillars of *obshchestvennost*.

A second profession with a public role and which grew in numbers and importance during this period was journalism. This benefited from the relaxtion of censorship and the moderate measure of glasnost introduced by Aleksandr II. Among the early beneficiaries had been Mikhail Katkov, the most influential journalist of his day. Of him, a contemporary would write:

> He entered the field of journalism at a time when the bonds that constricted Russian thought had been loosened and journalism had gained a position of major importance. By his own talent and intelligence he won first place among his fellows.[2]

Polovtsev, the secretary to the State Council, at the end of 1886 describes Katkov's role at the height of his career:

Alongside the legal government of the state there has been established a kind of shadow government in the person of the editor of the *Moscow News*. He has a great number of accomplices at the highest administrative levels, including Delianov, Ostrovsky, Pobedonostsev, Vyshnegradsky and Pazukhin. This entire cabal gathers at Katkov's ... and openly discusses the necessity of replacing such-and-such a minister with some other person, or of pursuing this policy with regard to that question. In short, they impudently issue their own commands, publish their censure or praise and, in the final analysis achieve their aims.[3]

No journalist, indeed, had since enjoyed a comparable influence. The profession, however, had prospered. Some half dozen major journals catering for cultural, economic and, in spite of censorship, political interests, were serving a growing number of readers. So did a popular boulevard press led by Alexei Suvorin's widely read *Novoe Vremya* (New Time).[4] Altogether, there existed in Russia at the end of the century some thousand periodical publications including 600 dailies. In St Petersburg alone there were 300 publications (including periodicals), in Moscow 100 and in Warsaw some 60.

Newspaper proprietors tended to cater for the tastes and preferences of their readers which would not necessarily coincide with those of government and bureaucracy. So long as circulation increased, they allowed journalists considerable latitude. Some editors enjoyed the patronage of ministers. Thus S. M. v. Propper, owner-editor of the *Birzhevye Vedomosti* (Exchange Gazette), was on excellent terms with Witte who made extensive use of journalists and publicists to propagate his policies.

Part of the significance of the major papers lay in the fact that they constituted autonomous nuclei composed of proprietors, editors, journalists and readers. These could contribute to the formulation of and give public expression to the views of *obshchestvennost* on major issues. Thanks moreover to improved railway communications, the press began to reach a wider, mainly urban, provincial public. A vexatious if only moderately efficient and sometimes capricious censorship ensured that a goodly part of the 'fourth estate' would be hostile to bureaucracy. It would be as oppositional as was safe without attracting the sanctions of suspension, fines or the prohibition of retail sales.

Another segment of *obshchestvennost* that increased both in numbers and importance was the medical profession. This grew with the spread of urbanization and with a rising demand from the *zemstva* for both qualified and semi-qualified medical personnel for rural areas. Repeated epidemics underlined the importance of medical services. Recruits were readily available as young people turned to medicine and midwifery from a strong urge to be of service to the common people, above all to the peasantry; such had been the inspiration of Turgenev's fictional Bazarov. It inspired Russia's most celebrated (largely non-practising) doctor, Anton Chekhov. The special significance of medics lay in the fact that many came into contact almost daily with different classes of the population and had a developed social conscience. Their profession made them semi-public figures while their status in society enabled them to help shape opinion, particularly on social issues. Moreover, in the Pirogov Society doctors possessed a professional body entitled to hold congresses and express collective opinions on professional and sometimes wider concerns. For all these reasons, the medical profession formed an important part of *obshchestvennost*.

Another group which over these years gained alike in size and visibility was the teaching profession. Time and again, former dons played a prominent role in public affairs. In general university teachers, notably professors, enjoyed a degree of independence as well as status and academic reputation. Although technically officials and, under the Reaction, hard pressed by curators to propagate conformist views, they were normally irremovable. Notwithstanding massive ministerial interference, university councils or senates preserved a measure of autonomy and a capacity for passive resistance. Professors also engaged in publicistic ventures. Indeed a leading St Petersburg daily, *Peterburgskie Vedomosti* (St Petersburg Gazette) was run largely by university professors. Furthermore, academic teachers, and more especially those holding dissident views, could influence at least some of their pupils.

Students, apprentice intellectuals, formed a major component of *obshchestvennost*. Living in close proximity in almost daily contact with one another, with intellectual and often political interests and filled with a youthful radicalism, they came to constitute something like the vanguard or cutting edge of *obshchestvennost*. Their numbers, notwithstanding the adoption of restrictive and socially selective admissions policies increased significantly. There was a growing demand from many quarters, not excluding the military, for trained lawyers, teachers, engineers, doctors and architects, surveyors, agronomists and veterinary surgeons. Students, moreover, had been setting up their own organizations. Not without a struggle, they succeeded in wresting from the authorities permission to form 'benevolent societies' (*zemliachestva*), that is, fraternities of students hailing from the same locality. They also set up clandestine unions which were led by activists and in touch with similar bodies at other institutions. Though generally tending to the lower end of the social scale, student society and its organizations could be described as classless.

A student sub-culture was formed by a sizeable body of widely dispersed ex-students expelled for unruly behaviour or academic failure. While some would gain eventual readmission, others, like Vladimir Ulyanov would take their degrees as external students. Still others, their careers damaged or destroyed, would become professional revolutionaries. They were joined by expellees from the classical gymnasia, who had fallen foul of school discipline, of Greek and Latin grammar, or both.

Some teachers in secondary schools like A. F. Kerensky's father, a headmaster in Simbirsk, who did his best to protect subversive pupils (including the Ulyanovs) from the consequences of their 'misdeeds', formed a further component of educated society. Not infrequently, their views would be liberal conservative. Few were in sympathy with the obscurantist educational policies of Dimitry Tolstoy and Delianov, which some at least successfully obstructed.

A further component of *obshchestvennost* was formed by the village schoolmasters employed by the *zemstva*. These everywhere were engaged in running battles with the local village priests. They were, as a rule, earnest and dedicated young men of 'advanced' political views, populist rather than Marxist, the midwives of a rising peasant intelligentsia. They would act as opinion formers in the villages, grouping around them small circles of older pupils or ex-pupils in opposition to *pope* (village priest), policeman, *kulak*, landowner and land captain.

The village teacher, if at times the most conspicuous, was not the only representative of the Third Element of *zemstvo* employees. The various *zemstvo* services were staffed by trained or part-trained professionals, many of them inspired by a populist philosophy of public service. Their influence would extend in two directions. In daily touch with the people in their capacity as social workers (in the widest sense of the term), they also co-operated closely with the often liberal-minded landowners who formed a number of *zemstvo* executives. Some of these, impressed with the public spirit and selfless idealism of their employees not only expressed a personal sympathy but may also have imbibed elements of their philosophy. *Zemstvo* employees also maintained contacts with their fellows elsewhere in loose and informal networks.

Yet another component of *obshchestvennost* was the rising profession of engineering. In the age of railway construction and industrial development this was of cardinal importance for Russian economic development. Career opportunities abounded, despite competition from sometimes better qualified foreign experts. Vyshnegradsky and Witte did their best to encourage technical education. The St Petersburg Institute of Technology, Russia's premier technological university, was the primary training ground. Not infrequently, Russian engineers like Turgenev's literary prototype, Solomin, or Witte's assistant and ally Prince Khilkov, either completed their studies or gained experience abroad, notably in England. Theirs was a Westernizing as well as modernizing profession with a belief in rationality, efficiency and progress. Critical, of Russian inefficiency and sloth, they tended towards political radicalism especially as students. Like those of the corresponding French École, alumni of the Institute of Technology would form a tightly knit group, a kind of freemasonry, patronized by Witte.

The growth of the professions, the backbone of *obshchestvennost*, was a significant (and inescapable) by-product of the perestroikas of Aleksandr II and Witte. Their members (other than those who entered state service) enjoyed a degree of autonomy and independent public standing. Their largely tolerated organizations escaped, at least in part, the control of the central bureaucracy. Unlike the bureaucracy, the professions did not in general have a hierarchical structure. Their organizations were democratic with a prevalence of the elective principle (anathema to bureaucratic centralizers). Professional cooperation between geographically separated units was likely to assume federal forms. Compared to earlier days, organization was now facilitated by improved means of communication, the fruit of perestroika: railways, trams, the railway telegraph and the telephone (the first telephone service was installed in Moscow in 1882).

Writers and poets should also be mentioned as constituting *obshchestvennost*. Prominent literary figures with a wide following, Korolenko, Chekhov, Gorky and, above all, Leo Tolstoy could mobilize opinion, particularly on moral issues. They would, on occasion, act as spokesmen for a wider public, the conscience of the nation. Unlike their peers in Germany and France, they were little given to *La Trahison des Clercs*, nationalist and anti-semitic aberrations. By and large they were a humanist moral force, opponents of persecution, intolerance, the ill-treatment of prisoners; against administrative arbitrariness and abuses. Tolstoy's *Resurrection* (1899), apart from being a work of literature was an impressive Dissident Manifesto. Though excommunicated by the Orthodox Church (1901), Tolstoy was too determined to be silenced and too famous to be touched. Chekhov and Gorky, equally resolute humanitarians, were like Tolstoy known beyond the confines of the Russian empire. Government and public alike were for different reasons highly sensitive to world opinion. Through Russia's writers above all, *obshchestvennost* acquired an international dimension.

Besides the professions and writers, *obshchestvennost* included some gentry landowners, notably those engaged in *zemstvo* work. Equally, it embraced members of the small but growing commercial community.

These ranged from well-educated younger industrialists of Moscow often with an Old Believer background, to entrepreneurs drawn from national or religious minorities, more particularly Jews, Armenians and Germans. Periodic fairs, above all that of Nizhni-Novgorod, and occasional congresses of industrialists brought together representatives of trade and industry to consider matters of common concern. Theirs was a voice which government, bent on modernization, could not afford to ignore. And though industry depended on government support, its representatives would feel increasingly irked by bureaucratic interventionism, the residual influence of the landed interest, and discrimination against minority groups. Many in the end would come to side with *obshchestvennost* rather than *vlast*.

II

Obshchestvennost had another significant dimension related only indirectly to the Great Reforms or the policies of Witte. In the economically and culturally more advanced borderlands of the empire the groups constituting *obshchestvennost* were always proportionally stronger than in the ethnically Russian heartland. They benefited from the quickening of the economic climate due to railway construction and increased in numbers – whether disproportionally or not it is impossible to say. Generally enjoying higher standards of education and literacy, a more cultured clergy than Russians, and closer contacts with the West, they included a higher proportion of readers and a wider educated public, and they benefited from the relaxation of censorship and ideological controls under Aleksandr II. Partly under the impact of the Italian *Risorgimento* and of rising national movements in other parts of Europe, part of the intelligentsia developed a growing consciousness of national identity and national aspirations.

The Polish rising of 1863, was followed by a violent Great Russian backlash. A policy of systematic Russification was introduced in Poland in which Polish education and administration were Russified. In 1869 the kingdom of Poland was renamed the Vistula Provinces. Under the influence of Katkov and Pobedonostsev, the policy of Russification was then extended to other ethnic groups. Baltic Germans, Finns, Armenians and Ukrainians were among the victims. Persecution and proselytism extended also to the Islamic populations. The Orthodox Church directed by Pobedonostsev played an active part and so did the anti-Semite and arch-Russifier Plehve. From the mid-1880s the persecution of minorities steadily intensified, and their leaders, in protest became a part of *obshchestvennost*.

The movements of non-Russian minorities divided Russian opinion. Whereas the bulk of liberals and radicals supported the aspirations of, particularly, Poles and Finns, a good few opposed them. While national movements on the one hand strengthened *obshchestvennost* they were, on the other, a potential source of division. Yet, even if members of *obshchestvennost* differed on some issues, they were united in their desire for change. For a time at least hostility to a common enemy, identified as the autocracy, outweighed all internal divisions and disagreements about ultimate objectives. All were united also in their desire for glasnost, for civil liberties and for political reform.

Obshchestvennost showed little interest in Witte and his perestroika. Though a reformer in the economic sphere, Witte associated himself with the reactionary politics of Aleksandr III and Pobedonostsev. He fought the *zemstva* and helped to topple the semi-liberal Goremykin. He financed Pobedonostsev's parish schools. At no stage did he show any sign of favouring political change. The small segment of the bureaucracy committed to economic reform was out of tune with the major aspirations of educated society. By the time Witte left the scene, *vlast*, as represented by Plehve, and *obshchestvennost*, in the shape of *zemstvo* constitutionalists, were on a collision course.

The looming confrontation of *obshchestvennost* and *vlast* fitted into a wider setting. In the wake of the Crimean War, Russia experienced two waves of perestroika, the Great Reforms and early industrialization. These resulted in an acceleration of change and an increased dynamism in a hitherto static society. Russia, in modern terminology, was transformed from a backward (or underdeveloped) into a developing country. She had entered the railway age. Society experienced a gradual transformation. While the landed gentry was in a state of terminal decline, the bureaucracy recruited from various social strata, had begun to replace it as the ruling class. The liberal professions (higher or bourgeois intelligentsia) and the entrepreneurial bourgeoisie were gaining in numbers and importance. The peasantry, meanwhile, saw an increasing differentiation within its ranks. Early industrialization had created a small but growing proletariat. By the turn of the century, the social changes set in motion by perestroika were beginning to have an impact on public affairs.

While economic and social change were accelerating, however, political change under the Reaction was minimal. Autocracy was preserved, the role of a centralized bureaucracy if anything increased. Though seeming political quiescence was achieved by repressive policies, tensions between the upholders (and beneficiaries) of the régime and representatives of *obshchestvennost* rose to danger point. The tsars and their ministers, by their policies, had unwittingly weakened the bases of their authority. Politically unprivileged *obshchestvennost* was demanding a share (if a junior one) in the exercise of power and the processes of decision-making.

Problems of a predominantly economic nature were meanwhile provoking unrest among the 'dark masses' of peasants, peasant workers and proletarians. Economic pressures due in part to the cost of perestroika and aggravated by the population explosion superimposed on the peasantry's perennial land-hunger, created a critical situation in the villages. Living and working conditions characteristic of early industrialization and worsened by a short term industrial crisis raised distress and discontent among the factory workers to a dangerous level. Resentment among ethnic and religious minority groups at official persecution was also on the rise. By the end of the century it was clear that a crisis was at hand.

NOTES

1. It is possible also to use the simpler term *obshchestvo*, society.
2. P. A. Zaionchovkovsky: *The Russian Autocracy under Alexander III* (Gulf Breeze, FL, 1976), p 36.
3. *Ibid.*
4. Whereas in 1860 there were 15 newspapers, five years later their number had risen to 28. By 1870 there were already 36 (D. M. O'Flaherty: *Tsarism and the Politics of Publicity 1865–1881*, unpublished PhD thesis, p 46–7).

Part V

Perestroika Under Duress: The Revolution of 1905

10

'Time of Troubles': The Run-Up

Towards the end of the century, perestroika entered a new phase. Hitherto it had been a restructuring from above, bureaucratic in character, the product of legislation and administrative fiat, accepted passively by the population at large. Nevertheless, the earlier perestroikas and their aftermath created *obshchestvennost*: educated public opinion. This, towards the end of the century, was beginning to transform itself into a broad oppositional movement. It was beginning to challenge *vlast*, the autocratic-bureaucratic state, calling for sweeping (at least in Russian terms) political reforms. Under intensifying pressure from below, bureaucracy would be forced to retreat step by step until at last forced to concede the political perestroika embodied in the October Manifesto and the subsequent Fundamental Laws of the Russian Empire.

Protagonists of a new political order, though their aspirations might differ in detail and the degree of their radicalism were agreed in their basic demands. They called for an end to autocracy, for participation in legislation by elected representatives of the Russian people and for the extension of civil liberties. The demand for ministerial responsibility to an elected body was at first confined to a minority. There was a general call for a régime of glasnost.[1]

To this core programme of political perestroika, other demands came to attach themselves. Prominent among these were calls for the partial or complete expropriation of remaining gentry estates for the benefit of the peasantry. Workers and their socialist supporters were clamouring for higher wages, shorter hours and improvements in living and working conditions. They also demanded the right to form legal trade unions. National movements on the periphery of the

151

empire called for an end to the policy of Russification and persecution. Demands were raised for autonomy and even independence. It was the subsidiary pressures of the more numerous groups seeking to advance their particular objectives which supplied the battering ram for the growing liberal movement. Together they forced the government to gradually concede a new political order. This could, in the mode of its introduction, be seen as Witte's second (political) perestroika.

Even if its introduction was bureaucratic and its character determined by the tsar and his ministers, it was the first perestroika which owed its origin to pressure from below. It was closely connected with the social transformation resulting from the policies of Aleksandr II and Witte, their necessary complement. Perestroika had become partially self-generating. Social change promoted by economic perestroika was fuelling a transformation also in the political sphere. Through the combination of a lost war and its inability to resist the strike weapon, the régime would eventually be forced into partial capitulation. Socio-economic restructuring produced in its turn a political perestroika. To what extent the sequence of the two is reversed in what was once the Soviet Union it is perhaps too early to say.

I

'The year 1901,' an observer noted, 'was probably the last year when reforms could have been introduced with perfect safety.'[2] Around that year, perceptive contemporaries noted with foreboding a radical change in the political climate. 'Now,' one of them commented awkwardly, 'together with much that was then hidden, it also becomes clear that a feeling of deep unease, of the volcanic condition of the political underground and lack of confidence in the immediate future were no strangers to even the most hard-bitten officials, the most inveterate foes of the revolutionaries.'[3] In 1900 the Minister of the Interior, undertook a trip through Russia during which 'he saw only the impressive side of things and met only representatives of the administration and of that part of Russian society which at that time had no revolutionary aspirations.' On his return, Sipyagin dumbfounded accompanying officials by observing that there was something radically wrong with Russia and that in fact the country stood on the verge of revolution.[4] By the following year, the feeling of alarm spread to other senior officials. Muraviev, the Minister of Justice declared that 'general discontent with the existing régime has seized all classes of society . . . things cannot continue like this for any length of time'.[5] And State Secretary Polovtsev noted in his diary: 'With every day, the situation grows not only more and more serious, but actually menacing.'[6] In August 1901, a resident in the Black Earth province of Voronezh painted a lurid (and somewhat fanciful) picture of conditions:

> Here something ill-boding hangs in the air: every day, the reflection of conflagrations illumines the horizon; a bloody haze drifts across the ground – it is difficult to breathe, to live, as it is before a storm. The peasant persists in sullen silence; and when he does speak occasionally, it is in such a way that a shiver runs down one's spine.[7]

It began in the universities. On 8 February 1899 on the occasion of its annual celebrations, the Vice-Chancellor (*Rektor*) of St Petersburg University issued an edict to the effect that this time the rowdy behaviour customary on the occasion would not be tolerated.[8] Angry students responded by interrupting the proceedings. Ejected from the building, they foregathered in the street outside where mounted police broke up their demonstration with extensive use of their whips (knouts). Student leaders then called a strike. Students were asked to boycott lectures and examinations and to prevent others from attending, if necessary by force. Students throughout the empire responded. Within a fortnight, the movement enveloped the other universities and by the end of March, every institution of higher education was strikebound.

The government tried to meet the challenge with a policy of repression interspersed with minor concessions. 'Temporary regulations' set up special boards under curators of educational districts with powers to suspend unruly students for up to three years. They would then be drafted into the army as common soldiers. Several academics, for having shown sympathy for the students were dismissed. Among the instigators of a hard line policy was Witte who proposed measures of such severity that even Pobedonostsev felt impelled to protest: 'No, Sergei Iulevich, that is impossible!' It was Witte who first proposed drafting students into the army, to the annoyance of the military who resented its use for penal purposes.[9]

Police brutality in dispersing the St Petersburg students shocked educated opinion and may even have worried the tsar. A commission of enquiry headed by a relatively liberal general recommended some modest concessions including the election of student elders and the authorization of occasional student meetings for educational purposes. Student societies under academic supervision would be permitted but no independent student unions.

When the heavily purged universities reassembled in the autumn, student anger persisted.[10] A source of particular resentment was the penal use of military service. The student movement continued. During 1900, a number of minor incidents culminated in more serious disturbances in Kiev. There a student demonstration was broken up by police and soldiers. Of the 500 odd students arrested, almost half were drafted into the army. Sympathy demonstrations swept the remaining universities. On 1 February 1901, in protest at the con-scripting of students, a twice-expelled former student shot and fatally wounded N. P. Bogolepov, the reactionary Minister of Education. Student meetings celebrated the exploit. Demonstrations continued. One outside Kazan Cathedral in St Petersburg was dispersed by mounted police where there were close on 800 arrests. French men of letters were roused to public protest at Russian police brutality.

Witte, by this time, appears to have changed course. Late in 1899, it was reported that he was now favouring leniency. Under the new Minister of Education, an aged general (79) of vaguely liberal disposition, a more conciliatory stance was adopted. During his year in office he was able at any rate to contain the movement.

If mounted police and the apparatus of repression generally experi-enced little difficulty in controlling unruly students, they found it harder, as in 1879–80, to deal with a different and more menacing manifestation. A terrorist group, the Fighting Organization (*Boevaya Organizatsia*) of the Socialist Revolutionary Party composed largely of students or ex-students was about to enter the stage.

In the spring of 1902, one of its members, dressed in the uniform of an imperial aide-de-camp, entered the Marinsky Palace in St Petersburg where a meeting of the committee of ministers was about to convene. At point blank range, he shot and fatally wounded Sipyagin, the Minister of the Interior. The murder, following on the heels of that of Bogolepov, alerted the authorities to the fact that they were once again faced with organized terrorism. Plehve, Sipyagin's successor then had recourse to one of his tried specialities, the recruiting of super-grasses in revolutionary organizations. His greatest catch was the second-in-command of the Fighting Organization, a former engineering student of Jewish extraction, Yevno Azev.[11] Azev, in fact, would turn out to be a double agent. While selectively betraying some fellow terrorists, he would, at the same time foil several terrorist attempts. The information he provided for the police department was invariably incomplete.

II

Meanwhile, in the Ukrainian Black Earth provinces of Poltava and Kharkov, peasant distress was approaching a climax. Here many peasants after 1861 had opted for 'beggarly allotments', one quarter of the local norm, free from redemption dues. Such allotments proved insufficient to support a peasant household. Moreover, peasant numbers had increased substantially since liberation, reducing the size of allotments. Additional land leased from neighbouring landowners – who exploited peasant distress – had to be paid for either in labour or from non-agricultural earnings. With the onset of industrial depression in 1901, outside employment opportunities diminished significantly.

In mid-March 1902, peasants in several districts simultaneously converged on manor houses, betokening a degree of organization. They demanded grain for themselves and fodder for their beasts. Where their requests were met, they departed peaceably. Elsewhere, they helped themselves. In some instances manor houses were set on fire at night and gutted. In the Poltava province, 70 estates suffered depredations, in Kharkov there were 27. Military detachments restored order. There was shooting in which some peasants lost their lives and more than a thousand were arrested, tried and flogged. Landowners who suffered losses were empowered to levy fines. The movement, surprisingly, did not spread. It was isolated and was easily suppressed, but it had been a warning.

III

Police activities, meanwhile, provoked unrest also among factory workers. On 19 February 1902, to commemorate the anniversary of the liberation of the serfs, the Moscow Workers' Association – an officially sanctioned organization – held a mass rally at the foot of a monument dedicated to the memory of the 'tsar-liberator'. Though most of the speeches were patriotic, there were also calls for an improvement in the workers' condition.

In the south, thanks to successful wage bargaining, an Independent Workers' Committee acquired support among metal workers. In November 1902, a strike in the rail yards of Rostov-on-Don developed into a local general strike. At mass demonstrations, speakers demanded wage increases and a nine-hour working day. There were calls also for an end to the autocracy.

The following summer, localized general strikes with epicentres in Odessa, Baku, Tiflis and Batum, coalesced. A quarter of a million workers downed tools. Though economic demands at first predominated, persistent calls were soon heard for the convocation of a constituent assembly. Red flags were beginning to appear. Cossack detachments, brought in to quell the unrest, hesitated to disperse striking workers though the strike was in the end broken, followed by mass arrests. The South Russian strike, in the main a spontaneous expression of discontent, also revealed evidence of rudimentary organization. What mainly disturbed the authorities was its extent and duration. An independent workers' movement was seen to be emerging, led by members of the intelligentsia and with mainly political objectives.

Though overt manifestations of popular discontent remained sporadic and isolated and were repressed with comparative ease, it was becoming apparent that the popular masses were getting restive. A new and elemental spirit of revolt was rising below the thin crust of Russia's Westernized ruling class.

IV

The growing ferment was extending also to *obshchestvennost*, the educated public.[12] With Goremykin, the then still semi-liberal Minister of the Interior (1895–9) turning a blind eye, some *zemstvo* men (*zemtsy*), under the leadership of D. N. Shipov, president of the Moscow provincial board, set up an informal secretariat and a loose regional organization. They held occasional informal meetings. The potential, if distant, threat to the autocracy inherent in even such modest beginnings was apparent to the authorities, not least to Witte and Plehve. The problem however, was that liberal landowners, some from aristocratic families, were a section of society difficult for the government to fight. Their activities could be – and indeed were – obstructed, but *zemstva* could be neither suppressed outright nor wholly absorbed into the bureaucracy. Their members were respected notables, sometimes popular figures, educated gentlemen, with a degree of local and regional influence who also enjoyed the support of the liberal press. If the government was to win its fight against terrorism, the support of public opinion, not least that of the *zemtsy*, would be essential. To gain it, some concessions to meet their aspirations might in the end become necessary. At first, however, under the aegis of Plehve, ministers chose instead a policy of containment and vexatious harrassment.

From its beginning the *zemtsy*-led Liberal movement was rent by divisions. The main disagreement concerned the objects to be achieved. While moderates (liberal-conservatives) favoured a roughly

German-style type of government with a strong monarchical executive, radicals preferred a limited constitutional monarchy on the Westminster model. Associated with this basic difference were others relating to workers' and peasants' demands, nationality issues, relations with socialist parties, attitudes to terrorism and to the use of force. While the moderates looked to achieving their aims through the pressure of opinion, radicals were prepared to make common cause with socialist and revolutionary groups. It was such divisions which would hamper the emerging Liberal campaign. The more astute among ministerial bureaucrats would sense the opportunities for exploiting them.

Since the 1890s, *zemstvo* activists had occasionally met in Moscow to discuss matters of common concern. Some of the more conservative *zemtsy* formed a group, calling itself *Beseda* (symposium). They contacted a number of academics and publicists with a view to a joint campaign. After much toing and froing it was decided to publish (abroad) a paper to publicize their views. Its editor would be Peter Struve an ex-Marxist and author of the founding manifesto of the Russian Social Democratic Workers' Party. In June 1902, the first issue of *Osvobozhdenie* (Liberation) was printed in Stuttgart and duly rolled off the presses. Copies were smuggled into Russia from Germany. The evolving views of the paper under the editorship of Struve, assisted by the historian Paul Miliukov, could be described as roughly left-liberal. They included an alliance of the Left (in today's parlance a Popular Front), democratic parliamentary government, respect for human rights and progressive social policies. The right of self-determination was to be granted to the non-Russian nationalities.

In May 1902, an unofficial all-Russian *zemstvo* congress convened in Moscow. It was attended by 52 *zemtsy* from 25 provinces, including 15 chairmen of provincial boards. Both moderate Slavophils and radical constitutionalists took part. The guidelines recommended for the forthcoming regular assemblies were moderate.

The moderates in the movement were, however, losing ground. In July 1903, a three-day meeting in Switzerland set out guidelines for the Union of Liberation, the nucleus of a future Liberal party. Of the 20 participants, seven were classified as 'gentry liberals' on the constitutionalist wing, six as 'intelligentsia liberals' and the remainder as 'intelligentsia socialists'. The movement, thus, represented a spectrum of the centre-left, with university professors and journalists prominent among intelligentsia representatives. The moderate liberal-Slavophils had already withdrawn from the movement.

In January 1904, the first congress of the Union of Liberation convened informally in St Petersburg. Some 50 participants were drawn from 22 cities. 'The first and main aim of the Union of Liberation,' they proclaimed, 'is the political liberation of Russia.'

Considering even a modicum of political freedom incompatible with the absolute character of the Russian monarchy, the Union would seek before all else, the abolition of autocracy and its replacement by a constitutional régime. Such a régime should be established 'in the spirit of extensive democracy'. It must embody the principles of 'universal, equal, secret, and direct elections', the famous *chetyrekh-vostka*. In the field of social policy the Union undertook to devote itself to 'the defence of the interests of the labouring masses'. As regards the nationalities, it acknowledged at any rate in principle 'the right of self-determination'. The Union had thus ranged itself on the right wing of a 'broad left' coalition.[13]

The Union of Liberation, in fact, represented an uneasy alliance of Moscow-based *zemstvo* constitutionalists and a St Petersburg contingent of populist/socialists grouped around a populist journal, *Russkoe Bogatstvo* (Russian Wealth) with a constituency in the Third Element of *zemstvo* employees. Ex-Marxists and liberal intelligentsia also played a considerable part. The council set up to organize the union's activities, including the clandestine distribution of *Osvobozhdenie*, was composed of ten members. Operating underground, the union was an organization of political activists backed by the sympathies and on occasion assistance of wider sections of the intelligentsia and constitutionalist gentry. Neither in political nor in social terms was it as yet clearly limited to either Right or Left. Something of a rainbow coalition, it formed the central core of a broad opposition movement.

While the Union of Liberation was in the government's view a potential threat, it is unlikely that it then caused serious alarm. Its members, however committed politically, were, of necessity, talkers as much as doers. So long as the government could satisfy at least the minimum demands of peasants and workers, it had little to fear from either the divided *zemtsy* or the politically engaged intelligentsia. The latter's contacts with peasants and workers remained limited, with 'the people' by and large distrusting and even disliking 'the students'. Any threat from this direction did not appear immediate. For the moment at least, there appeared no urgency for combating the liberal movement. The fight against terrorism, the resolution of economic problems and the conduct of foreign affairs must have priority.

V

In consequence of the tsar's imperialist ventures on the Yalu river, early in 1904, Russia became embroiled in war with Japan, a war which from the start went badly. In the summer Plehve, who had done his best to provoke it, fell victim to a terrorist bomb. Azev facilitated the assassination to punish Plehve for his role in brutal pogroms in Kishinev the previous year. Under the impression of the killing (and possibly of the war), the government decided to change course. Indeed well before the removal of Plehve, a conviction had been gaining ground in governing circles that repression alone no longer sufficed to arrest the creeping disorder. The concessions resulting from this realization had, however, been minimal. An imperial manifesto of 26 February 1903 reiterated the inviolability of autocracy but hinted at cosmetic changes. Though the village commune would be maintained, means would be sought to facilitate secession. There were vague hints about future co-operation between central government and *zemstva*. Possible concessions to religious minorities were mentioned. There was a reference to the need for improving the material position of (Orthodox) village priests. The possibility of financial assistance for land purchases by peasants was adumbrated. Vague 'offerings' of this kind had however done nothing to slow down, let alone arrest, the mobilization of liberal opinion.

The assassination of Plehve (July 1904) following hard on that of his Finnish representative, Bobrikov, and combined with news of Russian defeats in the Far East induced the tsar and his advisers to review their policies. A further influence may have been the birth, on 31 July, of the tsarevich Aleksei. In August, after some vacillation, Nikolai II appointed Plehve's successor. His choice, probably guided by an aristocratic lady of his acquaintance, fell on Prince P. D. Sviatopolk-Mirsky, Governor-General of the northwestern provinces. The prince, a man of honour and principle, wanted to effect a *rapprochement* between *vlast* and *obshchestvennost*. He would presently tell Witte that, at an interview with the tsar, he had stressed the urgent need to heal the division between government and public. This, he claimed, could be achieved only by meeting the just wishes of society and by pacifying the national minorities. The tsar, according to Mirsky, replied that he shared these aspirations. He would place no obstacles in the way of their realization. It was on this understanding that Mirsky had agreed to serve.

On assuming office, Mirsky proclaimed his conviction that government must rest on confidence in the public, and that he would be guided by that principle. Some representatives of *obshchestvennost* began to speculate hopefully on an approaching political thaw. The extent of the thaw would be put to the test when Mirsky authorized a congress of *zemstvo* delegates in St Petersburg. With some hundred participants already assembled, permission to hold the congress was suddenly withdrawn. In the end, it was again authorized but only as a private gathering in a private residence. The incident is significant as an indication of the government's vacillations. In principle, the right to hold a legal all-Russian *zemstvo* congress had been conceded. At the same time there was uncertainty, reflected in the rapid transition from authorization through prohibition to unofficial toleration. These equivocations bear witness alike to the sincerity of Mirsky's intentions, the strength of his opponents, the congenital indecision of the tsar and the lack of a clear line of policy.

The *zemtsy* in their turn proved no less divided. While all agreed on the need for full civil liberties, no consensus could be reached on the constitutional framework required. There was agreement on the need for representative institutions, but opinions differed about their functions. While a majority favoured a legislative assembly, a moderate minority led by Shipov preferred a purely advisory body. In the end, the *zemstvo* men formulated their aspirations in the form of 11 theses to be communicated to the tsar and the government. They were intended to serve as the basis of a concerted political campaign. Faced with growing political pressure and with further bad news arriving from the East, it was necessary for the government to formulate a reply.

Accordingly, Mirsky submitted a draft *ukaz* for consideration by the tsar. Among minor concessions envisaged, it held out promises of the addition of elected members to the State Council and for the removal of disabilities from Old Believers. To consider these matters, the tsar convened a meeting of ministers and other senior bureaucrats – Witte, in his memoirs, lists 17 participants. He himself, seemingly against the tsar's wishes, was invited to participate at the instance of Mirsky. The tsar explained that he had called the meeting to deliberate on the measures to be adopted in the face of a revolutionary movement that was growing by the day. The wishes of moderate and sensible elements in society must be satisfied. First, however, it must be decided in principle whether to meet some wishes of the public or to continue the recent policies. Witte, according to his own report, replied that the second course must lead to disaster. Five liberally inclined bureaucrats shared his views. Mirsky hardly spoke. Pobedonostsev, as was his wont, while criticizing the views of others, hesitated to oppose them directly.

Predictably, the most serious discussion revolved around the proposal to reform the State Council. A majority were sympathetic, while Pobedonostsev demurred. Witte, pressed by the tsar to declare himself, gave a characteristically ambivalent reply. While it may in fact have represented his true opinion, he must have known that it would inevitably turn the tsar against the proposal. The present form of government, Witte argued, neither met the needs of the empire nor reflected the self-awareness of the educated classes. On these grounds, he shared the view of those supporting the proposal. He could not, however, agree that what was proposed would leave the existing state structure in a secure position. It was, on the contrary, his profound conviction that the continuous, organized participation in legislative work of elected representatives would inevitably lead to what was called a constitution.

The meeting eventually agreed on the need to restore legality, to promote new legislation on religious minorities and, above all, to abolish the harsh laws against Old Believers. Stress was laid on the need for religious toleration and freedom of religious belief. The competence of *zemstva* and municipal councils must be enlarged. In short, what was recommended was the dismantling of the 'Plehve system' and a gradual return to the spirit of the Great Reforms. After the meeting, Witte recalls, participants expressed profound emotion at what they considered the promise of a new era. In deeply felt words Solski, the senior permanent official of the empire, expressed to the tsar the heartfelt gratitude of those present. Two ministers are reported actually to have burst into tears. The tsar then instructed Witte to draft an *ukaz* embodying the views of the majority. It was signed by all participants, though Witte does not recall whether, in the end, Pobedonostsev appended his signature. The document headed 'Guidelines for the amelioration of the state order' was then submitted to the tsar.

Some days elapsed. Then, on the morning of 11 December 1904, Witte was called to Tsarskoe Selo. On arrival, he found the tsar closeted with his brother the Grand-Duke Sergei. When they were seated, the tsar said to Witte: 'I approve of this *ukaz* but have misgivings about one of the points.' This, predictably, was the reform of the State Council. Witte was invited to give his frank opinion on whether this provision should be retained. He replied that the draft had been prepared under his personal direction. He therefore stood officially by this point and considered the proposal opportune. However when it came to offering personal advice he felt he should repeat the following: the involvement of elected representatives in legislative work would be the first step on a road along which every civilized country was moving – that is, towards popular representation and a constitution. No doubt, the present measure would be no more than a first modest step but, in time, it could lead to others. His advice, therefore, was that if the tsar had reached the sincere and irrevocable conclusion that it was impossible to go against the worldwide historical trend, the point must remain in the *ukaz*. If, on the other hand, he did not consider constitutionalism the right form of government for Russia, if he personally was resolved never to admit it, then it would be more prudent to drop the proposal. After hearing this double-edged advice, the tsar looked towards the smiling grand-duke. Turning to Witte, he declared categorically: 'Yes, I will never and in no circumstances whatever consent to a constitutional form of government because I consider it harmful for the people confided by God to my care. I will therefore follow your advice and cut out this point.'

Witte returned to St Petersburg with the draft *ukaz* with the controversial point omitted. That evening, he informed a saddened Mirsky of what had occurred and on 12 December 1904, the truncated *ukaz* was formally promulgated.

In the incident, as recalled by Witte, a number of points are significant. The first is the light it throws on the personality of the tsar. A few short months before he had, perhaps in all sincerity, promised Mirsky his support. Now, behind the prince's back, and listening to reactionary advisers, he rejected the key feature of Mirsky's programme approved, moreover, with near unanimity by the rest of his official advisers. It is interesting but fruitless to speculate on how he would have acted without Witte's equivocal advice. In all likelihood, the reactionary entourage exploiting the tsar's known predilections would, in any event, have carried the day. Even had the decision gone the other way there would have been endless opportunities for obstruction over matters of detail.

On Witte's motives, one can only speculate. He had, in fact, devised an ingenious way to enable him to state his honest opinion while at the same time humouring the tsar's prejudices and keeping on good terms with the reactionary camarilla. He did this without formally denying his own more liberal predilections and his views of historical necessity. In some ways, it was a masterly performance. Whether his intervention was for the ultimate good of Russia and its peoples is of course a very different matter. It is at any rate conceivable that a Melikov-type arrangement promptly implemented under the aegis of Mirsky and Witte might even at this late hour have succeeded in achieving an accommodation between *vlast* and *obshchestvennost*. On what difference this might have made to subsequent developments one can only speculate. It is at least possible that relations between government and public might have been changed for the better. On the other hand, it appears doubtful whether even firmly declared intentions would by then have satisfied the opposition. Time was running out for the kind of modest concessions still considered substantial by the tsar and his advisers. Greeted with raptures in 1896 at the time of the coronation, they might still have helped to defuse the situation between 1899–1903. Now things had almost certainly gone too far for Melikov-style proposals to influence the course of events. Even had Nikolai II not struck out the 'constitutional' clause, the proposals might have proved too little and too late. And yet when, under pressure from the grand-duke and influenced by Witte's ambiguous advice the tsar took what may have been a fateful decision, the outcome could not be known. He was overruling the almost unanimous recommendation of his ministers who, guided by Mirsky, were sincerely seeking an accommodation with the public. Ironically, when Nikolai II struck out the Melikov clause, not one of those present could foresee the future course of events. The death sentence had already been passed on the grand-duke. And, within less than a year, faced with a similar constitutional issue, Witte would proffer different advice and the tsar reach a very different decision.

The *ukaz* of 12 December, instructing ministers to examine possible modifications of some recent oppressive measures, while reiterating the inviolability of the Fundamental Laws of the empire proved predictably ineffective. The hapless Mirsky tendered his resignation which was, for the moment, refused. His brief political spring was over.

VI

While Mirsky was fighting his losing battle, radical elements of the opposition were mobilizing. During the autumn delegates representing a wide spectrum of radical and revolutionary opinion met in Paris on the initiative of a left-wing Finnish group. The Union of Liberation sent four members. Two represented Polish organizations, one nationalist, the other socialist. There were delegates also from Latvian, Georgian and Armenian groups. The Social Revolutionary Party was represented but Social Democrats declined to take part. Prominent among the speakers were the Social Revolutionaries Chernov and Azev. What was significant was the collaboration of left liberals, national minorities and populist socialists; that is, of moderate socialists, intelligentsia, ethnic minorities and (at any rate potentially) the peasantry. It was agreed that the overriding objective must be the overthrow of the autocracy and its replacement by 'a free democratic system on the basis of universal suffrage'. A further aim would be national self-determination for minority groups.

At the same time, there were further developments unwelcome to the government. The war in the East was going badly. A major battle at the end of September proved inconclusive with heavy losses on both sides. A Japanese assault on Port Arthur in November was repulsed, but time was running out for the defenders. On 20 December, Russia's great bastion in the Far East was forced to capitulate. The impact of its loss was comparable to that of Sevastopol during the Crimean War.

Meanwhile, a more immediate threat was developing nearer home. On 3 January 1905, workers at the Putilov arms and engineering works in St Petersburg downed tools. Those in the locomotive shops put forward demands for a minimum wage and an eight-hour working day formulated by the Assembly of Russian Factory and Mill Workers, a trade union founded late in 1903 by one Father Gapon, a former prison chaplain. The assembly had been sanctioned by Plehve and indeed supplied with police funds. When, on 3 January the Putilov management dismissed some of its members, the entire workforce came out. Within days, the strike had spread to other St Petersburg establishments, involving tens of thousands of workers.

Encouraged by his followers, Gapon decided to lead a mass procession to the Winter Palace to present a petition to the tsar. Drawn up by several hands it bore some 135,000 signatures. It contained, besides specific workers' demands others like an end to the war, full civil rights, a general amnesty and the convocation of a constituent assembly. It also called for the separation of church and state, universal education and the introduction of a graduated income tax to replace indirect taxation. The tsar had left St Petersburg with his family for one of his neighbouring residences. Ministers, not expecting major problems and having refused his request to declare martial law, decided to meet possible danger by throwing an armed cordon around the Winter Palace. On reaching it, demonstrators would be summoned to disperse. In case of refusal, the troops would execute the order. As the reliability of the garrison was suspect, units were drafted in from outside. It is difficult to imagine that these plans would have been made without the tsar's prior approval.

As the precautions taken would be fraught with future consequences, it may be asked what had been the alternatives. It was evident that the coming demonstration would be huge. It was also far from certain whether it would be peaceful. It would take place against the background of a growing strike movement. Since Friday 7 January, no newspapers had appeared in St Petersburg, a fact promoting widespread unease and the circulation of rumours. Although unauthorized demonstrations were illegal, no permission was sought for the approaching event. Could the tsar, in these circumstances, have received the deputation and accepted its petition? What reply, moreover, could he have returned to revolutionary demands largely of a political nature? How also would the huge crowd have reacted to inevitable prevarication? How safe, notwithstanding Gapon's personal assurances, would have been the person of the tsar? Again, how would the demonstrators react were some official personage to receive them on the tsar's behalf? Might not there be thoughts in the minds of some about certain episodes of the French Revolution? And who would claim that such fears were entirely groundless? The decisions taken by the ministers were, in the circumstances understandable. While, as it turned out, they may have been unwise, they may equally have prevented the outbreak of revolution. From the point of view of the authorities, they may have appeared the lesser evil. When the decisions were taken they were perhaps prudent precautions. Nor were alternatives easy to find.

No two accounts agree about the exact details of what did in fact happen on 'Bloody Sunday', 9 January 1905. What appears certain is that during the morning a crowd of some 150,000 composed of workers, students, women, children, cab-drivers, riff-raff and curious spectators converged in five vast columns on the square fronting the Winter Palace. One of the columns was led by Gapon himself. Of the marchers, some were carrying ikons, church banners or pictures of the tsar. Some were chanting religious hymns (according to one account the Russian national anthem). Witte, watching from a balcony, would later characterize one of the columns as a procession. The great majority of the demonstrators were unarmed. At the approaches to the Palace Square, skirmishes broke out with the military. Accounts differ as to the location of the major incidents, nor is there agreement on what precisely occurred. According to one account, the marchers were stopped by cordons of troops and, on refusing to halt, were fired upon. According to another, demonstrators converging upon the square were stopped at five check points and ordered to disperse. When the front ranks, which had been marching with arms linked, refused to budge, troops fired a volley of blanks, followed by salvoes of bullets. Yet another account claims that the mass of demonstrators actually reached the Palace Square. A horn signal was then sounded and troops fired on the densely massed crowds. There is a report of street fighting. It is also reported that after the crowds had been dispersed, the military engaged in brutal mopping-up operations well into the night. Some workers had secured arms at some stage by plundering an arsenal or armourer's shop. They tried to erect barricades but soon desisted. The official casualty figure of 130 dead and several hundred wounded is generally considered well below the truth. No official count was taken and estimates vary according to political sympathies. There are claims that the number of dead exceeded 1,000 with some 2,000 wounded. The true figure may well have been between 130 and 160. What is incontrovertible is that casualties were substantial and that the force employed was grossly in excess of what was required to disperse the demonstrators.

'Bloody Sunday' was a significant event, never to be forgotten or forgiven. This was the moment when the bulk of the Russian working class shed its residual monarchism and the religious sentiments surviving from its peasant origins. Nikolai II, in the eyes of Russian workers, had become the 'bloody tsar'. Many workers, it is claimed – one wonders on what evidence – destroyed his picture which had until then decorated their rooms, saying: 'We no longer have a tsar.' Henceforth, there could be no further question of officially-sponsored trade unions. With the disappearance, discredit and ultimate liquidation by revolutionaries of the unstable and confused Gapon, leadership of the workers' movement passed finally into the hands of socialist intellectuals of differing persuasions. By their clumsy and brutal handling of a difficult situation the authorities had irrevocably alienated a major element of the population. They also, as would soon appear, had provided the liberals with a weapon, ready to hand.

In the aftermath of 'Bloody Sunday' the strike movement intensified. By the end of January the number of strikers may have exceeded half a million. A general walk-out in St Petersburg was followed by a wave of sympathetic strikes throughout the empire. Increasingly workers joined forces with intellectuals outraged at the massacre – 'Down with the autocracy' was the battle cry. Nor did indignant protest stop at the frontiers of the empire.

The urgency of the situation was brought home to the government by the assassination on 4 February of the Grand-Duke Sergei. The killing had been facilitated by Azev's loathing for a fanatical and brutal anti-Semite. The murder of a prominent member of the dynasty, the first since 1881, shook Nikolai II and his advisers. On how to meet the situation, however, opinions were divided. While Pobedonostsev, the empress and occult influences at court called for firmness, ministers (other than Pobedonostsev) urged a policy of conciliation. The tsar, as usual, tried to run with the hare and hunt with the hounds. His inability to provide firm leadership was strikingly demonstrated by his erratic proceedings.

Nikolai once again convened the usual gathering of senior advisers to reconsider Mirksy's scheme for the inclusion of elected representatives in the legislative process. Three ministers favoured the proposal, one (Kokovtsev), as an essential prerequisite for an urgently needed foreign loan. Bulygin, the Minister of the Interior, in turn considered the measure essential in view of Russia's internal situation. He was instructed by the tsar to prepare a draft project.

Before Bulygin could complete his task, the official gazette carried a 'fire-eating' imperial 'manifesto on disorders and rebellion' castigating the instigators of disorder and treason and calling on all 'true Russians' to join in the fight against the inner enemy. With God's help, the tsar announced, he would 'under the banner of autocracy' lead the empire out of all difficulties and into 'a new and indestructible greatness'. Only Pobedonostsev, suspected by Witte of actually being its author (he had certainly approved it) had had prior knowledge of the document.

On the same day, 18 February, at a further ministerial meeting, the tsar blandly assured his advisers that he had not changed his views. He stood, he declared, by the policies enunciated in his *ukaz* of 12 December. Ministers with one voice warned that rebellion was spreading apace and that steps to pacify the public had become imperative. The only measure promising success was some form of popular representation, even if only through an advisory body. Bulygin then read his draft which, following a lunch break, received the imperial signature. In the Rescript the principle of an advisory legislative body was at long last formally conceded.

VII

While Bulygin – at a pace fast by normal bureaucratic standards – was elaborating his project, creeping chaos was engulfing the empire. Almost every class or section of the population was involved in protests, demonstrations, lawlessness and violence, at the very least the formulation of far-reaching demands. Numerous towns and villages were the scene of disorder. A rash of strikes of varying duration, often economic in origin but on occasion turning political, and which were accompanied by demonstrations and scuffles, involved ever widening strata of the Russia proletariat. Workers in increasing numbers were joined by members of the intelligentsia. From the end of January, every institution of higher education was closed. Students thus had time to engage in political activism. They were free to join any demonstration or political meeting they chose. Established members of the professions, while perhaps reluctant to take part in street demonstrations, did not hide their sympathies for a movement aimed at transforming the Russian state. Employers, notably in Moscow, were openly supporting the workers' movement. While some gave money to oppositional and revolutionary parties, others flooded the Ministry of Finance with petitions to the effect that only democratic freedoms and a parliamentary régime could create conditions favourable to the growth of Russian industry. In the borderlands, the wider movement was reinforced by demands for an end to Russification and for the extension of local autonomies.

In the countryside also, disorder was rapidly mounting. Before long large parts of rural Russia would become engulfed. Early demands were again mainly economic; a reduction in rents and the renting of land to smallholders rather than better off peasants. By the autumn plunder and arson, directed against the manor houses and accompanied by occasional violence and even murder would follow. It was, in the main, a spontaneous movement. In May a congress of peasant deputies set up an All-Russian Peasant Union, largely under the influence of the Union of Liberation.

In June, two dramatic events highlighted the chaotic situation. On the 14th, in the course of a general strike in Odessa, the crew of the battleship *Potemkin*, the jewel of Russia's Black Sea fleet, mutinied. Sailors hoisted the red flag, to be lowered 11 days later in a neutral Rumanian port. It was spectacular evidence – if indeed such were needed – that the loyalty of parts of the armed forces was now in serious doubt. And hardly had the *Potemkin* episode reached its conclusion when a terrorist succeeded in killing the military governor of Moscow. Not a single representative of authority could feel safe.

The last hopes for a favourable turn of events in the Far East were evaporating. A vast battle at the gates of Mukden showed that no Russian victories on land could be looked for. At sea, events were taking a still more disastrous turn. On 9 May, the Russian Baltic squadron under the command of Admiral Rozhdestvensky, having sailed halfway around the world, was intercepted in the straits of Tsushima and all but annihilated by Japanese speed and power.

Even before the disasters, the government had decided on the need for further concessions. An *ukaz* of 17 April had relieved Old Believers and Molokane (members of a dissident Orthodox sect) of the most oppressive disabilities. A Russian subject would henceforth be permitted to leave Orthodoxy for another form of Christianity without incurring penalties or losing his civil rights.

Developments within the *dvorianstvo*, meanwhile, were holding out some hope for the beleaguered régime. At the end of April, following months of increasingly uneasy co-operation, Shipov's moderate Slavophile minority finally broke away from the more radical *Zemstvo*-Constitutionalists.[14] There was now a group prepared to settle for some form of advisory body. An accommodation between them and liberal-minded bureaucrats entered the realm of possibility.

Dialogue was started also with representatives of the constitutionalists. On 25 and 26 May, under the impression of Tsushima, a congress of delegates of *zemstva* and municipalities, convened in Moscow. Under the leadership of liberal aristocrats, it adopted an address to the tsar stating that not only the empire was now in danger, but even the throne itself. Criminal negligence and mistakes had brought on the Japanese war and a string of humiliating defeats. Even more threatening than the international situation was the growing domestic chaos. The good intentions proclaimed in the December Rescript had not been realized. Instead, the powers of the police had been increased as well as its arbitrariness. While there was still time, representatives of the people must now be called to decide the grave issues of war and peace and, in agreement with the monarch, to 'erect a new state structure' (this, of course, came close to a demand for a constituent assembly). In an emotional conclusion, the petitioners adjured the tsar, in the hour of trial, to shoulder his responsibilities. Though couched in moderate language, the address amounted to nothing less than a call for a constituent assembly, an Estates General. Ten prominent delegates including no fewer than four princes, requested an audience of the tsar in order to present the address.

Over the objections of General Trepov, his chief confidential adviser, the tsar took the unprecedented step of receiving the deputation. On 6 June its spokesman, Prince Sergei Trubetskoy, professor of philosophy at Moscow university, asked for the introduction of democratic freedoms (of speech, of the press and of assembly, in short glasnost) and for the election of any future assembly by means of a democratic franchise (as against one based on separate *curiae*). The tsar's reply was twofold. First he assured the deputation of his irrevocable resolve to convene representatives elected by the people. He then, equivocally, expressed a pious hope that agreement between tsar and people, as in times past, would form the basis of a political order 'in accordance with Russia's traditional principles'. Clearly, he had no intention of abandoning the principle of autocracy: the promised assembly would be a purely advisory body. There was here no meeting of minds.

A fortnight later Nikolai received a second deputation, this time of conservative *zemstvo* men. This urged him to eschew Western-style parliamentary institutions and to call instead a traditional *zemsky sobor* to hear the people's views. Included in this delegation were a village elder claiming to speak for all peasants, and a member of the petty bourgeoisie allegedly representing all factory workers. The tsar graciously replied that the only strong states were those which preserved as sacred the traditions of the past. While the conservative delegation as yet represented little, it nonetheless was designed to give the tsar confidence in the loyalty of the 'true' Russian people. To an extent, indeed, it foreshadowed the shape of things to come. A threefold division was emerging within the landed gentry, Shipov's liberal Slavophils, Trubetskoy's constitutionalists and Bobrinsky's small but growing group of right-wing monarchists.

Meanwhile, in this state of domestic uncertainty, the Russian government entered into peace negotiations with Japan. For different reasons, the governments of the major powers watched with growing unease the wholly unforeseen progress of Japanese arms. Nudged by the German Emperor, the President of the USA offered his mediation. The Japanese government, feeling the financial strain and conscious of the strategic futility of a further advance in Manchuria, accepted the offer. The hard-pressed Russian government in its turn was eager to liquidate an unfortunate episode. On 26 May, Theodore Roosevelt accordingly invited the belligerents to a peace conference. Nikolai II chose as his First Plenipotentiary his ablest servant, Witte, whose skill and international reputation held out the best hope of minimizing Russian sacrifices. On 28 July the peace conference opened at Portsmouth, New Hampshire. Witte, seconded by the Americans, negotiated tenaciously and secured a treaty which, given the magnitude of the Russian defeat, was relatively lenient. It was signed on 23 August. On his return journey Witte was fêted in both Paris and Berlin. A grateful tsar conferred on him the coveted title of count. By securing comparatively lenient terms, he had rendered signal service to both the emperor and to Russia. The conclusion of peace, in no small measure, would help secure the survival of the tsarist régime.

By the time of Witte's return to St Petersburg, Bulygin and his assistants had concluded their labours. The 'Bulygin Duma' would be based on three electoral colleges. Nobility, burghers and peasants, would each choose their representatives in separate elections. These would be indirect, with two stages for nobility and townsmen and three for the peasantry, allowing a high degree of manipulation. A high property qualification in the urban *curia* effectively disenfranchised workers and intelligentsia. In government circles the (erroneous) view prevailed that the peasants overall were the only loyal element on which the government could rely. Peasants, accordingly, were allocated 43 per cent of seats as against 34 per cent for large-scale landowners and 23 per cent for the urban bourgeoisie. Legislative recommendations of the new body would be referred to the State Council. On 6 August 1905, the tsar signed the law establishing the Duma, which was then promulgated by imperial *ukaz*.

The reception was predictably discouraging. On the Right, the law was criticized as going too far in yielding to popular clamour. Radicals, on the other hand, differed only on whether the coming Duma should be boycotted altogether or used for agitational purposes to be destroyed from within. Not even moderates were prepared to accept the Bulygin Duma as the basis of a constitutional settlement. Yet objectively, and considering recent history, the Bulygin Duma constituted a substantial concession wrung from an unwilling tsar by the forces of opposition. Elected deputies representing a major part of the population would henceforth be permitted to participate, however modestly, in the preparation of legislation. And had Witte not been right in the view that even such small beginnings might open the door for constitutionalism? A national elective body, however restricted in its function and however unrepresentative – there are contemporary parallels – was, for Russia, a daring innovation going well beyond the *zemstva* and the Melikov proposals. However, a concession which might still have gained the government some goodwill the previous December, had now come too late to satisfy the bulk of public opinion. Without radical modifications in respect of both composition and competence, the Bulygin Duma could not resolve the political crisis. Nor could this be done by a wholly unexpected concession when, on 27 August, according to Witte at the instance of Trepov, the universities had their autonomy restored.

VIII

The new university statute, which debarred the police from entering university precincts without the consent of the elected university authorities merely helped to fan the flames of unrest. Lecture theatres, placed beyond police reach, now became venues of uninterrupted public oratory before large mixed audiences composed of students, factory workers, housewives, tradesmen, officials, society ladies and other curious spectators, journalists, professional people, artisans, soldiers and even school children. A. S. Khrustalev-Nosar, first chairman of the St Petersburg Soviet of Workers' Deputies would later claim that this body also had its roots in university autonomy. Strong peasant and agricultural labour movements, relatively well organized by social democrats were developing in the Baltic Provinces, particularly Latvia.

When Witte returned to Russia in September, he found the country in turmoil. The government, he recalls, had lost all power of decision.[15] Those in charge were either passive or worked against each other. The authority of the régime and its highest representative was trampled in the mud. Unrest was growing by the day, indeed from hour to hour (Witte, of course, had some interest in exaggerating the extent of the disorders to justify his subsequent conduct). All classes of the population were affected. The entire upper class was dissatisfied and embittered. The young, not only university students but even high school pupils no longer recognized any authority and listened only to those who preached the most radical doctrine. The great majority of academics also castigated the government and pronounced with authoritative voice: 'Enough! everything must be radically changed.' The representatives of *zemstva* and towns had long ago declared: 'The only salvation is a constitution.' The men of commerce and industry, wealthy people, took the same side. Some, at great financial sacrifice, supported not only the Liberation Movement but even the revolution. The workers, Witte claims, had fallen completely under the spell of the revolutionaries and were most active where physical force was involved.[16] All non-Russians in the empire, some 35 per cent of its population, when they saw the weakening of the central authority, raised their heads and concluded that the moment had come for the realization of their aspirations. The Poles cried 'autonomy', the Jews 'equal rights', – and, Witte might have added, cultural autonomy. All and sundry demanded removal of the oppression under which they had lived until then. Peasants once again raised the issue of their landlessness (better land shortage) and of their generally miserable condition. Officials, who had had a close view of the disorders prevailing in government offices as well as of the system of protection and nepotism which under Nikolai II had assumed gigantic proportions (had Witte himself been guiltless in this regard?) took their stand against the system they were serving.

The army in turn was indignant at its ignominious defeats and rightly blamed the government for everything. There was a further grievance especially among troops which had remained in Russia. By law, conscripts called up for war service should have been demobilized the moment peace was concluded. As this would have left Russia denuded of troops they were not discharged. This naturally created discontent and enabled revolutionaries to gain access to the soldiers (most of whom, Witte omits to mention, were actually civilians in uniform). There were cases of insubordination, even of active intervention on the side of the revolution. Many therefore believed that the troops were not to be relied on and dreaded the return of the defeated army from the East.

There was, in Witte's list of revolutionary elements, one notable absentee. Complete demoralization of the government would have ensued had a terrorist succeeded in killing the tsar (followed by a regency on behalf of the infant tsarevich by his uncle Mikhail).[17] Any attempt at regicide was frustrated by the intervention of Azev. Indeed, in the face of persistent failure and wearied by prolonged tension, the Fighting Organization was itself becoming demoralized. It could be argued that the methods of the late Plehve had, in the last resort, paid dividends.

As Witte noted, the major physical thrust had now shifted from student terrorists and their intelligentsia leaders to the proletariat. A railway strike in Moscow on 7 October spread rapidly to the rest of the network and to the telephone and telegraph lines associated with it. On 10 October Moscow was gripped by a general strike and effectively cut off from communication with the rest of Russia. By the 11th, the last factory still working in St Petersburg had shut down. Newspapers ceased to appear; schools, hospitals, shops, offices and the law courts closed their doors. Bakers went on strike. Demonstrators waving red flags filled the streets. Orators addressed the crowds. The police were powerless. Demonstrators skirmished with detachments of gendarmes. As the result of a spontaneous strike movement, the cities and towns of the empire were paralysed. On 13 October, some 40 delegates of striking workers met to form the St Petersburg Soviet of Workers' Deputies.[18] Originally a council of strike committees, the soviet would presently deal with the public authorities over a variety of matters involving the interests of St Petersburg workers. The chairman Khrustalev-Nosar was a radical lawyer, Leon Bronstein (Trotsky) a prominent member. On 17 October the soviet published the first issue of its official organ *Izvestia* (News). Another soviet was formed some time afterwards in Moscow. The importance of the soviets of 1905 has been exaggerated in retrospect.[19] Actions they undertook were relatively unsuccessful. As soon as the authorities regained some confidence, they would brush the soviets aside with comparative ease.

Paralysis and chaos on the other hand, brought about by the elemental mass movements of peasants and workers, did cause near-panic in government circles. Preparations were in hand for the imperial family to leave Russia. Even communications between ministers at St Petersburg and the tsar at Peterhof were possible only by sea. In this emergency, a delicate minuet was performed by the official decision-makers. The choice before the tsar and his advisers now lay between, on the one hand, the ruthless suppression of disorder by any means available or, on the other, a judicious mixture of resistance and concession. Were the second strategy to be adopted, the question would be one of the nature and extent of concessions needed to appease at least the more moderate elements of the opposition. The third choice, that of sitting it out until winter would dampen revolutionary ardour, was ruled out by the rapidly deteriorating situation with the forces of law and order in imminent danger of collapse. The growing signs of disaffection among conscripts still detained in the army in European Russia against their wishes (and against the law) lent added urgency to the situation.

In face of the deepening crisis the views at the top were, as usual, divided. The tsar was clinging with the determination of despair to the empty simulacrum of autocratic power. In practice, he was resigned to the minimum of concessions needed to weather the storm. Torn between the two, he failed to follow a consistent policy, swayed as he was by the advice in turn of hawks and doves. He hesitated, vacillated, listened to conflicting advice from people more resolute than himself, only, in the end, to have his hand forced by events.

Trepov, the 'dictator', a man unfitted for any position of responsibility, was lost in a situation for which he was in no way prepared. To organize straightforward repression and military or police rule was a comparatively easy task in even semi-normal times. To deal with what was now occurring, however, required qualities beyond those possessed by a mediocre if well-connected guards officer. Confronted with a major crisis, the general lost his head. One moment, he would publicly urge troops and police not to spare the bullets, then seized by panic, he would advocate the most far-reaching concessions. In the role of chief adviser to a tsar as weak and irresolute as Nikolai II, the smart but brainless and unstable soldier was a misfit.

Nikolai Nikolayevich, recommended to Nikolai II, his cousin once removed, by his staunch personal loyalty, had replaced the Grand-Duke Sergei as the tsar's familiar mentor. Like Sergei, he was big and determined, a soldier capable of inspiring confidence and a badly-needed sense of self-assurance. His, earlier on, had been a steadying influence. However, at the climax of the crisis, he too would lose his nerve.

Witte, lastly, was playing his usual deep and equivocal game. Familiar from bitter experience with the tsar's volatile character, his treachery (often involuntary) and unreliability he can have felt little confidence in the steadfastness, or judgment of his 'master'. At the same time, he was conscious of his own influence and responsibility. His success at Portsmouth and enthusiastic reception in European capitals had given him a good and almost certainly exaggerated opinion of himself. The title of count bestowed by a grateful sovereign had given inordinate pleasure. To the fury of his numerous enemies in the higher echelons of the bureaucracy his elevation suddenly turned him into a near-courtier. An element of unwonted servility entered his relations with a man whom at heart he despised. The difficulties of the monarch however, presented him with a golden opportunity for a political comeback.

NOTES

1. The term glasnost, as currently used, is rather vague. In its narrow sense, it may be considered as an absence of censorship and a free flow of information. In a wider sense, it may be held to include the right of dissent, freedom to criticize those in authority, to express opposition views, and to organize opposition parties. Whether political democracy and the rule of law are necessary parts of glasnost must remain an open question.
2. A. D. Kalmykov: *Memoirs of a Russian Diplomat* (New Haven and London, 1971), p 153.
3. Mark Vishnyak: *Padenie russkago Absoliutizma, Sovremenniye Zapiski* (Paris, 1924), vol VIII, p 261. (Translation is my own.)

4. V. I. Gurko: *Features and Figures of the Past* (Stanford, 1939), pp 85ff. 'But intuition,' Gurko adds, 'was not enough with which to govern Russia. The realization that there was "something rotten in the State of Denmark" was no substitute for finding a sane and solid correction for the decay.'

5. Quoted in Vishnyak: *Padenie russkago*, p 262.

6. *Ibid*.

7. Quoted in P. Maslov: *Agrarnyi Vopros v Rossii* (St Petersburg, 1906), vol II, p 106.

8. Already the previous March, in the fortress of St Peter and Paul in St Petersburg, a girl student had burnt herself alive after soaking her clothes in lamp oil. Student youth was shaken. A wave of protest meetings swept educational institutions. The police dispersed a gathering outside the Kazan Cathedral in St Petersburg, where it had been intended to hold a protest meeting (A. F. Kerensky: *The Crucifixion of Liberty*, London, 1934, p 84).

9. At the same time, he did not do this where he could have done, in the St Petersburg Polytechnic.

10. A ditty making the rounds among the students ran: 'Oh little Knout, oh little Knout, oh little Knout so merry, do you remember, little Knout, the eighth of February?'

11. For the remarkable career of Azev, see Boris Nicolaievsky: *Aseff: the Russian Judas* (London, 1934), translated from the Russian by George Reavey.

12. For the history of the liberation movement, see George Fischer: *Russian Liberalism* (Cambridge, MA, 1958).

13. *Ibid*, p 147.

14. Under the pressure of events, he later rejoined the general *zemstvo* movement to the extent of attending to its congresses.

15. For the history of events during the revolution of 1905, the (not always reliable) memoirs of Count Witte are an invaluable source. A. L. Sidorov, ed: *S. Yu. Vitte: Vospominania* (Moscow, 3 vols, 1960).

16. In fact they displayed considerable independence, to the annoyance of social democrats, particularly the Bolsheviks.

17. Witte records in his memoirs a comment by the dowager empress, to whom he had complained – cautiously – of the tsar's vacillating policies. 'You mean to say the emperor has neither willpower nor character. This is true, but see, should the occasion arise he would be replaced by Misha [the Grand-Duke Mikhail]. I know you love Misha but, believe me, he has still less willpower and "character".' *Graf Witte Erinnerungen* (Berlin, 1923), p 341. The section containing this quotation was omitted from the Russian edition.

18. It was not the first of its kind. The earliest Soviet had been set up months before in the textile centre of Ivanovo-Voznesensk.

19. They could perhaps be presented as a dress rehearsal for things to come.

11

Witte's Second Perestroika:
The Imperial Duma

There was, however, a problem. In accordance with his philosophy of history Witte despite his publicly professed autocratism considered autocracy to be an outdated form of government. Sooner or later, Russia must be drawn into the European mainstream of industrialization, constitutional government and parliamentary democracy. Moves in these directions therefore accorded with his concept of historical evolution. They were, in his view, inevitable. Yet he had earlier opposed the *zemstva*. He professed a cult of Aleksandr III and was a protégé of his widow, the dowager-empress. He had also believed that only autocratic power could implement the policies required for the development of Russian power and greatness. He shared, probably sincerely, the monarchist ideology of the Russian Orthodox Church. Thus, on the main political issue of the day Witte's own position was profoundly ambivalent. He was at the same time a determinist liberal even if in a somewhat modified form, and an empirical champion of autocracy. While promoting bourgeois policies, he may still have believed in divinely ordained monarchical absolutism. Small wonder that few believed in the sincerity of his convictions.

Witte's dilemma also had a strictly political aspect. As he was only too well aware, concessions he considered imperative on practical grounds, would be swallowed by the tsar with distaste and even resentment. Sooner or later Nikolai II, of whose personal ill-will Witte could feel assured, would blame him for any dovish advice. Not only was he familiar with the tsar's fickle character but he was aware also of the pervasive influence of his entourage. The empress in particular felt an implacable resentment towards a man capable in her view of eclipsing her beloved 'hubby'.

Politically Witte was isolated. Personally unpopular, he had incurred the lasting hatred of the political right for having ceded to the Japanese half the island of Sakhalin. (Witte's enemies, alluding to his new title, had dubbed him 'Count half-Sakhalin'.) Nor was the bureaucrat, supporter of erstwhile autocracy, opponent of the *zemstva*, patron of capitalist entrepreneurs and latter-day courtier, trusted by the moderate Left. Goremykin, his bureaucratic rival, was hovering in the wings. In the circumstances, any role Witte might still hope to play would depend on the notoriously transient support of the tsar and on his own indispensability of which he was sincerely persuaded. On his return from Portsmouth Witte was hampered by formidable handicaps.

I

While Witte was negotiating at Portsmouth, a committee of senior bureaucrats chaired by Count Solski, the president of the State Council, was studying possibilities of institutional reform. Among its objectives was to impose at least a semblance of unity on the competing ministerial interests. This was to be achieved by increasing the hitherto purely nominal authority over ministers of their chairman; since 1903 none other than Witte. A glaring weakness of the Russian political system would thus be mitigated. While a majority of its members accepted the need for more unified government, the committee was not unanimous. Kokovtsev was critical, according to Witte motivated by personal jealousy. Other opponents argued that the proposal would diminish the role of the tsar in the eyes of the people. Their true motive, probably, was the understandable fear of a threat to their own authority. Neither did they relish the prospective premiership of the unpopular Witte. The proposals which emerged from the deliberations were a compromise under which the Chairman of the Council of Ministers would exercise a limited authority over his ministerial colleagues.

On 6 October Witte, as Chairman of the Council, requested an audience with the tsar to present his view on the threatening situation. Nikolai replied that he had already decided to consult him. At their interview on the 9th, Witte submitted a hastily prepared report. He also told the tsar that there were only two choices – the concessions outlined in the report, or a military dictatorship with orders to suppress the rebellion at any cost. The first course, Witte remarked diplomatically, appeared to him the more appropriate, but in this he could be mistaken. He prudently advised the tsar to consult other ministers and members of his family.

Following his return to St Petersburg Witte revised his report. He concluded that whichever course was decided on it could be pursued only by someone firmly convinced of its rightness. On 10 October the tsar once more received Witte, this time in the presence of the empress. Witte, in presenting his revised report reiterated his views and once more alluded to the possibility of proclaiming martial law. The tsar indicated that Witte's report might form the basis of an imperial manifesto.

On the 13th, the tsar sent Witte a telegram quoted verbatim in his memoirs:

> I instruct you to unify the work of ministers, whom I charge with the restoration of order even before confirmation of the law about the [reform of the] Council of Ministers. Only with a quiet course of public life is there the possibility of common creative labour of the government and the freely [underlined] to be elected representatives of my people.[1]

It was an ambiguous instruction. Witte was to see to the immediate 'restoration of order' prior to the reformation of the Council of Ministers. On the morning of the 14th, Witte repeated to the tsar that decisive steps in one or other direction were needed. The crisis, in fact, was escalating. St Petersburg was without light, telephones or railway connections. Many shops were closed. Witte called an informal meeting of some ministerial colleagues. Rediger, the War Minister, and Trepov reported that troops in the capital were sufficient to suppress any armed uprising and to protect the outlying imperial residences. There were no units capable of restoring communications. Reservists whose demobilization had been delayed were restive. Troops in European Russia were demoralized by employment on police duties.

On the evening of the 14th the tsar instructed Witte to report the following morning with the draft of an imperial manifesto. This should convert Witte's proposals from promises into concrete facts to be presented as a personal favour from the tsar. Nikolai II thus wished to offer an *octroyé* constitution which could, if necessary, be modified or even withdrawn. He also wished to secure for himself such gratitude as might accrue. On presenting himself with his draft manifesto the next day, Witte was received by the tsar surrounded by his 'kitchen cabinet'. On the tsar's orders, he presented his report and answered a number of questions. Then, following a luncheon break and some further discussion, he submitted a revised draft manifesto, after which the tsar adjourned the meeting.

On the 16th towards evening Baron Fredericksz, the Minister of the Imperial Court informed Witte that he would call on him that night. To Witte's intense disgust, he brought with him two alternative drafts prepared on the tsar's orders by members of the State Council. Witte objected to both. The tsar, he said, should simply sign his report. Fredericksz countered that the decision to issue an imperial manifesto was not irrevocable. Witte rejoined that whichever version was finally adopted, its author should also become prime minister. Since the tsar appeared to doubt the justice of his (Witte's) views, it would be better for him to relinquish the post. He was ready to serve in some other capacity, if only as a provincial governor. Witte, in fact, was issuing an ultimatum.

When on the 17th it became clear that the Grand-Duke Nikolai not only declined a military dictatorship but urged instead the adoption of Witte's proposals, the tsar realized he no longer had a choice.[2] Witte's draft, the 'October Manifesto', was published that day accompanied by the report outlining his political programme. Two days later, Witte's appointment as President of the Council of Ministers was officially announced. On the same day, censorship, already ineffective de facto was abolished. On the 22nd there followed the proclamation of an amnesty. Pobedonostsev and Bulygin resigned. A new perestroika was approaching.

II

In the manifesto of 17 October, Nikolai II gave three undertakings. In the first place he promised to grant as 'unshakeable' foundations of civil freedom, 'real' inviolability of person, freedom of conscience, of speech, of assembly and of association. Secondly, he undertook to extend the franchise for the coming elections ('so far as the shortness of time till the calling of the Duma permits') to sections of the population at present disenfranchised. The definitive application of universal suffrage however must await the introduction of the new legislative order. Finally, it was 'unshakeably' established that no new law would enter into force without the prior approval of the Imperial Duma. Moreover, the elected representatives would receive the possibility of a 'real participation' in supervising the legality of the acts of the imperial authorities.

The promises of the manifesto, though in appearance substantial remained limited in scope. Civil liberties would be hard to implement under the régime of 'temporary regulations' imposing states of emergency. Inviolability of person likewise, could not be assured, given on one hand the deeply ingrained tradition of police brutality, on the other the persistence of widespread chaos bordering on civil war. The promise to extend the franchise for the coming elections, though hedged around with qualifications was, however, real and concrete. In principle at any rate universal suffrage was formally conceded. The undertakings regarding the functions of the future parliament – a crucial issue – were ambivalent, in keeping with the tsar's predilections. In the first place, as would soon emerge, the manifesto did not preclude the setting up of a far from democratic second chamber to balance the influence of the lower house. Secondly, the tsar did not abandon his right to legislate by imperial decree. Finally, the future parliament would lack effective control over the executive. The right to watch over the legality of executive actions was as vague as it was unlikely to be effective. Which of his prerogatives, it may be asked, was the autocrat actually giving up? Formally he was abandoning the plenitude of legislative power. Under the new system, the Duma would be a constant if junior partner in the legislative process – a substantial innovation. Secondly, the autocracy was permitting deputies to question, in however limited a form, the legality of official proceedings. To permit even the slightest questioning in public of the actions of officialdom must have been sufficient to make Aleksandr III positively gyrate in his grave.

The main loser in the approaching perestroika might well prove to be less the autocracy than senior officialdom. Ministers, henceforth, would no longer shepherd their legislation through only the State Council behind closed doors (even that, at times, a tricky operation) but also publicly through a critical Duma. An element of glasnost enshrined in the constitution would be introduced into the legislative process. Again, the actions of executive agents from ministers downwards would become subject to intermittent public scrutiny. The perimeters of arbitrary bureaucratic action were being significantly narrowed. This would still more be the case in the event of an attempt to implement the promises about civil liberties. However limited and at times ill-defined the undertakings which Witte had wrested from the tsar, and however uncertain their future implementation, they yet marked a major change in the character and spirit of Russian government. The days of the Sipyagins and Plehves were over. How far autocracy itself had been modified however, only the future would show.

III

Two days after signing the manifesto the tsar, in a long apologetic letter, explained the circumstances to his mother in Copenhagen.[3] 'Through all those horrible days,' he wrote, he had constantly met

Witte. 'We very often met in the early morning to part only in the evening when night fell.'

> There were only two ways open: to find an energetic soldier and crush the rebellion by sheer force. There would be time to breathe then but, as likely as not, one would have to use force again in a few months; and that would mean rivers of blood and, in the end, we should be where we had started. I mean to say, government authority would be vindicated, but there would be no positive result and no possibility of progress achieved.[4]

The alternative was concession:

> The other way out would be to give to the people their civil rights, freedom of speech and press, also to have all laws confirmed by the State Duma – that, of course, would be a constitution. Witte defends this very energetically. He says that, while it is not without risk, it's the only way out at the present moment. Almost everybody I had an opportunity of consulting is of the same opinion.[5]

However unwilling to take 'this terrible decision', he was left little choice:

> Witte put it quite clearly to me that he would accept the Presidency of the Council only on the condition that his programme was agreed to, and his actions not interfered with. He and Alexei Obolensky (Assistant Minister of Finance and Witte's close collaborator) drew up the Manifesto. We discussed it for two days and in the end, invoking God's help, I signed. My dear Mama, you can't imagine what I went through before that moment. In my telegram I could not explain all the circumstances which brought me to this terrible decision, which nevertheless I took quite consciously. From all over Russia they cried for it, they begged for it, and around me many – very many – held the same views. I had nobody to rely on except honest Trepoff. There was no other way out than to cross oneself and give what everyone was asking for.[6]

'My only consolation,' Nikolai concluded, 'is that such is the will of God [that] this grave decision will lead my dear Russia out of the intolerable chaos she has been in for nearly a year.'

Turning to the future Nikolai remarked that the situation was still very serious 'in spite of the fact that I am receiving declarations of very touching loyalty and thankfulness. The people seem to have gone mad – some from joy, others from discontent.' The local administrations did not quite know how to act 'under the new régime'. The tsar then commented on the change of government. 'The very next day,' he observed with wry satisfaction, 'Witte found out what he was in for – many to whom he offered positions under him in one capacity or another now refused to accept.' 'Old Pobedonostsev' had resigned and would be replaced by Alexei Obolensky. Glazov the Minister of Education also resigned but no successor had yet been found. 'All the ministers are resigning and we have to find new ones, but Witte must see to that.'[7] At the same time it was essential to keep order in the towns where both loyal and hostile demonstrators were involved in bloody clashes.

> We are in the midst of a revolution with an administrative apparatus entirely disorganised and in this lies the main danger. But God Almighty will be our help. I feel him supporting me and putting strength in me which gives me courage and does not allow me to lose heart. I assure you we have lived *years* in these days, such torments doubts and indecisions.[8]

A number of points are significant. One is the tsar's evident reluctance to sign the manifesto. He conceives himself as yielding only to force majeure. Before his mother, he exculpates himself by placing the blame on Witte. Next to Witte, however, responsibility is shared by God as what occurred was by His will. At the same time, Nikolai adds that he took the decision to sign in full awareness of its gravity. In the tsar's view, the manifesto was a revolutionary act, replacing the autocracy with something like constitutional government. Indeed he confesses to his mother that he has granted a constitution. He had no choice but to commit a reprehensible act. No more than Charles I or Louis XVI before him was Nikolai II resigned at heart to the role of a constitutional monarch.

Characteristically, Nikolai felt himself betrayed by all around him 'except honest Trepoff'. Curiously, there is no mention of the tsaritsa. What clearly emerges is the crucial part played by Witte. Not only did he prepare the programme of the new government but he also had the major share in drafting the manifesto. By presenting Nikolai with an ultimatum moreover, he had finally broken the tsar's resistance. In semi-retirement since his dismissal, Witte's star had been in the ascendant since Portsmouth. Now he would occupy the position of prime minister in a partially unified cabinet. He would have some authority over colleagues largely to be chosen by himself. By force of circumstance he had become the man of the hour. Yet Witte's position was insecure. Though the tsar for the moment could not do without him, his involvement had not endeared him to the imperial couple. 'Honest Trepoff' remained a threat as did the intriguer Goremykin. The task of pacifying an empire while at the same time initiating a major perestroika was indeed a daunting one. The odds on a successful outcome were hardly favourable.

NOTES

1. *Graf Witte Erinnerungen* (Berlin, 1923), p 322.
2. On the morning of the 17th, Fredericksz told Witte that he had reported their overnight conversation (i.e. Witte's ultimatum) to the tsar, who had made no comment. Fredericksz assumed that he wanted to consult the grand-duke. Hardly had he returned to his home when the grand-duke called, on his way to see the tsar. Fredericksz reported what had occurred and told him, 'It is necessary to set up a dictatorship and you must be the dictator.' Thereupon the grand-duke melodramatically drew a revolver from his pocket and declared: 'You see this revolver. I will go straight to the emperor and implore him to sign the manifesto and Count Witte's report. Either he signs or I will shoot myself in front of him.' With these words the grand-duke rushed away, to return presently with an order from the tsar to make fair copies of the two documents. When Witte arrived, he was to present them for signature. Mosolov, Fredericksz's head of chancery, later told Witte that the grand-duke had virtually forced the tsar's hand. He also reported remarks made to him by Fredericksz after his conversation with the grand-duke: 'No, I see no other way out except to accept Witte's programme. I had always assumed that it would end in a dictatorship and had considered the grand-duke the natural candidate. He is unreservedly devoted to the tsar and I considered him a courageous man. I have just seen that I was mistaken in him. He is a timid and scatter-brained person. No one is ready to assume the responsibility of dictator-ship. Everyone is afraid, all have lost their heads. There is nothing left now except to capitulate to Count Witte.' While Witte, when writing his memoirs, spared no pains to stress the part played by the grand-duke, by then an extreme reactionary and his political enemy, there is no reason to doubt the substance of the accounts of Witte, Fredericksz and Mosolov. The grand-duke's role in making up the tsar's mind had been a crucial one. There is evidence that he in his turn had been influenced by one Ushakov, leader of a small and (relatively) moderate workers' organization. See A. L. Sidorov, ed: *S. Yu. Vitte: Vospominania*, vol III, pp 41–2.
3. The tsar's letters to his mother, the Dowager Empress Maria Fedorovna, are an invaluable source for the personality of Nikolai II, his reactions to events and his relations with his ministers, particularly Witte. As they were not intended for publication, they are notably uninhibited and spontaneous. Why indeed should the tsar seek to misinform his mother? Edward J. Bing, ed: *The Letters of Tsar Nicholas and Empress Marie* (London, 1937).

4. What the tsar concealed from his mother was that he had toyed with the idea of instituting a military dictatorship but had failed to find a dictator.
5. Bing, ed: *Letters*, Nikolai to Maria, 19 October 1905, pp 188–91.
6. *Ibid.*
7. *Ibid.*
8. *Ibid.*

12

Witte's Second Perestroika: Towards a New Régime

Witte's first task as prime minister was to form his cabinet. For this he had to find men who, while acceptable to the tsar, were ready to carry out the policies outlined in his report. They must at the same time enjoy some credibility and public support. Yet they must also be prepared to share responsibility for the measures needed to stamp out the widespread revolt. Judging by the tsar's letters, Witte appears to have laboured under a number of illusions in this regard. In the first place, he may have expected that the disorders would gradually subside under the impression of the manifesto. He may also have cherished the expectation that respected public figures would be eager or, at any rate willing, to join the team. Finally, in the hour of his seeming triumph, he almost certainly underestimated the force of the impending right-wing backlash and its effect upon the tsar. Caught between revolutionary violence on the one hand and right-wing excesses on the other, Witte, as a moderate reformer, was in a weak position from the start. Though entering on the new phase of his career with his usual panache and self-assurance, he would soon become disillusioned. His second perestroika would become his political grave.

I

Witte's strategy – a seemingly promising one – was to bring about a coalition between progressive bureaucrats and moderate public figures. Prominent in the first group would be A. D. Obolensky, Pobedonostsev's successor as Procurator, and N. N. Kutler, the new

Minister of Agriculture. Existing bureaucratic incumbents acceptable to moderate opinion, would retain the technical portfolios of foreign affairs, finance, war and marine. Among public men Witte intended to offer the Ministry of Trade and Industry to A. J. Guchkov, the post of State Controller to D. N. Shipov, the Ministries of Education and Justice respectively to Prince E. N. Trubetskoy and Senator A. F. Koni. Had he succeeded, he would have presided over a ministry supported by moderate opinion and capable of guiding the transition to a pseudo-constitutional régime.

What predictably presented problems, however, was finding a successor at the Ministry of the Interior for the departing Bulygin. The candidate favoured by A. D. Obolensky was Prince S. D. Urusov, a liberal bureaucrat and consistent critic of the late Plehve. Urusov unfortunately lacked experience of police work. On interviewing the prince whom he had not met before, Witte formed a favourable impression. He doubted nonetheless whether Urusov would command the authority needed for the post. Instead, Witte's choice fell on P. N. Durnovo, former head of the police department and since 1900 Assistant Minister of the Interior, a leftover from the Plehve era. Witte would later defend the choice on the grounds of Durnovo's personality and experience and the absence of a more suitable candidate. Already during preliminary discussions, the 'public men' Witte approached had declined to serve with Durnovo. When asked to suggest alternatives, some, somewhat naively, mentioned Witte himself. The wily old fox knew better than to assume direct responsibility for inevitable future repression. Nor could he ignore the danger to life and limb.

When, during the conversations, someone incidentally dropped the name of P. A. Stolypin, governor of Saratov, the reaction was favourable. Witte, who did not know him personally, observed that as a governor he enjoyed an excellent reputation. One of those present, however (Witte thought it may have been Shipov), characterized Stolypin as 'a man of indeterminate profile'. The matter was pursued no further. With it disappeared the chance of a successful premiership. Stolypin was perhaps the only person who combined acceptability to the public men, with a proven ability to check popular disorder. A triumvirate composed of Witte, Stolypin and Guchkov might well have become the backbone of a government capable of putting an end to revolution while at the same time inaugurating a liberal spirit and, with widespread public support, the new political perestroika.

For their part, the public men may not have been wholly heartbroken when Witte's choice of Durnovo provided them with a respectable let out. The prospect of becoming associated with inevitable repression was not enticing. Nor did the record and personality

of Witte inspire unbounded confidence. While ready to accept Urusov
or possibly Stolypin as a colleague, they understandably balked at
working with an heir of the late Plehve. In appointing Durnovo, Witte,
as a considered decision, chose to abandon the strategy of coalition
government. Instead, he gave precedence to the restoration of order.
Urusov was weak if well-intentioned, Stolypin an unknown quantity.
Durnovo's qualifications on the other hand were undeniable. Given
the tsar's unconcealed preferences and those of the still influential
Trepov, Witte in fact had little choice. Like others before him
therefore, he was obliged to form a government composed exclusively
of bureaucrats.

II

While the workers' movement in the capital was slowly losing momentum, the tsar gleefully noted the emergence of a strongly anti-semitic
monarchist ground swell. 'In the first days after the Manifesto,' he
reported to Copenhagen, (27 October), 'the subversive elements
raised their heads, but a strong reaction set in quickly and a whole
mass of loyal people suddenly made their power felt.' Predictably, the
rising reaction had manifested itself, among others, in anti-Jewish
pogroms. These the tsar sought not only to explain but even to defend.
'The impertinence of the Socialists and revolutionaries had angered
the people once more; and because nine-tenths of the trouble-makers
are Jews, the people's whole anger turned against them. That's how
the pogroms happened.' He naively expressed his 'amazement' that
pogroms had occurred *simultaneously* 'in all the towns of Russia and
Siberia', suggesting something like a popular mass movement rather
than the probably centrally-orchestrated diversionary manoeuvre.
However, as Nikolai noted with satisfaction, suffering had not been
confined to the Jews: 'Some of the Russian agitators, engineers,
lawyers and such-like bad people suffered as well.'[1]

The tsar's observations are revealing. With only limited justification,
he chose to regard the revolutionary movement as predominantly
'Jewish' and saw in the pogroms loyalist outbursts of popular indignation. They were in fact encouraged, indeed on occasion instigated,
by local officials and/or clergy. There was little attempt to restrain the
hooligans. While deep-rooted anti-Jewish prejudices (and lust for
plunder) pervaded wide strata of the Russian population (notably the
petty bourgeoisie, but also clergy, lower officialdom and elements of
the peasantry residing on the outskirts of urban centres), anti-
Semitism, manipulated for political purposes, formed perhaps the
most effective weapon in the arsenal of counter-revolution. For

Nikolai II, monarchial loyalty and anti-Semitism came close to being synonymous. If Jewish populations suffered, they had in his view, 'brought it upon themselves'. At the same time, while Jews were singled out, they were not, of course, the only 'enemy'. The professional intelligentsia also, 'engineers, lawyers and such-like' had aroused the tsar's ire. Perhaps surprisingly, students were omitted from the list, unless subsumed under 'such-like bad people'.[2]

The tsar, by this time, was heartened by the receipt of loyal addresses. 'I am receiving telegrams from everywhere,' he wrote, 'with touching gratitude for the liberties conceded, but also many indicating that they want autocracy to be preserved. Why were they silent before, the good people?'[3] Of course, Nikolai must have understood that the two kinds of loyal address were contradictory. To anyone who knew him, including his mother, there could be no doubt which type of message it was that particularly warmed his heart.

At the same time, Nikolai reported on the problems confronting Witte. Not all his candidates for ministerial posts had finally agreed to serve. His difficulties had proved greater than expected. 'It is strange', Nikolai mused, 'that such a clever man should be wrong in his forecast of an easy pacification.' He did not, he added, quite like Witte's way of talking to various extremists 'especially as all these talks appear in the press the next day, and as often as not are distorted . . . I spoke to him about it, and hope he will not go on with it.'[4] Witte, had, however, achieved an apparent success though one that would hardly endear him to the tsar. 'To my regret,' Nikolai wrote, 'Trepoff is leaving.' It had always been his opinion that Trepov and Witte could not work together. For the first few days, everything seemed all right between them. Witte himself was full of praise for Trepov's activities. Nevertheless, constant friction and all kinds of difficulties soon arose. Nikolai had, reluctantly, to give in to Trepov's insistent demand to be released from his duties, 'painful though it is for me'. Trepov was quite overworked and beginning to lose heart as no other minister would help him. 'His conduct was brilliant all through the troublesome days in Petersburg' and it was only thanks to him and the astonishing discipline of the troops that horrible bloodshed had been averted.[5] Officers and men were very indignant at demonstrators carrying red and black flags and indulging 'in the most impossible speeches in the street' including calls for the proclamation of a democratic republic.

The dowager-empress, in a letter of 1 November, while expressing sympathy for her son in his tribulations also added some good advice. She wrote: 'I am sorry for Witte too. He has his measure of terrible difficulties . . . it is essential for you to show him all your confidence now, and to let him act according to his programme.'[6] To which Nikolai II replied that, while trying to help Witte, he was disappointed at his lack of energy. 'In your letter my dear Mama, you ask me to show all my confidence to Witte: I assure you I am doing my very best to ease his very difficult position and he knows it. But I must confess that I am disappointed with him in a way.'[7] Witte, with everyone else, had the reputation of being 'a very energetic and even despotic man', one who would straight away do his utmost to re-establish order. In fact, at the weekly Council of Ministers, there was much talk but little else.

> They talk a lot but do little. Everybody is afraid of taking courageous action . . . I keep on trying to force them – even Witte himself – to behave more energetically. With us, nobody is accustomed to shouldering responsibility, all expect to be given orders which, however, they disobey as often as not.[8]

A lot, the tsar observed, depended on the conduct of local authorities. Where governors were capable and honest, things were quiet, with Saratov, under Stolypin, a shining example. However, a number had done nothing at all. Worse, some actually led the mob 'red flag in hand' and had, of course, already been dismissed. In St Petersburg, the authorities seemed to have 'less courage than anywhere else'. Witte and Durnovo were permitting peaceful demonstrations and were determined to avoid bloodshed. This, more than anything else, was deepening the impression that the government 'out of fear and indecision' did not dare to state openly what was permitted and what was not.[9]

In fact, while Witte and Durnovo were temporizing, the workers' movement in St Petersburg was ebbing. Feeling that it was in danger of losing control the Soviet, on 1 November, called a new general strike in protest against the proclamation of martial law in the Kingdom of Poland and the suppression of some military disorders in Kronstadt. The strike, a fiasco, was called off on 5 November. Factory owners informed workers that they would no longer be paid for days or hours of absence. On 13 November, the Soviet failed to reach a decision about calling another strike. It simultaneously supported the 'temporary suspension' of an eight-hour day workers had unilaterally operated in some factories. From this moment, according to Witte, it began to lose its credibility and prestige. When strikes finally ceased four days later, Nikolai II congratulated the premier. 'I am happy that the senseless strikes have stopped. This is a great moral success for the government.'[10] On 26 November, Witte sanctioned the arrest of Nosar, the Soviet chairman, who was replaced by a triumvirate including Trotsky. The new praesidium considered calling a strike to protest against the arrest of Nosar but desisted in the face of worker opposition. It announced, however, that preparations were continuing for an armed uprising.

Following the arrest of Nosar, Witte ordered that of the entire Soviet. Durnovo delayed on the grounds that the arrest of individual members would allow others to escape. He preferred to await a plenary session which the Soviet, fearing arrest, was delaying. On 2 December, the Soviet praesidium called on the Russian people to withhold taxes, withdraw deposits from banks and savings banks and to demand payment in gold. It was a forlorn attempt to weaken the economy and to undermine Russia's international credit during critical negotiations for a massive foreign loan. The following day with the Soviet finally meeting in plenary session, Witte and Durnovo struck. Some 190 deputies, including Trotsky, were arrested as were numbers of other revolutionary leaders. The tsar rejoiced: 'Everyone was delighted when 250 important leaders of the workmen's committees and other organizations were arrested the other day. Furthermore 12 newspapers have been suppressed and their editors will be prosecuted for the odious things they have printed. In this case again everybody was agreed that such measures were long overdue!'[11] St Petersburg remained quiet. The authorities had regained control – indeed they had never lost it – and without any shedding of blood. Witte would later claim that during the whole of his premiership there was only one instance of the use of armed force. It was undertaken by the military against his wishes and with relatively small casualties.

The revolutionaries, meanwhile, were venturing on a last desperate throw. Their centre of activities had always been Moscow rather than St Petersburg. In Moscow the decision to rise was taken on 9 December. The authorities were not unprepared. As early as 9 November Witte learnt from a private source of the revolutionaries' plans. The government thereupon replaced the somnolent governor-general by Witte's candidate the moderate admiral Dubasov. Bulygin, the tsar's choice, prudently declined the honour. Dubasov at once appealed for reinforcements and the hard-pressed authorities on the tsar's peremptory orders unwillingly acceded to the request. Part of the remaining elite troops, the Semenovsky Guards regiment, entrained for Moscow. The arrival of the Guards on 15 December had been preceded by days of desultory skirmishing. The Semenovtsy succeeded with relative ease in recapturing the city centre. Artillery bombardment reduced 'Red Presnya', the last working-class stronghold overlooking the Moskva river. Following the 'victory', the soldiers indulged in some predictable excesses. On 22 December, the tsar could tell his mother that 'thanks to the faithful determination of our glorious troops' armed rebellion had been crushed. Government casualties had been light: ten killed and eleven seriously wounded.

The rebel losses were 'terrific', though actual figures were unobtainable as the dead and injured were taken away by their comrades.[12]

Though Witte's government had achieved some successes, its tribulations were far from over. Several sources of anxiety remained. The agrarian movement approached a climax during November and December. A wave of unrest swept the armed forces. In the most spectacular of the incidents, mutinous soldiers in Sevastopol occupied their barracks on 11 November. Two days later a cashiered officer, Lieutenant Schmidt, hoisted the red flag on the cruiser *Ochakov*. The rising, however, was quickly suppressed. More serious and persistent were the disorders along the Siberian railway where mutinous troops, incensed at the slowness of repatriation, seized a number of centres. The railway was eventually reopened by the despatch from both ends of the line of troop-carrying armoured trains. On 1 December advanced echelons of troops returning from the East reached Moscow. Violent disorders at the same time continued in the borderlands, notably Poland, Livonia and Kurland but also in the Caucasus and in Finland. However with the reopening of the Siberian line and with troops returning from Manchuria, the ultimate defeat of revolution, became merely a matter of time. Witte's policy of combining moderation with firmness saved the day.

III

Whether the régime, despite the near universal panic of its representatives, had ever been seriously threatened must remain a matter of some doubt. The St Petersburg Soviet proved feeble and ineffectual once the October strikes had fizzled out. The strike weapon, though effective in the short run and for agitational purposes, revealed its limitations: strikes, for economic and other reasons, could not be sustained for any length of time. When it came to armed confrontation, revolutionary skirmishers were no match for regular troops. Occasional mutinies against the background of wider discontents (delays in demobilization, the insensitivity of commanders, poor leadership and military defeat) were insufficient to break the morale of the armed forces as a whole or to undermine their general readiness to obey orders. Loyal troops and vessels easily overcame mutineers. Troops were thinly spread, preventing, before December, pacification of rural areas and the borderlands. They sufficed however to maintain control of the major centres. Nowhere did anti-government forces gain the upper hand for any length of time.

A major element in the victory of the government was the sporadic, indeed episodic character of revolutionary activity. There was neither central direction nor co-ordinated action. Indeed, there is more than a little justification for the view that what occurred in Russia in 1905 was less a revolution than a *Smuta*, a 'Time of Troubles'. While there were massive disorders threatening universal chaos, there was no determined or organized attempt to overthrow the government. Any number of largely isolated episodes did not amount to a revolution. Revolutionary violence in rhetoric as much as action had played into the hands of the government. The state of mind of the people, the tsar noted as early as 8 December had 'lately changed altogether'. The 'old heedless Liberals', always so critical of firm measures on the part of the authorities were now clamouring loudly for 'decisive action'. Such developments gave Witte the courage to keep to 'the right line of action'.

A final factor enabling the government to survive was the soundness of Witte's financial management. Though under some pressure, Russian finances and credit successfully withstood the strains of both the war and domestic disorders. Fortuitously, the simultaneous Franco-German clash over Morocco reminded France of the value of its Russian ally. Russia's prestige as a Great Power, if shaken, remained unimpaired. Witte therefore, would be able presently to negotiate another urgently needed French loan. Just as French politicians, bankers and investors had backed Russian imperialism in the Far East, so they would now provide the resources to tide the tsarist régime over its domestic crisis. The cards were thus stacked in favour of the government. Witte, though never completely in control, had played them skillfully.

IV

While fighting the revolutionaries, Witte's government was at the same time wrestling with several burning issues: the agrarian problem, the financial crisis and last, not least, the transition to the new quasi-constitutional order. Its achievement in all three spheres was considerable.

During November and December, with peasant disorders approaching their climax, steps for dealing with the rural situation appeared urgent. Panic-stricken landowners and officials were convinced that compulsory expropriation of some privately owned land could no longer be avoided. As Trepov told Witte: 'I am a landowner myself and I shall be happy to give up half my land without compensation as the only way of saving the other half.' Dubasov, after visiting the provinces of Kursk and Chernigov advised Witte to legalize such 'wild' occupations of estates as had already occurred. That might still pacify the peasants and prevent them from seizing the rest. After studying the land question Kutler concluded that compulsory expropriation had become a necessity. Witte, while not wholly unsympathetic to Kutler's programme, resisted such panic measures. In a matter of such gravity, he argued, careful legislation was needed. Such legislation, moreover, under the terms of the manifesto, must await the convocation of the Imperial Duma. Other considerations not mentioned in his memoirs may well have been in Witte's mind. A hasty agrarian perestroika – there are contemporary parallels – was likely to reduce still further the already low productivity of Russian agriculture. Serious damage might thereby be done to Russia's balance of trade. Moreover, once the panic subsided, the author of an agrarian law involving expropriation would be a 'marked man'.

Land reform was formally placed on the agenda when the tsar, at the end of an audience, handed Witte a memorandum for discussion by the Council of Ministers. In it P. P. Migulin, a professor of economics, proposed the immediate compulsory expropriation by imperial decree, of some land for the benefit of the peasantry. Trepov 'as a landowner' was urging Witte to implement Migulin's suggestion as a matter of urgency before the peasants could appropriate all the land. When the memorandum came before the Council of Ministers, the general view was that a matter of such importance must be weighed carefully. It could not, in any case, be resolved without the concurrence of Duma and State Council. In the meantime, all outstanding redemption payments should be cancelled and the scope of activities of the Peasants' Land Bank increased. An *ukaz* of 16 November accordingly reduced redemption payments due on 1 January 1906 by one half and thereafter cancelled them altogether. A commission chaired by Kutler was charged with exploring further measures to assist the peasantry. Its recommendations would be presented to the future Duma.

With the tsar urging expedition in all matters pertaining to the peasantry, Kutler presented proposals for increasing peasant landholding. These included the expropriation against compensation of all land permanently leased to peasants. His proposals, however had no chance of being adopted. Towards the end of December, the peasant movement was waning, and officials and landowners were beginning to recover from their panic. At a private meeting of ministers all, including Witte, rejected compulsory expropriation. Private property, they declared, must remain inviolate. Witte also argued that the measure would further damage Russia's already shaky finances. It was agreed that the Kutler commission, reinforced by opponents of compulsory expropriation, should reconsider the matter. Shortly after this, the tsar informed Witte that since everyone opposed Kutler he wished to replace him. On 14 February 1906, the minister was unceremoniously dismissed.

The abandonment of Kutler's project was not, however, to be the government's last word. At a meeting on 5 March, the Council of Ministers discussed legislative measures to be submitted to the coming Duma. These included a bill on rural reorganization on which preparatory work had already begun. By mid-April a preliminary draft was completed. It would eventually form the basis of the celebrated law on land settlement of 9 November 1906, associated with the name of Stolypin (to be discussed in a later chapter).

V

Of more immediate importance than long-term agrarian reform were the negotiations conducted by Witte and Kokovtsev for a large international loan. This had become a matter of urgency. The Japanese war had cost the Russian Exchequer some 2,450 million rubles. Note circulation had risen from 578 million rubles on 1 January 1904 to 1,207 million two years later. Wealthy Russians had transferred abroad hundreds of millions of rubles. The war, moreover, had necessitated heavy foreign spending which had depleted Russia's gold reserve. The convertible currency, so painfully established by Witte, was placed in jeopardy.

Witte – like his contemporary counterpart – knew that the grave economic crisis could be overcome only with the help of a large foreign loan. Furthermore, to give the government some leeway in its dealings with the Duma negotiations must, if possible, be concluded before its convocation. When Kokovtsev first discussed the matter with the French Prime Minister, he was told that nothing could be finalized until after the settlement of the Moroccan issue. All he was able to obtain immediately was an advance of 100 million rubles. Germany, meanwhile, in a bid for Russian diplomatic support, accepted a modest rescheduling of Russia's short-term debts. The conference of Algeciras, on the outcome of which the fate of the loan depended, dragged on until the end of March. The Russian government gave cautious diplomatic support to France and her British ally. Its reward was a loan of 2,250 million gold francs formalized in Paris on 3 April 1906. The terms were onerous, reflecting Russia's diminished international credit. However, the Russian government would now be able to weather the financial and economic crisis.

The loan also had a political dimension. Diplomatic support in exchange for financial assistance strengthened Russia's ties with France. Diplomatic solidarity at the conference marked the beginnings also of a tentative *rapprochement* with Russia's old rival Great Britain. British financial interests participated in the loan. The German government, on the other hand, annoyed at the Russian stance, instructed its banks to withdraw from the international consortium (though Russia's leading German banker, the house of Mendelssohn & Co. nevertheless participated unofficially). American interests also withdrew.

Though the terms of the loan were disadvantageous, Witte and Kokovtsev had negotiated with skill in difficult circumstances. Witte's personal credit abroad, unlike that of his country, stood unimpaired. The negotiations were, moreover, conveniently concluded before the Duma convened. On the other hand, Witte's preferred diplomatic strategy of uniting Russia, France and Germany in a continental league failed. Instead of the Franco-German reconciliation he sought, Algeciras brought the beginnings of a Russo-British *rapprochement*. Russo-German relations, on the other hand, received a setback. Russia's foreign policy was beginning to take a new direction, a logical consequence of the Russo-French alliance of 1894, and the *entente cordiale* concluded between France and Britain in 1904.

VI

Both the draft law on land reform and the international loan were part of the preparations for the transition to the new constitutional order. In regard to this the most urgent task was the preparation of an electoral law. Two drafts were prepared. One, described by Witte as the 'Moscow project' was elaborated by the public men whose collaboration Witte had vainly sought: Shipov, Guchkov and Prince E. N. Trubetskoy. The second project, a bureaucratic concoction was drawn up under Witte's direction by one of his senior officials. While the Moscow draft came close to implementing the democratic ideal of *chetyrekhvostka* (universal, direct, secret and equal suffrage – in today's parlance 'one man, one vote') the bureaucratic version merely added tenants and workers to the Bulygin franchise. The complicated multi-stage elections for peasant deputies were retained.

When the two drafts were discussed at an ad hoc meeting of ministers, members of the State Council and public men, a predictable majority opted for the Witte project. The public men on the other hand (other than the right-winger Count Bobrinski) led by the future Duma president Professor S. A. Muromtsev, preferred the democratic version. They were joined by a handful of liberal bureaucrats prominent among them State Controller Filosofov and Procurator, Prince A. D. Obolensky.

The matter was then discussed at an ad hoc meeting chaired by the tsar. In addition to the earlier participants, some grand-dukes and a number of more conservative State Councillors attended. At Witte's suggestion, four public men, Shipov, Guchkov, Count Bobrinski and Baron Korff had also been invited. Witte in advance assured the tsar that Bobrinski at least would support the bureaucratic version. To his surprise and the tsar's annoyance, the count in fact backed the Moscow project. After an adjournment, the meeting reconvened without the public men. During the interval Witte had challenged Bobrinski and received the following reply: 'Your Excellency, after the meeting of the Committee of Ministers I spent some time in the country. I met many people and gained the conviction that none except an extreme democratic law would now satisfy Russia. That is why I supported the Moscow Project.'[13]

At the resumed meeting, the difference of views persisted. A majority, as before, supported the Witte draft. In the end, no decision was reached. The tsar appeared undecided. Witte told the empress – the only occasion he claims to have spoken to her on matters of state – that the adoption of the democratic version would be a mistake. At a further meeting, with opinions still divided, Witte finally abandoned what had hitherto been a specious neutrality and urged what was, after all, his own project. The tsar then declared that he would confirm the bureaucratic proposal. To Copenhagen, he reported:

> I am very busy this week with a number of important but tiring conferences dealing with the electoral law for the Duma. The whole future of that institution hangs on the right solution of this problem. Alexei Obolensky with some others proposed universal suffrage, but I, acting on my firm convictions, declined to agree to it. God alone knows how far people will go with their fantastic ideas![14]

The preparation of detailed regulations defining the modus operandi and competence of Duma and the State Council was entrusted to an enlarged ministerial committee. A manifesto of 20 February 1906 announced the rules that would govern the proceedings of the two chambers. It laid down, among others, the arrangements for urgent legislation during a Duma recess. These would form the basis of the celebrated (or notorious) Article 87 of the future Fundamental Laws.

In the prolonged discussions concerning these laws, Russia's basic constitutional charter, Witte did his best to limit the Duma's competence. To prevent it from discussing constitutional issues and turn itself into a quasi-constituent assembly, he insisted on the publication of the Fundamental Laws before its convocation. The laws were thus an *octroyé* constitution, a fact later used to justify unilateral modifications (or violations). It was also on Witte's insistence that matters of foreign policy and military command were excluded from the Duma's competence. In general, Witte would later claim with the object of pacifying his critics that he used his influence to emasculate the more radical proposals. Not only did he seek to defend the tsar's prerogatives but he also watered down the modest rights granted to the Duma in its dealings with ministers.

The Fundamental Laws, as promulgated on 23 April, consolidated a number of piecemeal enactments. They contained several significant features. In the first place, as already indicated, the new arrangements were introduced unilaterally by the autocrat. To the extent that they set limits on his prerogatives these were formally self-imposed. Nikolai II accepted them unwillingly, perhaps with a genuine 'bad conscience'. At the same time, as his reluctance appears to indicate, he probably did so in good faith. Yet were there mental reservations on his part? It would indeed have been surprising if there were not. 'To the emperor of all Russia', read the first article of the Fundamental Laws, 'belongs supreme autocratic power. Submission to his power, not from fear only but as a matter of conscience, is commanded by God himself.' Only the word 'unlimited' before 'autocratic power', which had figured in an earlier draft, was omitted – with the tsar's agreement. (A limited autocratic power was, of course, a contradiction in terms.)

A second feature of the laws was that the hastily prepared document was exclusively the work of bureaucrats. No one outside official circles had been involved in their elaboration. Since *obshchestvennost* subscribed to the doctrine of popular sovereignty and called for a democratically elected Constituent Assembly, the omission is hardly surprising.

With both tsar and premier seeking to limit the competence of the Duma, detailed arrangements favoured the executive. Ministers, as hitherto, would be appointed by the emperor. They would be responsible to him alone, to be dismissed at his good pleasure. They would not (with some later exceptions) be members of the Duma. The Duma's rights would be limited to parliamentary questions ('interpellations') concerning the legality of ministerial actions. In theory, the Duma could, by a two-thirds majority, pass a vote of censure on the government. A corresponding resolution could then be submitted to the tsar who, however, was at liberty to ignore it. The executive, as hitherto, would remain under his sole control. The Duma's legislative 'powers' would essentially be negative. The constitution laid down that no bill could become law without the consent of its majority. Equally, no law could be enacted without the concurrent approval of the State Council and the tsar. Each of the three would therefore enjoy – at least in theory – a power of veto. The tsar, however, retained ill-defined powers of legislation by imperial decree (*ukaz*). Moreover, echoing the constitution of the Habsburg Monarchy, Paragraph 87 of the Fundamental Laws empowered the government to legislate by decree on matters it considered urgent while the chambers were in recess. Such decrees had to be submitted within a relatively brief timespan to the following Duma session. The Duma's rights of budgetary control were also circumscribed.

Not content with these institutional 'safeguards' the bureaucrats also did their best to ensure solid conservative majorities in both houses. This was easy enough to arrange in relation to the reformed State Council. Half its members would be nominated by the tsar, subject to periodic reappointment, while the remainder would be elected by nobility, clergy, *zemstva*, universities, merchants, industrialists and the Academy of Sciences. A permanent right-wing majority, if not necessarily a homogeneous one, seemed guaranteed.

Matters were less simple in the case of the lower chamber. Here three safeguards against radical majorities were incorporated. In the first place, on the mistaken assumption of the peasants' basic loyalty, they were granted a generous representation. A four-stage electoral process moreover created wide openings for administrative manipulation. A further safeguard, the under-representation of factory workers, would offer only marginal relief. Even with a relatively high urban property qualification, members of the professions and the radical intelligentsia were unlikely to be disenfranchised. Finally, there would be discrimination against members of minority groups which, however, could have only a limited effect. (Witte, however, in the face of opposition, secured voting rights for many Jews.) Given the state of Russian opinion any assembly based on popular voting was certain to have an oppositional majority. Clashes between Duma and government in fact were built into the new pseudo-constitutional structure. In the all but inevitable conflict between ministers and chambers the cards, thanks largely to Witte, were stacked in favour of the former.

Even if the régime of the Fundamental Laws, bastard offspring of autocracy and October Manifesto, was unlikely to operate smoothly it yet contained some notable innovations. In the first place, while the constitutional position was changed only marginally, the Fundamental Laws yet raised a question mark over autocracy as operated in the days of Aleksandr III. No 'restoration' could fully restore the shaken prestige of absolute monarchy, particularly with a monarch like Nikolai II who had lost all personal credibility. A further effect of the Fundamental Laws was the creation of a new and revolutionary glasnost, centred on a national forum. Enshrined in the constitution were freedom of speech for Duma deputies, personal immunity and relatively free parliamentary reporting. In consequence, oppositional and even revolutionary views could henceforth receive unprecedented publicity. Public criticism of ministers and their policies was formally institutionalized through the device of 'interpellations'. Public opinion thus received a legal and widely publicized mode of expression of a kind hitherto undreamt of.

Moreover, the creation of the Duma had important side effects. In the first place, further mild constraints, in addition to the only partially effective courts, were now placed on the arbitrary proceedings of officialdom. Bureaucratic misdeeds could be pilloried in public. Ministers and others would henceforth have to watch their step with somewhat greater care. Again, the new pseudo-parliamentary régime involved the legalization of political parties and their organization, however obstructed by administrative chicanery. Inefficiently and somewhat chaotically, even radical parties would now be able to organize not only in the capitals but also in the provinces. More particularly this would apply to the liberal-constitutionalist Party of People's Freedom, presently to be known as the Constitutional Democrats or Cadets. Within limits, electoral campaigning, however hampered by officialdom, would permit the propagation of their views at public meetings and in a party press.

Pseudo-constitutional politics, moreover, involved of necessity the growth of an alternative political elite; alternative, that is, to the official bureaucratic one. Party and Duma leaders could acquire national reputations whether through parliamentary speeches, journalistic activities or public oratory. Rank and file deputies would be known, at any rate, in their constituencies. If the members of *zemstvo* boards had once constituted the nucleus of a new political leadership, Duma deputies might now acquire a higher profile as a result of parliamentary activities. Guchkov, Miliukov, Rodzianko and others could achieve wider national recognition.

What is more, the political perestroika and accompanying glasnost enshrined in the Fundamental Laws was, as widely foreseen (or feared) likely to prove irreversible. The bureaucracy, resisting great temptations, had never seriously damaged, let alone abolished, the *zemstva*. Even less was it likely to do away with the Duma. The utmost it could attempt would be to tamper with its composition, to contest its competence and to fight it with an arsenal of bureaucratic chicanery. Henceforth it would have to coexist and work with a national representative body of a novel kind. The Fundamental Laws, even if they did not themselves inaugurate a fundamental constitutional shift, at least created the possibility. However strong the surviving influence of the old forces, there could now be no return to the undiluted autocracy of Aleksandr III.

VII

The promulgation of the Fundamental Laws marked the effective end of Witte's political perestroika. Constant intrigues by Trepov and Durnovo, combined with the fickleness of Nikolai II, had from the start placed him in a parlous position. Distrusted and disliked in equal measure by conservatives and liberals, landowners and bureaucrats, he found it difficult to steer a steady course. Any inclination towards liberal policies (other than, perhaps, opportunistically with regard to Jews) were checked by the need to appease the conservatives and to atone for the manifesto. Yet the conservatives, feeling threatened by the new order and under the fresh impression of recent terrors, were unwilling to forgive. Witte – not unlike Gorbachev – manoeuvred opportunistically from expedient to expedient, aware that time was running out. With the promulgation of the Fundamental Laws following on the successful loan negotiations, his usefulness to the tsar was at an end.

On 12 January, Nikolai reported to his mother that, since the abortive Moscow rising, Witte had radically altered his stance. He now wanted to 'hang and shoot everybody'. 'I have never', wrote the tsar, 'seen such a chameleon of a man.' That was the reason why no one believed him any more. Witte was absolutely discredited with everybody, 'except perhaps the Jews abroad'. Nikolai had praise only for the insignificant Minister of Justice, who had already 'cleaned up his poisonous ministry' and for Durnovo who was 'doing splendid work. I am very pleased with him too.' A fortnight later he added that Trepov had become 'absolutely indispensable' to him. 'He is experienced and clever and cautious in his advice. I give him Witte's bulky memoranda to read, then he reports on them quickly and concisely.'[15]

Floundering in a morass of intrigue, even the normally thick-skinned Witte finally realized that the time had come to quit. During February, he began to talk of his approaching dismissal. The tsar however asked him, both personally and through Trepov, to complete the loan negotiations and the arrangements for the Duma. Witte mentions another uncompleted task, the repatriation of the armies from Manchuria. He was still needed. For a further two months he remained indispensable. Thereafter, the tsar and his camarilla were free to 'kick him out'. Witte, it is clear, assessed the character and personality of Nikolai II no less accurately than the tsar assessed his own.

On 14 April 1906, Witte finally sketched out his letter of resignation. He had, he wrote, over the last two months disagreed profoundly with Durnovo's brutal policy of repression at a time when the revolution was largely defeated. On important issues like the peasant – Jewish – and religious questions, there was profound disagreement among ministers and 'influential spheres'. He felt incapable of defending policies which ran counter to his convictions. He was unable to share the views of extreme conservatives which, '*latterly*, have become the political credo of the minister of the interior'.

He had been, during the preceding six months, the target of attack for every 'screamer and scribbler' in the Russian public and for extreme elements with access to the tsar. Revolutionaries cursed him because during the revolution he introduced the most decisive measures with full conviction and with his entire authority. Liberals persecuted him because true to his oath and conscience, he defended the imperial prerogatives and would do so to the grave. Conservatives detested him because they wrongly blamed him for all the changes in the state order since the appointment of Sviatopolk-Mirsky. What had most damaged the public good was the distrust of his policies on the part of extreme conservatives, aristocrats and high officials who 'naturally' always enjoyed access to the tsar. These were able to raise doubts about the actions and even the intentions of those who did not suit them. The government must now either seek a modus vivendi with the Duma or resolve to employ extreme measures. In the first event, new men would be useful because they would be free from the odium incurred by present ministers in the course of the revolution. In the second, the role of the Ministers of the Interior, Justice and War would be decisive. In that event, he himself could only be an obstacle. Whatever attitude he chose to adopt, the extreme conservatives would savage him.

Witte was thus resigning in the stance of a moderate in protest against the policies of Durnovo (and Trepov) seconded by the tsar. As the letter contained thinly veiled criticism of Nikolai and his entourage and was unlikely ever to see the light of day, there can be little doubt that it accurately reflected his views at this time. The tsar accepted Witte's resignation in forms that were outwardly civil, indeed almost gracious. However unpopular Witte had made himself, his immense services in saving the régime could hardly be overlooked.

Thus departed, his reputation in tatters, the architect of the most significant tsarist perestroika. In contemporary terms, Witte would perhaps be best described as a modernizing technocrat. Neither a routine bureaucrat nor yet a politician or a courtier, he was, in important respects, a misfit in the tsarist régime. His modernizing policies, confined at first to the economic sphere, in the end extended also to the political. Both Siberian railway and Imperial Duma could be considered his children. Like the Miliutin brothers before him, Witte made use of the autocratic power to effect a major economic transformation. He also used that same power to combine the suppression of the revolutionary movement with significant political change. Potentially, at any rate, he thereby cleared the way for measured constitutional advance. Overall, his policies advanced Russia's defeudalization, her slow march towards Western bourgeois forms. Under his guidance a Russia underdeveloped had turned into a developing one. As already indicated, Witte believed in the inevitable evolution of Russia through a bourgeois to a democratic and perhaps socialist phase of development. Within the limits of the practicable, he could be described as a progressive, moving with what appeared to him the inevitable march of history. There may here be parallels with the views of Mikhail Gorbachev.

However, much as he might have liked to, Witte could not pursue his policies in a political vacuum. Rather, he had to operate within the narrow parameters of the autocratic-bureaucratic system with its elements of residual feudalism. He was obliged, moreover, to carry out his reforms in a desperately poor, backward and still largely undeveloped country and, furthermore, in a difficult international climate. It was these constraints which, besides limiting Witte's possibilities of achievement, contributed also to his failures. Against his wishes, recklessness and irresponsibility turned successful economic imperialism in the Far East into the Japanese debacle. Russian poverty forced him to overstrain the country's economic and fiscal resources helping, thereby, to provoke a political upheaval. Economic modernization under a still largely feudal régime involved inescapable political risks. However, the economic foundations well and truly laid by Witte survived the essentially political earthquake, to be built upon by others. In these respects also there may be contemporary parallels.

The narrower everyday constraints which Witte had cause to lament, were those of a political system based more particularly under the fickle Nikolai II on intrigue and backstairs influences; the obscure machinations of grand-dukes, policemen, guards officers, obscurantists, soothsayers and adventurers of every sort, as well as the Empress Alexandra Fedorovna. Himself an adept trained in the hard school of intrigue, Witte would in retrospect regret the time and energy he was forced to waste in futile internecine warfare.

Given the conditions within which he was forced to operate, Witte's achievements were formidable. Over and above his industrial policies, he successfully liquidated the Far Eastern adventure and organized the relatively speedy and safe return of the Russian armies from Manchuria. He helped to defeat the revolutionary movement and saved the régime by a constitutional compromise and his vast international credit. His perestroika had laid the foundations for something like a new start in both the economic and political spheres. And yet, when Witte – like Gorbachev a moderate reforming centrist – quit the scene of his labours, he had, almost certainly, exhausted his usefulness. His abrasive personality never made for easy popularity. Now, as a result of his recent policies, he was widely disliked and distrusted, for his virtues as a statesman as much as for his vices. At the height of the revolutionary movement, he appeared a saviour. With its waning, he was blamed on all sides for the policies which helped to achieve pacification. As he indicated in his letter of resignation, he was aware that the new pseudo-constitutional order would start under happier auspices under the direction of others. When writing his letter of resignation, the normally robust Witte was worn out and ailing though destined to regain his health and spirits. There was little left for him to contribute. It appears doubtful whether he would have been able to reach an accommodation with the Duma more easily than would his successors. The ambassadorship in a major European capital offered to him at his own request but never forthcoming would have provided a fitting conclusion to a distinguished career. Instead, periodic attempts at a comeback on an extreme conservative Germanophile ticket would do nothing to enhance Witte's reputation. They had, moreover, little chance of success. All that remained for him after 1906 was the composition of his voluminous memoirs, embittered, vindictive, apologetic and not wholly reliable yet an invaluable source for future historians.

Overall, Witte's career could be held to illustrate the limits of Russian reformability. The autocratic-bureaucratic régime showed itself capable of accommodating the reforming outsider and rough diamond. If Witte could not achieve everything he wished, he was yet given the opportunity to accomplish a great deal and the tsarist régime would emerge from the Witte era at least partially restructured. Although the original 'Witte System' helped to bring about a revolutionary crisis, Witte also contributed greatly to its relatively successful termination. Both his perestroikas struck root and, between them created the conditions for something like a new start. At the same time, Witte's political career was twice cut short by conservative (anti-perestroika) opponents he had no chance of defeating. Major aspects of the old autocratic-bureaucratic order proved ineradicable, not least the autocracy and a semi-autonomous bureaucratic officialdom. The reformer was forced to operate within the parameters set by Russian historic development. Anything new had to be established in a largely hostile environment.

In the shorter term, Witte left behind formidable problems not entirely of his making. Disorders continued. The agrarian crisis persisted. The working class was left sullen and resentful. The liberals were disgruntled. More specifically it remained to be seen how far ministers answerable to the tsar could combine this with a limited accountability to an elected legislative assembly. And, in a different sphere, how could a poor and recently humiliated country rebuild its armed forces, recover its self esteem and regain its international prestige? The problems Witte's successors would have to tackle were nothing if not formidable.

NOTES

1. Edward J. Bing, ed: *The Letters of Tsar Nicholas and Empress Marie* (London, 1937), Nikolai to Maria, 27 October 1905, pp 190–2.
2. *Ibid.*
3. *Ibid.*
4. *Ibid.*
5. *Ibid.*
6. *Ibid*, p 193.
7. *Ibid*, Nikolai to Maria, 10 November 1905, pp 194–5.
8. *Ibid.*
9. *Ibid*, p 195.
10. *Graf Witte: Erinnerungen* (Berlin, 1923), p 395.
11. Bing, ed: *Letters*, Nikolai to Maria, 8 December 1905, pp 200–2.
12. *Ibid*, Nikolai to Maria, 22 Dec 1905, pp 205–6.
13. A. L. Sidorov, ed: *S. Yu. Vitte: Vospominania* (Moscow, 1960), vol III, p 129.
14. Bing, ed: *Letters*, Nikolai to Maria, 8 December 1905, p 201.
15. *Ibid*, Nikolai to Maria, 12 January 1906, p 212.
16 A. L. Sidorov, ed: *Vitte: Vospominania*, vol III, pp 337–41.
17. *Ibid.*

Part VII

P. A. Stolypin

13

Stolypin and the Duma

Witte's resignation, contrary he claims to his expectation and wishes, brought with it that of the bulk of his cabinet. The tsar and Trepov preferred to face the coming Duma with a new team. When Nikolai II consulted the outgoing premier on the choice of a successor Witte, as was his wont, had offered two alternatives. If the tsar intended sincerely to implement the manifesto in the spirit as well as the letter, he advised, a suitable candidate would be the outgoing State Controller Filosofov. If, on the other hand, he intended to interpret the manifesto in a restrictive sense Akimov, the retiring Minister of Justice would be the proper choice. Nikolai therefore approached Akimov who, however, declined the honour. After consulting Prince Meshchersky and encouraged by Trepov, the tsar's choice then fell on Witte's old rival Goremykin. Confident that Goremykin – elderly, indolent and by this time cynical – would at all times unquestioningly take his orders from the Palace, Nikolai, invited him to head the new government.

Three key ministries remained to be filled, those of the interior, justice and finance. At Durnovo's first interview following Witte's resignation, the tsar asked him to stay on. Within two days, however, an imperial *ukaz*, announced his retirement (with, according to Witte, a golden handshake of 200,000 rubles). Some time before Durnovo had fallen out with Trepov who, in any case, had his own candidate. Already the previous August, he had drawn the tsar's attention to the Governor of Saratov, P. A. Stolypin. It was to Stolypin's 'energy, complete efficiency and entirely sensible actions' coupled with his great physical courage and the ability to calm unruly mobs that Trepov attributed the restoration or order in that province. Stolypin's reputa-

207

tion as an administrator combining courage, firmness and tact (in some ways a second Loris-Melikov) had in fact been spreading in bureaucratic circles. Yet when Nikolai II and Trepov took their 'leap in the dark' Stolypin was still, so far as the St Petersburg bureaucracy at large was concerned, an unknown quantity. Unlike the majority of his predecessors, he had never served in the police department. Member of a prosperous gentry family in the northwestern province of Kovno, Stolypin had started his career as the government-appointed marshal of nobility for that province.[1] In 1903 he was appointed Governor of the neighbouring province of Grodno. The following year, he was transferred to the restive Volga province of Saratov. His service experience, like Witte's, differed from that of the typical St Petersburg mandarin.

This was not the case with V. N. Kokovtsev, reappointed after a brief interlude, as Minister of Finance. A competent official with a judiciously low political profile, Kokovtsev would continue Witte's economic policies. On his reappointment, a new Ministry of Trade and Industry was carved out of Witte's overgrown empire and placed in the charge of D. A. Filosofov. The continuity of economic policy seemed assured.

To fill the Ministry of Justice vacated by Akimov, Trepov and the tsar once more turned to that reservoir of reactionary ministers, the law faculty of Moscow university. Their choice fell on I. G. Shcheglovitov, a professor by a strange irony considered a liberal sympathizer. Could Nikolai II and Trepov have anticipated that during his nine-year tenure he would do his best to emasculate the judicial reforms, to flout legality and to tamper with the independence of the Russian judiciary?

A further appointment of significance was that of a new Foreign Minister, a post which Lamsdorff, scapegoat for the Japanese fiasco, was obliged to vacate. His chosen successor was a career diplomat, A. P. Izvolsky, an erratic and vain opportunist, a dandy and snob with a craving for social recognition and diplomatic coups.

With Witte and Durnovo, the two 'strong men' of the previous administration removed and Goremykin a cypher, what emerged was effectively a cabinet headed de facto by Trepov. That the new administration was politically to the right of Witte's was symptomatic of this, while being to some extent fortuitous.[2] What was significant was that Trepov, who in the past had shown evidence of tactical flexibility, might now be expected to oversee the implementation of Witte's political perestroika.

I

The principal task facing the new administration would be that of initiating relations between the government (the tsarist bureaucracy) and the Duma representing a substantial part of the Russian people. The elections still held under the auspices of Witte and Durnovo without undue administrative interference had produced a chamber containing two major political groupings. The Constitutional Democrats or Cadets had secured some 180 seats out of a total of 524. Together with their allies, they commanded a near majority. Their major objectives included, besides an amnesty for political offenders, the introduction of ministerial responsibility, an extension of the franchise, a change in electoral procedures and the full implementation of civil rights; in short a radical democratization of the political system. For this purpose, they wished either to convert the Duma into a constituent assembly or to have such an assembly elected. In addition to such far-reaching constitutional changes, the Cadets were committed to an agrarian reform programme including, if necessary, the expropriation of a large part of privately-owned land with compensation well below its market value.

A second group of deputies consisted of some 200 peasant representatives (both working peasants and members of the growing peasant intelligentsia). Of these 107 formed a loosely knit grouping calling themselves *Trudoviki* (Toilers). Their principal object, besides a general amnesty (above all for offenders sentenced in connection with agrarian crime), was the expropriation of privately-owned estates without compensation and their distribution among the peasantry. Although the social policy of the Trudoviks was thus more radical than that favoured by the Cadets and though they cared less for parliamentary niceties and procedures, the objectives of the two groups overlapped sufficiently to make possible a large measure of co-operation between them. The government was thus faced with a solid oppositional phalanx whose demands it could not concede. Confrontation was inevitable.

On 27 April 1906 Nikolai II received members of Duma and State Council at the Winter Palace. His decorous if brief allocution was confined to banal platitudes. After returning to their own chamber, Duma deputies then chose with near unanimity Sergei Muromtsev, a prominent Cadet and former professor of Roman Law as their president. A passionate personal plea for a general amnesty by the veteran leader of the Liberation Movement and oldest Duma deputy Ivan Petrunkevich concluded the day's proceedings. It was becoming clear that the question of an amnesty which, under the Fundamental Laws was a royal prerogative, would provoke the first clash between Duma and ministers.

Following the example of the British House of Commons, the Anglophile Cadet leadership, ignoring the differences in the respective situations, decided to reply to the tsar's vacuous speech with an Address to the Throne. In respectful language it called for a number of constitutional changes. Of these, two were of special significance. Faith in the government the address declared, could be strengthened only by a ministry enjoying the Duma's confidence. Such faith, essential to 'peaceful and proper working' would emerge only with ministers 'responsible before the people's representatives' and no longer permitted to 'commit violence while hiding behind the name of your Imperial Majesty'. This was a request which struck at the very basis of the political system set up by the Fundamental Laws. If conceded, monarchical prerogative would, effectively, be superseded by popular sovereignty. To this, the principal desideratum of the Cadets, was added that of the peasantry. The most pressing task before the Duma, the address declared, was the satisfaction of the peasants' desperate need for land. To alleviate that need it was necessary, besides drawing on state, monastic and royal lands, to envisage also 'the compulsory confiscation of private estates'.

In addition to these basic desiderata, the address, for good measure, called also for the abolition of the State Council, an enlargement of the Duma's legislative competence, a radical democratization of the franchise, the abolition of states of emergency and of the death penalty, legalized freedom for workers to organize and to strike and the removal of every form of discrimination on grounds of religion, nationality, sex or class. To crown all, there was a request for a 'full political amnesty, as the first pledge of mutual understanding and co-operation between tsar and people'. The nation, the address added, awaited 'the immediate suspension of all death sentences' until such time as the Duma should abolish capital punishment forever. In fact, as passed by the Duma in the small hours of 5 May without opposition (with some ten abstentions) the document was less an address to the tsar than a revolutionary manifesto addressed to the electorate, to the Russian public and indeed to the country at large. So far as the government was concerned it was a declaration of war.

The official reaction was predictable. The tsar refused to receive the deputation chosen to present the address. It was instead handed to one of the ministers. On 13 May, Goremykin presented himself in the Duma at the head of his colleagues to deliver the government's reply. He did so in a monotonous voice, in the words of one present like 'a schoolmaster reading a lesson'. The Duma's major requests, he declared, involved radical amendments to the Fundamental Laws. These, however, were not susceptible to revision on the initiative of the State Duma. As regards land reform, any measure involving compulsory expropriation of privately owned land was 'absolutely inadmissible'. The principle of the inalienability and inviolability of private property was the fundamental rule of government throughout the world. Private property, the 'cornerstone of public well-being' must be upheld as without it, the existence of the state was unthinkable. To alleviate peasant poverty which he did not deny, Goremykin listed a number of palliatives already adopted without significant impact.

Following Goremykin's statement, deputies exploded with indignation. One furious speech followed another, while the premier 'sat silently smoothing his whiskers'. Presently, taking advantage of a recess, the ministers withdrew. One, on returning later, declared in reply to the debate, that the government took its stand on the laws of the empire. Where these were imperfect they might, in time, be amended. In the meantime, however, they must be obeyed as they stood. In the subsequent debate, Cadet speakers called for the resignation of the government. In conclusion the Duma, by an overwhelming majority, expressed its lack of confidence in the government and called on it to resign. Deadlock had been reached. Ministers, of course, had no intention of resigning. At the end of a ministerial meeting, Goremykin declared that it was their common duty 'to bear up patiently under our intolerable situation until we should clearly see that there was nothing more to hope for'.[3]

Ministers, however, were looking for a way out of the impasse. During June, on the initiative of Trepov and Izvolsky and with the tsar's blessing, exploratory talks were opened about the possibility of a change of government. Those involved included Stolypin and, on behalf of the Duma Muromtsev, Shipov and Paul Miliukov, leader of the Cadet Party. Accounts of the exchanges held in great secrecy present a confusing picture. They opened, it appears, with Trepov on authorization from the tsar approaching Miliukov about the possibility of forming a Cadet ministry. About Trepov's motives and degree of sincerity there has been inconclusive speculation. It might, however, be reasonably surmised that the general, who had before then shown tactical flexibility, considered that the tsar would have little to lose in installing a Cadet administration. In the first place, it appeared almost certain that Stolypin, whose calm, rational and authoritative speeches in the Duma gained him respect even among Cadets would remain at the Ministry of the Interior. A Cadet ministry, moreover, was likely if successful to drive a wedge between the Cadets – obliged to support continuing repression and their Trudovik and peasant allies. If, on the other hand, the ministry proved a failure, the Cadets would be discredited and a pretext furnished for a dissolution of the Duma. The risk from the government's point of view was likely to be slight.

It may be that Trepov had made his first approach with considerations such as these in mind.

In the meantime, Izvolsky was engaged in soundings about the formation of a coalition government of open-minded bureaucrats and carefully selected public men. Again, the tsar authorized exploratory talks. Izvolsky and Stolypin approached Shipov a key figure in any possible coalition. Shipov replied that no such government was possible without the participation of Cadets. Clearly a handful of isolated moderates would have found themselves in an impossible position, caught between the bureaucratic majority on the one hand and the Duma majority on the other. They themselves represented little more than the eleven abstainers on the no-confidence motion. Shipov then sent his friend, Count P. A. Geiden to consult Miliukov, who expressed the view that the only rational solution would be the formation of a Cadet ministry. Muromtsev was mentioned as a possible premier. Shipov then approached Muromtsev with the suggestion that he might head a new government with a strong Cadet representation. Muromtsev demurred, suggesting that any ministry containing Cadets must be headed by their leader Miliukov. Nothing daunted, Shipov in an audience with the tsar (28 June), advised the appointment of a Cadet ministry under Muromtsev. The Cadets in office, he argued, would be tamed by responsibility while the Duma would be ready to co-operate with a Cadet ministry. Shipov left the interview under the impression that the tsar was favourably inclined. Indeed, it appears that both Miliukov and Muromtsev may have been expecting an imperial summons. The call never came. Instead, after some days, the tsar opted for the alternative solution. On Sunday 9 July, an official proclamation announced the dissolution of the first Imperial Duma.

The question has been raised by historians as to the sincerity of the tsar and Trepov in initiating these exploratory talks. In fact, there can be little doubt in the seriousness of their intentions. No reason has ever been advanced why Trepov, Stolypin and the tsar should have engaged in an elaborate charade. Why, in particular, should the tsar have received Shipov as late as 28 June? Again, why was the dissolution of the Duma delayed? The possibility had been considered for weeks. It could have been carried out with a degree of justification any time after the end of May. The evidence suggests the seriousness of the attempt to reach an accommodation.

Why then did the tsar change his mind? Conventional wisdom has sought the explanation in contrary influences, palace influences, the admonitions of Kokovtsev and possibly of Stolypin. A Duma proclamation on the agrarian question (6 July) has been considered the proximate cause of its dissolution. However, the true reason for the abandonment of the talks, bearing in mind the subsequent course of events, may well have been a different one. It is clear that the tsar, when authorizing the soundings, had already decided to get rid of the ineffectual Goremykin. He had also made up his mind that, in any new government Stolypin, with his proven skill at handling the refractory Duma, must occupy a key position. Stolypin's star was in the ascendant as demonstrated by his role in the conversations. He would, at the very least, remain Minister of the Interior. It is possible that Miliukov may, at some stage, have indicated his unwillingness to include so stern a counter-revolutionary in a possible Cadet cabinet. Stolypin himself may have argued against the formation of a Cadet ministry from which he might conceivably have been excluded. For either side, the difficulties of co-operation would have been great, perhaps insurmountable. This, in all probability, was understood by both parties. The exploratory talks, almost certainly, were doomed to failure.

In this situation someone, it may have been Stolypin himself, hit on a different solution. Stolypin in all probability would become the new premier while at the same time retaining the Ministry of the Interior. He would then resume the attempt to form a coalition ministry, possibly without the Cadets. In these circumstances it might help to dissolve the Duma and, in due course, trust to the luck of the ballot. During the interval between dumas, it would be possible to legislate under Article 87 of the Fundamental Laws. Some legislative projects would then be ready for submission to the new Duma, thus remedying a notable earlier deficiency. This was a plausible scenario to have formed in Stolypin's mind. It was, in any event, what would actually occur.

The suspension of the exploratory talks by the dissolution of the Duma has been widely seen as a missed opportunity. In all probability it was not. For the reasons indicated, the talks were almost certain to fail. With widespread disorder still rampant, the tsar would in no circumstances have handed over the Ministry of the Interior to an inexperienced and untrustworthy Cadet, nor have parted with his new favourite Stolypin. No opportunity was in fact lost – the exploratory talks would simply be resumed in somewhat different circumstances.

The story of the demise of the first Duma and with it the eclipse of Trepov, of Goremykin and of Muromtsev, is quickly told. (Trepov had been losing influence and would die in the course of the autumn.) On 20 June, the government published a statement outlining in broad terms its future agrarian policy. It ruled out the expropriation of privately-owned land. In reply, the Duma on 6 July reminded the Russian public that any legislation on the land question would require its approval. Everyone therefore should calmly await its future legislation. In addressing a direct appeal to the Russian people the Duma almost certainly exceeded its constitutional competence. Within two days, after consulting Goremykin and Stolypin, the tsar decided to dissolve it. The decree was published on 9 July.

On receiving notice of the dissolution some 200 deputies (120 Cadets, the rest mainly Trudoviks) repaired to Vyborg in nearby (autonomous) Finland. From there, they appealed to the Russian nation, pending the convocation of a new Duma, to withhold taxes and refuse enrolment as recruits. The appeal fell on deaf ears. Deceived by their own rhetoric, the deputies had misjudged the popular mood. The main result of the Vyborg appeal would be the prosecution of the signatories, automatically debarring them from future Duma service. Their trial with prison sentences of three months would not take place until late the following year. Leading Cadets would thus be excluded from the new Duma.

Shortly before the dissolution, Goremykin informed his ministerial colleagues that he had been relieved of his duties. His successor would be Stolypin, who would also retain the Ministry of the Interior. Stolypin at once resumed his soundings about the formation of a coalition government. On 15 July he met some public men including the pivotal Shipov. The terms they demanded were stiff. Of a total of 13 ministerial posts, the public men claimed seven: the interior, justice, education, agriculture, trade, the procuratorship and state control. They also laid down conditions on major policy issues. The government must publicly declare its resolve to reorganize and extend peasant landownership where this was recommended by local agricultural authorities. Compulsory expropriation however was to be avoided. No more death sentences should be carried out. A sweeping political amnesty would exclude only those guilty of murder or of serious offences against property. A new Duma must convene no later than 1 December. Stolypin understandably rejected these terms. The demands of the so-called moderates like those for the Ministry of the Interior and for a majority of seats in the new cabinet were unrealistic. Local option land reform with possible expropriations and a sweeping political amnesty also could hardly be entertained. The proposed date for the convocation of a new Duma was outside the realm of possibility. Indeed, the nature of the terms demanded must raise doubts as to the sincerity of Shipov, Lvov and those they represented.

With 'collective' negotiations thus stalled Stolypin, with the tsar's approval approached individual moderates. On 20 July, the tsar received N. N. Lvov, a moderate *zemstvo* leader and A. F. Guchkov, to both of whom Stolypin had offered portfolios. Both refused to serve. So did A. D. Samarin, a respected public figure, twice received by the tsar and offered the procuratorship. 'They hold their own convictions in higher esteem than patriotism,' Nikolai II reported, 'and seem to be guided by false modesty on the one hand, and fear of committing themselves on the other. We will manage without them never fear!'[4] The exploratory talks had thus broken down, never to be resumed.

What is significant about the exchanges is the persistence of ministers in pursuing them and the backing they received from the tsar. Equally worth noting are the unrealistic demands put forward by the public men as the price of their co-operation. The reluctance of individual moderates to serve with a majority of bureaucrats and to share responsibility for inevitable repression is however only too understandable. What the exchanges demonstrated was the lack of any basis for the formation of a coalition government. Stolypin now knew that his object of seeking an accommodation with political moderates must be pursued by other means. His ministry, following the departure of three leading reactionaries moved somewhat towards the centre.

II

Having reconstituted the government, Stolypin could turn to urgent public business. The foremost task for many months to come would be the restoration of public order. The suppression of the December uprising in Moscow did not end the revolutionary disorders. According to official figures, some 1,600 people, mainly officials, were killed by terrorists during 1906. The figure for 1907, would exceed 2,500. There were still some major incidents. In July a three-day mutiny took place in the garrison of Sveaborg. Kronstadt and the battleship *Pamiat Azova* were also affected. Then on 12 August, a hitherto unknown terrorist group, the Maximalists, a faction of the Socialist Revolutionaries, blew up Stolypin's summer residence in St Petersburg. Twenty-seven lives were lost including those of the dynamiters. Among the injured were Stolypin's young daughter and baby son, though he himself escaped unhurt. The following day a female terrorist killed General Min, equerry to the tsar, who had led the suppression of the Moscow rising.

Stolypin answered terror with terror. On 19 August a state of emergency was declared covering the greater part of the empire. Under Article 87 of the Fundamental Laws provincial governors were empowered to set up field courts-martial authorized to try suspects within 24 hours of a criminal act. Sentence would be carried out immediately. Between September 1906 and April 1907, when the courts-martial were abolished, 683 death sentences, according to official statistics, were carried out. The true figure was almost certainly considerably higher.

The revolutionaries replied in kind. On 30 August the tsar reported to his mother an alleged attempt to kill him. (It may have been a half-hearted operation, possibly foiled by Azev). During the months which followed, two provincial governors, the Governor-General of Warsaw, the Military Commandant of St Petersburg and the Chief Military Prosecutor fell victim to terrorist attacks.

Nor were these the only acts of violence. The dissolution of the Duma was followed by a series of so-called expropriations, armed robberies organized by parties of the far Left in association with criminal elements. Among the more spectacular was one in October 1906 when Maximalists armed with bombs and revolvers attacked and robbed an official carrying state funds outside a bank in St Petersburg. They escaped with booty of 400,000 rubles. It was such expropriators together with killers of officials and perpetrators of peasant violence who appeared before the courts-martial. In a desperate struggle between terror and counter-terror, legality inevitably went by the board. There was little room for legal niceties. Not until well into 1907 did the government with an extensive use of *agents provocateurs*, super-grasses and various covert operations, finally gain the upper hand. It may be questioned whether historians are justified in castigating Stolypin's illegalities, as they have consistently done. This was a cruel civil war waged ruthlessly by both sides and one in which Queensbery Rules did not apply. So far as the government was concerned, the plea of self-defence could, with some plausibility, be advanced. A ruthless represion was, moreover, a necessary prerequisite for Stolypin to retain the tsar's confidence.

The law of 9 November, the centrepiece of Stolypin's agrarian reform legislation, had a long and chequered pre-history. Ever since the 1870s reformers had become increasingly convinced that the problem of peasant farming in Russia was less one of land shortage than of inefficient land use.[5] The peasants were 'backward' and unable or unwilling to change their wasteful and unproductive farming methods. Three aspects of traditional peasant farming in particular were blamed for the backwardness of the Russian village: three-field crop rotation, open-field land utilization and communal landholding with its system of intermingled strips and, in many cases, periodic redistributions. It was these obstacles to efficient farming which, in the view of the reformers had to be removed.

After much inconclusive discussion and some bureaucratic investigations the government, under the impression of a partial famine in 1901 finally resolved on the need for legislative action. On 23 January 1902, Nikolai II had set up, under the chairmanship of Witte, the

'Special conference on the needs of agriculture'. The conference, consisting at the beginning of 19 members including the Ministers of the Interior and Agriculture, was instructed to

> discuss all questions relating to agriculture and all related areas of the people's work in order to propose measures to His Imperial Majesty concerning the most immediate needs, including the ways and means for their practical accomplishment and to submit the opinions of the Conference and of its separate members to His Imperial Majesty on questions of general administrative character where they have significance to the rural economy.[6]

This was an extensive brief. From the start, it revealed the dichotomy in the government plans between providing relief for the poorest peasants and measures for the improvement of rural productivity.

The conference proceeded to set up a network of local committees at both *uezd* and provincial level composed of local officials selected by the government and others chosen by local interests, notably *zemstvo* assemblies. During the first part of 1903, the conference received their reports and recommendations. An abridged version of the reports was published in 58 volumes, a boiled down version divided into topics in 23. Early in 1905, the conference began preparing a draft law. On 30 March it was unceremoniously disbanded.

In fact, a rival organization had long preceded it. Already in 1894, the Ministry of the Interior (MVD) had addressed an elaborate questionnaire on peasant matters to provincial governors who had, in turn, consulted local officials. The replies – filling a mere four volumes – had been published in 1897. In 1901 the tsar had asked Sipyagin to submit the collected materials together with his considerations on what should be done. On 14 January 1902, Sipyagin was instructed to prepare a draft law on the reform of village administration. After his assassination, Plehve reconvened the original editing commission of 1894. By October 1903 the MVD had published its draft laws. On 8 January 1904, the land section of the Ministry instructed governors to convene local conferences to discuss the drafts. Many did so, but proceedings were delayed by the Japanese War. When the replies were finally analysed, it emerged that many reports were missing and that those which had been received were confused and inconsistent.

The chaotic and unco-ordinated proceedings of those inveterate enemies the Ministries of Finance and the Interior, while producing a mass of materials, were ill designed to lead to consistent legislation. Indeed activities since 1902 had been nothing so much as a power struggle between Witte and Plehve for control of the coming reform.

Nonetheless, as Yaney concludes, in spite of their inconclusive results, 'the MVD's editing commission and Witte's special conference constituted the foundation from which the reform laws evolved'. In spite of the lack of concerted policies, both were in broad agreement that 'private property should somehow replace communal landholding'. Peasants should not be coerced but should be permitted to take part in the transformation of landholding. This was to be 'enabling' legislation.

On 26 February Nikolai II issued a manifesto which Yaney compares to Aleksandr II's Rescript to Nazimov. In it, the tsar committed himself publicly to the introduction of major changes in the rural economy. While the coming reforms would be based on the inviolability of communal landholding they would at the same time provide means by which peasants could depart from the village. (The parallels with today's attempts to privatize parts of *kolchozy* and *sovchozy* hardly need pointing out.)

Action, however, was slow to follow. In the spring of 1905, a conference was set up under the chairmanship of Goremykin with instructions to work out the principles on which the coming reform should be based. The proceedings of the conference dragged on until January 1906. Its proposals, when they did emerge, were largely ignored. It did, however, sketch out a plan for the creation of a land reform organization which would form the basis for future activities. Finally a decree of 6 May 1905 set up an inter-ministerial Committee on Land Problems with the remit to draw up legislative proposals. In a compromise between the rival pretensions of the MVD and Ministry of Finance, it was resolved that the Ministry of Agriculture (MZ) should be the chief executive agent of the coming reform. Agents of the MVD (governors and land captains), and those of the Ministry of Finance (the Peasant Land Bank and, curiously, the *zemstva*) would co-operate with the central land settlement organization of the Ministry of Agriculture. That Ministry was, at the same time, demoted to the rank of a chief administration, allegedly to provide an opportunity for removing Witte's long-standing ally, the minister, Ermolov. Another object may have been to strengthen the position of the MVD.

Three men played the major part in drafting the reform legislation: Witte, A. V. Krivoshein and V. M. Gurko. Witte, between 1896 and 1899 had become convinced of the need for radical changes in peasant society. The object must be 'to make more farm products available for urban and foreign markets and contribute more revenue to the government'.[7] Agrarian reform was needed to support industrial growth. It was here that Witte's priorities differed radically from those of the MVD which was concerned primarily with the welfare of the poorer peasants in the interest of social stability. In Witte's view, the bulk of the peasantry should be left to fend for itself. It was the small minority of the more prosperous and enterprising which should be encouraged. If they wished, they should be enabled to secede from the village commune. Individual peasants should also be encouraged to dispose of their strips and to move from their villages to new consolidated homesteads, *khutors*. Where Witte stood for progress, measured mainly in terms of productivity, Plehve and the MVD placed the emphasis instead on peasant welfare. They would therefore seek to preserve the traditional village commune likely to be preferred by the bulk of the peasantry and to mitigate land shortage by the provision of additional land for peasant settlement. Interestingly, in his battle with the MVD Witte sought the alliance of elements in the hitherto detested *zemstva*. A law of 1901 had given him a large measure of control over their finances. The following year, he not only offered them generous subsidies but, as chairman of his conference encouraged them to put forward their views on peasant reform. They would form some counterweight to the land captains, the principal local agents of the MVD.

A second 'father' of the reform was A. V. Krivoshein of whom Yaney writes that if any one man could be called 'the creator of the "Stolypin" Reform it would be he'. Since 1887 Krivoshein had made his career in the Land Section of the MVD. In 1896, he became a vice-director of the department in charge of peasant resettlement in Siberia. In 1902, he became its director. When in 1905 the department was transferred to the Ministry of Agriculture, Krivoshein moved with it, now with the rank of deputy minister. In October 1906, he changed ministry once more. He became deputy minister in the Ministry of Finance, this time to head the Peasant and Gentry Land Banks. In May 1908 he was appointed director of the newly-created Department of Land Settlement and Agriculture, a post he would fill until 1915. It made him overall director of the reform.

Critics claimed that Krivoshein was an opportunist who changed opinions in accordance with changing political circumstances. Witte considered him a scoundrel and even threatened resignation in 1906 to prevent his appointment as minister. Krivoshein, Yaney observes, 'had more experience at dealing with the ups and downs of peasant reform than either of his fellow-enactors'. He was essentially a pragmatist. In February 1906 he stated his views on reform:

'The government must leave off proclaiming promises and begin at last to act. It must begin to carry out its laboriously prepared, exhaustively studied, but until now very little implemented measures to improve peasant conditions. The important thing is to act, to begin the reform, and let action itself show us the best means to accomplish our aims.'[8]

The third major figure, placed 'at the heart of the government's efforts at land reform' V. I. Gurko, had for several years served in the imperial chancery, the nerve centre of bureaucratic administration. He then transferred to the MVD to become the head of its Land Section from 1902 to the end of 1906. In a book written in 1902, Gurko advocated permitting individual peasants to claim their strips as private property and to convert them into consolidated *khutors*. He would later claim that his 'hidden agenda' at the time had already included dismantling the village commune. The weaker peasants should no longer be protected as hitherto. Left to themselves, they might perhaps perish, but their demise would have little significance for human progress and for the vital strength of a people and its government. In fact, their removal might even prove beneficial. By enabling a few individual peasants to exchange their strips for *khutors*, with their example hopefully being followed by others, the reform would in time break up the entire communal system of landholding. Gurko's object was 'the rationalization of peasant land-use by reforms carried out directly on allotment land'. Consolidation was to be achieved by means of a succession of radical distributions of communal land. The eventual 'Stolypin Reform' would largely reflect Gurko's approach.

Omitted from Yaney's list of major architects of the reform is none other than Stolypin himself. Of three major reforms, two had already been enacted before he came to St Petersburg in April 1906. The outlines of the third, the crucial law of 9 November, with whose objects he was in sympathy, had by then been generally accepted by the government. Stolypin had thus been absent from the capital when the reform legislation was being drafted.

Three measures prepared under the aegis of Witte in November 1905 paved the way for the liberation of peasants from communal control. While the first created the legal framework for private ownership of communal land, the second provided resources for the setting up of *khutors*. The third set up the machinery for implementing the reform. Together they formed the basis for the law of 9 November. That law, reflecting the views of Krivoshein and Gurko rather than those of Witte and Kutler was less radical than earlier proposals. 'All the elaborate schemes for a rural legal order that were drafted and half-drafted between 1902 and 1904 were buried.' With the law of 9 November Stolypin and Krivoshein finally succeeded, after the endless 'palavering' and in-fighting, in getting land settlement on the road. Its operation and results will be considered later.

By the *ukaz* of 9 November, the government committed itself to the weakening and progressive abolition of communal landownership in favour of private property in land. 'Every head of household', the first crucial paragraph laid down, 'who owns *nadel* [allotment or communal] land in accordance with the custom of the *mir* [village commune] has the right at any time to demand that his share of this land should be confirmed to him as private property.' Paragraph 12 provided for the second stage of the process; the consolidation of plots and the establishment of compact farmsteads. 'Every householder,' it ran, 'to whom parts of the communal land have been allocated as indicated has the right to demand at any time that the commune in exchange for his shares shall allocate to him an equivalent holding so far as possible in one place.' While the intention of the legislators was clear, the manner of its implementation was not. Some major details would not be finally settled until 1911. In the meantime those charged with supervising land settlement, would have to proceed in the spirit adumbrated by Krivoshein, operating from case to case guided less by defective laws than by peasant reactions and the light of their own judgment.

The potential implications of the rural perestroika envisaged by the legislators were far-reaching. What Stolypin would demagogically describe as his 'wager on the strong' would, hopefully, free a minority of enterprising peasants from the shackles imposed by traditional methods enforced by the commune. Private property in land, and with it an embryonic land-market in allotment land, would be established. Consolidation of strips into compact plots would become a possibility. In the longer term, a minority of peasant households might become the nucleus of a new, reasonably prosperous 'property-owning democracy'. In Stolypin's mind, the political implications of land settlement in the longer term would almost certainly outweigh its purely economic aspects.

III

The government, meanwhile announced that the new Duma would convene on 20 February 1907. The announcement was followed, almost immediately, by the opening of the election campaign. Unlike those for the first Duma, the new elections were no longer confined to Cadets and the somewhat amorphous Trudoviki. Further contestants stood ready to enter the fray. On the left, both Social Democrats and Social Revolutionaries, who had boycotted the previous elections, would enter the campaign. In the centre the Union of 17 October, generally known as Octobrists, was challenging the Cadets, more particularly in rural areas in the *curiae* of landowners. Led by Aleksandr Guchkov, the Octobrists, heirs to the moderate *zemstvo* men, adopted as their platform the full implementation of the October

Manifesto within the framework of the Fundamental Laws. More specifically, they called for a string of 'organic reforms' in areas like the safeguarding of civil rights, religious toleration and the reform of local government. The Octobrists, in fact, were putting forward a programme not greatly different from that of Stolypin. On the extreme Right, monarchist organizations were campaigning on a platform of undiluted autocracy, Great Russian chauvinism and hostility to Jews, Poles and Finns. The leading monarchist organization, the Union of the Russian People, dating from October 1906 and headed by a doctor, Aleksandr Dubrovin, enjoyed the patronage of elements of the aristocracy, the court, the senior bureaucracy and last, not least, the sympathies of Nikolai II himself. The union in its turn patronized the notorious 'Black Hundreds', gangs of militant thugs dedicated to the instigation of anti-Jewish pogroms and to the fight against revolutionaries, students and liberals.

The election campaign fought during January and February and marked by harassment of Cadet clubs and meetings, while still leaving the Cadets the dominant influence, greatly strengthened the parties of the Left. Social Democrats, Socialist Revolutionaries, People's Socialists and Trudoviks between them won a total of 214 seats as against 92 for the Cadets, 32 for Octobrists and other moderate conservatives and 22 for Right extremists. Some 160 deputies were without party affiliations or represented national or local interests. Some 90 deputies might be classified as government supporters. There was little prospect that a Duma thus constituted would work smoothly with Stolypin's government.

Convening on 20 February, deputies turned their attention to the legislation promulgated under Article 87 of the Fundamental Laws. While opposition members savaged the field courts-martial, ministers in their turn castigated revolutionary terror and vainly called on Cadet deputies to join them. The differences between government and opposition were once more shown to be irreconcilable.

On 6 March 1907, Stolypin presented the government's legislative programme. Besides its centrepiece, the agrarian law, this included proposals for the reform of local government in rural areas, reform of the lower courts and the legalization of trade unions; all except the first modest in scope. Duma deputies were little interested in such chicken-feed.

The main clash with the government came over the bill on land reform. When it became clear that this keystone of his legislative programme would be thrown out, Stolypin resolved on another dissolution. To secure a more pliable future Duma, moreover, he decided to alter the electoral system. Ever since his appointment as Minister of the Interior, his assistant Kryzhanovsky had in fact been working secretly on a new electoral law. Well before the elections for the Second Duma, this had already been approved by the Council of Ministers. Since its prospective defeat over the agrarian bill (the true cause of the dissolution) would damage the government's standing, a pretext had to be found. During the budget debate, a Social Democratic deputy had launched an intemperate attack on the army and, by implication, the tsar. Outrage had been expressed by right-wing deputies. Dubrovin and his cohorts launched a campaign of telegrams calling on the tsar to dissolve the Duma. 'I am getting telegrams from everywhere,' Nikolai II noted, 'petitioning me to order a dissolution; but it is too early for that. One must let them do something manifestly stupid or mean, and then – slap! And they are gone!'[9]

The Duma, however, proved slow in furnishing the desired pretext. Then, on 4 May the police, after raiding the flat of a Social Democratic deputy, claimed to have found documents implicating SD deputies in a conspiracy to provoke military mutinies. The documents were soon found to be forgeries which, however, did not prevent Stolypin from demanding the lifting of parliamentary immunity from 55 SD deputies. The Duma decided to appoint a commission of 22 members to examine the charges and report within 48 hours. Before its report unmasking the documents as forgeries could be completed, the government dissolved the Duma for having failed to lift SD immunity immediately. On the morning of 3 June 1907 an imperial manifesto announced the dissolution. Elections for a new Duma would be held on 1 September. Simultaneously, the government promulgated its new electoral law. Sixteen SD deputies had already been arrested, a fate that now befell any others who failed to go into hiding. Nikolai II improved the shining occasion with a telegram to Dubrovin expressing agreement with the views of the union and rejoicing in its support.

Stolypin's proceedings were morally indefensible. Even the attempts of Social Democrats and Socialist Revolutionaries to set up revolutionary cells in the armed forces and intemperate speeches by left-wing deputies could not justify the manufacture of a shady and dishonourable pretext for dissolution. The promulgation of the new electoral law, in a manner specifically prohibited by the Fundamental Laws, was an unconstitutional act, later inaccurately described as a coup d'état. It was an indication of the readiness of tsar and government to play fast and loose with the new constitution. The tsar's telegram to Dubrovin, leader of a band of right-wing hooligans was a gratuitous insult, more especially to moderate centrist elements eager for the successful operation of the new semi-constitution. As against this, Stolypin could plead the political expediency of his proceedings. Two radical dumas, it could be argued, had demonstrated the impossibility of co-operation between a more or less democratically elected assembly and the government. There was no reason to believe that a third duma, elected under the same franchise, would produce different results. Stolypin, unlike extreme right-wingers, was however determined to preserve the Duma as an elective legislative body. He wished neither to abolish it nor yet to reduce it to a purely advisory role. His object in altering the electoral law was to secure an assembly prepared to co-operate with the government within the framework of the Fundamental Laws.

Linked to Stolypin's parliamentary strategy was the future of his agrarian perestroika. If the Duma rejected the agrarian bill as it had clearly been about to do, the government would be forced either to abandon the principal aim of its policy or to implement it in defiance of the legislature. Stolypin, for 'reasons of state', chose to cut the Gordian knot by unconstitutional means. The result would fulfil his expectations. Whether it also justified his proceedings must remain a matter of opinion. The Third Duma elected under the new franchise would, unlike its predecessors, be prepared to work with the government. The agrarian bill would be passed and the policy implemented within the terms of constitution.

IV

Kryzhanovsky's electoral law involved manipulation of a high order. Nearly all the towns which had elected radical deputies lost their separate representation and were merged with surrounding rural districts. In such towns as were permitted to keep their representation, electors were divided, by property, into two numerically unequal *curiae* with each electing the same number of deputies. As a deputy representing St Petersburg in the first (wealthy) *curia* would explain, his constituents could be gathered together in one room – something of an exaggeration. In rural areas also, a relatively small number of landowners would choose a majority of electors. Through joint electoral colleges, they had a voice even in the election of peasant deputies. Under the old electoral law peasants in European Russia had elected 2,529 delegates, landowners 1,963. Under the new law, the respective figures would be 1,168 and 2,644. The number of workers' delegates was reduced from 208 to 114. As a result, 230 landowners would elect one elector. So would 1,000 rich business men, 15,000 lower middle class voters, 60,000 peasants or 125,000 urban workers. By the use of separate national *curiae* in areas with ethnically mixed populations, Great Russian representation was artificially increased. Thus in Warsaw, while a handful of Russians elected one deputy, the mass of the Polish population chose the other. Overall, Polish representation was reduced from 36 deputies to 14. Similar discrimination was visited on other minorities. Some categories like migrant workers, previously disenfranchised by senatorial decisions, now formally lost the vote. Again, while the verification of mandates had until then been in the hands of the Duma, this was now transferred, in contravention of the Fundamental Laws, to the Minister of the Interior.

The end result of these manipulations was a large over-representation of the landed gentry at the expense of every other group; of the urban bourgeoisie in relation to the rest of town dwellers; of Orthodox Great Russians as against religious or ethnic minorities. The bureaucracy, disappointed in the peasant vote, was now seeking instead a political alliance with the loyalist gentry and the urban bourgeoisie.

The outcome of the elections fulfilled the government's expectations. Before analysing the results certain facts have to be borne in mind. Party organization was loose. With many deputies coming to St Petersburg without clear party affiliations, they would only with time join one or other of the Duma factions (the term used for parliamentary groups above a minimum size). Some, to the end, never did. Again, the lines of division between adjoining factions were fluid and some deputies would pass from one to another. Some deputies died and were replaced by others. Factions were loosely organized, particularly those of the political Right. Covering a spectrum of political opinion some would show a tendency to fragment. By the end of its five-year term, the Duma would have substantially changed its composition.

Bearing in mind the fluidity of political allegiances, the composition of the Duma was as follows. The strongest group, numerically, was that of the Octobrists, with some 150 deputies elected in 1907, reduced to 120 by 1912. To their right, with some 70 members, sat the closely allied factions of the moderate Right and the Nationalists. By the end of the legislative period, their numbers had risen to 90, mainly at the expense of the Octobrists. Octobrists, moderate Right and Nationalists with an aggregate strength of some 220 deputies, constituted together a centre-Right working majority. From its ranks, the Duma would elect as its president an Octobrist, Nikolai Khomiakov, a moderate Slavophil. Octobrists would become chairmen also of the major Duma committees. The extreme Right mustered some 40–50 deputies, led by an unbalanced demagogue, V. M. Purishkevich. The unstrained language and scandalous behaviour of its deputies would disgust even the more gentlemanly representatives of the moderate Right. On the centre Left, the Cadet faction had shrunk to 50 (eventually 54) deputies. Together with the closely allied Progressists with 28 members (later increased to 40) they constituted a left-centre opposition with a combined strength of some 80–90. The decimated far Left consisted of 13 Trudoviks and 20 (eventually 14) Social Democrats.

The crucial groupings in the new Duma were, on the one hand, the Octobrists, on the other the Nationalists and moderate Right. The former, a heterogeneous group spanning a wide range of political opinions represented, as shown by their constituencies, mainly the landed gentry of the central provinces. Landowners of Baltic-German origin also played a prominent part. Ninety-nine Octobrist deputies belonged to the landed gentry, 10 were drawn from the peasantry, 15 connected with industry, commerce or banking. Many, at one time or another, had seen service in central or local government. In the words of Miliukov, the Octobrists were 'chiefly the party of former bureaucrats and functionaries'.[10]

While the moderate Right and Nationalists did not differ greatly from the Octobrists in their social profile, they were distinguished by the fact that they were drawn mainly from the Western provinces of the empire. There Great Russians often formed a minority among Ukrainians, White Russians, Poles and Jews. The Nationalists in particular besides monarchism, were protagonists of Great Russian ascendancy and of Russia one and indivisible. With farming methods superior to those of landowners in the interior, they also represented the interests of capitalist farming. The moderate Right and the Nationalists favoured reforms in matters like education and local government and indeed a general modernization of Russian society. Theirs was a grouping to which Stolypin, himself a landowner from the ethnically mixed northwest, had natural affinities.

The key figure in the new Duma was the Octobrist leader Aleksandr Guchkov. Grandson of a serf and son of a textile manufacturer and banker, he was himself associated with several commercial enterprises. He was a crucial link between the Octobrist landowners of the central provinces and sections of the Moscow commercial bourgeoisie. With Octobrists in control of the major Duma committees, he would become Stolypin's ally in the attempt to operate the modified semi-constitutional system. Their views were sufficiently close to provide the basis for an effective if temporary partnership. Government and Duma would now be able to collaborate. Work in the new Duma would also help to tame the Cadets, turning erstwhile allies of revolution into a parliamentary opposition. Moderate opinion was moving to the Right.[11] Stabilization would make Stolypin's centrist renovation a practical possibility.

V

While Stolypin was ruthlessly stamping out the last embers of revolution, he was determined, at the same time, to pursue a policy of renovation and reform. This extended to four main areas: agrarian reform, the armed forces, Russian control of the restive borderlands and miscellaneous reforms in education, local government, and the treatment of religious minorities. While there would throughout be some activity in all these spheres, the emphasis would change from time to time in accordance with political circumstances. The political forces involved in shaping the new measures were the tsar with his unofficial advisers, Stolypin himself and his ministerial colleagues, and the right-centre Duma groupings.[12] An important part would be played also by the reformed State Council with its permanent conservative majority.

The first task facing the new Duma was consideration of the *ukaz* of 9 November 1906. When the debates opened on 28 October 1908, no fewer than 210 deputies expressed a desire to be called. A majority, with Octobrists in the van, gave the bill enthusiastic support. It appeared to foreshadow the possibility of an extensive agricultural perestroika without compulsory expropriation. It held out the remoter promise of a growing conservative, self-reliant and relatively prosperous element among the peasantry. In the words of S. I. Shidlovsky, the Octobrist spokesman on peasant affairs: 'We have to develop in the village an environment that will educate the peasantry to be economically efficient and enterprising and therefore it has to be educated to respect private property.'[13] And again: 'The basis of a state of law is the free, energetic and independent individual. You will not get such an individual without providing him with the natural right of private property. I think that those who really strive to make our country a state ruled by law cannot oppose the private ownership of land.'[14] Private property, individual self-reliance and a rule of law and, with them, enterprise and economic efficiency were the keynotes of Octobrist policy. The collectivist commune, they argued, had been a negative influence alike on the peasantry and on the state.

Opposition to the bill came from several quarters. The Cadets (unconvincingly) called for its rejection on the ground that the *ukaz* of 6 November had, in their view, been improperly promulgated. Again, Miliukov argued that its object was merely to protect the selfish interests of some 130,000 gentry landowners. Criticism was voiced also by some Octobrist deputies. One, who however declared his intention of voting for the bill, expressed misgivings about the possible effects on Russian farming of overhasty privatization.[15] Another objected to amendments introduced by the Duma's Agrarian Committee with the object of facilitating secession from the commune. Peasant deputies – including Octobrists – predictably clamoured for further allocations of land. 'The peasants need land,' one speaker declared, 'and we as men of the land put our trust in the Duma that it will give us the land, peacefully and justly.' Others expressed misgivings about strengthening a small class of *kulaks* at the expense of the rest. 'We peasants,' one deputy declared, 'have to recognise with regret that this bill will not give land to those who do not have it or have very little. In consequence the agrarian problem, the burning problem of the peasants' life, will not be solved by this *ukaz*.'[16]

The debate dragged on until guillotined on 15 November. The bill would finally receive its third reading only on 24 April 1909 in the form submitted by the Duma's Agrarian Committee. In due course it was passed also by the reformed State Council and received the royal assent, a monument to the co-operation of government and Duma majority. Besides this major legislative act, the Duma would devote much of its time and energies to lesser agrarian measures. It would pass hundreds of government bills and vote the resources needed for the implementation of the new policies. In 1908, A. V. Krivoshein, the chief architect of the land reform programme, was appointed Director of a newly created Department of Land Settlement and Agriculture, a post he would occupy for a period of seven years.

VI

By the time the agrarian bill had finally passed into law, a new issue, that of military reorganization and re-equipment had forced itself on the attention of government and Duma. The Japanese War, like its predecessors, revealed weaknesses in Russian military organization. There were heavy losses of materiel, notably in the navy. A diplomatic confrontation with Austria-Hungary and her ally Germany in 1908–9 over the Austrian annexation of Bosnia and Herzegovina ended in a painful Russian defeat. Russia's armed forces were unable to contemplate the possibility of conducting a major war. Already before the Bosnian crisis Stolypin and Guchkov had agreed that a strengthening of the armed forces was an urgent necessity. Following the Bosnian affair, military reform and rearmament became the order of the day.

National defence was a field where tsar, government and Duma majority could co-operate. It was at the same time, a highly delicate sphere given the tsar's predictable touchiness about his military prerogative. More than once in an area where a precise delimitation of functions was difficult to achieve and, without forbearance on both sides, impossible, serious conflicts would arise. The tsar, throughout, would put the defence of what he conceived to be his prerogatives before the sometimes indiscreetly presented demands of military efficiency. Stolypin, placed between the tsar on one side, the impetuous Guchkov and his supporters on the other, would find himself in an increasingly difficult position.

On 10 November 1907 the Duma formed a Committee of National Defence, consisting of 33 members. All were loyalists – Cadets and deputies further to the Left had been excluded by decision of the chairman. The committee rapidly became the forum for co-operation between ministers, military leaders and deputies. This automatically aroused the suspicions of the tsar, the camarilla and right-wing politicians. Did it not raise the treble spectre of a threat to the sacred prerogatives, a degree of ministerial responsibility and of a government based on parliamentary support? From the point of view of the extreme Right there was indeed ground for concern. Prominent members of the committee had, from the start, established a close working relationship with ministers and high-ranking officers. The War Minister himself, General A. F. Rediger was regularly holding meetings with leading committee members. Stolypin supplied official data. Late in 1907, some deputies assisted him in preparing plans for a far-reaching military perestroika. Guchkov's preoccupation with national defence, meanwhile, gained him golden opinions in St Petersburg society and among personnel of the War Ministry. Staff officers joined informally with members of the committee in examining problems of military organization and financing. 'Strong ties,' Guchkov later recalled, 'were gradually established between me and my colleagues in the National Defence Committee and military-naval circles, thanks to which our work became more productive.'[17] In 1909 Rediger's successor, Sukhomlinov, would uncover the existence of an 'informal committee', of military officials sponsored by Guchkov.[18] At his request the tsar would suppress the 'underground institution'.

In its financial support for military reorganization and rearmament, the Duma coalition was unstinting. A bill in 1908 increased officers' pay. Others provided funds for strategic railway development (double-tracking the Siberian railway and constructing a line on the river Amur). The following year, on its own initiative, the Duma increased by some 40 million rubles an allocation for military re-equipment. Every demand for army appropriations was met, with the support of all deputies except those of the extreme Left. (Matters were somewhat different when it came to naval budgets.) 'In the field,' declared an Octobrist deputy, 'our expenditures have to be lavish; the resources have to be found and will be found.'[19] And found they were, thanks not least to buoyant government revenues.

However, the Duma majority, and here the trouble began, expected value for money. That, inevitably, meant the overhaul of an archaic organization that had so signally failed, and a reduction in nepotism, corruption and sheer incompetence. 'When we considered the necessary reforms in the army,' Guchkov later recalled, 'it soon became apparent that no serious reforms could be accomplished with the existing structure of the War Ministry.'[20] His first target was the recently set up National Defence Council which during the Japanese War, had signally demonstrated its incompetence. Reformers wished to see its functions transferred to the Minister of War. A second target was a gaggle of redundant grand-dukes occupying various positions (as 'inspectors') in the armed forces. Beyond a reform of personnel, Rediger and the Duma committee planned a variety of technical changes designed to increase efficiency. The tsar, who resented its very existence, watched the proceedings of the Defence Committee with growing apprehension. On 27 May 1908 Guchkov, on behalf of the committee, spoke in the Duma on the military budget. His speech (which Finance Minister Vladimir Kokovtsev claimed had been cleared with Stolypin) was a withering indictment of the defects of military organization revealed during the recent war. In it, he blamed the central authorities for provoking a war for which the Russian armed forces were ill-prepared. The war had shown up deficiencies in the structure of the War Ministry. It had revealed a High Command riddled with incompetents, many of whom continued to occupy important positions. Little had changed since then, with the same nepotism persisting and the same court influences determining senior appointments. Reforms planned by the War Ministry were frustrated by the Council of National Defence, the major obstacle to improvement. To bring about the necessary changes, the government must separate itself unequivocally from the representatives of the past. Since the war, the chaos had, if anything, worsened. In particular, the presence in key positions of grand-dukes 'who are by definition not responsible to anyone in government' was 'an unnatural situation'. While deputies recognized their inability to provide remedies, it was their duty to call it by its true name, 'irresponsibility'. As the Duma was ready to sacrifice much in the cause of national defence, they had the right to expect 'at least a little self-denial of some material benefits on their (the grand-dukes') part'.

Prolonged applause greeted parts of the speech. Some deputies of the moderate Right, however, expressed disquiet at its tone while the extreme Right exploded. Purishkevich declared it 'utterly impermissible to discuss in the Duma subjects that constitute the prerogative of the autocratic leader of the Russian army.'[22] The Right must protest in the strongest terms possible against a precedent that might set the Duma on 'an undesirable and extremely dangerous road'. Rediger, in replying for the government, declared that many of the defects pilloried by Guchkov were well-known to his ministry. 'I have to admit', he confessed, 'that to my regret much of the criticism expressed here is justified.'[23] Efforts were, however, in hand to remedy the matters complained of. Stolypin also, according to Guchkov's later recollections, expressed to him, necessarily in private, his satisfaction at the speech.

Guchkov's attack on the grand-dukes formed the prelude to a more serious incident. In May 1908 the Duma voted credits for the setting up of a naval General Staff in ·accordance with plans prepared by a group of young naval officers. When later in the year the Naval Staff Bill came before the State Council, it was criticized as infringing the royal prerogative. Spokesmen of the extreme Right chose the occasion for a frontal attack on Stolypin's co-operation with the Duma on military matters. It was insinuated that there was a conspiracy afoot to restrict the tsar's prerogatives. In December, the State Council threw out the Naval Staff Bill. On 19 December, the Duma passed the bill a second time. The State Council with much 'arm-twisting' by Stolypin, then accepted it by a narrow majority (87:75). Witte, during the debate, once more insinuated that Stolypin was harming the tsar in order to curry favour with the Duma. The Right, through its court connections, then persuaded the tsar (who perhaps did not need much persuading) to refuse his assent. A vigorous public campaign was, at the same time, unleashed against Stolypin and his Octobrist allies.

Matters had reached this pass when the international crisis provoked by the Austro-Hungarian annexation of Bosnia supervened. War with Austria and her ally Germany looming on the horizon, Rediger warned his ministerial colleauges that the possibility of such a war could not be contemplated. On 8 March Russia had to bow to a brutal ultimatum.

'Once the matter had been put as definitely and unequivocally as that,' wrote the tsar (18 March), 'there was nothing for it but to swallow one's pride, give in and agree. The ministers were unanimous about it . . . Our decision was all the more inevitable as we were informed from all sides that Germany was absolutely ready to mobilise. Against whom? Evidently not against Austria!'[24]

Although there had been no choice, the Russian surrender caused widespread indignation. The Russian public did not realize the necessity and it was hard to make them understand how ominous things had looked. Now they would go on 'abusing and reviling poor Isvolsky even more than before!' '*Nobody* except the bad people,' wanted war now. They had been very close to it. Once the danger had passed, people immediately began shouting about humiliation and insults. True, the form and method of Germany's action was brutal 'and we won't forget it'. They had been trying again to separate Russia from France and England but, once again, they had failed. Instead, Nikolai concluded, such methods tended to bring about the opposite result.[25]

It was in the atmosphere of resentment following the Bosnian surrender that the Duma set about debating the annual budget of the War Ministry. Guchkov in an impassioned speech accused the government of having failed in its duty to prepare the country to face an international crisis. Instead, there were wrangles about relatively minor matters, a 'vain attempt by men of the past to try to undermine our great effort by raising secondary issues of rights and prerogatives'. Had not the time come, Guchkov asked, for 'a radical reorganization of our entire military system'?[26] Purishkevich in a rage rounded on the Octobrist leader accusing him of undermining Russia's international standing. Russia needed neither new ways, nor new men, nor yet any special brand of 'cotton-patriotism' (a delicate allusion to Guchkov's origins in the textile industry). Markov, another right-winger, accused Guchkov of harbouring ambitions to emulate the Young Turks (who had carried out a military coup the previous year) and of being an ally of the Social Democrats. The session, not surprisingly, ended in uproar.

This was the moment chosen by the tsar to reassert his control over military matters. As he reported to Copenhagen, he had been obliged 'to dismiss the Minister of War who twice in the Duma not only did not refute the speeches of Guchkov but even agreed with him and so did not defend the honour of the army.'[27] He replaced Rediger with Sukhomlinov whom he had known for 20 years. The Chiefs of Staff were changed at the same time. Sukhomlinov, a man of sub-mediocre talents in the military sphere, was socially acceptable to the tsar and even more to the empress, who valued his talents for entertaining the royal children. Nikolai presently would tell Sukhomlinov not to pay too much attention to the Duma: 'You are my minister. There is nothing to discuss with them.' Sukhomlinov was only too willing to oblige. He would incompetently, but with imperial favour, fill his post until 1915. His appointment marked the end of Stolypin's military perestroika with consequences to be revealed in 1914. It marked the end also of co-operation between military leaders and the Duma's Defence Committee. It gravely weakened the position of the reform-minded Stolypin.

Disheartened by vitriolic right-wing attacks, Stolypin may have indicated a wish to resign on the ground that he had lost the tsar's confidence. This, by his right-wing foes, was stigmatized as a scandalous, unprecedented action since in Russia ministers did not resign but awaited their dismissal. Stolypin's resignation was refused. When, on 25 April, the tsar rejected the Naval Staff Bill, he used the occasion to remind Stolypin that they were living in Russia and not abroad or in Finland. He would not so much as consider the idea of resignation. The 'hysterical clamour' of Stolypin's opponents would soon die down. He must now prepare regulations defining the competence of the Duma in military and naval matters. 'I warn you,' Nikolai added gratuitously, 'that I reject in advance your or anyone else's request to be relieved of their responsibilities.'[28] On 29 August 1909 the government promulgated unilaterally the 'August Regulations' restricting the Duma's right to discuss military and naval budgets. 'I have not created the Duma to command me,' the tsar chose to inform Sukhomlinov, 'but only for advice.'[29]

VII

Stolypin was therefore obliged to soldier on. In an extensive interview granted to a French journalist early in the year, he had expounded his domestic programme. 'I have taken the revolution by the throat,' he proclaimed 'and I will succeed in strangling it . . . if I survive.'[30] It was necessary, above all, to carry out in their entirety the reforms promised in the October Manifesto. Before this could be done, however, it would be necessary to restore absolute order. Demands were being made on the government for an end to arbitrary proceedings, for ending the state of siege where it still existed, for revoking extraordinary police powers and for ending administrative exile. No! The government could not, without abdicating, relinquish its special powers so long as the revolution was not completely dead. Even if calm was slowly returning, banditry, the result of almost two years of total anarchy, had not yet ceased. Revolutionary propaganda was as active as ever. Only recently, an attempt had been made to organize a seditious movement among the young, more especially in the universities. It was there the revolution had begun in 1905. Anarchy continued to be preached in the factories, the army, and especially the officer corps. In these conditions, while recognizing and deploring certain arbitrary acts committed by its officials, how could the government abandon weapons still needed to achieve a final victory over the revolution, perhaps moribund but not yet dead? It would mean giving new hope to the agitators just at the moment when every means must be employed for their final liquidation (*pour les écraser définitivement*).

Stolypin knew well that the revolutionaries taxed the government with cruelty and charged them before European opinion with implacable repression. He also cited figures. In 1906, 4,742 acts of banditry and terrorist attempts claimed the lives of 738 officials and 640 private persons and injured 948 officials and 777 others. In 1907, 12,102 acts of banditry and terrorism cost 1,231 officials their lives and injured 1,284; 1,768 private individuals had died, 1,734 been injured; 2,771,000 rubles were stolen from the exchequer and private persons. In 1908, 365 officials, one per day, were killed in 9,424 incidents, 571 injured. For non-officials, the figures were 1,349 and 1,384; 2.2 million rubles were stolen. The total for the three years amounted to 26,268 attempts claiming a total of 6,091 lives, and more than 6,000 injured. The exchequer and private persons were robbed of more than 5 million rubles.[31]

What, compared to this, were the 20,000 condemnations for so-called political offences of which the government stood accused? What were 3,000 death sentences and 2,000 executions charged against them? Was it not in fact a mark of great leniency that in 1908, when 365 officials and 1,349 others were killed by 'anarchist bandits' there had been only 697 executions? Was it their fault that the gaols were full and that police and officials, exasperated by constant attacks, sometimes took a cruel revenge? And it was in a country still in such turmoil and divided against itself, so vast and moreover inhabited by members of such different races that they were being summoned with execrable threats to introduce forthwith the latest refinements of political liberty as practised in the democracies of the West: a parliamentary régime, universal suffrage, ministerial responsibility, freedom of association and assembly; a solution to the agrarian question by compulsory expropriation of landed estates, and uniting of very diverse and sometimes little civilized nationalities which composed Russia in a federation within which they would enjoy an absolute autonomy! Could the government responsible for guiding and administering the country give in to demands such as these backed by armed menace? 'No,' Stolypin exclaimed, 'our watchword is and must be: order, again order and always order!'[32]

They were nonetheless, so far as conditions permitted, doing everything possible not only to return Russia to a normal state but also to realize the reforms promised in the manifesto. Wherever the situation improved, they abolished the state of siege and the states of emergency. Wherever a diminution of acts of banditry and anarchy permitted, they were controlling the actions of their agents. Administrative exile of which, during 1908 there had been 10,000 instances, was diminishing rapidly. In the current year, if calm continued to return, Stolypin hoped cases would not exceed 3,000. For the rest, preoccupied as they were with defeating the revolution, they were engaged with the approval of the sovereign, in realizing the promises of the manifesto. They had already introduced in Duma and State Council projects of law which would incorporate in the Russian Code the reforms granted in principle by the emperor: draft laws on freedom of conscience, freedom from arrest, inviolability of domicile and of correspondence. There already existed provisional laws on freedom of conscience and freedom of the press which would be replaced by permanent ones now in preparation.

Stolypin then outlined his future programme. As soon as order was fully restored they would realize without haste, which in the actual circumstances would be fatal, the promises of the manifesto. They would then resolve 'naturally in the Russian sense, but moderately and without violence' the 'so-called national questions' concerning Finland and Poland. They would secure the passage of an agrarian law which took landownership away from the *mir* or commune to give it to the inhabitants of the villages. It would transfer to the Russian peasant the private property of these lands and provide him, by means of appropriate credit institutions, with the means for cultivating them by modern methods. They would, wherever possible establish elementary and professional schools. Above all, they would concern themselves with the economic development of the country. This would be promoted by the extension of the railway network, by the creation of credit institutions that would allow municipalities and *zemstva* to proceed with works of sanitation, drainage, road building and the construction of local tram and railway lines. All this would be impossible without a solid financial base. In agreement with his colleague and friend Kokovtsev, Stolypin would nurse and further consolidate the country's finances. These happily, three years after an unfortunate war and on the morrow of a severe revolutionary crisis were in a sound condition; striking testimony to Russia's vitality. In short, Stolypin concluded, they would act in agreement with a formula current in France 'ni réaction, ni révolution: le progrès politique et économique dans l'ordre, sans lequel il n'est pas possible'.[33] His Majesty entirely approved of these views, and gave Stolypin all the support and encouragement he could desire for realizing them.

Such, early in 1909, had been the programme expounded by Stolypin. Its salient features would be order, implementation of the manifesto, agrarian reform, development of Russia's infrastructure, smooth working of the legislative mechanisms and restrictions on the autonomies of Finland and Poland.[34]

The execution of Stolypin's programme would, however, be beset with difficulties. Under the stress of political conflict, his Duma majority based on the Octobrists and indeed the Octobrist party itself were splintering. While strict constitutionalists among Octobrist deputies, exasperated at some of Stolypin's proceedings, were moving towards a *rapprochement* with Cadets and Progressists, right wingers presently to break away as Right Octobrists, were seeking new partners to the Right. Between the two there remained an indeterminate centre group. The great days of Octobrism were over. When in March 1910, in disgust at the antics of the Right and the proceedings of ministers, the moderate non-partisan Khomiakov resigned the Duma presidency, the majority, in a gesture of defiance, elected Guchkov in his place. The presidency, however, had by this time become an empty shell offering its occupant little except frustration.

Indeed, inability to carry out significant reforms in the face of obstruction from the State Council and the scandalous conduct and rowdyism of right-wing deputies had damaged the Duma in the eyes of the country. Greeted with high hopes at the time of its installation, it had since lost much of its credibility. As a forum for questioning ministers and for castigating abuses under the protection of a fragile immunity, it continued nonetheless as an important instrument of glasnost. This was an activity ministers made little attempt to curtail. Duma proceedings would retain some interest particularly from 1910 onwards, for politically engaged members of *obshchestvennost*.

On the face of it, it was the tsar who would be the principal beneficiary from the malaise afflicting the Duma, Stolypin, the Octobrists and Guchkov. Nikolai had, with the suppression of the revolutionary movement, regained much of the ground he appeared at one time to have lost. While Stolypin continued to occupy his post on sufferance, the docile Sukhomlinov was conducting military affairs to the tsar's satisfaction and Russia's future discomfiture. The few pieces of 'undesirable' legislation that would still issue on occasion from a dispirited Duma could be blocked in the State Council. The Duma was now largely emasculated. Ministers were again the tsar's obedient servants with instant punishment for any sign of disobedience. Duma criticism of ministerial actions could be safely disregarded as could public opinion at large. The economy, as will presently be shown, was buoyant. And yet the tsar was uneasy in his mind. The international situation was threatening. Despite Sukhomlinov's soft soap there were worrying questions about Russian military preparedness. Nor was the domestic situation completely reassuring so long as major social issues remained unresolved. Anarchic manifestations and disorders of various kinds continued, the work in the main of right-wing demagogues and gangs.

VIII

In the light of his experiences over military reform and faced with the disintegration of the Union of 17 October Stolypin, from dire necessity, decided to change course. Instead of concentrating on perestroika he would now seek to strengthen the empire and, hopefully, rebuild his coalition, by measures to enhance the Russian position in the borderlands. Assertions of Russian supremacy, while enlisting the enthusiastic support of Nationalist deputies, would appeal also to the patriotic sentiments of a majority of Octobrists. They were likely at the same time to commend themselves to the tsar and to members of the extreme Right in Duma and State Council. Moreover, the two major strands of the new nationalist policy, the strengthening of Russian influence in the western provinces and the curtailment of Finnish autonomy were personally congenial to Stolypin. As a landowner in the ethnically mixed western provinces, he shared the anti-Polish sentiments of the Nationalists. He disliked Finnish autonomy at the very gates of St Petersburg. This, during the revolution, had posed a real threat, with Finland a safe haven for every revolutionary and terrorist in the empire. Although the question of the western provinces was of longer standing, that of restricting Finnish autonomy seemed the one less likely to arouse controversy. It was to Finland, accordingly, that Stolypin first turned his attention.

On 16 March 1910, the tsar issued a manifesto regulating legislative procedures with regard to matters common to the grand duchy and the rest of the empire. Taxation, military service, state security, commercial policy, railway communications, education and language policy among others were withdrawn from the cognizance of the Finnish Diet and transferred to the Russian authorities. Finnish autonomy, which had not fully operated since 1898, was abolished. With enthusiastic Octobrist support, a bill passed through the appropriate Duma committee almost without discussion. It was presented to a plenary session on 7 May. On 21 May, the debate on the bill was opened in the presence of all the ministers. Stolypin, in a forceful speech attacked Finnish nationalists and their Cadet sympathizers. The Finns, he charged, had joined in and encouraged the revolutionary movement. Russian interests in Finland had been shown to lack legal safeguards. While the Finns should continue to enjoy a broad local autonomy, matters involving Russian interests must be placed 'beyond the competence of the Finnish Diet'. In what affected the empire as a whole, the Finnish Diet would henceforth be limited to advice. Five Finnish representatives would be elected to the Duma.

During the debate the split became apparent in the ranks of the Octobrists. While their official spokesmen indulged in wild flights of chauvinist rhetoric, men of the party's left wing led by the thoughtful Baron Alexander Meyendorff joined the Cadets in opposition. No one, Meyendorff argued, had the right to claim a monopoly of patriotism. Russo-Finnish relations were too complex a subject to be dealt with in so hasty and perfunctory a manner. The constitutional rights of the grand-duchy should be respected. 'Strong arm' tactics against national minorities would only breed hatred and separatism. For himself, he had no wish to share in this national achievement. On 26 May 1910, the opposition including 23 left-Octobrists walked out in protest against the unconstitutional proceedings and the violation of Finland's historic rights. The bill, in the end, was passed by a large majority. Its passage helped to consolidate Stolypin's shaken position while at the same time further weakening the loose-knit Octobrist faction.

Before Stolypin could turn to the western provinces a new issue supervened; that of the Orthodox parish schools. On 15 October 1910, the government introduced in the Duma a bill 'on the introduction of universal education'. This, as it emerged from the relevant Duma committee enshrined two basic principles. As Von Anrep, the Octobrists' principal spokesman on educational matters emphasized, the Russian school must be a state school under the permanent supervision of the civil authorities. Furthermore, the successful development of education could be achieved only with the fullest co-operation of the institutions of local government, the *zemstva* and municipal councils. These must be given the broadest responsibilities in educational matters. The bill, thus, in effect, provided for the full secularization of elementary education and for its control by the (no longer left-wing) organs of local government. The committee had rejected a clause appointing local marshals of nobility chairmen of District (*uezd*) Educational Councils.

On the delicate subject of the language of instruction in areas with non-Russian majorities, the committee recommended arrangements which could be considered *relatively* liberal. Instruction during the first two years could be in the native tongue, though Russian would from the start form part of the curriculum. Use of the native language could be extended beyond two years, in special cases, by legislative enactment. What was proposed would amount in its effects to a policy of persistent, if gradual Russification. Three controversial issues emerged during the debates: the control of parish schools, the chairmanship of Educational Councils and the status of non-Russian languages.

The Right, Nationalists and government united in opposition to amendments to the original bill introduced in a liberal spirit by the Octobrist-dominated committee. They demanded greater attention to

Russian national interests and more control over primary education by gentry and clergy. The subjection of parish schools to secular control, it was argued, would have a disastrous effect on the religious sentiment of the masses. It would foster the spread of revolutionary ideas. 'You flirt with revolution,'a right-wing spokesman shouted, 'and the revolution will destroy you.' For the government, the Procurator of the Synod contended that the Orthodox Church and its educational institutions were the principal guardians of morality and order. Their autonomy must be safeguarded. In a similar vein, the Minister of Education criticized even minor liberal amendments inserted by the committee.

Faced with a concerted onslaught from the Right, the Octobrists again revealed their divisions. Right Octobrists indulged in nationalist rhetoric: 'all the peoples living in Russia have to be acquainted with the Russian language, Russian literature and attracted to Russian culture . . . Our major goal and the most important national interest has to be the strengthening of Russian nationalism.'[35] Von Anrep, in defending the amendments, launched into a violent attack on the Orthodox Church, its subservience to the authorities, the corruption of its higher dignitaries, its stifling influence and its loss of moral authority. Peasant deputies seconded the attack, citing from their own experience instances of deficiencies and corruption in parish schools.

Battle lines were drawn. Amid violent arguments, the education bill went through its readings. The bulk of the Octobrists voted with the opposition. The Duma then became embroiled with the State Council. In February 1912, the Council finally accepted the Education Bill insisting however, at the instance of the Procurator, on the continued autonomy (that is church control) of parish schools. Moreover, such schools were to receive a share of the subsidy. The Council's amendments thus amounted to an attack on a basic principle enshrined in the Duma bill. When the conciliation commission of the two chambers proved unable to produce a compromise, the Council threw out the measure on educational finance. Decision on the organizational bill meanwhile was held up until it lapsed with the end of the legislative period in 1912. However, although no new law could be passed, the money for the expansion of schools was appropriated and spent. For 1923, universal compulsory education was envisaged. The necessary budgetary arrangements were made.

IX

The issue which finally undermined Stolypin's already shaky position was a proposal for the introduction of *zemstvo* institutions in six western, ethnically mixed provinces. The programme had come from the Octobrists and been accepted by Stolypin. On 6 May 1910 the government accordingly submitted to the Duma a bill for the introduction of *zemstva* in six provinces. Peasants, landowners and townsmen would choose the deputies jointly. Electors would however be divided into national *curiae*, one for Poles, the other for Russians. Representation would be weighted in favour of the Russian element. A fixed number of seats would be reserved for the Orthodox clergy. Presidents of the new *zemstvo* boards must be Russians, as must at least half the members and half the employees. Jews who outnumbered the Poles were disenfranchised.

The Octobrist-controlled Duma Committee on Local Self-Government introduced a number of amendments. These, while somewhat increasing Polish representation, reduced that of Orthodox priests. The quota stipulations for *zemstvo* boards and employees were dropped. A new clause somewhat unrealistically permitted Polish and non-Polish *curiae* to hold joint elections if both expressed a desire by two-thirds majorities. In theory, Poles might thus take part in the election of non-Polish deputies. Already in committee, Nationalists and Right Octobrists had fought these liberalizing amendments.

When the amended bill came before the plenum, it at once ran into difficulties. Stolypin, in rejecting the bulk of the changes, set out to establish his nationalist credentials. The object of the measure he declared, was to protect Russia's 'historic principles' and to affirm 'openly and without hypocrisy' that the western region was and would forever remain Russian. The Right and the Nationalists expressed similar sentiments. The object, one of their spokesmen declared, was to decide 'who will be the master of the western provinces – the Russians or the Poles'. The law needed to destroy once and for all any Polish hope of ever annexing these provinces. The Left opposed the entire bill on grounds of principle, with the Cadets reiterating the view that, like other nationalist measures this one would only help the separatists. The government, they charged, was exacerbating national antagonisms in order to divert attention from real and burning issues. The Octobrists were, as usual, divided. Twenty-two finally voted with the Left against the amended bill. When, in the course of the readings, individual amendments were voted on, the disarray among the Octobrists was complete and one vote was lost due to Octobrist divisions. Another amendment was defeated by the combined vote of Right, Nationalists and many Octobrists. In other votes, however, Union deputies rallied to support the amendments. The bill was finally passed with Octobrist support. Some Rightists voted with the Left in protest against the surviving amendments.

What followed came as a bombshell. On 4 March 1911 the State Council by 92 votes to 68 rejected the provision setting up separate national *curiae*. Two factors combined to produce this unexpected vote. One was the Right's intense hatred of Stolypin, another the 'democratic' elements in the law and a fear that it might lead to a further restriction on the tsar's prerogatives. Stolypin, had staked the future of his government on the passage of the bill without major changes. The clause on national *curiae*, he insisted, was central to it. Down to the last moment, he had expected to carry the day. The President of the Council had indicated that the tsar desired the passage of the bill. Privately, however, Nikolai had told some opponents that they were free to vote 'according to their conscience'.

Following the adverse vote in the State Council, Stolypin once more tendered his resignation. It was widely believed that this time it would be accepted. However, somebody convinced the tsar that it was still too early to part with his forceful prime minister.[36] Nikolai therefore – one can imagine with what enthusiasm – agreed to Stolypin's terms. Among his reasons may have been a reluctance to accept a resignation resulting from an adverse parliamentary vote. Nor could he have been happy with Stolypin's remark, on gaining his point, that the Duma would feel satisfaction 'that the law, which it worked out with such care, was saved by Your Majesty'.[37] The device adopted at the instance of Stolypin, was simple, if barely constitutional. Duma and State Council were adjourned for three days. The *Zemstvo* Bill was then enacted under Article 87. As a 'lesson' to the State Council, two of the bill's leading opponents were suspended.

The method adopted by Stolypin placed a further strain on his relations with the Octobrists. When news of his resignation first reached them, there was among them and moderate Rightists a feeling of regret. Had not Stolypin proved himself a friend of the Duma and within limits an upholder of constitutional government? When, on 10 March, it became known that he would stay at his post, more than 200 signatures were collected within hours for the reintroduction of the bill. When, however, rumours spread about the intention to enact it under Article 87, Octobrist deputies were concerned. A delegation went to see Stolypin, who assured them that he had no intention of harming the Duma. The bill would be promulgated exactly as they had passed it. His object, he claimed, was to teach the State Council a lesson and to curb its reactionary anti-Duma tendencies.

Stolypin seriously misjudged the deep-rooted Octobrist commitment to constitutional government. The steering committee of the

Octobrist faction at once denounced the use of Article 87 when the bill could in fact have been enacted by normal legislative methods. The precedent about to be created could in future be used also against the Duma. In any case, both the adjournment and its purpose constituted an abuse of the Fundamental Laws. Were Stolypin to persist, the Octobrists would vote against the bill. Guchkov would resign the Duma presidency and no Octobrist would agree to take his place. The die however, was cast. On 12 March, the Duma was adjourned. Two days later the bill was officially promulgated. Guchkov resigned the presidency despite Stolypin's attempts to dissuade him. 'The Octobrists', a Nationalist deputy recorded in his diary, 'have pleaded in vain with Stolypin not to act in such an unlawful manner. This is the end of Stolypin; he had such a convenient party on his side and how foolishly he has lost it.'[38]

The extent of Octobrist disenchantment emerged in the interpellations after the intermission and during the debates which followed. Stolypin could produce only a lame defence. The chambers, he contended, while entitled to reject the government's bills could not question the legality of its legislative initiatives. The use of Article 87 was not subject to constitutional limitations. While the Duma considered the action of the State Council legitimate, the government thought otherwise. The rejection of the bill by the State Council had, in its view, created an emergency. The misery of the Russian population in the western provinces had given rise to a situation which justified its proceedings. The conduct of the State Council in obstructing bills passed by the Duma was intolerable. It had forced the government chosen by the tsar to act and not evade its responsibilities towards the nation. All Stolypin gained for his pains was some desultory applause from the Nationalist benches.

Somewhat more convincingly, Stolypin would defend his proceedings in private conversation. Had he, he told a confidant, tried again 'to guide the bill through the legislative institutions, then of course there never would have been elected zemstvos in the western and south-western provinces'.[39] Overall, Stolypin was now widely discredited and his impending dismissal the common 'talk of the town'.

X

Perhaps spurred on by his increasingly precarious situation, Stolypin decided to submit to the tsar a memorandum on a systematic restructuring of the Russian administration.[40] In May 1911 in great secrecy, he dictated its outlines to Aleksandr Zenkovsky, a financial expert attached to the Kiev provincial *zemstvo* to be turned by him into a more elaborate document.[41] The underlying philosophy emerges from Stolypin's explanation of his reasons for the unlikely choice of confidant in preference to some St Petersburg *chinovnik*. He reported Stolypin as having said,

> that you are not a mere bureaucrat like many of my colleagues but a genuine zemstvo leader who can draft my project of a report to the Emperor and accurately illustrate my ideas to expand zemstvo activities as well as to transfer to them responsibility for many measures now carried on not by zemstvo workers but by state officials.[42]

He planned, he said, 'to transfer to the zemstvos many of those activities presently handled through local public institutions by departments of the Ministry of Internal Affairs'.

The decentralization of governmental functions, their debureaucratization and transfer to elective bodies was to be part of a radical reorganization of central government. It would affect both existing ministries and involve the creation of new ones, whose functions and responsibilities Stolypin outlined. In regard to commerce and industry, Stolypin observed that 'if one compares Russian industry with that of such other countries as Germany, Austria-Hungary, England and others, the picture is dismal.' Russia's feeble development, particularly in metallurgy and machine construction resulted from on the one hand 'the economic policy practised by the Ministry of Finance, and, on the other, restrictions on the rights of the Jews'. Jews were undeniably

> talented financiers and merchants. In the central European countries, industry and commerce and banking operations quickly advanced when Jews were granted full rights. Therefore it seems desirable to remove all restrictions on Jews in Russia, enabling them to form new joint-stock undertakings. The industry of Russia would immediately begin broad development.[43]

This would create a demand for workers, and also enable some agricultural workers to improve their material conditions. A decrease in the need for imports would mitigate the outflow of gold and currency. Exports on the other hand would increase, swelling the Russian reserves. Clearly, Jews were allotted a part in Stolypin's planned perestroika. The perestroika would involve the creation, from 1912 onwards of a number of new ministries with responsibility respectively for labour, local self-government, nationalities, social security, creeds, natural resources and public health care.[44]

In this comprehensive programme of reform there was, however, one notable omission. Not a word was said about the armed forces, their size, administration and equipment. In the light of bitter experience, Stolypin knew better than to complicate still further a task that would, in any case, be formidable. He appears to have envisaged a wholesale restructuring of government institutions extending over two decades.[45]

Stolypin, it appears, planned to submit his memorandum 'about enacting reforms and renovating the state administration of Russia' to the tsar not later than the autumn of 1911. Evidence suggests that after the celebrations in Kiev, he intended to repeat his offer of resignation. Perhaps, having read his memorandum the tsar would, for patriotic reasons, ask him to continue in office. In case of difficulties with Duma or State Council, Stolypin again contemplated a resort to Article 87. In this connection, he pointed to the fact that it had taken three and a half years of parliamentary debates to convert the *ukaz* of 9 November into a definitive law.[46]

While making these plans, Stolypin was conscious of the fact that time was running out. Intrigues following the *zemstvo* crisis persuaded him that there was no time to lose. At the Kiev festivities when explaining his plans to the local governor-general, he complained 'with deep bitterness' about his recent treatment. It was, of course, unlikely that the tsar would again ask Stolypin to continue in office in the event of another resignation. Yet might he not perhaps, seduced by Stolypin's vision and from a sincere concern for Russia's future welfare have fallen in with Stolypin's proposals? Might not the still influential dowager-empress, Stolypin's staunch friend and supporter, have once more persuaded her son to keep his prime minister? Were in fact Stolypin's hopes and aspirations totally unrealistic?

These were questions never to be answered. On 1 September 1911, during a gala performance at the Kiev city theatre, Stolypin was shot and fatally wounded by one Dimitry Bogrov, an ex-revolutionary turned police agent. Though warned of the likelihood of an attempt, the Kiev police chief had actually provided the assassin with a ticket of admission. Almost certainly, there had been connivance by men in the *Okhrana*. Bogrov, moreover, was hanged before investigators from St Petersburg could reach Kiev – forestalling any possible revelations. Ironically, an autopsy carried out on Stolypin's body appears to have revealed that he was suffering from an incurable disease and had in any case only a few more months to live.

P. A. Stolypin was succeeded as chairman of the Council of Ministers by the plodding Kokovtsev who had almost certainly plotted against him. His plan for a major administrative perestroika died with him. The policy of land-settlement which he had helped to implement would survive him for some years. As early as April 1908 Lenin noted in an article in *Proletarii* that the 'Stolypin constitution' and Stolypin's agrarian policy marked 'a new phase in the breakdown of the old semi-patriarchal and semi-feudal system of tsarism, a new movement towards its transformation into a middle-class monarchy.'

> If [Lenin went on] this should continue for very long periods of time . . . it might force us to renounce any agrarian programme at all. It would be empty and stupid democratic phrase-mongering to say that the success of such a policy in Russia is 'impossible' . . . It is possible! If Stolypin's policy is continued . . . then the agrarian structure of Russia will become completely bourgeois, the stronger peasants will acquire almost all of the allotment land, agriculture will become capitalistic, and any 'solution' of the agrarian problem will become impossible under capitalism.[47]

Lenin saw the situation as a race between Stolypin's perestroika and the next major upheaval. 'I do not expect to live to see the revolution,' he would more than once declare pessimistically during Stolypin's final years. With the accelerating movement towards bourgeois-capitalist forms, and with some consolidation of semi-parliamentary government, peaceful evolution was indeed a possible outcome. Had the Provisional Government, successor to the Imperial Duma, been able to maintain itself in power, it might have become the legitimate heir of the transformation brought about by Witte and Stolypin.

How far Stolypin, with whose name the land settlement policy is commonly associated can be considered an independent exponent of perestroika must remain a matter of opinion (or of semantics). His reform programme broadly continued that originated by Witte. When Stolypin took charge, he found the land reform legislation ready to hand. Similarly, it was Witte who initiated the policy of seeking an accommodation with public men and a coalition government. Stolypin would at first be responsible merely for implementing Witte's pro-gramme. Gradually he would add some new features mainly to secure a parliamentary majority. When his alliance with Guchkov and the Octobrists based primarily on military reform became unstuck, he switched to Great Russian nationalism backed by a centre-Right majority. Finally, *in extremis*, he prepared the comprehensive proposals outlined in the Zenkovsky memorandum.

A 'man of the centre', Stolypin was assailed by critics from both the Right and the Left. While for the former he was too liberal, the latter would not forgive his brutal methods of repression. Tsar, empress, camarilla and State Council majority were numbered among his opponents. Towards the end, he could maintain his position only by offers (threats) of resignation. By 1911 however, his dismissal was generally expected. Land settlement, the centrepiece of his programme was, by this time, beginning to run out of steam. Major parts of a legislative programme sanctioned by the Duma had been 'scuttled' by the State Council. In fact, by 1911 the impulse towards perestroika once originated by Witte, had waned. A new age of reaction, personal rule and right-wing politics was approaching. Under the *aegis* of Rasputin, the final phase of the Russian monarchy was about to open.

NOTES

1. In a small number of provinces the Marshals of Nobility were appointed by the government and not, as was usual, chosen by the *dvorianstvo*. This was an arrangement directed against Polish landowners in the western provinces.
2. Noted reactionaries now occupied the posts of Procurator of the Holy Synod, Director of the Administration of Land Affairs and State Controller.
3. Ann Erickson Healy: *The Russian Autocracy in Crisis 1905–1907*, (Hamden, CT, 1976), p 196.
4. Edward J. Bing, ed: *The Letters of Tsar Nicholas and Empress Marie* (London, 1937), Nikolai to Maria, 21 July 1906, p 213.
5. For the following, see George Yaney: *The Urge to Mobilize: Agrarian Reform in Russia, 1861–1930* (Urbana, IL, Chicago and London, 1982).
6. Yaney: *The Urge to Mobilize*, p 195.
7. *Ibid*, p 210.
8. *Ibid*, pp 227–8.
9. Bing, ed: *Letters*, Nikolai to Maria, 29 March 1907, p 229.
10. Quoted in Ernst Birth: *Die Oktobristen (1905–1913): Zielvorstellungen und Struktur* (Stuttgart, 1974), p 26. S. Elpatevsky, in *Russkoye Bogatstvo* (1907), describes the Octobrists as 'predominantly serving nobility. They serve in government offices and ministries, in science and culture, in municipal and *zemstvo* self-government' (Birth, *op cit*, p 26).
11. Early in 1907, the formerly coordinated forces of *obshchestvo* were beginning to fall apart. Every new election moved the *zemstva* further to the Right. On 11 June a loyalist congress of *zemstvo* leaders met in Moscow (Alexander V. Zenkovsky: *Stolypin: Russia's Last Great Reformer*, Princeton, 1986, p 8).
12. It is worth noting that the Duma, on 13 November 1907, rejected by 201 votes to 146 the use of the term 'autocrat' (*samoderzhets*) in an address to the tsar (Zenkovsky: *Stolypin*, p 10).
13. Ben-Cion Pinchuk: *The Octobrists in the Third Duma 1907–1912* (Seattle and London, 1974), pp 59–60.
14. *Ibid*.
15. Fears were expressed that the new agrarian policy would undermine

efficient estates and lower agricultural standards (see Zenkovsky: *Stolypin*).

16. It is worth noting that during 1908–9, at Stolypin's insistence, the Peasants' Land Bank acquired some nine million desyatins from large landowners for resale to peasants (Zenkovsky: *Stolypin*, p 12). It may, however, be doubted how far the bank's land sales benefited the poorest peasants.
17. Pinchuk: *The Octobrists*, p 65.
18. Among the regular participants was General F. F. Palytsin, Chief of Staff from 1905 to 1908, an ardent supporter of reform.
19. Pinchuk: *The Octobrists*, p 65.
20. *Ibid*, pp 66–7.
21. *Ibid*, p 68.
22. *Ibid*, p 69.
23. *Ibid*, p 69.
24. Bing, ed: *Letters*, Nikolai to Maria, 18 March 1909, p 240.
25. *Ibid*, Nikolai to Maria, 19 March 1909, p 241.
26. Pinchuk: *The Octobrists*, p 78.
27. Bing, ed: *Letters*, Nikolai to Maria, 18 March 1909, p 240.
28. Pinchuk: *The Octobrists*, pp 76–7.
29. *Ibid*, p 76.
30. Pierre Poléjaïeff [Polezhayev]: *Six années: La Russie de 1906 à 1912* (Paris, 1912), p 48.
31. *Ibid*, pp 49–50.
32. *Ibid*, p 52.
33. *Ibid*, p 54.
34. In an interview in 1909 with the Saratov newspaper *Volga*, Stolypin declared: 'When the roots of the State become healthy and robust the Russian government's statements will sound entirely different to Europe and all the world. Give our nation 20 years of external and internal peace and then you will not recognize the Russia of today!' (quoted in Zenkovsky: *Stolypin*, p 20).
35. Pinchuk: *The Octobrists*, p 129.
36. Throughout the crisis, Stolypin enjoyed the support of Witte's old patron, the Dowager Empress Maria Feodorovna (Zenkovsky: *Stolypin*, p 25).
37. Pinchuk: *The Octobrists*, p 141.
38. *Ibid*, p 144.
39. Zenkovsky: *Stolypin*, p 29.
40. 'All subsequent events connected with the intrigue persuaded Stolypin to consider the necessity, not later than fall 1911, of presenting a report to the Sovereign about enacting reforms and renovating the state administration of Russia' (*Ibid*, p 28).
41. *Ibid*, pp 25–6, 96, 120 and 141–2.
42. *Ibid*, p 96.
43. *Ibid*, p 43. There may be some doubt both about the accuracy of Zenkovsky's reporting and perhaps also about the degree of Stolypin's sincerity, particularly with regard to the Jews. However, many who disliked Jews have paid glowing tribute to their economic 'usefulness'.

44. In this context, Stolypin once more returned to the Jews. He was convinced that, immediately on being granted full civil rights, they would form large joint-stock banks and concessionary enterprises to exploit Russia's natural wealth (Zenkovsky: *Stolypin*, p 36).
45. The functions of the new ministries are set out in some detail (see *ibid*). They give a good idea of the scope of the intended perestroika.
46. Zenkovsky: *Stolypin*, p 29.
47. V. I. Lenin: *Sochinenia*, 3rd Russian edn (Moscow, 1928–37), vol XII, p 29.

14

Fruits of Perestroika:
The Witte Legacy

By the end of 1908 the effects of the revolution of 1905 were wearing off. 1909 would see the beginnings of an economic upsurge that would gather pace during the following years. Both industry and agriculture would prosper. Government finances would benefit from steadily rising tax revenues. Foreign capital would pour into Russian industries. Indeed rapid industrial expansion would in the end produce 'over-heating' in the economy, bottlenecks, shortages and signs of inflationary pressure. There would be some rise in real wages, an increase in farm incomes and a patchy all round prosperity. The sustained boom could be seen as a posthumous vindication of the original 'Witte System', with Witte himself, embittered and cantankerous, watching developments from the sidelines.

There was, nevertheless, a difference. Whereas in the 1890s industrialization had been largely a hothouse growth, induced from above and sheltered by high protective walls, the new spurt would increasingly be a spontaneous product of Russian capitalism and entrepreneurship. Witte, at vast cost to the Russian people, had primed the pump. His successors as well as some sections of the population were reaping the benefits. Land settlement, while contributing to the economic upturn, was not its cause. The government still helped with large military contracts and also engaged in some regulatory intervention. It was, nonetheless, the private sector with private entrepreneurship at the helm which was beginning to take the lead.

I

British consular and diplomatic reports present a detailed picture of Russia's economic progress during these years.[1] The 'more normal and progressive tendencies' in Russian agriculture observable in 1907–8 noted H. M. Groves, the British Consul in Moscow, had been even more marked in 1909. The improvement had occurred mainly in the second half of the year thanks to an abundant grain crop enabling peasants in a very large area to pay off arrears of taxation, to carry out repairs of their buildings and to replenish their stock of cattle. In the Volga and northeastern provinces peasants increased the amount of cattle kept for the winter, the increase being mainly in cows for milking purposes. In other districts, they took up more land. They increased their stock of agricultural implements at the autumn and winter fairs. Carts and wheels were also in good demand. The most marked symptom was the increased purchase of sowing seed by comparison with 1908, both of grain and of grass.

Agricultural wages for the summer season showed an increase of 30–50 per cent over the average for the three preceding years. This, Consul Groves considered, might to some extent be explained by the reduced number of spare hands caused by steady emigration to Siberia. Improved agricultural methods were also marked during this year, notably in the preparation of the soil. The traditional three-field system (with the use of fallow) was being replaced by regular crop rotation. The demand for fertilizer, met through the *zemstva*, looked like exceeding that of 1908 by 35–45 per cent.

The year 1909 was 'especially rich' in examples of every kind of co-operative venture. Co-operative associations of various kinds were formed to assist in the disposal of crops. Co-operative credit associations offered advances on grain, largely with the help of loans from the State Bank. A whole series of new co-operative associations of various kinds were formed in connection with bee keeping, sale of fruit, wine making, the purchase of goods at fairs and from factories, poultry farming, and cattle-fattening among other things. *Zemstva* were actively promoting this rural progress by collective purchases of sowing seed, by supplying improved agricultural machinery and fertilizers and by sending out instructors to assist in improvements of cattle breeding and poultry raising.

One of the most prominent features of the year was the tendency of peasants to start new farms or allotments. During the first nine months of the year, 560,000 peasants applied to the Land Commission for land for such purposes. They were helped by both *zemstva* and the Peasant Land Bank with the latter holding, by 1 October, a land fund in excess of four million desiatines. Among the beneficiaries of the good harvest were both the Russian Treasury and the money market. As Sir Arthur Nicholson, the ambassador reported, the year 1909 was 'extremely beneficial in its effects on the general financial and economic situation in Russia'.[2] In addition to an international loan (at 4.5 per cent) issued in January, the collection of ordinary revenue surpassed the estimates considerably. For the first eight months, revenue collected exceeded that for the same period of 1908 by 3.5 million pounds.

From July, when the favourable yield of crops had definitely been ascertained, 'the foreign exchanges moved rapidly in Russia's favour, until they touched the specie point – remittances of gold commenced from abroad and as the proceeds from the harvest began to be realized the balance of trade remained strongly in Russia's favour'.[3] The value of gold in the State Bank, on 29 September, had risen to 140 million rubles, compared with 127.1 at the same time the previous year. This was 115.8 per cent of the paper in circulation as against 109 per cent a year before. The rise in the gold reserve represented increased deposits by private banks and individuals, enabling the State Bank to enlarge the facilities extended to industry.

Deposits in private commercial banks, meanwhile, rose from 105 million rubles in July 1908 to 124 million in July 1909, even before the bonus of the harvest. Banks, at the time of reporting, were said to be conducting 'a largely increased business in bill-discounting, at rates more favourable to borrowers'.[4] Between 1 January 1908 and 1 July 1909, 40 private banks were reported to have reopened 60 branches closed in recent years. Mutual credit institutions were reporting a rapid extension of their operations. 'The satisfactory feature of the year 1909, from a financial point of view,' Nicholson summed up, 'consists ... in the strengthening of the national fund of capital (as the consequence mainly of a good harvest) and the beneficial effects accruing to the different branches of industry from a more plentiful supply of capital and easier conditions of credit.'

During 1910 while the benefits of the previous harvest were still pulsating through the Russian economy, a second good harvest provided a further booster. Its effects on the agricultural economy were again reported in detail by Consul Groves.

Industry, like agriculture, was booming. For the iron industry, Groves reported, 1910 was again a record year for production, 'surpassing even 1904'. Output failed to keep pace with demand, especially for iron girders, heavy rails and roofing iron. Production of cast iron, however, increased little. 'At the same time, manufacturers of agricultural and constructional machinery were demanding larger quantities of cast-iron with the result that a 'famine' in cast-iron ensued.'[5] Another result was that the import of various forms of machinery increased by nearly three million pounds.

The building industry was also experiencing a boom. The abundance of money and cheap credit in 1910 gave a strong impetus, especially in the two capitals, to urban house building. There was a great rise in the output of bricks, cement and other building materials. This also affected the production of roofing iron and helped to balance the effect of reduced demand from the villages. Roofing iron was still looked on as a luxury by the peasants, who preferred instead to apply their earnings from two good harvests to meeting more pressing needs: arrears of rents, instalments for taking up fresh land, livestock and plant, household expenses. There was an abundance of straw for thatching with extremely rainy weather minimizing the fire risks.[6]

Ambassador Nicholson reported that 1910 saw a remarkable further improvement in Russia's financial position. It resulted mainly from an excellent harvest in 1909, followed by one slightly above average in 1910. For the first time for some 18 years the budgetary estimates for 1910 showed a surplus without recourse to loans either internal or foreign. A surplus remained even after providing for extraordinary expenditure of £12.3 million mainly for railway construction and military re-equipment. The revenue collected during the year exceeded the estimates by £16.7 million.[7]

Of the ordinary expenditure for 1910, 30.5 per cent was devoted to national defence, over 23 per cent to servicing the national debt, 20 per cent to general expenses of administration and 5.2 per cent to education. Agriculture and land reorganization absorbed 2.6 per cent, ways and communications other than railways 1.7 per cent. The education budget, modest by the standards of the late twentieth century, exceeded by more than one-third the amount spent in 1907, while the agricultural budget more than doubled. The two key items of ordinary revenue – profits from the spirit monopoly and railway receipts – showed large increases over 1909, £5.7 and £3.5 million respectively, in the first six months. Much of the new disposable income, clearly, was being spent on alcohol. There were also considerably increased receipts from customs and excise.[8]

The enormous value of grain exports from two good harvests caused an inflow of gold from abroad. This commenced in the latter part of 1909 and continued, almost without interruption, throughout 1910. The stock of gold held by the State Bank both in Russia and abroad rose from £133.6 million on 1 July 1909 to 152.9 million on 1 January 1911. The abundance of money enabled the bank to lower its discount rate towards the end of 1909 from 5 per cent to 4.5 per cent. During the first half of 1910 deposits in savings banks exceeded withdrawals by £3.6 million – double the average rate of savings for the preceding six years.[9]

The favourable developments reported for 1909 and 1910 would continue, if more patchily, until the eve of World War I. Among significant aspects reported by British diplomats were increased managerial efficiency, improvement in methods of production and in the distribution, sale and transport of goods, great increases in electrification and buoyant government finances. For the year 1912, for instance, government revenue, favoured by a good harvest exceeded all earlier records. 'Ordinary' receipts, according to provisional estimates of the ministry of finance, reached the 'enormous total' of £324.6 million. This exceeded by 12 million, the amount raised in 1911, and was due almost entirely to increased yields from existing taxes (the only new tax being an increased levy on real estate which yielded an additional £700,000). The other chief sources of revenue that showed greatly increased yields were, once again, the spirit monopoly, the state railways, the industrial tax and excise duties on tobacco and petrol.[10]

Expenditure on military and naval armaments rose 'in impressive proportions'. Ordinary expenditure on the army increased by £1 million compared with 1911, by £3 million over the previous five years. The budget, moreover, provided an extra £7.4 million for the renewal of equipment, stores, and materiel. Supplementary estimates of a further £2.5 million were sanctioned during the year. In short, Russia was trying to hold her place in the international arms race. The budget also provided for a further £11.65 million for the construction of state (largely strategic) railways, an increase of £1.6 million over 1911. As against this, the education budget reached £12.4 million, exceeding by £2.2 million that for the previous year and by £4.4 million that of 1910. An allocation of £6.2 million was made to agriculture and land reform – a relatively modest sum – and £3.7 million to means of communication other than railways. The prospective budget for 1913 envisaged a defence expenditure totalling £93.3 million as against £79.8 (£62 million military, £17.8 naval) in 1912. To facilitate pushing forward its military and naval preparations in 1913 as rapidly as possible, the government decided temporarily to abandon its recently adopted policy of reducing the national debt. An armaments boom was in prospect.[11]

For the year 1913 the British ambassador (now Sir George Buchanan) reported that the buoyancy of the revenue had enabled Russia 'without any perceptible strain on her finances' to shoulder the enormous defence expenditure of £93.7 million. This buoyancy, the ambassador attributed on the one hand to the growth of population, on the other to a good harvest that had favoured revenue collection. Receipts for the first nine months of 1913, showed an excess of £25.5 million over the corresponding figure for 1912. The sources of revenue showing large increases were the spirit monopoly (£6.8 million), the state railways (£4.5 million) and the sugar excise (£2.8 million). It was a blot on the Russian scene, the ambassador observed, that so large a proportion of the ordinary revenue was derived from the consumption of alcohol. The total receipts from this source during 1913, from returns so far available, were likely to exceed £95 million; more than a quarter of the total ordinary revenue and equalling total defence spending. Peasant drunkenness, Sir George considered, was an economic evil (if hardly a fiscal one). Whether this was either a desirable or a safe basis for government finance must remain an open question.[12] At all events, peasant (and other) drunkenness helped to finance £100 million of military expenditure, including the cost of a partial mobilization against Austria–Hungary, compared with £62 million in 1912. The budget for 1914 envisaged a further increase in revenue of some £30 million. It also provided for an increase in military expenditure of another £11.1 million, raising the total to £104.8 million. Estimates for the Ministry of Transport for 1914 provided for an increase of over £10 million, for education and agriculture of an extra £2 million each. The Ministry of Trade and Industry would receive an additional £1.2 million. Arrangements were in hand for a large loan for joint-stock railways to be raised in 1914 with a government guarantee. During 1914, in fact, except for the building industry, the positive trends persisted.[13]

II

Would economic growth have continued at the same hectic pace had war not intervened? It is a question which, of course, cannot be answered with certainty. One reason for this is the decisive impact of the ever unpredictable harvest. Whether diversification of crops and a turn to specialist production noted in the consular reports would significantly reduce overall dependence on the vagaries of the Russian climate must remain doubtful. The increased use of fertilizer and of more sophisticated implements, the introduction of various cash crops and the spread of improved agricultural methods were raising productivity. Such modernization was producing a modicum of peasant prosperity, thus enlarging the market for some consumer goods. However, much of the increased farm income was clearly spent on spirits. Increasing urban populations and a modest rise in real wages were producing a growing demand for agricultural produce. Overall thus, though setbacks in the shape of poor harvests were to be expected, the outlook for the longer-term future of Russian agriculture was bright. Nor did the prospects for industry look less promising.

True, for reasons that are not entirely clear, the great building boom had, by 1914, run out of steam. Yet municipal projects, like major developments planned by the Moscow City Council were likely to be resumed sooner or later. Again, with the progress of agriculture, fireproof building in the villages was likely to continue. The move towards *khutors*, farmsteads outside the village proper, would stimulate building activities.

More significant for the future health of Russian industry was the government's rearmament programme. In March 1912, a leading German industrialist reported from St Petersburg that the government had just decided on its programme of future naval construction. Over the next ten years, it was intended to build 16 battleships of 30–40,000 tons, 8 battle cruisers of 30,000 tons, 16 smaller cruisers of 8,000 tons, 64 destroyers (torpedo boats) and 24 submarines. The estimated cost was 900 million rubles, 500 to be spent during the first quinquennium. This, the industrialist noted, would fill the order books of large sections of Russian industry and accelerate further an industrial upsurge that was already extraordinary. The boom moreover was reinforced by the fact that French banks were willing to invest any amount of capital. Continued orders for armaments seemed assured. Even if some of these would go to government arsenals and shipyards, private enterprise, from the extractive industries upwards, was certain to secure its share. Similarly the demand for energy and hence for electrical equipment seemed set to grow – enhanced moreover by the steady exhaustion of Russia's oil reserves.

For the textile industry, a developing popular market, the product of population growth, urbanization and some improvement in living standards, would ensure a steady progress. A growing middle class was at the same time developing a taste for 'quality goods'. In the Asian market also there was a growing demand for textiles.

Buoyant public revenue was virtually guaranteed by the thirst for vodka of the fast-growing population. This would enable the government to invest in agricultural improvement as well as armaments. A growing market for articles of mass consumption, notably tobacco and sugar, would further swell the government's coffers.

Overall, whatever the shorter-term fluctuations, the longer-term outlook for the Russian economy in 1914 was bright. The upward phase of the business cycle begun in the mid-1890s still had several years to run. Thanks to an effective economic perestroika, Russia had embarked on her industrial and commercial 'take off'.

III

The economic developments between 1909 and 1914 described in detail by the British diplomats can be illustrated more broadly from statistical data.[14] Between 1909 and 1914 inclusive, the population of the empire grew from 157.1 to 175.1 million. The railway network expanded from 66,300 to 73,000 kilometres. Output of cast iron rose from 176.8 to 264.1 million *pud*, reaching in 1913, a peak of 283 million. In the southern industrial region, Russia's most productive, the production of cast iron grew from 122.9 million tons in 1909 to 189.7 million in 1913, that of pig iron and steel for the whole of the empire from 162,870 million to 246,551 million. In the southern region alone it had jumped from 88,973 million pud in 1909 to 141,044 million in 1913. The overall output of bituminous coal 1,526.3 million pud in 1909, exceeded 2000 million in 1912 and 1913. In the Donbas alone, Russia's major coal-mining region, it rose from 1,082.7 million pud in 1909 to 1,561 million four years later. Other statistics, if less striking, tell a similar tale. Thus the amount of raw cotton employed in Russian manufactures, 21.3 million *pud* in 1909, had in 1913, reached 25.9 million. Overall, the picture was one of rapid industrial expansion. For the years between 1890 and 1899, the height of the 'Witte boom' the annual rate of industrial growth has been estimated at 8.03 per cent, close to 9 per cent during the second quinquennium. The average growth rate for 1907–13 is put at 6.25 per cent, at 7.5 per cent for the years 1910–13. Moreover, whereas between 1901 and 1907 it was mainly large-scale industry that grew, between 1907 and 1912 small and medium sized enterprises expanded at an equal rate.

No less impressive were the figures relating to Russia's foreign trade. Total turnover (imports and exports) valued in 1908 at 912.6 million rubles reached 1,591 million in 1911 and 1,520 million two years later. Healthy export surpluses ranged from 521 million rubles in 1909 to 364.6, 429.7, 347 and 146 million respectively in succeeding years. From 1909 onwards, there was a steady slight rise in the value of imports from 906 million rubles in 1909 to 1,374 million in 1913. Both the needs of modernization and domestic shortages contributed to the increase. The value of exports, during the same period, rose less sharply, from 1,428 million rubles in 1909 to 1,520 million four years later. The relative importance of grain exports declined from 52.5 per cent in 1909 to 39.1 per cent in 1913. On the other hand, the export of other agricultural produce, notably eggs and butter, showed a marked increase. So did the relative value of exported timber and paper products. Exports, if still on a modest scale, were beginning to reflect an increasing diversification of agricultural production. As regards imports, the relative value of machinery and apparatus rose from 8.9 per cent in 1909 to 12.3 per cent in 1913. Their percentage of the total had however, since 1911 remained almost stationary. The bulk of Russia's growing imports came from Germany, exceeding those from Great Britain (Russia's next most important trading partner) in a ratio of about 3:1.

The buoyancy of the revenue reported by the diplomats is borne out by the statistical data:

Sources of government revenue (in million rubles)

	1908	1909	1910	1911	1912	1913
Total revenue from all ordinary sources	2,418.0	2,526.0	2,781.0	2,952.0	3,106.0	3,417.0
from direct taxes	194.2	198.7	216.1	224.1	243.3	272.5
from state railways	512.5	567.9	625.9	708.0	742.4	813.6
from spirits monopoly	709.0	718.9	767.0	783.1	824.7	899.3
from postal services	52.5	58.2	63.8	68.2	72.7	79.0
from stamp duties	65.6	72.7	82.8	92.9	101.8	111.8

Source: P. A. Khromov: *Ekonomicheskoye Razvitie Rossii v XIX–XX vekakh* (Moscow, 1950)

While increases in the yields from direct taxes, state railways, the postal services and stamp duties bear witness to the quickening pace of economic life, that in the growth of profits from the spirits monopoly attests to the growing population's unquenchable thirst.

As regards government expenditure, besides the heavy outlay on defence spending described by the diplomats, the most significant items are those relating to the three modernizing ministries, of finance, education and agriculture:

Budgets of modernizing ministries

	1908	1909	1910	1911	1912	1913	1914
	(in million rubles)						
Education	53.0	64.3	79.8	97.9	118.1	143.1	153.6
Finance	432.5	459.8	409.4	403.2	424.7	482.3	445.7
Agriculture	58.0	71.2	85.6	103.5	119.9	135.8	146.2

Source: P. A. Khromov: *Ekonomicheskoye Razvitie Rossii v XIX–XX vehakh*

Finally, some details from the banking sector speak an eloquent language. The gold reserve of the state bank which until 1914 consistently exceeded by a comfortable though not a growing margin the value of notes in circulation, showed a steady if erratic increase. Its annual value from 1908 to 1914 in million rubles is given as 1,169; 1,220; 1,415; 1,450; 1,435; 1,556, and 1,695. Meanwhile, deposits in Russian joint-stock banks for the same period rose from 239.8 million rubles through 290.1, 334, 422 and 528.9 million to 657.7 million in 1913, to reach 752.9 million the following year. There was a rapid increase also in savings:

Growth of deposits in state savings banks 1900–1914

	1900	1910	1911	1912	1913	1914
number of savings books in thousands	3,145	6,940	7,436	7,973	8,455	8,992
deposits in million rubles	608.3	1,283	1,397	1,503	1,595	1,835

Source: Olga Crisp: *Studies in the Russian Economy before 1914* (London, 1976)

Thus, while the number of savers increased rapidly, the amount of savings remained modest.

One element alone in the financial situation might have been a matter for concern. The specie in circulation (gold and high grade silver) which had been at a high level (absolutely and relative to paper money) from 1900 until 1908, in 1909 showed a drastic fall in absolute terms. It then took until 1912 for it to pass the level of 1907. It again fell slightly in 1913. The value of paper money in circulation meanwhile had been rising slowly but steadily from 1,087 million rubles in 1909 to 1,495 in 1913. In this respect Witte's 'golden age' appeared to be on the wane. Yet, had normal conditions prevailed, this need not in itself, have posed a threat to the Russian economy.

IV

How far the 'Stolypin Reforms' contributed to the improvements in Russian agriculture described by the British diplomats and confirmed by the wider statistics it is impossible to say. While the land-settlement programme produced substantial results before its operation was suspended in 1915, it would be hard to claim that it fully justified the high hopes of its promoters. On paper indeed, the results achieved were impressive. Before the end, close on three million heads of households had requested the transformation of their allotment holdings into private property. Applications, however, fell off steadily following a peak in 1908:

Households seceding from the village commune

	1907 (incomplete)	1908	1909	1910	1911	1912	1913	1914
(in thousands)	212	840	650	342	242	152	160	120

Source: L. A. Owen: *The Russian Peasant Movement 1906–1917* (London, 1937)

A similar decline occurred in the number of households abandoning the village commune for individual farming:

Households setting up individual farmsteads

	1907 (incomplete)	1908	1909	1910	1911	1912	1913	1914
(in thousands)	48	508	580	342	145	122	135	98

Source: L. A. Owen: *The Russian Peasant Movement 1906–1917*

In his annual report for 1910, with the land settlement programme already past its peak, Sir George Buchanan reported on its progress. It was estimated, he wrote, that by the close of the year 1910, newly constituted separate farms would number 507,000. The total number of separated farms, whether owned by households remaining in the village or by those moving to separate farmsteads (*khutors*), was officially estimated at 4 per cent of the total number. Some 10 per cent of the new owners had sold their land, usually to other peasants. 'In these circumstances,' Buchanan opined, 'it is, of course, premature to speak, as is sometimes done, of a transformation of rural Russia. A newly created 'hutor' or separate farmstead, was still a rarity looked on with curiosity by the peasants.'[15]

The extent to which peasants had taken advantage of the enabling legislation to have their separate strips consolidated into single holdings varied in different parts of the empire.[16] In a survey he produced early in 1913, A. A. Kofod[17] worked out the percentage of consolidated holdings by regions:

Percentages of consolidated holdings

	percentage holding
Southern steppe	16.2
Southeastern steppe	11.3
West (two areas)	9.5
	10.4
Central agricultural provinces	3.4
Southwestern provinces	3.3
Eastern provinces	3.0
Northern provinces	1.5

Source: L. A. Owen: *The Russian Peasant Movement 1906–1917*

The average for all provinces covered by land settlement legislation was 5.7 per cent. Its comparative success in the southern steppe Kofod attributes to a combination of relative uniformity of the soil (uniformity of soil and level land facilitated division), a comparative abundance of land and the partly industrial character of even small-scale farming. Similar conditions had favoured the process in parts of the southeastern steppe. In the western provinces, meanwhile, private ownership and consolidated holdings to some extent predated Stolypin's legislation. Land settlement, however, made relatively little headway in the crowded central agricultural provinces where there was a strong attachment to the commmune and to traditional farming methods. In the southern part of the region this was in part also a product of land shortage (consolidated plots would have been too small for subsistence). In the north the prevalence of industrial and migratory employment made agriculture a subsidiary activity. Experience proved that in large parts of the empire, and especially in the crucial central provinces, the wholesale transition from communal to individual farming would be at best a matter of decades.

Bernard Pares paints a somewhat rose-coloured picture of the effectiveness of the reform when he writes: 'The results were astonishing. By 1914 there was already a yeoman population of 8,700,000 households with a strong sense of property, and consequently with a strong instinct of public order. On the new farms the men were full of a new and businesslike energy. The cattle took on an altogether healthier appearance. Districts outside the village, which might therefore at any time have changed ownership under the old dispensation, were now for the first time carefully cultivated and planted with fruit trees. Such peasants as had no taste for agriculture and sought other work were now quite free to do so; they made their way to the towns with the capital obtained from the sale of their holdings and added materially to their prosperity ... the principle of co-operation flourished everywhere, for once the peasant had some property with which to co-operate, he sought association with his fellows for buying machinery or for marketing goods. No instinct is more in the genius of the Russian peasant than that of co-operation.' In this the common life under the old system had played its part, but now co-operation was free and voluntary. '... in this form it grew up of itself and flourished everywhere.'[18]

Yaney also takes an optimistic, possibly over-optimistic, view: '... in the early summer of 1914 the Stolypin Land Reform was flourishing. Land settlement commissions were working far more efficiently than in their early years, and they were responding to peasant needs with a much finer sensitivity. The movement for agricultural improvement was growing rapidly; specialists were intensifying their work where they were already established, and they were extending new agencies to every corner of the empire ... the way seemed clear for the specialists to proceed with the full-scale modernization of Russian agriculture.'[19] In its later stages, according to Yaney, there had occurred 'the virtual takeover of the reform organization by agricultural specialists, chiefly surveyors, agronomists, and statisticians.'[20]

As Yaney notes:

> For purposes of survival the 'primeval' community was a practical, going concern if it could somehow get enough land. Land hunger ... was something more than a product of ignorance that could easily be swept aside by enlightenment. It was an attitude that made sense in many areas and would go on making sense until the general situation changed in rural Russia.[21]

The mass of the Russian peasantry, nothwithstanding official encouragement and indeed 'persuasion', was unwilling to take advantage of the enabling legislation devised by the bureaucrats in St Petersburg. A critical and perhaps more realistic assessment of the reform is provided by Robert McKean:

> Even before 1914 the incidence of the reform was most uneven. After the first explosive rush to leave the commune between 1908 and 1910, the rate of applications declined continuously. By 1915 only 11 per cent of all households (1.25 million) had consolidated their strips and a mere 103,364 peasant households had set up individual farms outside the commune. Contrary to official expectations, the commune failed to disintegrate after 1906 – despite all the pressures and blandishments of the bureaucracy. Three quarters of all consolidations of scattered strips into

enclosed plots of land were implemented by entire villages (i. e. communes) rather than individual peasants. The effects of the reform also least affected the poorest and most densely populated regions, viz. the south-west and central agrarian provinces. And the enclosure of allotments by itself merely represented a first step towards the promotion of the crucial technical changes alone capable of raising the abysmally low productivity of peasant farming.[22]

Following a vigorous beginning, the movement for secession slowed down dramatically. It nonetheless contributed, as had been Stolypin's intention, towards increasing the still small number of relatively prosperous and enterprising peasant-freeholders. As Polezhaev, eulogizing Stolypin's achievement (for the benefit of French investors) wrote in 1912:

> It is certain that it is impossible to assess fully (*de se rendre compte*) by means of some statistical data the degree of success achieved by the rural economy of a vast country . . . it is necessary to recall that, at this point of time, the development is only beginning and one can as yet speak only of a movement towards progress (*d'une sorte de tendance vers le progrès*) and not of precise results towards which this tendency must lead.[23]

V

In the years before the war Russia was, in the aftermath of Witte's perestroika, in the throes of both a relatively rapid industrialization, and a longer-term rural transformation. She was, markedly if unevenly changing from an underdeveloped into a developing country. Self-sustaining development appeared to be accelerating, to an increasing extent with the aid of native capital and entrepreneurship. Exports were growing in value and becoming increasingly diversified. Moreover, thanks to the efforts of Witte and Stolypin, Russia was, at the same time, experiencing a measure of political modernization. This found expression in the quasi-parliamentarism of the now securely established Duma and in the growing role of the no longer revolutionary *zemstva*. A multi-party system, a relatively free press and the immunity of Duma deputies combined to ensure a fair degree of glasnost. If this was not the freedom of western political culture and institutions and if the rule of law was not yet of the kind obtaining in politically advanced nations, it was yet a far cry from the practices that had prevailed so recently under the Great Reaction. Only the liberal decade of Aleksandr II had prefigured comparable conditions. A strengthened public opinion moreover, ensured that such glasnost and political evolution as had been achieved had now become difficult to subvert. However hard tsar, camarilla and subservient ministers would try to conceal the growing influence of Rasputin, their success would prove incomplete. Under a régime of semi-glasnost Rasputin would become a 'semi-public' figure. He would be referred to even in Duma speeches. Nor was it as easy as it had been before to hide a variety of bureaucratic abuses. Neither official encouragement of anti-Jewish pogroms nor the use of *agents provocateurs* would remain unpilloried.

A novel and significant feature of the pseudo-constitutional régime was the close co-operation of Duma and press.[24] This reflected the elementary interests of both parties. The more serious papers would print full reports of Duma debates. On major occasions, even during the actual sessions, Moscow papers would have details transmitted by telephone. Especially in the first two years of the Duma and again during the parliamentary battles of 1910 verbatim reports or summaries of major speeches filled the columns of the political sections. The reporting depending on a paper's political affiliations, could be selective. The risk of prosecution by the authorities was minimal. In the last resort, editors could always shelter behind the official stenographic protocols published by the state printing house. Nicholson, the British ambassador, reported in June 1909 that 'in 1909 in St Petersburg and Moscow there was outspoken criticism of the government, and the proceedings of the Duma were freely reported and reproduced.'[25]

In the measure that Duma and State Council acquired access to once zealously guarded matters of state, relevant information and opinions became available also to the press. As a rule, even the proceedings of closed sessions (usually devoted to military matters) could not be kept a secret. Oppositional deputies, including those of the far Left participated in the discussions. Each faction, moreover, maintained direct links with a friendly editor. At the same time, it may be noted that most papers retained their independence. However passionate their political engagement, they were not 'party organs'.

Leading journals also tried independently to influence political attitudes. As even a revolutionary had to admit 'certain parliamentary characteristics . . . were trickling into political life' and the 'carefully selected Duma' had become 'a public forum in which the numerically weak opposition could give vent to its grievances. It could do so in the main because the Right majority was not insensitive to the voice of the press'.[26] The political opposition was thus able to compensate, to some degree thanks to the press, the numerical weight lost through alterations in the franchise and electoral manipulation. Without the interaction of Duma opposition and press the spread of oppositional views in the last years before 1914 would be inexplicable. Glasnost also, in this manner, achieved its modest successes.

Thus between the end of the Crimean and the outbreak of the Great War perestroika and glasnost had transformed the face of Russia. It is difficult to visualize an 'iron-autocrat' like Nikolai I in the age of Witte and Stolypin, Guchkov and Miliukov. Within the space of two generations, not only the 'old Russia' of Nikolai I and Gogol, but also the 'sunset' gentry Russia of Turgenev and Tolstoy had ceased to be. In his *Cherry Orchard* Chekhov, even before 1905, had written its symbolic epitaph. The day of the Lopakhins appeared to be dawning.

NOTES

1. FO 371, Russia, PRO, London.
2. Sir Arthur Nicholson to Sir E. Grey, 30 December 1909, No 683, Annual Report on Russia for the Year 1909, PRO, London.
3. *Ibid.*
4. *Ibid.*
5. Consul H. M. Groves: Annual Commercial Report for 1910, PRO, London.
6. A. L. Sidorov, ed: *S. Yu. Vitte: Vospominania* (Moscow, 1960), vol III, pp 337–41.
7. *Ibid.*
8. *Ibid.*
9. *Ibid.*
10. *Ibid.*
11. *Ibid.*
12. *Ibid.*
13. *Ibid.*
14. For invaluable statistical material, see P. A. Khromov: *Ekonomicheskoye razvitie Rossii v XIX–XX vekakh* (Moscow, 1950).
15. Sir George Buchanan to Sir E. Grey, 22 March 1911, No 683, Annual Report on Russia for the Year 1910, PRO, London.
16. For details of the effectiveness of land settlement in different parts of the empire, see especially *Komitet po zemleustroitelnym delam 1906–1916* (Petrograd, 1916), Appendix 3; P. Maslov: 'Zemledel cheskoye Khoziaistvo posle revoliutsii' in L. Martov, P. Maslov and A. Potresov, eds: *Obshchestvennoye dvizhenie v Rossii v nachale XX veka* (St Petersburg 1909–10), vol IV, pp 1–32; A. Kofod: *Russkoye zemleustroistvo*, 2nd edn (St Petersburg, 1914), p 123; and Launcelot A. Owen: *The Russian Peasant Movement 1906–1917* (London, 1937).
17. Yaney describes him as 'the first propagandist for land settlement on village land and ultimately chief inspector of the reform organization'.

George Yaney: *The Urge to Mobilize: Agrarian Reform in Russia, 1861–1930* (Urbana, IL, Chicago and London, 1982).

18. Sir Bernard Pares: *The Fall of the Russian Monarchy* (New York, 1939), p 114.
19. Yaney: *The Urge to Mobilize*, p 399.
20. *Ibid*, p 387f.
21. *Ibid*, p 214.
22. R. B. McKean: *The Russian Constitutional Monarchy, 1907–1917*, The Historical Association General Series 91 (London, 1977), pp 21–2.
23. Pierre Poléjaïeff [Polezhayev]: *Six Années: La Russie de 1906 à 1912* (Paris, 1912), p 122.
24. For the following, see Manfred Hagen: *Die Entfaltung Politischer Öffentlichkeit in Russland 1906–1914* (Wiesbaden, 1982), pp 130–2.
25. *Ibid*, p 131.
26. Hagen: *Die Entfaltung*, p 132.

Part VII

Conclusion

15

The Anatomy of Tsarist Perestroika

/

I

What were the impulses that set in motion successive attempts at perestroika? The broad answer to the question is: the Russian need to coexist with more advanced societies and nations. This coexistence, ever present to the mind of thinking Russians, had a number of important corollaries. First and foremost, an underdeveloped Russia found herself involved in permanent diplomatic and military competition with more highly developed countries. Moreover, it was an unequal competition with Russia, owing to her backwardness, in constant danger of defeat. As soon as manpower and size ceased to provide adequate protection and a sufficient power base, the problem of national 'fitness' or preparedness for possible conflict presented itself. This in theory involved a constant need for modernization, military and economic in the first place, but extending also into the cultural and political spheres. In practice, and more especially during the period covered by the present study, when more dynamic competitors were making rapid economic and technological strides and with crude manpower losing much of its edge, the need for keeping up with potential rivals became for Russia a matter of survival, at least as a Great Power. Successive Russian defeats underlined the urgency of the problem. Modernize or decline was the ineluctable choice. That choice for a proud and patriotic Russian could not for a moment be in doubt. At whatever cost, Russia must maintain her position among the Powers. A desperate near-permanent perestroika was a precondition of ability to compete if far from a guarantee of success. The stimulus to perestroika thus was in the first place external.

A second impulse is related to the first, though not synonymous with it; that of 'the Western model'. At every step and in many different spheres Russia was confronted with more successful, perhaps more fortunate, societies. This had been a permanent feature of her history and its impact, if anything, was increasing during the period here considered. The achievements of other nations in many fields, not least the military, invited comparison and emulation. So did their living standards, their economic progress, their technology and their cultural institutions. There was a constant temptation for Russians to borrow, to copy, to imitate. Moreover, fatally from a Russian point of view, the Western model was constantly evolving, dynamically progressive. 'To catch up with and overtake' and 'we will bury you' were impotent cries of desperate boasting from that day to this, from Peter the Great to Nikita Khrushchev. Russian xenophobia, in fact, was fighting a constant and losing battle both with the seductions of the Western model and with the perceived need to follow it to remain competitive. Serious nativist alternatives, as Westernizers since Chaadaev and indeed well before him realized, did not exist. And where a Marxist model was adopted by some even that, within its own dialectic, did not envisage jumping the bourgeois-capitalist stage of development.

But was the Western model in fact relevant to a country with Russia's distinctive cultural physiognomy, or, indeed, to underdeveloped countries like her in general? It was a question some Russians did ask themselves, yet, whatever the philosophical answer, practical necessity made at least selective borrowing imperative. The mere existence of a Western model forced Russian policy makers into copying 'the West'. Moreover, for most educated Russians the Western model possessed a seductive appeal. Western life was easier, more comfortable, more civilized. Western culture was widely held to be superior or, at the very least to be a necessary complement to the Westernized elements of Russian culture. Western institutions – a Roman legacy – were admired by Russians who had never known them.

How far then could a Western style society be created in Russia? How far could the achievements and amenities of the West be transplanted into a harsher clime? Whatever the practical possibilities and whatever the theoretical objections of Slavophile nationalists and patriots, a Westernization or further Westernization of Russian life and society was desired by increasing numbers of the already Westernized. Their wishes, including a desire for glasnost, individual freedom and political rights, also created a further impetus for reform, perestroika. A culture perceived to be superior or, if value judgments are to be avoided 'more attractive', constituted a constant spur to the desire for change.

It is at this point that new impulses for perestroika supervened. A widespread desire for change mainly among parts of the upper classes would, in the face of resistance, provoke dissatisfaction, criticism, dissent, demands, clandestine organization, demonstrations, and culminate in terrorism and revolution. Western ideologies which could not be stopped at the frontiers would threaten to undermine social and political stability. Political prudence and the instinct of self-preservation or, alternatively, irresistible pressure from below might indicate the need for concession. So might rational reflections and even the personal predilections of policy-makers. Men like Aleksandr II with his Hohenzollern heritage or Witte, equally of German descent, were by conviction partisans of Western cultural forms whether social, political or economic. Personal preferences here would go hand in hand with a wider quest for social and political stability.

The different impulses behind perestroika interacted and combined in varying degrees. They could be more cultural or more utilitarian, emotional or rational. According to differences of emphasis, they could be directed more towards material or towards idealistic objectives, to material improvement or to 'civil rights', glasnost and a rule of law. In the last resort, whatever the emphasis, the different motives intertwined.

II

Perestroika involved the combined efforts of a number of agencies. First and most important was the autocratic power. No Miliutin or Loris, no Witte or Stolypin could have pursued his policies without the constant backing of the tsar. The tsars selected their reforming ministers, often non-bureaucrats from unorthodox backgrounds. They maintained them in office in the face of frequently bitter criticism and opposition – but would also dispense with them on occasion. The tsars played a decisive role also in the implementation of reforming policies (as well as others), from Aleksandr II's active involvement in the liberation of the serfs through his signature of the 'Melikov constitution' to Nikolai II's introduction of the gold standard and his promulgation of the October Manifesto. At important junctures, Nikolai II used his powers to promote the 'Stolypin reform'. Thus, when the old State Council in the spring of 1906 rejected by a narrow majority proposed credits for the new Committee for Land Settlement Affairs, he signed the minority report. 'One of the last contributions of the old autocracy', it has been said, 'was to allow the Stolypin Reform to begin.' Again, under the new dispensation the reform had gone ahead thanks to the use of Article 87 for promulgating the *ukaz* of 9 November 1906. The Naval Staff Bill in turn, was enacted by means of the autocratic power. At many crucial junctures, perestroika was possible only through the intervention of the tsar. Changes promoting glasnost, judicial reforms, university autonomy, the introduction of *zemstva* were products of imperial resolve. Without it no major legislative initiative was possible. Many reforms also would have been strangled at birth or emasculated by opponents without continuing imperial support. Perestroika, in fact, required throughout the exercise of the autocratic power. Except for the 'extorted' October Manifesto and the subsequent Fundamental Laws the extent of glasnost would (largely through censorship and press regulations), depend equally on the tsar's good pleasure.

Aleksandr II and Nikolai II had some grounds for claiming that autocracy was both necessary and beneficial. No Russian parliament, however constituted, would have liberated the peasants with land. Again, the Loris-Melikov constitution which might have set Russia on the road of peaceful constitutional reform could only have been instituted by imperial *ukaz*. When Aleksandr III, under the influence of Pobedonostsev rejected it, the plan at once collapsed. It was the same tsar who authorized the Russo-French alliance, the indispensable financial base of perestroika.

Next to the autocratic power, the reforming section of the high bureaucracy was an indispensable agent. While the tsar was able to initiate, he was unfitted by training, experience and lack of legislative expertise and technical knowledge either to plan (except in the broadest outline) or execute reforms. To do this, he required competent assistants. Significantly, these were usually available, whether in the shape of Nikolai Miliutin and his entourage; of the circle of Loris-Melikov and Catherine Dolgoruky; of the former railway managers and engineers gathered around Witte; or the Krivosheins, Gurkos and their helpers in the Land settlement operation. There would always emerge from the ranks of the large St Petersburg bureaucracy small nuclei of determined reformers. In the early days – surprisingly in view of later developments – these might emerge in the Ministry of the Interior. Later, they would find a home in the Ministry of Justice, still later in that of Finance. Finally, by the nature of the technical requirements, reforming circles would develop in the Ministry of Agriculture and, until the dismissal of Rediger, in the Ministry of War. A characteristic of such reforming bureaucrats was their readiness to work with non-bureaucratic experts brought in from outside and with representatives of the 'educated public'. Indeed with the tacit approval of Krivoshein's Commission for Land settlement Stolypin's agrarian reform would, in the end, be executed by technicians: agronomists, surveyors and statisticians.

Bureaucratic reformers in spite of some overlap, must be distinguished from groups of bureaucratic liberals which also existed throughout. Not all partisans of perestroika were necessarily also liberals. The latter, as distinct from reformers, had as their main platform the defence of legality and civil liberties. They would, as senior statesmen and members of the old State Council seek to preserve intact or even extend the Great Reforms which they had earlier helped to elaborate. Until decimated by repeated purges, they would find a home in the Ministry of Justice. As senior bureaucrats they would, like the early Goremykin, favour the activities of the *zemstva*. Later, like Sviatopolk-Mirsky or Urusov they would seek to check arbitrary administrative acts and to co-operate with moderate representatives of *obshchestvennost*. They were sympathetic to a measure of political reform and public participation. With the decline and eventual replacement of the old State Council, the liberal bureaucrats would lose their collective focus. Henceforth, they could act only as individuals. Overall, the role of liberal bureaucrats would, following their active and enthusiastic participation in the Great Reforms, diminish steadily in successive phases of perestroika.

Autocracy for initiative, political authority and direction; the modernizing or reforming groups in the bureaucracy and their helpers as planners and executors formed the essential infrastructure of perestroika. For some reforms with a socio-political aspect, more particularly during the era of the Great Reforms, they would receive support from liberal bureaucrats outside the immediate sphere of perestroika.

Besides such key elements, other agents of perestroika and glasnost deserve mention. Not least among these were the *zemstva*, at the same time products and instruments of reform. Their essential feature, emphasized by Stolypin during his dealings with Zenkovsky was the fact that they stood largely outside the bureaucratic structure. Deriving much of their moral authority from popular election on an attenuated all-class basis, they helped over the years to transform rural Russia. They did this through the promotion of secular elementary education, and of rudimentary welfare services. In the later stages they would play a key role also in promoting agricultural improvement, furthering co-operatives, and in the provision of rural credit. In the political transformation, the role of the *zemstva* would be crucial. *Zemstvo* work was the training ground for a generation of progressive politicians. These would form the backbone of the Liberation Movement during the critical years 1904–5. Reform-minded bureaucrats would, if unsuccessfully, try to enlist their co-operation. Without them, the Cadet party would have consisted simply of professional men with little influence. In addition, the *zemstva* would make a major contribution also to forming the leadership of the political Left. They provided the organizational framework and favourable surroundings for the radical Third Element. Their educational activities helped the formation of a new politically aware peasant intelligentsia. It would play a prominent part in the Trudovik factions of the first two Imperial Dumas. If Russia was able to develop from an autocracy into a quasi-constitutional state with loosely organized but not wholly ineffective political groupings this, in no small degree was thanks to the *zemstvo* experience. This, in several different ways was an important agent in the transformation of the Russian state and Russian society.

Like the *zemstva* both product and agent of reform, *obshchestvennost* also helped to promote perestroika. It gave moral support and encouragement to Aleksandr II in his struggle for emancipation with land and promoted his later reforms. A growing band of newspaper proprietors, publicists and journalists fought a running battle against censorship. Under the Reaction, this was a discouraging experience. Freedom of information was not tolerated, as emerged only too clearly after the Khodynka tragedy of 1896. A liberal newspaper owner-editor would years later publish his memoirs abroad under the title of *What did not appear in the Paper (Was nicht in die Zeitung kam)*. In the run-up to the revolution of 1905, the educated public would agitate for constitutional reform, among others in a banqueting campaign. Its professional associations, notably the venerable Imperial Free Economic Society of St Petersburg, the Moscow Society of Jurisprudence and the Pirogov Society of Russian Doctors founded in 1885 served, until either closed or gagged at the end of the century, as vehicles of free discussion. *Obshchestvennost* created a network of professional organizations operating with some degree of autonomy. Attempts in the Sipyagin-Plehve era to destroy them came too late and were only partially successful. Through them, *obshchestvennost* contributed to the beginnings and growth of the liberation movement. While the influence of *obshchestvennost* on the course of events is difficult to evaluate, there is no doubt that it was a significant force for political change and glasnost. The liberation movement helped to ensure that civil rights would figure prominently in the October Manifesto.

Another agent of perestroika was the West. With Russia, a developing country too poor to finance fundamental reforms single-handed, she had little choice but to rely on foreign capital. Foreign loans at crucial points helped successive Russian governments to finance reforming policies. Private foreign investment, principally French and German, played a major part in railway construction, in the development of induced industries and in financing military expenditure. Moreover, as Witte was at pains to point out to Nikolai II, foreign capital invested in Russian industry brought with it know how, technology and management skills in which Russia was deficient. Indeed no serious industrial development was possible without the services of numerous foreign experts, engineers and managers.

Dependence on Western loans and investment made the Russian government more sensitive to Western opinion. Thus some of the worst anti-Semitic excesses were eventually checked by the authorities when banking circles in Berlin and Paris reacted. More generally, the Russian government had to take some account of indignant Western reaction to events like the excommunication of Leo Tolstoy or the massacre of 'Bloody Sunday'. While considerations of Western sensitivity would never restrain the activities of policemen in the Ministry of the Interior, of the *Okhrana* or of the punitive detachments – they did not prevent even a long and ludicrous trial for ritual murder in 1913 – they at least put the Russian government under the necessity of seeking to defend its actions.

More significantly, *any* Russian perestroika in any sphere whatever was dependent on Western models. When Aleksandr II decided to modernize the archaic judicial system, experts were sent abroad to study the legal practices of more advanced countries. Witte's economic philosophy was borrowed from Friedrich List. With a desire to emulate the successful Danish peasantry, a major role in the Stolypin Reform was entrusted to the Dane (or rather, Bornholmer) Kofod. The Duma, in its procedures, tried to model itself on the parliament of Westminster. Exchanges of parliamentary delegations underlined the link. (Sir) Bernard Pares was proud to act as Gentleman Usher to the First Duma. Young Russians and not only political radicals went abroad to study at foreign universities and technical institutions. When, at the end of the period, Stolypin dictated to Zenkovsky his blueprint for reform, he envisaged sending experts abroad to study Western social institutions. In short, the Western input was throughout an essential ingredient of perestroika.

Finally the Duma, an institution based on Western models (as against the Muscovite-Russian *zemsky sobor*) was again, like the *zemstvo* both product and agent of modernization. In the first place, together with the Fundamental Laws, it accustomed the Russian public to some form of constitutional government, for Russia a major innovation. There was now something like a written constitution as well as a national forum for public debate. Moreover, even after Nikolai II had reverted to a system of personal rule, the constitutional arrangements survived. Plans not long after the death of Stolypin to turn the Duma into a purely advisory body were speedily abandoned. The Duma would retain its legislative functions, its status and a measure of prestige. In due course it would guide the February Revolution and give a degree of legitimacy to the Provisional Government composed mainly of its members. It survived, formally unscathed, the vicissitudes of its chequered history.

The Duma's major contribution to the political transformation of Russia was its role in creating and training an alternative political elite. Parliamentarians, whatever their political allegiances, got to know and occasionally to esteem one another. A majority among them, moreover, would develop some feelings of solidarity in the struggle with bureaucracy, government and the 'dark forces'. When the old political elite was finally overthrown, the new one stood ready to replace it. There existed a shadow ministry, the portfolios already neatly allocated. Whether the common link was in fact parliamentary or, as has been suggested, Masonic, the formal framework of the new government and such legitimacy as it possessed, stemmed from the Duma.[1] It would be the Temporary Committee of the Duma which would assume authority when power fell from the hands of Nikolai II.

A further contribution of the Duma was its role as an agent of glasnost. Debates were relatively free and, no less important, could be and were reported. A two-way exchange existed also between electors and their deputies. Circumstances were arising when illiteracy rather than censorship would reduce the effectiveness of glasnost. Glasnost inevitably, and perhaps not in Russia alone, was confined to 'the educated' and to urban populations, notably in the two capitals. The oppositional sub-culture of Moscow in its hostility to St Petersburg bureaucracy of which Guchkov was the flamboyant spokesman, would benefit more particularly from the Duma and its proceedings.

Finally the Duma, however imperfectly, represented the principles of popular sovereignty and democracy which were new to Russia. Duma deputies were responsible not to tsar or government but to their electors and, indeed to the nation at large. They did not look to the government for preferment. Some, however, would seek re-election. They would have to take into account the views of their electors. While parts of the population now enjoyed formal representation the interests of groups deprived of the vote would, to an extent, find self-appointed spokesmen among Duma deputies. However imperfect in practice, the institution of the Duma thus marked a shift in the balance of Russian government. As Witte had correctly forecast, the October Manifesto would prove a step on the road to constitutional government. A mere 11 years were to separate the Duma from the Provisional Government and the Constituent Assembly.

Important agencies, thus, were throughout the period promoting perestroika and glasnost in their various manifestations. If heterogeneous in character they constituted a potentially powerful coalition committed to modernization in many spheres of Russian life.

III

If the forces for change were formidable, so also were the obstacles. Foremost among these was Russian poverty. Perestroika cost money which had either to be squeezed out of the population or borrowed, largely from abroad. For both methods, there was a price to pay. For the first, it consisted in low living standards and periodic famine, for the second in dependence on foreign capital markets and governments, with some loss of independence in the field of foreign relations. The effects of poverty were compounded by a high rate of military expenditure. Russia's armed forces, inevitably, claimed a larger share of national resources than those of other major countries. This was the necessary price to be paid for Great Power status and participation in imperialist competition. It was raised further by the need to re-equip after repeated disasters. Aleksandr III's policy of 'peace at any price' had a sound economic base. So had the unsuccessful attempt of Nikolai II at the end of the century to secure a halt to the arms race. Vast expenditure on the armed forces was, at least from the 1890s onwards, part of the price to be paid for French financial assistance.

Further obstacles to perestroika were the size (and diversity) of the empire, the gigantic nature of the task and the nature of Russian administration and its procedures. Variations in local conditions had to be considered. Control of local agents from remote 'ex-centric' St Petersburg presented problems. Not all provincial governors, the key administrative agents, would prove either competent or co-operative. At the centre, there was often a lack of unity or direction, exemplified most notably in the prolonged feud between the Ministries of the Interior and Finance, and in the role of unofficial advisers chosen by successive tsars. There was, in general, a lack of effective control whether at the centre or by the centre over the periphery. Almost any reform would be denatured to a greater or lesser extent in its application by men of often doubtful capacity, motivation and public spirit. Corruption in the bureaucracy was endemic. It is surprising that, in spite of the flaws in administration, a public-spirited minority was able to achieve an extensive if patchy modernization of an archaic system.

A corollary of size combined with the bureaucratic centralization of government was a powerful force of inertia. The Russian bureaucracy, with the exceptions already noted, was wedded to routine, to an easy life and to the pursuit of individual self-interests. The efforts required for perestroika were the last thing the bulk of officialdom wished to engage in. The aim was to be left undisturbed, to have as little change as possible and to be spared even the semblance of responsibility. Moreover the semi-paralysis induced by the reign of routine at the centre was matched by a different kind of inertia in the vast interior provinces. Here a traditional and declining rural society proved resistant to changes cooked up in remote government offices by men unfamiliar with local conditions. Peasants, except for a small minority, were attached to the old ways, preferring the village commune to new-fangled *khutors*. Known collectivist institutions and traditional methods with their co-operative farming operations engendered a sense of security in many as well as favouring the self-interest of some.

In general, there was the widespread *oblomovshchina*, still to be lamented by Lenin, *nekulturnost*, illiteracy, the total absence (except perhaps among people of foreign origin) of a work ethic. Among the hallmarks of Russian life in general were sloth and inefficiency abetted by climatic extremes. However modernizers might regret it, Russians would not be Germans. In over-romanticized but widely used terms, Russians often put spiritual above material considerations. 'Prussianism' and 'Germanism' and their efficiency, the model for perestroika, were viewed by the bulk of the Russian population with extreme distaste. So in particular was the discipline which, in the interest of efficiency, people of German origin sought to impose whether in factory or regiment. In what degree ineradicable corruption was a dysfunctional factor, in relation to perestroika, is an interesting matter for speculation. Perhaps it was neutral. It may even have contributed to bending legislation by the centre to suit local conditions and preferences.

As regards glasnost, this was, of course anathema to Russian officialdom (as it is, indeed to any bureaucracy). In the Russian case, the normal aversion to the 'light of day' of officialdom everywhere was intensified by a pathological secretiveness deeply ingrained in the Russian administrative tradition. The mass of the Russian people, on the other hand, with its still large if diminishing percentage of illiterates, was disinterested in the glasnost so highly prized by members of the urban intelligentsia. In the face of general bureaucratic hostility and widespread popular indifference, glasnost in Russia would always be a precarious and somewhat exotic plant with only shallow roots.

The more specific obstacles to political reform, on the other hand, were of a different nature. Not least among them was the ambivalent attitude of the tsars. These were, and considered themselves to be, autocratic rulers bearing a mythical responsibility towards 'God and their conscience'. Autocracy by its very nature, did not blend with popular sovereignty. Ministerial responsibility, other than to themselves, must be repugnant to autocrats. Even where reluctantly conceded, political perestroika granted at the good pleasure of the ruler, was always considered, at least in theory, revocable. The rights and functions of *zemstva* could be restricted, personnel, elections and proceedings interfered with. It was possible for Ministers of Education to play fast and loose with university autonomy. Shcheglovitov, as Minister of Justice, would severely denature the judicial reforms of 1864. Stolypin, with the tsar's approval would, in 1907, arbitrarily alter the electoral law. Five years later, plans to turn the Duma into a purely advisory body were seriously discussed. Non-bureaucratic political institutions throughout remained at the mercy of the auto-cracy even in its new constitutional guise.

A more specific opposition to perestroika would at times come from the 'law and order' men. These, from their point of view not without justification, considered major reforms as dangerous experiments, a threat to the existing order. The effects of perestroika on public order were unpredictable. Social and national issues would be raised with disorders a likely consequence. Moreover, as conservatives like Pobe-donostsev and opportunists like Witte argued with some cogency, any move in the direction of constitutionalism would place the régime on an inclined slope, expose it to new pressures and force it into further concessions. Change, once initiated, would be difficult, per-haps impossible to arrest. From at least the 1870s onwards the Ministry of the Interior, responsible for the security forces and extending its tentacles into many areas of public life, would be a serious obstacle to perestroika. Not accidentally, Stolypin in his blueprint for reform, while 'boosting' the role of the *zemstva*, proposed to confine that of the Ministry of the Interior to police and propaganda activities.

A final obstacle and not the least, was the resistance of vested interests. This, in the literature, is often represented as a form of perverse wickedness. It is, of course, nothing of the sort. It is perfectly natural for people to defend with single-minded determination their possessions, privileges and status. Landowners, understandably, would seek to preserve their estates, officials to retain their perks. Local officials would defend their authority against the claims of the *zemstva*, those manipulating village meetings, the *obshchina* (land commune) against seceders. Any perestroika, must needs hurt a variety of interests. It would inevitably infuriate those whose interests would suffer. Moreover, many of those who stood to lose belonged to influential groups or occupied important positions. It was with power-ful forces indeed that outsiders like Loris-Melikov, Witte or Stolypin, not to speak of lesser reformers, must contend. Thus if perestroika and glasnost were to be effective, a whole phalanx of obstacles and obstructions would have to be overcome. To bring about more than cosmetic change, to alter and modernize Russia more than superficially would, in view of the obstacles to be faced, be a Herculean task.

IV

How successful, it may be asked, were the efforts here considered to restructure the Russian *ancien régime*? In its overall effects, perestroika could, with equal justice, be considered to have been either a qualified success or a qualified failure. The patchy modernization brought about by Aleksandr II, Witte and Stolypin sufficed, in spite of setbacks, to preserve Russia's place among the great powers. This was achieved with difficulty and at heavy cost for the Russian people. In more specific terms, perestroika made a major contribution to the provision of an infrastructure in communications, banking and industrial equipment which formed the basis for Russia's industrial-commercial take-off. Perestroika, during this period, transformed Russia from a backward or underdeveloped into a developing country. Not least, it turned a country of largely servile labour into one of 'free' workers whether in village or town. Again, perestroika and glasnost brought about a considerable advance in Westernization. In important respects between the Crimean and Great wars, Russia moved rapidly closer to the Western model. Such, notably, was the case in the economic sphere, but only a little less so in the political. Here, first *zemstva* and then the Duma took root as elements in the political system. A Western-style political culture with elections, parties, a variegated press, with professional associations and pressure groups arose. Glasnost, however obstructed, played an essential part. A spirit of enterprise developed, through Witte's industrial policies and through the 'decollectivization' of the Stolypin reform. Within a relatively short period of time, a great deal was accomplished. Perestroika and glasnost with all their blemishes and flaws could not be considered failures.

And yet there can be no doubt that fundamental and lasting success eluded the 'perestroikists' faced perhaps with an impossible task. It would be difficult to argue that there had been a truly radical transformation of Russian society. What emerged was less a 'new order' than an old one which had been revamped. Change was gradual, on the whole, intermittent and patchy, with the old and the new existing uneasily side by side. There was constant danger of a relapse into stagnation and, indeed regression. The forces of inertia proved impossible to overcome, old attitudes hard to modify. Neither national character nor traditional attitudes could be changed in a day. Glasnost, unsupported by a firm institutional framework, remained precarious and at all times vulnerable. A philosophy of individualism, of individual rights, duties and responsibilities failed to establish itself. It lacked any foundation in the Muscovite/Russian tradition. Nor could it be said that however great the advances due above all to Aleksandr II, a rule of law became securely established. In short, what might perhaps be described as the Russian psyche or cultural ethos was only incompletely and perhaps only superficially modified. Individual exceptions there had, of course, always been. Yet Russians could not collectively jump over their own shadow. Centuries of historic and collective experience with the attitudes they had engendered could not be wiped out in the space of two generations by governmental fiat. Indeed one of the weaknesses of both perestroika and glasnost was that, unavoidably, they were the products of St Petersburg bureaucracy. Attempts at involving or consulting a wider public invariably yielded disappointing results. So did efforts to involve non-bureaucrats in government. *Vlast* and *obshchestvennost* proved in essence irreconcilable, with perestroika remaining unavoidably the province of the former.

As significant was the failure to achieve perestroika's overall objective, that of finally 'catching up' with the more advanced countries. There were a number of reasons for the failure. One was that, while reforms were being carried out in Russia, her major competitors also did not stand still. The rate of relative advance, industrial, technological, military, like the advance in living standards invariably favoured Russia's rivals. They had both the higher starting levels and the more dynamic societies, greater resources, greater expertise and a greater spirit of initiative among their subjects. At the same time Russian progress, unlike Western, never became fully self-sustaining. To achieve the continuance of even patchy modernization required constant effort by the state, an effort, moreover, that would not always be forthcoming. Without it, there was a constant tendency to sink back into stagnation. Central planning, control and prodding on the other hand, inhibited all initiative at lower levels. While a degree of individual entrepreneurship did indeed develop in the final decade, it was still confined to few. Industry in particular still depended, to some extent, on the state or public bodies, on government orders whether for armaments or strategic railway construction or on municipal projects. Dependence on foreign capital and expertise persisted, as, indeed, it does to the present day. The relatively weak education system moreover – its projected expansion remained largely on paper – was insufficient to sustain an advanced economy or a society of a Western kind. The Great War, in certain respects a testimony to Russian strength would, at the same time, expose many areas of unredeemed backwardness, inefficiency and general incompetence. Russia's strength, as before, would still lie largely in vast territory and numbers. It would be wrong, at the same time, to ignore the successful economic operations of the unions of *zemstva* and towns fruit, to a great extent, of perestroika. But both the economy and the political system would in the end collapse under the strain. The central object of perestroika would prove unattainable.

A certain aura of ambivalence, inevitably, hung over both perestroika and glasnost. In the case of the first, the obstacles to its implementation which have been considered, could be overcome only by the strongest of governments and the use of unfettered power. Yet that essential power, would at the same time impede perestroika by preventing, or at least hindering political modernization, and all but ruling out popular participation, let alone initiative. At the same time, any effective perestroika, more particularly in the political sphere, would tend to undermine the authority needed to effect further, particularly economic, change. Similarly successful economic restructuring would undermine stability and bring about social changes likely to weaken the central authority. Autocratic power again was both essential for bringing about economic change and a curb on economic development through centralized legislation, planning and control – without which however, perestroika from the centre would be impossible. Perestroika was thus full of contradictions and to a degree self-defeating. Complete success, in the circumstances, would prove beyond the reformers' reach.

In the same way, there were inherent contradictions with regard to glasnost and civil rights. Glasnost would involve free unfettered discussion and the right to criticize the actions of authority. It would involve freedom of association, the right to set up intermediate organizations independent of the state. Glasnost in short, was inherently incompatible with the existence of the absolute (totalitarian) state. Yet it was, arguably, only such a state which, in the face of formidable obstacles could advance the progress of perestroika. In any case, in practical terms, the highest representatives of state power, and not least those determined on restructuring, would be naturally impatient of criticism, discussion and delay holding up their programme of reform. And how often would not glasnost facilitate even obstruction from its opponents? Those convinced of the need for perestroika and determined to carry it through against all opposition, would be naturally inclined – like Stolypin – to ride roughshod over obstacles presented by the practice of glasnost. Glasnost and perestroika did not necessarily go hand in hand, indeed were more likely sooner or later to clash. In any case psychologically, the wielders of absolute power would be unlikely to concede with good grace to a 'natural right' of individuals and groups to enjoy the benefits of glasnost. The great historian V. O. Kliuchevsky could speak of 'tsarism's hopeless struggle for progress without dissent'.[2] Glasnost also, when used to the full, was partly self-defeating, more particularly in an atmosphere of intensive perestroika. In conjunction with nationality problems and with social issues thrown up or aggravated by restructuring, it carried with it a threat of disintegration, of a weakening of authority; an end to all prospect of an ordered perestroika. The role of glasnost with perestroika was problematic. Could any practitioner of perestroika be, at the same time, a sincere protagonist of glasnost?[3] There were profound reasons why, owing to inherent contradictions, radical restructuring and an effective policy of glasnost were, in practice, all but incompatible.

It need not perhaps be pointed out that the October Revolution and its aftermath did little to change the basic situation. No more than Aleksandr II, Witte or Stolypin could Lenin, Stalin and Khrushchev achieve the restructuring that would enable Russia to compete internationally on equal terms whether in the technological, the economic, the scientific, the cultural, or, in important respects, the military sphere. The basic problems continued under the new régime to be similar to those under the old. Under both, it is possible equally to speak according to taste, of partial success or partial failure. The great goal of 'catching up' with and overtaking Russia's more advanced competitors would elude her rulers under the new régime as it had done under the old. No perestroika could abolish or overcome the historic past. Glasnost, when allowed to operate, could do little more than explain it.

In any event, whatever the degree of success or failure of contemporary perestroika, it comes too late in the day. The twenty-first century almost certainly belongs to the eastern neighbours of what was once the Soviet Union. They accomplished their modernization to better effect decades ago or are rapidly doing so. It is improbable that the Russia of the republics will ever 'catch up' with the leaders.

NOTES

1. George Katkov: *Russia 1917: The February Revolution* (London, 1967), pp 163–73 and 378–9.
2. Quoted in D. M. O'Flaherty: *Tsarism and the Politics of Publicity 1865–1881* (unpublished PhD thesis), p 14.
3. 'This was the ambivalence, never satisfactorily resolved, between the autocracy's drive to increase its power in the arena of international competition by stepping up the pace of material progress, and its instinctive and furious resistance to the social change and unpredictable intellectual activity which grew out of material progress.' *Ibid*, pp 10–11.

Bibliography

A. E. Adams, ed: *Imperial Russia after 1861 – Peaceful Modernizaton or Revolution?* (Boston, 1965)

Aleksandr Mikhailovich, Grand-Duke: *Vospominania* (Paris, 3 vols, 1933)

Gregor Alexinsky: *Modern Russia* (London and Leipzig, 1913)

E. M. Almedingen: *The Empress Alexandra 1872–1918* (London 1961)

P. L. Alston: *Education and the State in Tsarist Russia* (Stanford, 1969)

O. Anweiler: *Die Rätebewegung in Russland 1905–1921* (Leiden, 1957)

A. Ya. Avrech: *Tsarism i treteiyunskaya sistema* (Moscow, 1966)

——: *Stolypin in tretia duma* (Moscow, 1978)

M. A. Baring: *A Year in Russia* (London, revised edn, 1917)

J. H. Bater: *St Petersburg. Industrialisation and Change* (London, 1976)

I. P. Belokonsky: *Zemskoye dvizhenie* (Moscow, 1910)

——: *Zemstvo i Konstitutsia* (Moscow, 1910)

P. A. Berlin: *Russkaya burzhuazia v staroye i novoye vremia* (Moscow, 1922)

I. V. Bestuzhev: *Borba v Rossii po voprosam vneshnei politiki 1906–1910* (Moscow, 1961)

A. D. Bilimovich: *Zemleustroitelnye zadachi i zemleustroitelnoye zakonodatelstvo v Rossii* (Kiev, 1907)

V. T. Bill: *The Forgotten Class: The Russian Bourgeoisie from the earliest beginnings to 1900* (New York, 1959)

E. J. Bing, ed: *The Letters of Tsar Nicholas and Empress Marie* (London, 1937)

E. Birth: *Die Oktobristen (1905–1913): Zielvorstellungen und Struktur* (Stuttgart, 1974)

C. E. Black, ed: *The Transformation of Russian Society since 1861* (Cambridge, MA, 1960)

C. E. Black: *The Transformation of Russian Society: Aspects of Social Change since 1861* (Cambridge, MA, 1970)

C. E. Black *et al*: *The Modernization of Japan and Russia: A Comparative Study* (New York and London, 1975)

W. L. Blackwell: *Russian Economic Development from Peter the Great to Stalin* (New York, 1974)

J. de Bloch: *Les Finances de la Russie* (Paris, 1899)

J. Blum: *Lord and Peasant in Russia from the Ninth to the Nineteenth Centuries* (Princeton, 1961)

———: *The End of the Old Order in Rural Europe* (Princeton, 1978)

A. K. Bogdanovich: *Dnevnik* (Moscow-Leningrad, 1924)

M. P. Bok: *Vospominania o moyem otse P. A. Stolypine* (New York, 1953)

M. Bompard: *Mon Ambassade en Russie, 1903–1908* (Paris, 1937)

Sir George Buchanan: *My Mission to Russia* (London, 1923)

T. Yu. Burmistrova and V. G. Gushakova: *Natsionalnii vopros v programmakh i taktike politicheskikh partii v Rossii 1905–1917 gg* (Moscow, 1976)

P. A. Buryshkin: *Moskva kupecheskaya* (New York, 1954)

R. F. Byrnes: *Pobedonostsev, His Life and Thought* (Bloomington, 1968)

The Cambridge Economic History of Europe, vol VI, chapter VIII, 'Agrarian Policies and Industrialisation: Russia 1861–1966' (London, 1966)

R. Charques: *The Twilight of Imperial Russia* (Oxford, 1958)

E. D. Chermensky: *Burzhuazya i tsarism v revolyutsii 1905–1907 gg* (Moscow 1939; 2nd edn, Moscow, 1976)

E. Chmielewski: *The Polish Question in the Russian State Duma* (Knoxville, 1970)

M. S. Conroy: *Peter Arkadyevich Stolypin. Practical Politics in Late Tsarist Russia* (Boulder, CO, 1976)

O. Crisp: *Studies in the Russian Economy before 1914* (London, 1976)

J. S. Curtiss (ed): *Essays in Russian and Soviet History* (New York, 1963)

E. de Cyon: *L'alliance franco-russe*, 2nd edn (Lausanne, 1895)

A. M. Davidovich: *Samoderzhavie v epokhu imperializma. Klassovaya sushchnost i evolyutsia absolutizma v Rossii* (Moscow, 1975)

V. G. Diakin: *Samoderzhavie, burzhuaziya i dvorianstvo* (Leningrad, 1978)

C. von Dietze: *Stolypinische Agrarreform und Feldgemeinschaft* (Leipzig, 1920)

E. J. Dillon: *The Eclipse of Russia* (New York, 1918)

N. M. Druzhinin: *Gosudarstvennie krestiane in reforma P. D. Kiseleva* (Moscow–Leningrad, 1946–58)

——: *Russkaya derevnia na perelome 1861–1880gg* (Moscow, 1978)

S. M. Dubrovsky: *Stolypinskaya reforma* (Leningrad, 1925; 3rd edn as *Stolypinskaya zemelnaya reforma*, Moscow, 1963)

G. A. Dzhanshiev: *Epokha velikikh reform*, 9th edn (St Petersburg, 1905)

R. Edelmann: *Gentry Politics on the Eve of the Russian Revolution. The Nationalist Party 1907–1917* (NJ, 1980)

T. Emmons: *The Russian Landed Gentry and the Peasant Emancipation of 1861* (Cambridge, 1968)

T. Emmons and W. S. Vucinich (eds): *The Zemstvo in Russia. An Experiment in Local Self-government* (Cambridge, 1982)

N. P. Eroshkin: *Istoriia gosudarstvennykh uchrezhdenii dorevoliutsyonnoi Rossii*, 2nd edn (Moscow, 1968)

Essad Bey: *Nikolaus II. Glanz und Untergang des letzen Zaren* (Berlin, 1935)

M. Falkus: *The Industrialization of Russia 1700–1914* (London, 1972)

E. M. Feoktistov: *Za kulisami politiki i literatury* (Moscow, 1929)

M. Ferro: *Nicholas II, the last of the Tsars* (London, 1991)

D. Field: *The End of Serfdom: Nobility and Bureaucracy in Russia, 1855–61* (Cambridge, 1976)

A. Finn-Enotayevsky: *Kapitalizm v Rossii 1890–1917* (Moscow, 1925)

G. Fischer: *Russian Liberalism from Gentry to Intelligentsia* (Cambridge, MA, 1958)

M. T. Florinsky: *The End of the Russian Empire* (New Haven, 1931)

K. Fröhlich: *The Emergence of Russian Constitutionalism 1900–1904. The Relationship between Social Mobilization and Political Group Formation in Pre-Revolutionary Russia* (The Hague etc, 1981)

S. Galai: *The Liberation Movement in Russia 1900–1905* (Cambridge, 1973)

M. Ganfman *et al*: *Svoboda petchati pri obnovlennom stroye* (St Petersburg, 1912)

M. Ya Gefter: *Ekonomicheskie predposilkii pervoi russkoi revoliutsii* (Akad. Nauk. SSSR Doklady i Soobshchenia Instituta Istorii Vypusk 6 Leningrad–Moscow, 1955)

A. Gerassimov: *Der Kampf gegen die erste russische Revolution* (Frauenfeld and Leipzig, 1934)

V. Gere: *Znachenie 3-ei gosudarstvennoi dumy v istorii Rossii* (St Petersburg, 1912)

A. Gerschenkron: *Economic Backwardness in Historical Perspective* (Cambridge MA, 1962)

——: *Continuity in History and other Essays* (Cambridge, MA, 1965)

I. V. Gessen: *V dvukh vekakh. Zhiznennii otchet* (Berlin, 1937)

D. Geyer: *Wirtschaft und Gesellschaft im vorrevolutionären Russland* (Cologne, 1975)

Giertz, H.: *Zur Frage des Scheinkonstitutionalismus in Russland zwischen den beiden bürgerlich demokratischen Revolutionen*, in *Jahrbücher für die Geschichte der UdSSR und der volksdemokratischen Länder*, 16, 1 (1972)

Ginden I. F.: *Banki i promyshlennost v Rossii* (Moscow, 1927)

——: *Russkie kommercheskie banki: Iz istorii finansogovo kapitala v Rossii* (Moscow, 1948)

——: *Gosudarstvennii bank i ekonomicheskaya politika tsarskogo pravitelstva 1861–1892gg* (Moscow, 1960)

Girault, R.: *Emprunts russes et investissements français en Russie 1887–1914* (Paris, 1973)

Golovin, F. A.: *Vospominania* in K(rasnii) A(rkhiv) 19 (1926) and 58 (1933)

Graham, S.: *Tsar of Freedom: The Life and Reign of Alexander II* (New Haven, 1935)

Greenberg, L.: *The Jews in Russia*, vol II, 1881–1917 (New Haven, 1951)

Gurko, V. I.: *Features and Figures of the Past*, in J. E. Wallace Sterling *et al* (eds): The Hoover Library on War, Revolution and Peace, Publication no 14 (Stanford, 1939)

Hagen, M.: *Die Entfaltung politischer Öffentlichkeit in Russland 1906–1914* (Wiesbaden, 1982)

——: *'Die russische Presse zur Regierungskrise im Frühjahr 1911'* in R. V. Thadden *et al*, eds: *Das Vergangene und die Geschichte. Festschrift für Reinhard Wittram* (Göttingen, 1973)

Harcave, S.: *First Blood. The Russian Revolution of 1905* (London, 1964)

Healy, A. E.: *The Russian Autocracy in Crisis 1905–1907* (Hamden, CT, 1976)

Hoetzsch, O.: *Russland. Zweite vollständig umgearbeitete Auflage (Berlin, 1917)*

——: *Russland: Eine Einführung auf Grund seiner Geschichte von 1904 bis 1912* (Berlin, 1913)

Hosking, G. A.: P. A. Stolypin and the Octobrist Party' in *SEER (Slavonic and East European Review)*, vol 47, 1969

——: *The Russian Constitutional Experiment. Government and Duma 1907–1914* (Cambridge, 1973)

Hutchinson, J. F.: *The Union of 17 October in Russian Politics 1905–1917* (PhD Thesis, London, 1966)

——: 'The Octobrists and the Future of Imperial Russia as a Great Power' in *SEER*, vol 50, 1972

A. Isvolsky: *The Memoirs of Alexander Isvolsky* (London, 1920)

Izgoev, A.: *Russkoye obshchestvo i revoliutsiiya* (Moscow, 1910)

Jablonowski, H.: 'Die russischen Rechtsparteien 1905–1915', in *Russland-Studien. Gedenkschrift für Otto Hoetzsch* (Stuttgart, 1957)

Kalynishchev, F. I.: *Gosudarstvennaya duma v rossii v dokumentakh i materialakh* (Moscow, 1957)

Karpovich, M.: *Imperial Russia 1801–1917* (New York, 1932)

S. D. Kassow: *Students, Professors and the State in Tsarist Russia* (Berkeley, 1989)

Katz, M.: *Mikhail N. Katkov: A Political Biography 1818–1887* (The Hague, 1966)

Khromov, P. A.: *Ekonomicheskoye razvitie Rossii v XIX–XX vekakh* (Moscow, 1950)

——: *Ocherki ekonomiki Rossii perioda monopolicheskogo kapitalisma* (Moscow, 1960)

Khrushchev, A. A.: *A. I. Shingarev: ego zhizn i deiatelnost* (Moscow, 1918)

Kiss, G.: *Die gesellschaftspolitische Rolle der, Studentenbewegung im vorrevolutionären Russland* (Munich, 1963)

Kizevetter, A. A.: *Na rubezhe dvukh stoletii–Vospominania 1881–1914* (Prague, 1929)

Kochan, L.: *Russia in Revolution 1890–1918* (London, 1967)

Koefoed, C. A.: *My Share in the Stolypin Agrarian Reforms* (Odense, 1985)

Kokovtsov, V. N.: *Iz moego proshlago. Vospominania 1903–1919* (Paris, 2 vols, 1933)

——: *Out of My Past – Memoirs of Count Kokovtsov* (Stanford, 1935)

Kolosov, A: *Aleksandr III, ego lichnost, intimnaya zhizn i pravlenie* (London, 1902)

Komitet Ministrov: *Nasha zheleznodoroshnaya politika* (St Petersburg, 4 vols, 1902)

Koni, A. F.: *Sergei Yulevich Vitte: Otryvok Vospominanii* (Moscow, 1925)

Korelin, A. P.: *Dvorianstvo v poreformennoi Rossii 1864–1904 gg.Sostav, chislennost, korporativnaya organizatsiya* (Moscow, 1979)

Kornilov, A.: *Obshchestvennoye dvizhenie pri Aleksandre II (1855–1881) Istoricheskie ocherki.* (Moscow, 1909)

——: *Modern Russian History* (New York, 1924; published in Russia 1912–14)

Korostowetz, V.K.: *Graf Witte, der Steuermann in der Not* (Berlin, 1929)

Koshko, I. F.: *Vospominania Gubernatora* (Petrograd, 1916)

Krasilnikov, N.: P. A. Stolypin i ego deiatelnost v pervoi, vtoroi i tretei Gosudarstvennoi dume (St Petersburg, 1912)

Kretchetov, P.: *P. A. Stolypin: Ego zhizn i deiatelnost* (Riga, 1910)

Krivoshein, K. A.: *A. V. Krivoshein (1857–1921) Ego znachenie v istorii Rossii nachala XX veka* (Paris, 1973)

Kucherov, S.: *Courts, Lawyers and Trials under the Last Three Tsars* (New York, 1957)

Kulomsin, A. N.: *Le Transsibérien* (Paris, 1904)

Kurlov (Komarov) P. G.: *Gibel imperatorskoi Rossii* (Berlin, 1923)

V. N. Lambsdorf: *Dnevnik V. N. Lambsdorfa 1886–1890* (Moscow–Leningrad, 1926)

Langer, W. L.: *The Franco-Russian Alliance 1890–1894* (Cambridge, MA, 1929)

——: *European Alliances and Alignments* (New York, 1931)

——: *The Diplomacy of Imperialism*, 2nd edn (New York, 1951)

von Laue, T. H.: *Sergei Witte and the Industrialization of Russia* (New York, 1963)

Laverychev, V. Ja.: *Krupnaia burzhuazia v poreformennoi Rossii 1861–1900* (Moscow, 1974)

Lehmann, C. and Parvus: *Das hungernde Russland: Reiseeindrücke* (Stuttgart, 1900)

Lemke, M.: *Epokha tsenzurnykh reform 1859–1865* (St Petersburg, 1904)

Lenin, V. I.: *The Development of Capitalism in Russia* (Moscow, 1956; translated from V. I. Lenin's *Works* vol 3, 4th Russian edn, prepared by the Institute of Marxism-Leninism of the Central Committee of the CPSU)

Leontovitsch, V.: *Geschichte des Liberalismus in Russland* (Frankfurt am Main, 1957)

Leroy-Beaulieu, A.: *Un homme d'état Russe (Nicolas Milutine) D'après sa correspondance inédite* (Paris, 1884)

——: *The Empire of the Tsars and the Russians* translated by Z. Ragozin (New York, 3 vols, 1898)

Levin, A.: *The Second Duma. A Study of the Social Democratic Party and the Russian Constitutional Experiment (New Haven, 1940)*

——: *The Third Duma. Election and Profile* (Hamden, CT, 1973)

Levitsky, S.L.: *The Russian Duma: Studies in Parliamentary Procedure 1906–1917* (New York, 1956)

Lincoln, W. Bruce: *Nikolai Miliutin: An Enlightened Russian Bureaucrat of the 19th Century* (Newtonville, MA, 1977)

Loewe, H.–D.: *Antisemitismus und reaktionäre Utopie. Russischer Konservatismus im Kampf gegen den Wandel von Staat und Gesellschaft 1890–1917* (Hamburg, 1978)

Lowe, Charles: *Alexander III of Russia* (London, 1895)

Lyashchenko, P. I.: *Istoriya narodnogo Khozyaistva SSSR* (Moscow, 1939; 2nd edn, Moscow, 1950)

McKay, J. P.: *Pioneers for Profit: Foreign entrepreneurship and Russian Industrialization 1885–1913* (Chicago and London, 1970)

Mackenzie Wallace, Sir D.: *Russia* (London, Paris, New York and Melbourne, 2 vols, 1905)

Maklakov, V. A.: *Vlast i obshchestvennost na zakate staroi Rossii* (Moscow, 1936)

Maurach, R.: *Der russische Reichsrat* (Berlin, 1939)

Medlicott, W. N.: *The Congress of Berlin and After* (London, 1938)

Y. Melnik, ed: *Russen über Russland* (Frankfurt am Main, 1900)

Menashe, L.: *Alexander Guchkov and the Origins of the Octobrist Party. The Russian Bourgeoisie in Politics* (PhD thesis, New York, 1966)

Meshcherskii, V. P.: *Moi vospominania*, Part III, 1881–94 (St Petersburg, 1912)

Miliukov, P. N.: *Russia and its Crisis* (New York, 1962)

Miliutin, D. A.: *Dnevnik* (edited by P. A. Zaionchkovsky, Moscow, 4 vols, 1947–50)

Miller, F. A.: *Dimitrii Miliutin and the Reform Era in Russia* (Vanderbilt, 1968)

Miller, M.: *The Economic Development of Russia 1905–1914* (New York, 1967)

Mosse, W. E.: *Alexander II and the Modernization of Russia* (London, 1958, Rev, London, 1992)

Nicolaievsky, B.: *Aseff: The Russian Judas* (translated by G. Reavey, London, 1934)

Nikolai II *Dnevnik Imperatora Nikolaya II (1890–1906)*

Nikolaya *Dnevnik Nikolaya II 1890–1906* in Krasnii Arkhiv, vols 20–22 and 27 (Berlin, 1923)

Nolde, B.: *L'Alliance franco-russe* (Paris, 1936)

Nötzold, J.: *Wirtschaftspolitische Alternativen der Entwicklung Russlands in der Ära Witte und Stolypin* (Munich, 1966)

Orlovsky, D. T.: *The Limits of Reform: The Ministry of Internal Affairs in Imperial Russia 1802–1881* (Cambridge, MA, and London, 1981)

Owen, T. G.: *Capitalism and Politics in Russia: A Social History of Moscow Merchants 1855–1905* (Cambridge, 1980)

Palme, A.: *Die russische Verfassung* (Berlin, 1910)

Pares, Sir Bernard: *My Russian Memoirs* (London, 1931)

——: *The Fall of the Russian Monarchy* (New York, 1939)

Pinchuk, B. S.: *The Octobrists in the Third Duma 1907–1912* (Seattle and London, 1974)

Pintner, W. M. and Rowney, D. K., eds: *Russian officialdom from the Seventeenth through the Twentieth Centuries: the Bureaucratization of Russian Society* (Chapel Hill, NC, 1980)

Pipes, R.: *Struve: Liberal of the Left 1870–1905)* (Cambridge, MA, 1970)

Pobedonostsev, K. P.: *Reflections of a Russian Statesman* (Ann Arbor, 1968)

——: *Pisma Pobedonostseva k Aleksandru III* (Moscow, 2 vols, 1925–26)

Poléjaïeff, P.: *Six Années. La Russie de 1906 à 1912* (Paris, 1912)

Polovtsev, A. A.: *Dnevnik A. A. Polovtseva* (Moscow, 2 vols, 1966)

Portal, R.: *La Russie industrielle de 1881–1927* (Paris, 1956)

——: *La Russie de 1894 à 1914* (Paris, 1963)

Preyer, W. D.: *Die russische Agrarreform* (Jena, 1914)

Propper, S. M. von: *Was nicht in die Zeitung kam* (Frankfurt am Main, 1929)

Raeff, M.: *Plans for Political Reform in Russia 1730–1905* (Englewood Cliffs, NJ, 1969)

Rieber, A. J.: *The Politics of Autocracy: Letters of Alexander II to Prince A. I. Bariatinski 1857–1864* (Paris and The Hague, 1966)

——: *Merchants and Entrepreneurs in Imperial Russia* (Chapel Hill, NC, 1982)

Riha, Th.: *A Russian European. Paul Milyukov in Russian Politics* (Indiana, 1969)

Robbins, R. Jr: *Famine in Russia, 1891–92: The Imperial Government responds to a Crisis* (New York, London, 1975)

Robinson, G. T.: *Rural Russia under the Old Regime* (New York, 1932)

Rogger, H.: *The Formation of the Russian Right 1900–1906 Californian Slavic Studies*, vol III (Berkeley, 1964)

——: *Russia in the Age of Modernization and Revolution 1881–1917* (London, 1983)

Saenger, M.: *Die Wittesche Währungsreform* (Frankfurt am Main, 1927)

Santa Maria Ph.: *The Question of Elementary Education in the Russian Third State Duma 1907–1912* (PhD thesis, Kent State University, 1977)

Scheibert, P.: *Die russische Agrarreform von 1861. Ihre Probleme und der Stand ihrer Erforschung* (Cologne and Vienna, 1973)

Schulze-Gävernitz, G. von: *Volkswirtschaftliche Studien aus Russland* (Leipzig, 1899)

Schweinitz, L. von: *Denkwürdigkeiten des Botschafters General von Schweinitz* (2 vols, Berlin, 1927)

Sering, M. Hrsg.: *Russlands Kultur und Volkswirtschaft* (Berlin and Leipzig, 1913)

Seton-Watson, G. H. N.: *The Decline of Imperial Russia* (London, 1952)

Simanowitsch, A.: *Rasputin: Der Allmächtige Bauer* (Berlin, 1928)

Soloviev, Yu.B.: *Samoderzhavie i dvorianstvo v kontse XIX veka* (Leningrad, 1973)

Starr, S. F.: *Decentralization and Self-Government in Russia, 1830–1870* (Princeton, 1972)

Stavrou, T. G. ed.: *Russia under the last Tsar* (Minneapolis, 1969)

Strakhovsky, L. I.: 'The Statesmanship of Peter Stolypin: A Reappraisal' in *Slavonic Review*, vol 37, 1959

Sumner, B. H.: *Tsardom and Imperialism in the Far East and the Middle East* (London, 1942)

——: *Russia and the Balkans 1870–1880* (London, 1937)

Szeftel, M.: *The Legislative Reform of August 6, 1905* (*the "Bulygin" Duma*) in Etudes presentées à la Commission Internationale pour l'histoire des Assemblées d'Etats (1967)

——: *Nicholas II's Constitutional Decisions of October 17–19 1905 and Sergius Witte's Role* (Namur, 1968)

——: The Reform of the Electoral Law to the State Duma of 1907: A new Basis for the Formation of the Russiana Parliament in Studies presented to the International Commission for the History of Representative and Parliamentary Institutions, vol 36, 1970

Tagantsev, N. G.: *The Russian Constitution of April 23, 1906* (Brussels, 1978)

Tatishchev, S. S.: *Imperator Aleksandr II. Ego zhizn i tsarstvovanie* (St Petersburg, 2 vols, 1903)

Tkatchenko, P. S.: *Moskovskii universitet v obshchestvenno-politicheskoi zhizni Rossii vtoroi poloviny XIX veka* (Moscow, 1956)

Tokmakoff, G.: *Stolypin and the Third Duma. An Appraisal of the Three Major Issues* (Washington, 1981)

Troyat, H.: *Daily Life in Russia under the last Tsar* (London, 1961)

Tuck, R. L.: 'Paul Milyukov and Negotiations for a Duma Ministry' in *Am. Slav. & E. European Review*, vol 10, 1951

Valuyev, P. A.: *Dnevnik P. A. Valuyeva, ministra vnutrennykh del* (Moscow, 2 vols, 1961)

Veselovskii, B.: *Istoriia Zemstva za 40 let* (St Petersburg, 4 vols, 1909–11)

Vinogradoff, Sir Paul: *Self-Government in Russia* (London, 1915)

Vucinich, W. S. ed.: *The Peasant in Nineteenth Century Russia* (Stanford, 1968)

Walkin, J.: *The Rise of Democracy in Pre-revolutionary Russia: Political and Social Institutions under the Last Three Tsars* (New York, 1962)

White, H. J.: *The Rise of Democracy in Pre-revolutionary Russia: Political and Social Institutions under the Last Three Tsars* (New York, 1962)

White, H. J.: *French international accounts 1880–1913* (Cambridge, MA, 1933)

Williams, H.: *Russia and the Russians* (New York, 1918)

S. Yu. Witte: *Vospominania* (edited by A. L. Sidorov, Moscow, 3 vols, 1960)

R. S. Wortman: *The Development of a Russian Legal Consciousness* (Chicago, 1976)

G. L. Yaney: *The Systematization of Russian Government: Social Evolution and the Domestic Administration of Imperial Russia 1711–1905* (Urbana, IL, 1973)

——: *The Urge to Mobilize: Agrarian Reform in Russia 1861–1930* (Urbana, IL, Chicago and London, 1982)

P. A. Zaionchkovsky: *Voyennye reformy 1860–1870 gg v Rossii* (Moscow, 1952)

——: *Otmena krepostnogo prava v Rossii* (Moscow, 1954)

——: *Provedenie z zhizn krestianskoi reformy 1861g* (Moscow, 1958)

——: *Krizis samoderzhaviia na rubezhe 1870–1880–x godov* (Moscow, 1964; translated and edited by G. M. Hamburg as *The Russian Autocracy in Crisis, 1878–1882*, Gulf Breeze, FL, 1979)

——: *Rossiiskoye samoderzhavie v kontse XIX stoletiia* (Moscow, 1970; translated and edited by D. R. Jones as *The Russian Autocracy under Alexander III*, Gulf Breeze, FL, 1976)

——, ed: *Spravochniki po istorii dorevolyutsionnoi istorii Rossii. Bibliografia* (Moscow, 1971)

——: *Samoderzhavie i russkaia armiia na rubezhe XIX–XX stoletii 1881–1903* (Moscow, 1973)

——: *Pravitelstvenii apparat samoderzhavnoi Rossii v XIX v* (Moscow, 1978)

A. V. Zenkovsky: *Stolypin: Russia's Last Great Reformer* (Princeton, 1986)

V. Zilli: *La Rivoluzione Russa del 1905. La formazione dei partiti politici (1881–1904)* (Naples, 1963)

Index

Shcherbina, Tatiana x
Shidlovsky, S. I. 227
Shipov, D. N. 156, 160, 168f., 186, 195f., 211ff. *passim*
Shuvalov, P. A. (Count) 58
Sipyagin, D. S. 111, 112, 123, 152, 154, 180, 217
Solski, D. M. (Count) 161, 177
Solzhenitsyn, A. I. xi, 132
Soviets 171, 173, 189f.
Speransky, M. M. (Count) 3, 34, 63, 112
Stalin, J. V. x, 3, 13, 14, 15, 83
State Council 198; and Naval Staff bill 231, 236, 239; and Western *zemstvo* bill 241
Stieglitz, A. L. (Baron) 26
Stolypin, P. A. 117, 186, 189, 207f., 211ff. *passim*; Land reform legislation 220, 222ff. *passim*; coup of 3 June 1907 223f., 226f.; and national defence 228ff. *passim*; resignation refused 233; attacks Finnish autonomy 237f.; and Western *zemstvo* bill 240ff.; reform programme, 242ff.; on Jewish entrepreneurship 243; death 244; appreciation 245, 273, 275
Stroganov, S. G. (Count) 80
Struve, P. B. 157
Sukhomlinov, V. A. 229, 232f., 236
Suvarov, A. A. 18
Suvorin, A. S. 141
Sviatopolk-Mirsky, P. D. (Prince) 159f., 163f., 166, 201, 273

Third Element 47, 143, 274
Third Section of H.M. Own Chancery 18, 58
Timashev, A. E. 63
Tocqueville, A. de 55
Tolstoy, D. A. (Count) 58f., 63
Tolstoy, L. N. (Count) 45, 51, 65, 113, 119, 131, 144
Totleben, E. I. 20
Toynbee, A. 136
Trepov, D. F. 169, 171, 173, 178, 181, 187f., 192f., 200, 207f., 211, 213
Trepov, F. F. 65, 71
Trotsky, L. D. 5, 173, 189f.
Trubetskoy, E. N. (Prince) 186, 195

Trubetskoy, S. N. (Prince) 169
Trudoviki 209, 274
Tsushima 168
Turgenev, I. S. 26, 37, 51, 56, 142, 144

Union of Liberation 157f., 163, 168
Union of the Russian People 222
Union of 17 October (Octobrists) 221f.; composition of faction in Third Duma 226; and agrarian reform 227; disintegration 236f.; 239; and Western *zemstvo* crisis 240f.
Universities reform 49f., 171
Urusov, S. D. (Prince) 186, 273
Uvarov, S. S. (Count) 19

Valuev, P. A. (Count) 45, 52, 55, 73, 77
Vyborg Manifesto 214
Vyshnegradsky I. A. 86; economic policies 90, 95, 96, 115, 117, 141, 143

Westernisation x, xi, 11f., 42
Wilhelm I 76, 86
Wilhelm II 86
Witte, Mathilde 96
Witte, S. Ju. (Count) x, xi, 3, 13, 15, 85, 95ff.; and Meshchersky 96; economic philosophy 98ff.; and currency reform 103; TransSiberian railway 105; industrial policy 106f.; expansion in Far East 108f.; on *zemstva* 110f.; and agricultural crisis 117ff.; industrial policy considered 126ff.; attitude to Jews 130, 133f., 143, 153f., 156, 160ff., 166, 170, 171f., 174, 176ff., 186ff., 190, 193, 195, 200ff.; resignation 200f.; achievements 201ff., 209; and Land reform 216ff. *passim*, 231, 249, 271, 274

Yaney, G. L. 218ff., 261
Yeltsin, B. ix, x, xi, 132

Zaionchkovsky, P. A. 76, 80
Zamiatnin, D. N. 42, 44
Zarudny, M. I. 42
Zasulich, Vera 65, 71
zemstva 46ff. 157, 159f., 168, 240, 273
Zenkovsky, A. V. 242f.
Zhukovsky, V. A. 37
Zubatov, S. V. 121